Brief Menu

More →

Rules *for* WRITERS

TENTH EDITION

Rules *for*

WRITERS

Diana Hacker

Nancy Sommers
HARVARD UNIVERSITY

bedford/st.martin's
Macmillan Learning

Boston | New York

Vice President: Leasa Burton
Program Director: Stacey Purviance
Senior Program Manager: Laura Arcari
Director of Content Development: Jane Knetzger
Senior Executive Editor: Michelle M. Clark
Development Editor: Melissa Rostek
Assistant Editor: Aislyn Fredsall
Director of Media Editorial: Adam Whitehurst
Marketing Manager: Vivian Garcia
Senior Director, Content Management Enhancement: Tracey Kuehn
Senior Managing Editor: Michael Granger
Executive Content Project Manager: Gregory Erb
Senior Workflow Project Manager: Jennifer L. Wetzel
Production Supervisor: Brianna Lester
Director of Design, Content Management: Diana Blume
Interior Design: Claire Seng-Niemoeller
Cover Design: William Boardman
Text Permissions Editor: Allison Ziebka
Photo Permissions Editor: Alexis Gargin
Photo Researcher: Krystyna Borgen, Lumina Datamatics, Inc.
Director of Digital Production: Keri deManigold
Senior Media Project Manager: Allison Hart
Copyeditor: Arthur Johnson
Indexer: Ellen Kuhl Repetto
Composition: Lumina Datamatics, Inc.
Printing and Binding: RR Donnelley

Library of Congress Control Numbers: 2021930724, 2021930758 (Writing about Literature)

ISBN 978-1-319-24425-5 (spiral-bound)

ISBN 978-1-319-39294-9 (paperback)

ISBN 978-1-319-39301-4 (Writing about Literature Edition)

Printed in China.

2   3   4   5   6   26   25   24   23   22

ACKNOWLEDGMENTS

Text acknowledgments and copyrights appear at the back of the book on page 585, which constitutes an extension of the copyright page. Art acknowledgments and copyrights appear on the same page as the art selections they cover.

For information, write: Bedford/St. Martin's, 75 Arlington Street, Boston, MA 02116

Contents

Preface for Instructors

Dear Colleagues,

Welcome to the tenth edition of *Rules for Writers*. This edition comes to you as a complete teaching program. You have the handbook you love, a trusted writing guide to answer students' questions and to solve their writing problems, available as both an interactive e-book and a print handbook. And you have **Achieve**, Macmillan's new digital course experience that helps you design assignments, comment on students' drafts, and measure students' writing progress. This program includes everything you need to make college success more achievable for all students.

Over ten editions, *Rules for Writers* has been shaped by the students and instructors who love the handbook. My Macmillan editors and I listen to students' questions about college writing; we listen to instructors' suggestions about new topics and examples to solve their instructional challenges. We listen and learn; we reimagine and revise — just like our students. With the help of 1,000 students and 600 instructors, we co-designed Achieve to offer an interactive e-book and digital platform to develop and deepen students' writing skills. Achieve answers students' basic question "How do I write a good college paper?" with a suite of tools, including adaptive quizzing, to support and personalize each student's success as a college writer.

These digital learning tools — and the handbook itself — are now more important than ever. Our classrooms and our face-to-face teaching were upended in 2020. Almost overnight, the pandemic required our students to become online learners, and we became online instructors. The intersections of racial, social, and public health issues widened students' worldviews and offered more to think and write about. The world needs to hear their voices, now more than ever. As my own teaching moved online, I found that *Rules for Writers* connected our online writing community. The book gave us a common language to talk about writing, acting as a trusted resource for students' big questions about quoting, summarizing, and paraphrasing sources and about building paragraphs and punctuating sentences. In any classroom, the handbook's explanations and examples anchor students, giving them the confidence to question sources, for example, or to craft more nuanced argumentative thesis statements. Especially for online learning, *Rules for Writers* gives students the courage to try something new, assured that they have their handbook's advice supporting them throughout their writing process.

Just as students need tools to navigate online learning, they need the guidance and confidence to express themselves in their writing — and that requires some flexibility. As national conversations around equity and inclusivity expanded, our editorial team took a closer, more critical look at the "rules" that the handbook's title suggests. We made it our mission to ensure that students can see themselves in the handbook and to no longer endorse one "standard" English. Our **Diversity, Equity, and Inclusion (DEI) Advisory Board**, a talented team of writing faculty, reviewed early manuscript, questioned some of our assumptions, and encouraged us to widen our instruction around language and usage — and we did so. In the tenth edition, we revised the handbook's coverage of noninclusive, stereotypical, and other harmful language to stress the importance of equity and respect in writing. We took a close look at how we phrased our grammar instruction and at the examples presented, revising where appropriate to emphasize flexibility and inclusivity. And we expanded our research instruction to show students how to incorporate diverse perspectives and underrepresented voices. Thanks to our DEI Board, students will find new instruction on widening the research conversation (see 51c), strategies for entering a research conversation and seeking out underrepresented voices. You can learn more about our DEI board on page xxix.

In the tenth edition of *Rules for Writers*, you'll find other new features, including more instruction on annotating, analyzing, and paraphrasing sources, and on how to write an argument about an argument. In our updated chapter on writing arguments, you'll find a new researched argument paper about the relationship between zoos and endangered animals. In Achieve, students will follow the student's writing process, see drafts and important documents from her research, and hear her talk about how she took a position on a debatable issue. Students have an opportunity to learn alongside the writer with scorable activities on establishing common ground, balancing rhetorical appeals, and contributing to research conversations.

The Hacker tradition is one of innovation, and the tenth edition of *Rules for Writers*, combined with Achieve's digital course experience, will transform the way we teach and the way students learn. I am eager to share the tenth edition with you, confident that you will find everything here that you and your students value about *Rules for Writers*. Our handbook remains a trusted resource to support students' progress as writers, providing structure and building confidence — especially in online classes. I can't imagine teaching without it.

Welcome to the Tenth Edition

Achieve with *Rules for Writers*

Achieve is an exciting and comprehensive set of interconnected teaching and assessment tools. It integrates the most effective elements from Bedford/St. Martin's digital content that you may be familiar with — including LaunchPad and LearningCurve — in a single powerful, easy-to-use platform.

Values we share.   We are proud to present Achieve with *Rules for Writers*, which rests on three core values:

- *Engaging students for better outcomes.* Prebuilt assignments include a variety of activities — from skill-building exercises to multidraft writing assignments — to engage students both in and out of class.

- *Supporting students of all levels.* Achieve was designed for all students, whether they are high achievers or they need extra support.

- *Partnering with teachers and learners.* Bedford/St. Martin's is dedicated to unparalleled customer experience. We depend on extensive learning research and rigorous testing, and we co-designed Achieve with instructors and students over several years and in hundreds of courses.

Superior content you trust.   We know that you have long depended on Bedford/St. Martin's to provide content from respected authors whose work is based on expert teaching, vetted scholarship, and bright-eyed innovation. The best, most effective, most thoroughly tested course materials — developed in the Bedford tradition — live in Achieve and provide a foundation for your course.

- *An interactive e-book for Rules for Writers* brings together the resources students need to prepare for your class. Students can download the e-book to read offline or to have read aloud to them.

- *LearningCurve adaptive quizzing* offers personalized question sets and feedback for each student based on correct and incorrect responses. Questions are conveniently tied back to the e-book to encourage students to access help when they need it.

- *Videos, writing prompts, and other activities* have been developed to support the Hacker/Sommers approach; are designed to deliver a coherent learning experience; and will make prep, practice, and review both easy and engaging. This edition features a case study around the new student argument essay, following the writer's process through videos, notes, drafts, and exercises.

- *Innovative writing videos* build students' confidence as they write analysis and argument essays and annotated bibliographies.

Writing tools that keep writing and revision at the center of your course.   Achieve with *Rules for Writers* gives teachers deeper visibility into students' writing processes so they can target instruction and feedback to help writers grow and develop across drafts, across assignments, and across courses. Students do the work of the course in a contained and active writing space that promotes revision, reflection, and peer review.

Assignments and units that make your life easier.   A flexible assignment building tool allows you to assign ready-made writing prompts — all fully customizable — or create your own. For *Rules for Writers*, Achieve includes the following assignments, all with rubrics and Draft Goals that you can use as is or tailor to your needs: annotated bibliography, argument essay, narrative essay, researched argument, and rhetorical analysis. Achieve for *Rules for Writers* also comes with a prebuilt course option that you can adapt to fit your needs; add, hide, and rearrange resources and assignments — conveniently available in a searchable library — until the course works for you.

Source Check plagiarism prevention that teaches.   This tool helps students become more responsible and ethical research writers.

It allows students to scan their work for potential plagiarism *before* they submit it for review so that they learn academic habits and citation practices in the context of their own writing.

Diagnostics and study plans that give students ownership. Promoting personalized learning, diagnostics for reading and sentence skills establish a baseline for student performance and point students to actionable study plans that build skills and confidence.

Reporting and insights that inform your teaching.   An innovative dashboard highlights student engagement, opportunities for intervention, and both whole-class and individual progress toward goals.

What's new in the book?

- *A new argument essay and a look into the writing process.* Section 7, Writing Arguments, features a new student essay. The chapter is built around examples from the writer's essay and process. A companion case study in Achieve brings the writer's process to life for students, from developing a working thesis and organizing an argument to selecting and integrating evidence. Videos, notes, and drafts from the writer illustrate concepts, and the corresponding exercises have students apply what they've learned and test their understanding.

- *More help finding and working with sources.* Updated chapters on finding and evaluating sources have a new focus on online research. Instruction on widening the research conversation helps students conduct research and seek out sources from diverse viewpoints (see 51c). Sentence guides give students a road map for integrating sources effectively (see 56c). Three new features in Academic Reading and Writing — a how-to box on annotating sources effectively, a guide for analyzing digital sources, and a case study of a student responding to an argument — provide much-needed advice on crafting analyses and arguments. A new chapter in Multilingual Writers and ESL Topics offers guided instruction in paraphrasing sources effectively, focusing on common concerns for writers who are new to writing in English.

- *Step-by-step help with grammar and punctuation.* New features guide students in building two important skills: revising run-on sentences (see 20a) and using quotation marks with other punctuation (see 56b).

- *Up-to-date MLA and APA formatting and documentation guidelines.* The advice, models, and student essays in the tenth edition of *Rules for Writers* align with MLA's 2021 update and APA's 2020 guidelines.

- *New affordable options.* To allow you to meet the price point that you and your students are comfortable with, Bedford/St. Martin's offers *Rules for Writers* in a number of options, all with our signature quality: Achieve with e-book, classic spiral-bound with and without tabs, paperbound with no tabs, and stand-alone e-book.

A new resource for corequisite composition

Writers develop over time — and some writers need more time and more practice to develop the skills and habits that help them meet the challenges of the first-year writing course. For those students enrolled in paired, corequisite, or ALP sections of composition, *A Student's Companion to Hacker Handbooks* offers practical support that will help them get up to speed and perform on-level. The workbook offers college success and reading strategies; graphic organizers for many kinds of writing; opportunities for reflection; and more than sixty exercises covering everything from thesis statements and plagiarism to fragments, run-ons, commas, and verb tenses.

A *Student's Companion to Hacker Handbooks* is available as a print workbook, as a convenient e-book, or as a module through Achieve. Even better, the print companion is available packaged with the handbook at no additional cost to students.

What hasn't changed?

Neither Google nor an OWL can give students the confidence that comes with a coherent reference that covers all the topics they need in a writing course. *Rules for Writers* supports students as they compose for different purposes and audiences and in a variety of genres, and as they collaborate, revise deeply, conduct research, document sources, format their writing, and edit for clarity. The ninth edition's authoritative and trustworthy instruction, brief and accessible explanations, and step-by-step help in writing guides and how-to boxes are still here in the tenth.

With examples that teach and plenty of boxes, checklists, and navigation tools, the book is easy to use and understand. It also comes with the service and support you have come to expect from Bedford/St. Martin's — including professional resources, training for digital tools, and quick, personal service when you need it.

Bedford/St. Martin's puts you first

From day one, our goal has been simple: to provide inspiring resources that are grounded in best practices for teaching reading and writing. For more than 40 years, Bedford/St. Martin's has partnered with the field, listening to teachers, scholars, and students about the support writers need. No matter the moment or teaching context, we are committed to helping every writing instructor make the most of our resources — resources designed to engage every student.

HOW CAN WE HELP YOU?

- Our editors can align our resources to your outcomes through correlation and transition guides for your syllabus. Just ask us.
- Our sales representatives specialize in helping you find the right materials to support your course goals.
- Our learning solutions and product specialists help you make the most of the digital resources you choose for your course.
- Our Bits blog on the Bedford/St. Martin's English Community (**community.macmillan.com**) publishes fresh teaching ideas regularly. You'll also find easily downloadable professional resources and links to author webinars on our community site.

Contact your Bedford/St. Martin's sales representative or visit macmillanlearning.com to learn more.

Digital and print options for *Rules for Writers*

DIGITAL

- *Achieve with Rules for Writers.* Achieve is a flexible, integrated suite of tools for designing and facilitating writing assignments, paired with actionable insights that make students' progress towards outcomes clear and measurable. Fully editable pre-built assignments support the book's approach and an e-book

is included. To order Achieve with *Rules for Writers*, use
ISBN 978-1-319-39295-6. For details, visit **macmillanlearning
.com/college/us/achieve/english**.

- *Popular e-book formats.* For details about our e-book
  partners, visit **macmillanlearning.com/ebooks**.

- *Inclusive Access.* Enable every student to receive their
  course materials through your LMS on the first day of
  class. Macmillan Learning's Inclusive Access program is
  the easiest, most affordable way to ensure all students have
  access to quality educational resources. Find out more at
  macmillanlearning.com/inclusiveaccess.

PRINT

- *Rules for Writers* (Classic), Tenth Edition. To order the spiral
  bound version, use ISBN 978-1-319-24425-5. To order *Rules
  for Writers* (Classic) spiral bound version packaged with
  Achieve, use ISBN 978-1-319-44385-6. To order the paperback
  version, use ISBN 978-1-319-39294-9. To order the paperback
  version packaged with Achieve, use ISBN 978-1-319-44389-4.

- *Rules for Writers with Writing about Literature,* Tenth Edition. To
  order the spiral bound tabbed version, use ISBN 978-1-319-39301-4.
  To order *Rules for Writers with Writing about Literature*
  packaged with Achieve, use ISBN 978-1-319-44387-0.

- *A Student's Companion to Hacker Handbooks*, Second Edition.
  To order the paperback workbook, use ISBN 978-1-319-24421-7.
  To package the workbook with the print handbook at no
  additional cost, contact your sales representative.

Your Course, Your Way

No two writing programs or classrooms are exactly alike. Our
Curriculum Solutions team works with you to design custom
options that provide the resources your students need. (Options
below require enrollment minimums.)

- *ForeWords for English.* Customize any print resource to
  fit the focus of your course or program by choosing from
  a range of prepared topics, such as **Sentence Guides for
  Academic Writers**.

- *Macmillan Author Program (MAP).* Add excerpts or
  package acclaimed works from Macmillan's trade imprints

to connect students with prominent authors and public conversations. A list of popular examples or academic themes is available upon request.

- *Mix and Match.* With our simplest solution, you can add up to 50 pages of curated content to your Bedford/St. Martin's text. Contact your sales representative for additional details.

Instructor Resources

You have a lot to do in your course. We want to make it easy for you to find the support you need — and to get it quickly.

Teaching with Hacker Handbooks is available as a PDF that can be downloaded from **macmillanlearning.com** and is also available in Achieve. In addition to chapter overviews and teaching tips, this instructor's manual includes sample syllabi, correlations to the Council of Writing Program Administrators' Outcomes Statement, and classroom activities.

Acknowledgments

I am grateful for the expertise, enthusiasm, and classroom experience that so many individuals brought to the tenth edition.

Meet our Advisory Board for Diversity, Equity, and Inclusion

The following fellow teachers of writing worked with us to make sure students can see themselves and their experiences represented in the tenth edition, to review terminology and instruction, and to promote inclusion and openness. We are grateful for their important contributions.

Kendra N. Bryant, North Carolina Agricultural and Technical State University

Javier Dueñas, Miami Dade College, North

Symmetris Jefferson Gohanna, Calhoun Community College

David F. Green, Howard University

Jamila Kareem, University of Central Florida

Esther Milu, University of Central Florida

Kristin vanEyk, University of Michigan

Reviewers

John Allen, Milwaukee ATC–Downtown; Dana Anderson, Indiana University Bloomington; Beth Baldwin, Prince George's Community College; Margaret Barnhart, Dickinson State University; Victoria Bowman, Camden County College; Amber Nicole Brooks, Georgia State University; Siobhan Craft Brownson, Winthrop University; Daniel S. Burt, Cape Cod Community College; Joseph Couch, Montgomery College–Takoma Park; Kirstin Cronn-Mills, South Central College; Michael G. Davros, Northeastern Illinois University; Christina Marie Devlin, Montgomery College–Germantown; Semire Dikli, Georgia Gwinnett College; Theresa M. Dolan, Los Angeles Trade Technical College; Elizabeth Donley, Clark College; Lisa DuRose, Inver Hills Community College; Anthony T. Fulton, Prince George's Community College; Robert Goldberg, Prince George's Community College; W. Gary Griswold, California State University–Long Beach; John Hansen, Missouri State University–West Plains; John L. Hare, Montgomery College–Germantown; Erik S. Hill, Davidson-Davie Community College; Mary Ann Leiby, El Camino Community College District; R. Elise Lozano, Tarrant County College–Southeast Campus; Amanda S. McBride, Davidson County Community College; Kevin P. Moore, County College of Morris; William Nessly, West Chester University of Pennsylvania; Clayann Gilliam Panetta, Christian Brothers University; Patricia Pantano, Medaille College; Elizabeth Quirk, Wake Technical Community College; Tristan Destry Saldaña, College of Marin; Jennifer Schaefer, Lord Fairfax Community College; Joshua Scheidler, Western Michigan University; Lisa M. Spaulding, Penn Valley Community College.

Contributors

I thank the following fellow writing teachers for important content and smart revisions. Our exciting new resource for corequisite composition, *A Student's Companion to Hacker Handbooks,* was made possible with the help of Sylvia Basile (Midlands Technical College), who wrote material on integrating sources; Sandra Chumchal (Blinn College), who wrote advice and activities for two chapters on active reading; Sarah Gottschall (Prince George's Community College), who contributed content to help students avoid plagiarism and write stronger thesis statements; and Paul Madachy (Prince George's Community

College), who wrote an important chapter on audience awareness. I am also grateful to colleagues who have contributed to the previous editions, as their important work informs the tenth edition: Margaret Price (The Ohio State University) helped us to think about gender and pronouns and inclusivity; Kimberli Huster (Robert Morris University and Duquesne University) updated advice for multilingual writers; and Sara McCurry laid the groundwork for the current version of *Teaching with Hacker Handbooks*.

Student Contributors

Including sample student writing in each edition of the handbook and its media makes these resources more useful for you and your students. I would like to thank these students for letting us adapt their work as models: Sophie Harba, Dan Larson, Michelle Nguyen, Margaret Peel, Julia Riew, Emilia Sanchez, April Bo Wang, and Ren Yoshida.

Bedford/St. Martin's

Developing handbooks, e-books, and digital writing tools is a highly collaborative business, and it is my pleasure to acknowledge and thank the enormously talented Bedford/ St. Martin's media and editorial teams, whose commitment to student success informs each new feature of *Rules for Writers* and Achieve for *Rules for Writers*. Leasa Burton, vice president for Humanities, generously offers her deep knowledge of composition to help us understand how the field continues to transform. Leasa's leadership is a source of inspiration and instruction for those who work with her. Stacey Purviance, program director for English, and Adam Whitehurst, director of media editorial for Humanities, led an extraordinary effort to develop and test the writing tools in Achieve. Stacey is a treasured source of thoughtful and innovative ideas, always quick to imagine digital solutions to support student writers. And Adam is a constant source of practical answers to our media questions. I thank them for their creative energy and their dedication to engaging instructors and students in the process of building Achieve. Laura Arcari, program manager for English, offers her superb judgment and big-picture thinking to make sure that *Rules for Writers* remains the handbook instructors trust and love. I am grateful for Laura's commitment to our handbooks, especially her deep understanding of our digital writing tools to build students' success and confidence. Many thanks to Bedford marketing colleagues Joy Fisher Williams and Vivian Garcia for their treasured advice and feedback. Doug Silver, product manager, helps us to reimagine writers' and teachers' opportunities with digital tools.

Michelle Clark, senior executive editor for handbooks, is the editor every author dreams of having. She manages to be exacting and endearing all at once — a treasured friend and colleague and an endless source of creativity. Michelle combines imagination with practicality and hard work with good cheer. Melissa Rostek, development editor and lead editor of the tenth edition, brings her excellent editorial instincts and bold questions to our collaboration. Always an advocate for students, she is a close reader extraordinaire who knows how to make every idea more interesting and every sentence more precise. Thank you, Melissa, for your unshakable optimism and steadiness, for being such an awesome editor, and for our friendship. Barbara Flanagan, recently retired as senior media editor, managed content development for Achieve and acted as our guide to all things digital. For more than 30 years, Barbara brought her unrelenting insistence on clarity and precision, as well as her expertise in documentation, to the Hacker/Sommers handbooks. Barbara set the bar high for all of us, and we benefited from her tremendous talents. We miss you, Barbara! Thanks also to Aislyn Fredsall, assistant editor, for developing the new researched argument paper, overseeing the review and permissions processes, and developing ancillary materials. Aislyn jumps in to assist on any project with her "can do" spirit, always showing us how to accomplish a task better than we imagined. She suggests innovative ways to make our handbook smarter.

Many thanks to the media production team, especially Allison Hart, senior media project manager, for delivering engaging and accessible handbook tools for students composing in the digital age. Thanks also to Gregory Erb, executive content project manager, for his experience with our handbooks and for his careful eye and smart management of the content production process; to Arthur Johnson, copy editor, for his thoroughness and attention to detail; to Claire Seng-Niemoeller, who kept our design clean, simple, and elegant — as always; and to Billy Boardman, senior design manager, who has created a striking new cover for this milestone tenth edition.

Last, but never least, I offer thanks to my own students who, over many years, have shaped my teaching and helped me understand their challenges. Thanks to my friends and colleagues Jenny Doggett, Sarah Garfinkel, Joan Feinberg, Suzanne Lane, Elisabeth McKetta, Maxine Rodburg, Laura Saltz, and Kerry Walk for sustaining conversations about the teaching of writing. And thanks to my family: to Joshua Alper, an attentive reader of life and literature, for his steadfastness across the drafts, and for his grace and good humor; to my parents, Walter and Louise Sommers, who encouraged me to write and set me forth on a career of writing and teaching; to my extended family, Ron, Charles, Mary, Demian, Liz, Devin, Yuval, Kate, Nik, Sam, Steve, and Alexander, for their encouragement and affection; and to Rachel, Alexandra, and Brian, world-class listeners, witty and wise beyond measure, always generous with their instruction and inspiration in all things that matter. They give point and purpose to writing and share my thrill when they hold this handbook in their hands. And to my grandchildren, Lailah and Oren, thanks for the joy and sweetness you bring to life.

Nancy Sommers

Scavenger Hunt

Using one of the five paths described on the inside front cover of this book, practice locating the help that writers typically need in college. Knowing how the book works and being able to quickly find answers means you get more for your money. Answers appear at the back of the book.

🔍 Finding answers to common writing questions

1 Your first assignment requires an effective thesis statement. This section of *Rules for Writers* covers drafting and revising a thesis statement.

_____
Book section numbers
(4a, 12d, for example)

2 You have been asked to format your essay in MLA style. Where in *Rules for Writers* can you find an example showing MLA format?

_____

3 You are writing a research paper and want to cite a short article from a website in your APA references list. Where will you find a model that shows you how?

_____

4 Where in the book will you find a two-page writing guide on how to write an argument essay?

_____

5 Where in *Rules for Writers* will you find advice that will help you to detect fake or misleading news?

_____

6 Locate the box that gives you advice on how to write better peer review comments.

_____

Q Using the Brief Menu, Contents, or Glossary of usage

Each of the following sentences includes an error. Identify the number of the section in *Rules for Writers* that includes advice that will help you edit the sentence. As a bonus, try to edit each of the following sentences correctly!

7 A verb have to agree with its subject. _____

Book section numbers (4a, 12d, for example)

8 Commas are useful, but are generally overused. _____

9 About sentence fragments. Academic writers should avoid them. _____

10 I plan to lay down for a nap before my shift begins. _____

11 Professor, will you except late papers? _____

12 The city felt the affects of the hurricane for months afterward. _____

A Process for Writing

1 Exploring, planning, and drafting

Welcome to *Rules for Writers* — your college writing guide. One of the pleasures of college writing is figuring out what you think and exploring questions to which you don't have answers. You may find that the process leads you in unexpected directions. The more you learn, the more questions you form. It's in the *process* of writing and thinking about ideas that you discover what's interesting in a subject and why you care about it.

Since it's not possible to think about everything all at once, start by assessing your writing situation and composing a piece of writing in stages — planning, drafting, revising, and editing.

1a Assess your writing situation.

Before composing a first draft, spend time asking questions about your writing situation. Each situation presents you with choices to make about your subject, purpose, audience, and genre. (See the checklist for assessing your writing situation on the next page.)

Subject

Often your subject will be assigned to you. When you are free to choose what to write about, select subjects that interest or puzzle you. What would you like to learn more about? What problems or issues intrigue you? Writing is much more interesting when you explore questions you don't have answers to.

Keep in mind that the length of your writing assignment will also affect your subject. A broad subject such as advertising can be a good starting point, but it is likely too general for a focused piece of writing. Choosing one aspect of that subject — in other words, narrowing to a more focused topic — will make the writing more manageable and effective. For example, you might narrow the subject of advertising to the use of pop songs in advertising or the influence of ads on body image.

CHECKLIST FOR ASSESSING YOUR WRITING SITUATION

Subject

- Has your subject been assigned, or are you free to choose your own?
- Why is your subject worth writing about?
- What questions would you like to explore?
- Do you need to narrow your subject to a more specific topic?

Purpose

- Why are you writing: To inform? To analyze? To argue? To call readers to action? For some combination of purposes?
- What message do you want to communicate?

Genre

- What genre or type of writing is required: Essay? Report? Speech or presentation? Something else?
- What are the expectations for your genre? For example, what type of evidence is typically used?

Audience

- Who are your readers? How well informed are they about the subject? What are their interests and motivations?
- What information do readers need to understand your ideas?
- Will your readers resist your ideas? What objections might you need to anticipate and counter?

Length and format

- Are there length requirements? Format requirements?
- What documentation style is required — MLA, APA, or another style?
- Do you have guidelines or examples to consult?

Deadlines

- Do you know the rough draft due date? The final due date?
- How should you submit your writing — by printing, posting, emailing, or sharing?

Purpose

In many writing situations, part of your challenge will be determining your purpose or reason for writing. The wording of an assignment may suggest its purpose. If no guidelines are given, you may need to ask yourself, "What do I want to accomplish?" and "What do I want to communicate to my audience?" Here are some common purposes for writing; identify which one or more of these aims you hope to accomplish:

to inform	to analyze
to explain	to synthesize
to summarize	to propose
to persuade/argue	to call readers to action
to evaluate	to reflect

Audience

You are always writing to readers, so take time to consider their interests and expectations. Ask questions such as these: Who are your readers? What kind of information will they need to understand your ideas? What do they know or believe about your subject? What style of writing will they expect — direct or indirect, personal or impersonal? What kind of response do you want from your readers? Make choices that show respect for your readers' values and perspectives.

Your audience is often wider than it first seems. For some pieces of writing, such as a class assignment, you will know your readers and their interests. Other pieces of writing have multiple audiences with different expectations; for example, at a job or an internship, you might write for both your supervisor and a customer. In more public writing, such as social media posts, you might never know your readers. The more your writing travels and your words stay in motion, the larger your audience grows. Whatever you write, whether digitally or in print, consider the words you choose and the tone you take so that you accomplish your purpose for communicating.

Genre

Pay attention to the genre, or type of writing, assigned. Each genre is a category of writing meant for a specific purpose and audience,

WRITING FOR AN AUDIENCE: EMAILS AND OTHER MESSAGES

Whether you're writing to an instructor, a classmate, or a potential employer, follow these guidelines for effective messages:

- Use a concise, specific subject line.
- State your main point at the beginning of the message.
- Keep paragraphs brief and focused.
- Avoid writing anything that you wouldn't say to your reader face to face.
- If you include someone else's words, let your reader know the source.
- Choose your words thoughtfully, and use considerate language. Without tone of voice and facial expressions to help convey meaning, a written message can easily be misinterpreted.
- Proofread for typos and errors.

with its own set of agreed-upon expectations for style, structure, and format. Sometimes an assignment specifies the genre — a researched argument essay in a writing class, a lab report in a biology class, a policy memo in a criminal justice class, a slide presentation in a business class. Sometimes the genre is yours to choose, and you need to consider how and why a specific genre will help you achieve your purpose and reach your audience.

EXERCISE 1–1   Narrow the following subjects into topics that would be manageable for an essay of two to five pages.

1. The minimum wage
2. Immigration
3. Cyberbullying
4. The cost of a college education
5. Internet privacy

EXERCISE 1–2   Suggest a purpose and an audience for each of the following subjects.

1. Medical experimentation using animals
2. Racial profiling
3. Genetically modified foods
4. Required vaccines in schools
5. Alternative sentencing for first-time offenders

1b Explore your subject.

When deciding on a subject, consider what you know and what you don't know. What would you like to find out? You might find it useful to explore your subject with sentence starters. In the examples below, "X" is the subject you're interested in:

Here's something I would like to understand about X: _____.

What doesn't make sense about X is _____.

Why hasn't anyone asked this question about X: _____?

The following strategies will help you generate ideas for your writing.

Asking questions

Questions are the engines of writing. They propel you forward, one question leading to another. Posing questions and exploring possible answers helps you investigate your subject. Try asking *why* and *how* questions that cannot be answered with a simple *yes* or *no*. Ask questions that allow you to enter interesting debates, gather multiple perspectives, and deepen your understanding of what's at stake.

Talking and listening

Talking about your ideas will help you develop your thoughts and discover what your listeners find interesting, what they are curious about, and where they disagree with you. If you are writing an argument, try describing it to listeners who have other points of view to hear their ideas.

Reading and annotating texts

Reading is an important way to deepen your understanding of a topic, learn from the insights and research of others, and expand your perspective. Annotating (making notes on) a text encourages you to read actively—to highlight key concepts, to note possible contradictions in an argument, or to raise questions for further research and investigation.

Brainstorming and freewriting

Brainstorming and freewriting are good ways to figure out what you know and what questions you have. Write quickly and freely, without pausing to think about word choice, to discover what questions are on your mind and what directions you might pursue.

Keeping a journal or a blog

A journal is a collection of informal or exploratory writing. You might pose questions, comment on an interesting idea from one of your classes, or keep a list of questions and observations that occur to you while reading. You might imagine a conversation between yourself and your readers or stage a debate to understand opposing positions.

Although a blog is a type of journal, it is a public rather than a private writing space. In a blog, you can explore an idea for a paper by writing posts from different angles. Since most blogs allow commenting, you can start a conversation by inviting readers to give you feedback in the form of questions, counterarguments, or links to other sources on a topic.

1c Draft and revise a working thesis statement.

For many types of writing, you will be able to state your central idea in a sentence or two. Such a statement, which ordinarily appears at the end of your introduction, is called a *thesis statement* or simply a *thesis*.

Understanding what makes an effective thesis statement

An effective thesis statement is a central idea that conveys your purpose, or reason for writing, and that requires support. An effective thesis should

- state a position that needs to be explained and supported
- use concrete language and be sharply focused
- let your readers know what to expect
- be appropriate for the assignment's length requirements, and not too broad or too narrow
- pass the "So what?" test (see p. 8)

Drafting a working thesis

As you explore your topic, you will begin to see ways to focus your material. You might try stating your topic as a question and then turning your question into a position. You'll find that the process of answering a question or taking a position on a debatable topic will focus your thinking and lead you to develop a working thesis.

For example, here are the efforts of a student, Jared, to pose a question and draft a working thesis for an essay in his ethics course.

QUESTION

Should athletes who enhance their performance through biotechnology be banned from athletic competition?

WORKING THESIS

Athletes who boost their performance through biotechnology should be banned from athletic competition.

This working thesis offers a useful place to start writing, a way to narrow the topic and focus a first draft. However, it doesn't respond to readers who will ask why this topic matters or why these athletes should be banned. To fully answer his own question, Jared pushed his thinking with the word *because*.

STRONGER WORKING THESIS

Athletes who boost their performance through biotechnology should be banned from athletic competition because biotechnology gives them an unfair advantage and disrupts the sense of fair play.

Revising a working thesis

As you move toward a clearer and more specific position you want to take, you'll start to see ways to revise your working thesis. As your ideas develop, your working thesis will change, too. You may find that the evidence you've collected supports a different thesis or that your position has changed as you have learned more about your topic. Or you might find instead that your position isn't clear and needs to become more specific.

One effective way to revise a working thesis is to put it to the "So what?" test below.

PUTTING YOUR WORKING THESIS TO THE "SO WHAT?" TEST

Use the following questions to help you revise your working thesis.

- Why would readers want to read an essay with this thesis?
- How would you respond to a reader who hears your thesis and asks "So what?" or "Why does it matter?"
- Is your thesis debatable? Can you anticipate counterarguments (objections) to your thesis?
- How will you establish common ground with readers who may not agree with your argument?

HOW TO

Solve five common problems with thesis statements

Revising a working thesis is easier if you have a method or an approach. The following problem/solution approach can help you recognize and solve common thesis problems.

1 **Common problem: The thesis is a statement of fact.**

Solution: Enter a debate by posing a question about your topic that has more than one possible answer. For example: Should the polygraph be used by private employers? Your thesis should be your answer to the question.

Working thesis: *The first polygraph was developed by Dr. John Larson in 1921.*

Revised: *Because the polygraph has not been proved reliable, even under controlled conditions, its use by private employers should be banned.*

2 **Common problem: The thesis is a question.**

Solution: Take a position on your topic by answering the question you have posed. Your thesis should be your answer to the question.

Working thesis: *Why did so many companies release ads about racism in 2020?*

Revised: *Because corporate social responsibility matters to both customers and employees, companies in the U.S. advertised their values more than their products in 2020, using their platforms to speak out against racism.*

→

HOW TO SOLVE FIVE COMMON PROBLEMS WITH THESIS STATEMENTS *(Continued)*

3 Common problem: The thesis is too broad.

Solution: Focus on a subtopic of your original topic. Once you have chosen a subtopic, take a position in an ongoing debate and pose a question that has more than one answer. For example: Should people be tested for genetic diseases? Your thesis should be your answer to the question.

Working thesis: *Mapping the human genome has many implications for health and science.*

Revised: *Now that scientists can detect genetic predisposition for specific diseases, policymakers should establish clear guidelines about whom to test and under what circumstances.*

4 Common problem: The thesis is too narrow.

Solution: Identify challenging questions that readers might ask about your topic. Then pose a question that has more than one answer. For example: Do the risks of genetic testing outweigh its usefulness? Your thesis should be your answer to the question.

Working thesis: *A person who carries a genetic mutation linked to a particular disease might or might not develop that disease.*

Revised: *Avoiding genetic testing is a smart course of action because of both its emotional risks and medical limitations.*

5 Common problem: The thesis is vague.

Solution: Focus your thesis with concrete language and clues about where the essay is headed. Pose a question about the topic that has more than one answer. For example: How does the physical structure of the Vietnam Veterans Memorial shape the experience of visitors? Your thesis—your answer to the question—should use specific language.

Working thesis: *The Vietnam Veterans Memorial is an interesting structure.*

Revised: *By inviting visitors to see their own reflections in the wall, the Vietnam Veterans Memorial creates a link between the present and the past.*

EXERCISE 1–3   In each of the following pairs, which sentence would be an effective working thesis for a short paper? Why would the other sentence be ineffective? Is it too factual? Too broad? Too vague? Use the problem/solution approach presented on pages 9–10 to evaluate each sentence.

1. a. Many drivers use their cell phones irresponsibly while driving.
   b. Current state laws are inadequate to punish drivers who use their cell phones irresponsibly to text, read email, or perform other distracting activities.

2. a. The electoral college creates imbalanced elections because it gives disproportionate decision-making power to states with fewer people.
   b. The electoral college was created to make presidential elections more balanced.

3. a. As we search to define the intelligence of animals, we run the risk of imposing our own understanding of intelligence on animals.
   b. How does the field of animal psychology help humans define intelligence?

4. a. The high cost of college needs to be reduced because it affects students and their families.
   b. To reduce the high cost of college, more students should be offered opportunities for dual-enrollment courses and a three-year college degree.

5. a. Opioid addiction affects people of all ages and from every socioeconomic group.
   b. The most effective way of treating opioid addiction is with combination therapies; often a single therapy is not enough.

1d Draft a plan.

To focus your ideas and develop your thesis, try listing and organizing supporting ideas. When you group and order your ideas, whether informally or formally, you identify how the different points fit together to support your thesis and organize your essay.

When to use an informal outline

An informal outline can be drafted and revised quickly to help you figure out a tentative organization. Informal outlines can take many forms. Perhaps the most common is simply the thesis followed by a list of major ideas. Here is one student's informal outline.

INFORMAL OUTLINE

Working thesis: Animal testing should be banned because it is bad science and doesn't contribute to biomedical advances.

- Most animals don't serve as good models for the human body.
- Drug therapies can have vastly different effects on different species — ninety-two percent of all drugs shown to be effective in animal tests fail in human trials.
- Some of the largest biomedical discoveries were made without the use of animal testing.
- The most effective biomedical research methods — tissue engineering and computer modeling — don't use animals.
- Animal studies are not scientifically necessary.

When to use a formal outline

Early in the writing process, rough outlines have certain advantages over formal outlines: They can be produced quickly, and they can be revised easily. However, a formal outline may be useful later in the writing process, after you have written a rough draft, to see whether the parts of your essay work together and whether your essay's structure is logical.

The following formal outline is the basis for the research paper that appears in 58b. The student's thesis is an important part of the outline. Everything else in the outline supports the thesis, directly or indirectly.

FORMAL OUTLINE

Thesis: In the name of public health and safety, state governments have the responsibility to shape public health policies and to regulate healthy eating choices, especially since doing so offers a potentially large social benefit for a relatively small cost.

I.   Debates surrounding food regulation have a long history in the United States.

A. The 1906 Pure Food and Drug Act guarantees inspection of meat and dairy products.

    B. Such regulations are considered reasonable because consumers are protected from harm with little cost.

    C. Consumers consider reasonable regulations to be an important government function to stop harmful items from entering the marketplace.

II. Even though food meets safety standards, there is a need for further regulation.

    A. The typical American diet—processed sugars, fats, and refined flours—is damaging over time.

    B. Related health risks are diabetes, cancer, and heart problems.

    C. Passing chronic-disease-related legislation is our single most important public health challenge.

III. Food legislation is not a popular solution for most Americans.

    A. A proposed New York City regulation banning the sale of soft drinks in servings greater than twelve ounces failed in 2012, and in California a proposed soda tax failed in 2011.

    B. Many consumers find such laws to be unreasonable restrictions on freedom of choice.

    C. Opposition to food and beverage regulation is similar to the opposition to early tobacco legislation; the public views the issue as one of personal responsibility.

    D. Counterpoint: Freedom of choice is a myth; our choices are heavily influenced by marketing.

IV. The United States has a history of regulations to discourage unhealthy behaviors.

    A. Tobacco-related restrictions faced opposition.

    B. Seat belt laws are a useful analogy.

    C. The public seems to support laws that have a good cost-benefit ratio; the cost of food/beverage regulations is low, and most people agree that the benefits would be high.

V. Americans believe that personal choice is lost when regulations such as taxes and bans are instituted.

    A. Regulations open up the door to excessive control and interfere with cultural and religious traditions.

FORMAL OUTLINE, continued

  B. Counterpoint: Burdens on individual liberty are a reasonable price to pay for large social health benefits.

VI. Public opposition continues to stand in the way of food regulation to promote healthier eating. We must consider whether to allow the costly trend of rising chronic disease to continue in the name of personal choice, or whether we are willing to support the legal changes and public health policies that will reverse that trend.

1e Draft an introduction.

Introductions are often called *hooks* because their purpose is to capture the attention of readers and give them a reason to say "Yes, I want to read your essay." Your introduction will usually be a paragraph of 50 to 150 words (in a longer paper, it may be more than one paragraph) and will include your thesis statement. The most common strategy is to open with a few sentences that engage readers, establish your purpose for writing, and lead readers to your thesis statement.

As you draft your introduction, try to avoid sweeping opening statements such as "Since the beginning of mankind . . ." or "In today's society . . ."; such broad statements don't hook readers or show them why your essay is worth reading. Also avoid dictionary definitions or a restatement of the assignment.

> **ACADEMIC WRITING** Depending on your past experiences with writing, you may feel that asserting a thesis in your introduction sounds impolite or even rude. Don't be afraid to use a direct approach. Make your position clear with a strong thesis in your introduction.

An effective way to hook readers is with an engaging question. In the following introduction, a student reaches out to her readers with this question: Should the government enact laws to regulate healthy eating choices? By showing the debate around the question, she establishes common ground with her readers. The thesis statement answers the question and takes a position. Notice how all the sentences in the introduction move clearly and logically to prepare readers for the student's thesis.

Opening question engages readers.

Should the government enact laws to regulate healthy eating choices? Many Americans would emphatically answer "No," arguing that what and how much we eat should be left to individual choice rather than to unreasonable laws. Others might argue that it would be unreasonable for the government not to enact legislation, given the rise of chronic diseases that result from harmful diets. In this debate, both the definition of reasonable regulations and the role of government to legislate food choices are at stake. In the name of public health and safety, state governments have the responsibility to shape health policies and to regulate healthy eating choices, especially since doing so offers a potentially large social benefit for a relatively small cost.

Shows two sides of the debate to establish common ground.

All the sentences lead readers to the thesis.

Thesis answers the question and offers the writer's position.

—Sophie Harba, student

TIP: For more examples of effective introductions, see the model essays in 5d, 7h, and 63b.

STRATEGIES FOR DRAFTING AN INTRODUCTION

- Offer a surprising statistic or an unusual fact
- Ask a question
- Introduce a quotation
- Establish common ground with readers
- Provide historical background
- Define a key term or concept
- Point out a problem, contradiction, or dilemma that needs resolution
- Use a vivid example or image

1f Draft the body.

As you draft the body of your essay, you might naturally ask: What should I say? How will I write an entire essay on my topic? You will find the process easier if you have a working thesis to guide the drafting process. If your thesis suggests a plan or if you have sketched a preliminary outline, try to organize your paragraphs accordingly. Draft the body of your essay by writing at least one paragraph about each supporting point you listed in the planning stage.

Remember that first drafts aren't finished drafts. They are just *first*, a place to begin. Find your momentum and keep writing.

Asking questions as you draft

As you draft, ask yourself who you are writing for and what points you want to get across. Try to anticipate what your readers might need to know to understand your thesis and follow your train of thought.

Keep these questions in mind as you draft:

- Who are my readers?
- What is my purpose?
- What does my thesis promise readers?
- How will I support my thesis?
- What evidence do readers need to understand my ideas?

For more detailed help with drafting and developing paragraphs, see section 2.

★ **Using sources responsibly**   As you draft, keep notes about sources you read and consult (see section 51). If you quote, paraphrase, or summarize a source, include a citation, even in your first draft. You will save time and avoid plagiarism if you do so.

Adding visuals as you draft

As you draft, you may decide that some of the support for your thesis would be most effective as a visual. Visuals can convey information concisely and powerfully. Graphs and tables, for example, can simplify complex numerical information. Images — including photographs and diagrams — often express ideas vividly. Keep in mind that if you use a visual from one of your sources or use published information to create your own visual, you must credit the source. Also, be sure to choose visuals to supplement your ideas, not to substitute for them.

The chart in this section describes eight types of visuals and their purposes.

★ **Using sources responsibly** If you create a chart, timeline, or other visual using information from your research, cite the source of the information even though the visual is your own. If you download a photograph from the web, credit the person or organization that created it.

CHOOSING VISUALS TO SUIT YOUR PURPOSE

Pie chart

Pie charts compare a part or parts to the whole. Segments of the pie represent percentages of the whole (and always total 100 percent).

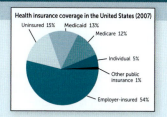

Health insurance coverage in the United States (2007)
Uninsured 15% Medicaid 13%
Medicare 12%
Individual 5%
Other public insurance 1%
Employer-insured 54%

Bar graph (or line graph)

Bar graphs highlight trends over a period of time or compare numerical data. Line graphs display the same data as bar graphs; the data are graphed as points, and the points are connected with lines. (The image shown here is a bar graph; see page 102 for a line graph.)

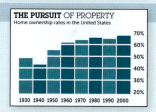

THE PURSUIT OF PROPERTY
Home ownership rates in the United States
70%
60%
50%
40%
30%
20%
1930 1940 1950 1960 1970 1980 1990 2000

Infographic

An infographic presents data in a visually engaging form. The data are usually numerical, as in bar graphs or line graphs, but they are represented by a graphic element rather than bars or lines.

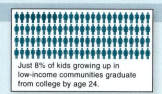

Just 8% of kids growing up in low-income communities graduate from college by age 24.

→

CHOOSING VISUALS TO SUIT YOUR PURPOSE, continued

Table

Tables display numbers and words in columns and rows. They can be used to organize complicated numerical information into an easily understood format.

Photograph

Photographs vividly depict people, scenes, or objects discussed in a text.

LIBRARY OF CONGRESS, PRINTS & PHOTOGRAPHS DIVISION [LC-DIG-HIGHSM-04024]

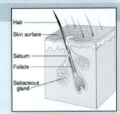

Diagram

Diagrams, useful in scientific and technical writing, concisely illustrate processes, structures, or interactions.

NATIONAL INSTITUTE OF HEALTH

Flowchart

Flowcharts show structures (the hierarchy of employees at a company, for example) or steps in a process and their relation to one another. (See also p. 125 for another example.)

Map

Maps illustrate distances, historical information, or demographics and often use symbols for geographic features and points of interest.

FROM *MAKING OF THE WEST: PEOPLES AND CULTURES*, 6E, BY LYNN HUNT, ET AL. COPYRIGHT 2019 BY BEDFORD/ST. MARTIN'S. ALL RIGHTS RESERVED. USED BY PERMISSION OF THE PUBLISHER MACMILLAN LEARNING.

1g Draft a conclusion.

A conclusion reminds readers of the essay's main idea without repeating it. By the end of the essay, readers should already understand your position, so the concluding paragraph is often relatively short. An effective conclusion rounds out an essay by giving readers a sense of completion or by issuing a call to action.

Always end your essay on a strong, positive note. You don't need to use phrases such as *In conclusion* or *In summary* because your readers will understand that your essay is concluding. The conclusion is your chance to have the last word on the subject and remind readers why your essay was worth reading.

To make your conclusion memorable and give a sense of completion, you might bring readers full circle by linking your last paragraph to your first one, returning to the thesis or including a detail from the introduction. To conclude his argument essay about the shift from print to online news, student writer Sam Jacobs returns to the hook from his introduction, the phrase *fit to print*, and echoes his thesis to show the broader importance of his argument.

Here are the introduction and conclusion from Jacobs's essay.

INTRODUCTION

"All the news that's fit to print," the motto of *The New York Times* since 1896, plays with the word *fit*, asserting that a news story must be newsworthy and must not exceed the limits of the printed page. The increase in online news consumption, however, challenges both meanings of the word *fit*, allowing producers and consumers alike to rethink who decides which topics are worth covering and how extensive that coverage should be. Any cultural shift usually means that something is lost, but in this case there are clear gains. The shift from print to online news provides unprecedented opportunities for readers to become more engaged with the news, to hold journalists accountable, and to participate as producers, not simply as consumers.

CONCLUSION

The Internet has enabled consumers to participate in a new way in reading, questioning, interpreting, and reporting the news.

Decisions about appropriate content and coverage are no longer exclusively in the hands of news editors. Ordinary citizens now have a meaningful voice in the conversation—a hand in deciding what's "fit to print." Some skeptics worry about the apparent free-for-all and loss of tradition. But the expanding definition of news provides opportunities for consumers to be more engaged with events in their communities, their nations, and the world.

TIP: For more examples of effective conclusions, see the model essays in 5d, 7h, 58b, and 63b.

STRATEGIES FOR DRAFTING A CONCLUSION

In addition to echoing your main idea, a conclusion might do any of the following:

- Briefly summarize your essay's key points
- Return to the hook used in the introduction
- Propose a course of action
- Offer a recommendation
- Suggest the topic's wider significance or implications
- Redefine a key term or concept
- Pose a question for future study

---

2 Writing paragraphs

A paragraph is a group of sentences that focuses on one main point or example. Except for special-purpose paragraphs, such as introductions and conclusions (see 1e and 1g), paragraphs are units of organization that develop and support an essay's main point, or thesis. Aim for paragraphs that are well developed, organized, coherent, and neither too long nor too short for easy reading.

2a Focus on a main point.

An effective paragraph is unified around a main point. The point should be clear to readers, and all sentences in the paragraph should relate to it.

Stating the main point in a topic sentence

A clear topic sentence, a one-sentence summary of the paragraph's main point, tells readers what to expect. It acts as a signpost pointing in two directions: backward toward the thesis of the essay and forward to the body of the paragraph.

Usually the topic sentence comes first in the paragraph.

> All living creatures manage some form of communication. The dance patterns of bees in their hive help to point the way to distant flower fields or announce successful foraging. Male stickleback fish regularly swim upside-down to indicate outrage in a courtship contest. Male deer and lemurs mark territorial ownership by rubbing their own body secretions on boundary stones or trees. Everyone has seen a frightened dog put his tail between his legs and run in panic. We, too, use gestures, expressions, postures, and movement to give our words point.
>
> — Olivia Vlahos, *Human Beginnings*

In college writing, topic sentences are often necessary for advancing or clarifying lines of an argument and introducing evidence from a source. In the following paragraph on the effects of a 2010 oil spill in the Gulf of Mexico, the writer uses a topic sentence to state that the extent of the threat is unknown before quoting three sources that illustrate her point.

> To date, the full ramifications [of the oil spill] remain a question mark. An August report from the National Oceanic and Atmospheric Administration estimated that 75 percent of the oil had "either evaporated or been burned, skimmed, recovered from the wellhead, or dispersed." However, Woods Hole Oceanographic Institution researchers reported that a 1.2-mile-wide, 650-foot-high plume caused by the spill "had and will persist for some time." And University of Georgia scientists concluded that almost 80 percent of the released oil hadn't been recovered and "remains a threat to the ecosystem."
>
> — Michele Berger, "Volunteer Army"

Sticking to the point

Sentences that do not support the topic sentence destroy the unity of a paragraph. In the following paragraph describing the switch to online learning at a high school, the information about the chemistry teacher is clearly off the point.

> As a result of the emergency move to online learning, students at Lincoln High School have had to make important adjustments. Students suddenly were put in charge of their own learning and working space, sometimes having to compete with siblings for a suitable place to do schoolwork, for example. Also, students in classes with hands-on labs, such as biology and chemistry, had to adjust to learning by simulation. The chemistry teacher left to have a baby halfway through the term, and most of the students didn't like the substitute. For students who learn better in groups, the move to online learning left them feeling disconnected and uncertain.

WRITING FOCUSED AND UNIFIED PARAGRAPHS

A strong paragraph supports a thesis, opens with a topic sentence, focuses on and develops a main point, and holds together as a unit. As you build and revise your paragraphs, ask these questions:

- Does each paragraph support the thesis?
- Does each paragraph open with a clear topic sentence?
- Does each paragraph focus on a main point and develop the point?
- Is each paragraph organized and coherent?
- Is each paragraph the right length for its topic?
- Does each paragraph contain transitions to help readers move from sentence to sentence and between paragraphs?

EXERCISE 2–1 Underline the topic sentence in the following paragraph and cross out any sentences that do not support the main idea.

> Quilt making has served as an important means of social, political, and artistic expression for women. In the nineteenth century, quilting circles provided one of the few opportunities for women to forge social bonds outside of their families. Once a week or more, they came together to sew as well as trade small talk, advice, and news. They used dyed cotton fabrics much like the fabrics quilters use today. Surprisingly, quilters' basic materials

haven't changed that much over the years. Sometimes the women joined their efforts in support of a political cause, making quilts that would be raffled to raise money for temperance societies, hospitals for sick and wounded soldiers, and the fight against slavery. Quilt making also afforded women a means of artistic expression at a time when they had few other creative outlets. Within their socially acceptable roles as homemakers, many quilters subtly pushed back at the restrictions placed on them by experimenting with color, design, and technique.

2b Develop the main point.

Though an occasional short paragraph is fine, particularly if it functions as a transition or emphasizes a point, a series of brief paragraphs suggests inadequate development. How much development is enough? That varies depending on the writer's purpose and audience.

For example, when Jane Brody, a health columnist, wrote a paragraph to convince readers that it is impossible to lose fat quickly, she knew that she would have to present a great deal of evidence because many dieters want to believe the opposite. If her paragraph was underdeveloped and light on evidence, she would not be able to persuade her readers and would leave them with more questions than answers. If Brody had left her paragraph at these few sentences, it would not be sufficient:

UNDERDEVELOPED PARAGRAPH

When you think about it, it's impossible to lose — as many diets suggest — 10 pounds of *fat* in ten days, even on a total fast. Even a moderately active person cannot lose so much weight so fast. A less active person hasn't a prayer.

This three-sentence paragraph states her main point but does not contain enough information to back it up. The paragraph that Brody *did* write builds on the main point and contains enough evidence to convince even skeptical readers:

WELL-DEVELOPED PARAGRAPH

When you think about it, it's impossible to lose — as many . . . diets suggest — 10 pounds of *fat* in ten days, even on a total fast. A pound of body fat represents 3,500 calories. To lose 1 pound of fat, you must expend 3,500 more calories than you consume. Let's say you weigh 170 pounds and, as a moderately active person, you burn 2,500 calories a day. If your diet contains only 1,500 calories, you'd have an energy deficit of 1,000 calories a day. In a week's time that would add up to a 7,000-calorie deficit, or 2 pounds of real fat. In ten days, the accumulated deficit would represent nearly 3 pounds of lost body fat. Even if you ate nothing at all for ten days and maintained your usual level of activity, your caloric deficit would add up to 25,000 calories. . . . At 3,500 calories per pound of fat, that's still only 7 pounds of lost fat.

— Jane Brody, *Jane Brody's Nutrition Book*

2c Make paragraphs coherent.

When sentences and paragraphs flow from one to another, logically and clearly, without noticeable bumps, gaps, or shifts, they are said to be coherent. Coherence can be improved by strengthening the ties between old information and new. A number of techniques for strengthening those ties are detailed in this section.

Linking ideas clearly

Readers expect to learn a paragraph's main point in a topic sentence early in the paragraph. Then, as they move into the body of the paragraph, they expect to encounter specific details, facts, or examples that support the topic sentence — either directly or indirectly.

If a sentence does not support the topic sentence directly, readers expect it to support another sentence in the paragraph and therefore to support the topic sentence indirectly. The following paragraph begins with a topic sentence. The highlighted sentences are direct supports, and the rest of the sentences are indirect supports.

There are several things that students can do to stay involved socially while attending school remotely. First, they can use technology to support their studies outside of the classroom. Instead of meeting in the library for a study session, students can meet over video. Class members can use chat software or social media groups to discuss the week's lecture, ask questions, or organize group work. Second, students can move their extracurriculars online alongside their classes. Clubs can meet virtually and complete club activities over video, or students can simply stay in touch with friends or dorm neighbors while unable to see them in person. Finally, students can stay informed on what is happening at their schools. Many schools and colleges have blogs, social media pages, or online newsletters. Such platforms deliver school updates, inform students of virtual activities or events that they can attend, and — through pictures, videos, and more — provide a piece of campus life, however small.

— Margaret Smith, student

Repeating key words

Repetition of key words is an important technique for gaining coherence. To prevent repetitions from becoming dull, you can use variations of a key word (*hike, hiker, hiking*), pronouns referring to the word (*gamblers . . . they*), and synonyms (*run, sprint, race, dash*).

In the following paragraph describing plots among indentured servants in the seventeenth century, historian Richard Hofstadter binds sentences together by repeating the key word *plots* and echoing it with a variety of synonyms.

> Plots hatched by several servants to run away together occurred mostly in the plantation colonies, and the few recorded servant uprisings were entirely limited to those colonies. Virginia had been forced from its very earliest years to take stringent steps against mutinous plots, and severe punishments for such behavior were recorded. Most servant plots occurred in the seventeenth century: a contemplated uprising was nipped in the bud in York County in 1661; apparently led by some left-wing offshoots of the Great Rebellion, servants plotted an insurrection in Gloucester County in 1663, and four leaders were condemned and executed; some discontented servants apparently joined Bacon's Rebellion in the 1670's.
>
> — Richard Hofstadter, *America at 1750*

Using parallel structures

Parallel structures are frequently used within sentences to underscore the similarity of ideas (see section 9). They may also be used to bind together a series of sentences expressing similar information. In the following passage describing folk beliefs, anthropologist Margaret Mead presents similar information in parallel grammatical form.

> Actually, almost every day, even in the most sophisticated home, something is likely to happen that evokes the memory of some old folk belief. The salt spills. A knife falls to the floor. Your nose tickles. Then perhaps, with a slightly embarrassed smile, the person who spilled the salt tosses a pinch over his left shoulder. Or

someone recites the old rhyme, "Knife falls, gentleman calls." Or as you rub your nose you think, That means a letter. I wonder who's writing?

— Margaret Mead, "New Superstitions for Old"

Providing transitions

Transitions are bridges between what has been read and what is about to be read. They help readers move from sentence to sentence and from paragraph to paragraph.

Sentence-level transitions Certain words and phrases signal connections between (or within) sentences. Frequently used transitions are included in the chart on page 27.

In the following paragraph about social psychology research, the authors use transitions to guide readers from one idea to the next.

> Social psychologists conduct research because many of the things we think we know to be true turn out to be false, or more nuanced than we originally thought, when subjected to investigation. For example, it seems reasonable that people who are threatened with punishment for doing something forbidden, illegal, self-defeating, or fattening might eventually stop, and the more severe the punishment, the more likely they will be to comply. After all, they would now associate the activity with fear or pain. But when tested empirically, this assumption turns out to be dead wrong.

— Elliot and Joshua Aronson, *The Social Animal*

ACADEMIC WRITING Choose transitions carefully and vary them appropriately. Each transition has a different meaning (see the chart on the next page). If you do not use a transition with an appropriate meaning, you might confuse your readers.

▶ Although opening the store may seem unappealing, working the
early shift has its advantages. ~~Moreover,~~ *For example,* staff members who
arrive early typically avoid the worst traffic and find the best
parking spaces.

COMMON TRANSITIONS

TO SHOW ADDITION   and, also, besides, further, furthermore, in addition, moreover, next, too, first, second

TO GIVE EXAMPLES   for example, for instance, in fact, specifically, to illustrate

TO COMPARE   also, in the same manner, likewise, similarly

TO CONTRAST   although, but, even though, however, in contrast, nevertheless, on the contrary, on the other hand, still, though, yet

TO SUMMARIZE OR CONCLUDE   in conclusion, in short, in summary, therefore, to sum up

TO SHOW TIME   after, as, before, during, finally, immediately, later, meanwhile, next, then, when, while

TO SHOW PLACE OR DIRECTION   above, below, beyond, close, nearby, opposite, to the left

TO INDICATE LOGICAL RELATIONSHIP   as a result, because, consequently, for this reason, if, since, so, therefore, thus

Paragraph-level transitions Paragraph-level transitions usually link the *first* sentence of a new paragraph with the *first* sentence of the previous paragraph. In other words, the topic sentences signal global connections.

Look for opportunities to echo the subject of a previous paragraph (as summed up in its topic sentence) in the topic sentence of the next one. In his essay "Little Green Lies," Jonathan H. Adler uses this paragraph-level transition strategy to link topic sentences.

> Consider aseptic packaging, the synthetic packaging for the "juice boxes" so many children bring to school with their lunch. One criticism of aseptic packaging is that it is nearly impossible to recycle, yet on almost every other count, aseptic packaging is environmentally preferable to the packaging alternatives. Not only do aseptic containers not require refrigeration to keep their contents from spoiling, but their manufacture requires less than one-10th the energy of making glass bottles.
>
> What is true for juice boxes is also true for other forms of synthetic packaging. The use of polystyrene, which is commonly (and mistakenly) referred to as "Styrofoam," can reduce food waste dramatically due to its insulating properties. (Thanks to these properties, polystyrene cups are much preferred over paper for that morning cup of coffee.) Polystyrene also requires significantly fewer resources to produce than its paper counterpart.
>
> — Jonathan H. Adler, "Little Green Lies"

Maintaining consistency

Coherence suffers whenever a draft shifts confusingly from one point of view to another or from one verb tense to another. (See section 13.) In addition, coherence can suffer when new information is introduced with the subject of each sentence. As a rule, a sentence's subject should echo a subject or an object in the previous sentence.

2d If necessary, adjust paragraph length.

Most effective paragraphs range between one hundred and two hundred words. Shorter paragraphs can require too much starting and stopping, and longer ones can strain the reader's attention span. There are exceptions to this guideline, however. Paragraphs longer than two hundred words frequently appear in scholarly writing, where writers explore complex ideas. Paragraphs shorter than one hundred words occur in business writing, in news articles, and on websites, where readers routinely skim for main ideas, and in informal essays to quicken the pace.

In an essay, the first and last paragraphs will ordinarily be the introduction and the conclusion. These special-purpose paragraphs are often shorter than other paragraphs in the essay. Typically, the body paragraphs will follow the essay's outline: one paragraph per point in short essays, several paragraphs per point in longer ones. Some ideas require more development than others, however, so it is best to be flexible. If an idea stretches to a length unreasonable for a paragraph, you should divide the paragraph, even if you have presented comparable points in the essay in single paragraphs.

Paragraph breaks are not always made for strictly logical reasons. Writers use them for all of the following reasons.

REASONS FOR BEGINNING A NEW PARAGRAPH

- to mark off the introduction and the conclusion
- to signal a shift to a new idea
- to indicate an important shift in time or place
- to emphasize a point (by placing it at the beginning or the end, not in the middle, of a paragraph)
- to highlight a contrast
- to provide readers with a needed pause
- to break up text that is too dense

Beware, however, of using too many short, choppy paragraphs that read like a list. Readers want to see how your ideas connect, and they become irritated when you break their momentum by forcing them to pause every few sentences. Here are a few reasons you might have for combining some of the paragraphs in a rough draft.

REASONS FOR COMBINING PARAGRAPHS

- to clarify the essay's organization
- to connect closely related ideas
- to bind together text that looks too choppy

2e Choose a suitable strategy for developing paragraphs.

Although paragraphs and essays may be developed in any number of ways, certain methods of organization occur frequently, either alone or in combination:

illustrations (p. 29)   analogy (p. 32)
narration (p. 30)   cause and effect (p. 33)
description (p. 30)   classification (p. 33)
process (p. 31)   definition (p. 34)
comparison and contrast
(p. 31)

These strategies for developing paragraphs have different uses, depending on the writer's subject and purpose.

Illustrations

Illustrations are extended examples and can be a vivid and effective means of developing a point. The writer of the following paragraph uses illustrations to support his point that Harriet Tubman was a genius at eluding her pursuers.

> Part of [Harriet Tubman's] strategy of conducting was, as in all battle-field operations, the knowledge of how and when to retreat. Numerous allusions have been made to her moves when she suspected that she was in danger. When she feared the party was closely pursued, she would take it for a time on a train southward bound. No one seeing Negroes going in this direction would for an instant suppose them to be fugitives. Once on her return she

was at a railroad station. She saw some men reading a poster and she heard one of them reading it aloud. It was a description of her, offering a reward for her capture. She took a southbound train to avert suspicion. At another time when Harriet heard men talking about her, she pretended to read a book which she carried. One man remarked, "This can't be the woman. The one we want can't read or write." Harriet devoutly hoped the book was right side up.

—Earl Conrad, *Harriet Tubman*

Narration

A paragraph of narration tells a story or part of a story. Narrative paragraphs are usually arranged in chronological order, but they may also contain flashbacks, interruptions that take the story back to an earlier time. The following paragraph recounts one of the author's experiences in the wilderness of Tanzania.

One evening when I was wading in the shallows of the lake to pass a rocky outcrop, I suddenly stopped dead as I saw the sinuous black body of a snake in the water. It was all of six feet long, and from the slight hood and the dark stripes at the back of the neck I knew it to be a Storm's water cobra — a deadly reptile for the bite of which there was, at that time, no serum. As I stared at it an incoming wave gently deposited part of its body on one of my feet. I remained motionless, not even breathing, until the wave rolled back into the lake, drawing the snake with it. Then I leaped out of the water as fast as I could, my heart hammering.

— Jane Goodall, *In the Shadow of Man*

Description

A descriptive paragraph sketches a portrait of a person, place, or thing by using concrete and specific details that appeal to one or more of our senses — sight, sound, smell, taste, and touch. Consider, for example, the following description of the grasshopper invasions that devastated the Midwestern landscape in the United States in the late 1860s.

They came like dive bombers out of the west. They came by the millions with the rustle of their wings roaring overhead. They came in waves, like the rolls of the sea, descending with a terrifying speed, breaking now and again like a mighty surf. They came with the force of a williwaw and they formed a huge, ominous, dark brown cloud that eclipsed the sun. They dipped and touched earth, hitting objects and people like hailstones. But they were not hail. These were *live* demons. They popped, snapped, crackled, and roared. They were dark brown, an inch or longer in length, plump in the middle and tapered at the ends. They had transparent wings, slender legs, and two black eyes that flashed with a fierce intelligence.

— Eugene Boe, "Pioneers to Eternity"

Process

A process paragraph is structured in chronological order. A writer may choose this pattern either to describe how something is made or done or to explain to readers, step by step, how to do something. Here is a paragraph explaining how to perform a "roll cast," a popular fly-fishing technique.

Begin by taking up a suitable stance, with one foot slightly in front of the other and the rod pointing down the line. Then begin a smooth, steady draw, raising your rod hand to just above shoulder height and lifting the rod to the 10:30 or 11:00 position. This steady draw allows a loop of line to form between the rod top and the water. While the line is still moving, raise the rod slightly, then punch it rapidly forward and down. The rod is now flexed and under maximum compression, and the line follows its path, bellying out slightly behind you and coming off the water close to your feet. As you power the rod down through the 3:00 position, the belly of line will roll forward. Follow through smoothly so that the line unfolds and straightens above the water.

— *The Dorling Kindersley Encyclopedia of Fishing*

Comparison and contrast

To compare two subjects is to draw attention to their similarities, although the word *compare* also has a broader meaning that includes a consideration of differences. To contrast is to focus only on differences.

Whether a paragraph stresses similarities or differences, it may be patterned in one of two ways. The two subjects may be presented one at a time, as in the following paragraph of contrast.

So Grant and Lee were in complete contrast, representing two diametrically opposed elements in American life. Grant was the modern man emerging; beyond him, ready to come on the stage, was the great age of steel and machinery, of crowded cities and a restless, burgeoning vitality. Lee might have ridden down from the old age of chivalry, lance in hand, silken banner fluttering over his head. Each man was the perfect champion of his cause, drawing both his strengths and his weaknesses from the people he led.

— Bruce Catton, "Grant and Lee: A Study in Contrasts"

Alternatively, a paragraph may proceed point by point, treating the two subjects together, one aspect at a time. The following paragraph uses the point-by-point method to compare speeches given by Abraham Lincoln in 1860 and Barack Obama in 2008.

Two men, two speeches. The men, both lawyers, both from Illinois, were seeking the presidency, despite what seemed their crippling connection with extremists. Each was young by modern standards for a president. Abraham Lincoln had turned fifty-one just five days before delivering his speech. Barack Obama was forty-six when he gave his. Their political experience was mainly provincial, in the Illinois legislature for both of them, and they had received little exposure at the national level — two years in the House of Representatives for Lincoln, four years in the Senate for Obama. Yet each was seeking his party's nomination against a New York senator of longer standing and greater prior reputation — Lincoln against Senator William Seward, Obama against Senator Hillary Clinton.

— Garry Wills, "Two Speeches on Race"

Analogy

Analogies draw comparisons between items that appear to have little in common. Writers use analogies to make something abstract or unfamiliar easier to grasp or to provoke fresh thoughts about a common subject. In the following paragraph, physician Lewis Thomas draws an analogy between the behavior of ants and that of humans.

Ants are so much like human beings as to be an embarrassment. They farm fungi, raise aphids as livestock, launch armies into wars, use chemical sprays to alarm and confuse enemies, capture slaves. The families of weaver ants engage in child labor, holding their larvae like shuttles to spin out the thread that sews the leaves together for their fungus gardens. They exchange information ceaselessly. They do everything but watch television.

— Lewis Thomas, "On Societies as Organisms"

Cause and effect

A paragraph may move from cause to effects or from an effect to its causes. The topic sentence in the following paragraph mentions an effect; the rest of the paragraph lists several causes.

> The fantastic water clarity of the Mount Gambier sinkholes results from several factors. The holes are fed from aquifers holding rainwater that fell decades — even centuries — ago, and that has been filtered through miles of limestone. The high level of calcium that limestone adds causes the silty detritus from dead plants and animals to cling together and settle quickly to the bottom. Abundant bottom vegetation in the shallow sinkholes also helps bind the silt. And the rapid turnover of water prohibits stagnation.
>
> — Hillary Hauser, "Exploring a Sunken Realm in Australia"

In the following paragraph, the topic sentence identifies a cause; the rest of the paragraph lists the effects.

> The rise of rail transport in the nineteenth century forever changed American farming — for better and for worse. Farmers who once raised crops and livestock to sustain just their own families could now make a profit by selling their goods in towns and cities miles away. These new markets improved the living standard of struggling farm families and encouraged them to seek out innovations that would increase their profits. On the downside, the competition fostered by the new markets sometimes created hostility among neighboring farm families where there had once been a spirit of cooperation. Those farmers who couldn't compete with their neighbors left farming forever, facing poverty worse than they had ever known.
>
> — Chris Mileski, student

Classification

Classification is the grouping of items into categories according to some consistent principle. The principle of classification that a writer chooses ultimately depends on the writer's purpose. The following paragraph classifies types of intelligence.

> Robert Sternberg has introduced his three-part theory of successful intelligence. *Analytical* intelligence is our ability to complete problem-solving tasks such as those typically contained in tests; *creative* intelligence is our ability to synthesize and apply existing knowledge and skills to deal with new and unusual situations; *practical* intelligence is our ability to adapt to everyday life — to understand what needs to be done in a specific setting and then

to do it; what we call street smarts. Different cultures and learning situations draw on these intelligences differently, and much of what's required to succeed in a particular situation is not measured by standard IQ or aptitude tests, which can miss critical competencies.

> — Peter C. Brown, Henry L. Roediger III, and Mark A. McDaniel,
> *Make it Stick: The Science of Successful Learning*

Definition

A definition puts a word or concept into a general class and then provides enough details to distinguish it from others in the same class. In the following passage, the writer defines *Punk* as a subculture.

> Quickly expanding beyond its garage rock origins, Punk was an attitude, subculture and übercult — an anti-authoritarian backlash of nihilist aggression. It began to take hold in New York around 1973 and by the end of the decade had cultivated not only its own abrasive sound, but also its own in-your-face visual aesthetics. Like the Hippies that came before them, the Punks, and their New Wave sidekicks, were ready to change the world, though less with peace and love than with a slap upside the head.
>
> — Ann Fensterstock, *Art on the Block*

3 Revising, editing, and reflecting

To revise is to *re-see*, and the comments you receive from reviewers — instructors, peers, and writing center tutors — will help you re-see your draft through readers' eyes. Asking your readers simple questions such as "Do you understand my main idea?" and "Is my draft organized?" will help you revise your draft to clarify and organize your ideas. Writing multiple drafts allows you to write in stages, seek feedback, and strengthen your work through revising and editing.

3a Use peer review: Give constructive comments.

Peer review offers you an opportunity to read the work of your classmates, pose questions and suggestions, and help them see their drafts through your eyes. When you review a peer's work, you not only help your classmate but also benefit from the process of thinking strategically about revision. As you offer advice about how to strengthen a thesis, for example, or how to use a visual to convey information, you are learning, too, about the purpose of a thesis or about the role of visuals.

HOW TO

Write helpful peer review comments

1 **View yourself as a guide, not a judge or an editor.**
Ask questions and propose possibilities instead of dictating solutions. Help your peer identify the strengths of a draft. Try phrasing comments this way: "Have you thought about . . . ?" or "How can you help a reader understand this point?"

2 **Pay attention to global issues first.** Focus on the big picture—purpose, thesis, organization, and evidence—before sentence structure, word choice, and grammar. You might, for instance, offer counterarguments to a peer's thesis, or you might suggest places where additional evidence would make an argument more persuasive. Use the checklist for global revision on page 42 to help you focus on global issues.

3 **Restate the writer's main idea.** As a reader, you can help your peer see whether points are expressed clearly. Can you follow the writer's train of thought? Restate the writer's thesis and main ideas to check your understanding.

4 **Be specific.** Point to specific places in a draft and show your classmate how, why, and where a draft is effective or confusing. Instead of saying "I like your introduction," say exactly what you like: "You use a surprising statistic in your introduction, and it really hooks me as a reader." Always end your peer review session with specific recommendations for revising.

3b Learn from peer review: Revise with comments.

Peer review gives you an opportunity to learn what's working and not working in your draft. Your peers will offer their suggestions, answer your questions, and help you strengthen your essay.

The following guidelines will help you learn from reviewers' comments and revise successfully.

- **Be active.** Guide reviewers to understand your purpose and goals for writing, including why you chose your topic and what you hope to accomplish in your draft. Tell reviewers your specific concerns so they can focus their feedback. Ask reviewers to show you what puzzles them about your draft and what is unclear. Always ask questions to make sure you understand your reviewers' comments.

- **Have an open mind.** After you've worked hard on a draft, you might be surprised to hear reviewers tell you it needs more development. Don't take criticism personally. Your readers are responding to your essay, not to you. Responding to readers' objections instead of dismissing them will strengthen your ideas and make your essay more persuasive.

REVISE WITH COMMENTS: WHAT DOES "BE SPECIFIC" MEAN?

Often the comments you'll receive are written as shorthand commands, such as "Be specific!" Such comments don't show you how to revise, but they do identify where you want to focus your attention. When reviewers say that you need to "be specific," the comment often signals that you could strengthen your writing by including additional evidence or by analyzing the evidence.

Strategies for Revising

- **Reread your topic sentence** to understand the focus of the paragraph. (See 2a.)

- **Ask questions.** Does the paragraph contain claims that need support? Have you provided evidence—specific examples, vivid details and illustrations, statistics and facts—to help readers understand your ideas and find them persuasive? (See 7f.)

- **Analyze your evidence.** Remember that details and examples don't speak for themselves. You will need to show readers how evidence supports your claims. (See 4d.)

- **Weigh feedback carefully.** Your reviewers will offer more suggestions than you can use, so be strategic. Sort through all the comments you receive with your original goals in mind, and focus on global concerns first — otherwise, you'll be facing the impossible task of trying to incorporate everyone's advice.

- **Keep a revision and editing log.** To help you become a stronger writer, make a list of the global and sentence-level concerns that keep coming up in your reviewers' comments. For more on improving your writing with editing logs, see pages 44–45.

Excerpt from an online peer review session

Juan (peer reviewer): *Rachel, your essay makes a great point that credit card companies often hook students on a cycle of spending. But it sounds as if you're blaming students for their spending habits and credit card companies for their deceptive actions. Is this what you want to say?*

Peer reviewer restates writer's main point and asks a question to help her clarify her ideas.

Rachel (writer): No, I want to keep the focus on the credit card companies. I didn't realize I was blaming students. What could I change?

Writer takes comment seriously and asks reviewer for specific suggestion.

Juan (reviewer): *In paragraphs three and four, you group all students together as if all students have the same bad spending habits. If students are your audience, you'll be insulting them. What reader is motivated to read something that's alienating? What is your purpose for writing this draft?*

Peer reviewer points to specific places in the draft and asks questions to help writer focus on audience and purpose.

Rachel (writer): Well . . . It's true that students don't always have good spending habits, but I don't want to blame students. My purpose is to call students to action about the dangers of credit card debt. Any suggestions for narrowing the focus?

Writer is actively engaged with peer reviewer's comments and doesn't take criticism personally.

Juan (reviewer): *Most students know about the dangers of credit card debt, but they might not know about specific deceptive practices companies use to lure them. Maybe ask yourself what would surprise your audience about these practices.*

Peer reviewer responds as a reader and acts as a coach to suggest possible solutions.

Rachel (writer): Juan, that's a good idea. I'll try it.

Writer thanks reviewer for his help and leaves session with a specific revision strategy.

POST COMMENT

3c One student's peer review process

Student writer Michelle Nguyen's assignment, a literacy narrative, asked her to explore this question: *How have your experiences with writing shaped you as a writer?*

Here is Nguyen's draft, along with the questions she gave her peer reviewers before they read her draft.

QUESTIONS FROM NGUYEN TO PEER REVIEWERS

Alex, Brian, and Sameera: Thanks for reading my draft. Here are three questions I have about my draft: Is my focus clear? Is there anything that confuses you? What specifically should I cut or add to strengthen my draft?

Rough draft with peer comments

My family used to live in the heart of Hanoi, Vietnam. The neighborhood was small but swamped with crime. Drug addicts scoured the alleys and stole the most mundane things— old clothes, worn slippers, even license plates of motorbikes. Like anyone else in Vietnam in the 1990s, we struggled with poverty. There was no entertainment device in our house aside from an eleven-inch black-and-white television. Even then, electricity went off for hours on a weekly basis.

> **Alex F:** You might want to add a title to focus readers.

> **Sameera K:** I really like your introduction. It's so vivid. Think about adding a photo so readers can relate. What does Hanoi look like?

> **Brian S:** You have great details here to set the scene in Hanoi, but why does it matter that you didn't have an "entertainment device"? Maybe choose the most interesting among all these details.

I was particularly close to a Vietnam War veteran. My parents were away a lot, so the older man became like a grandfather to me. He taught me how to ride a bicycle, how to read, how to take care of small pets. He worked sporadically from home, fixing bicycle tires and broken pedals. He was a wrinkly man who didn't talk much. His vocal cords were damaged during the war, and it caused him pain to speak. In a neighborhood full of screaming babies and angry shop owners and slimy criminals, his home was my quiet haven. I could read and write and think and bond with someone whose worldliness came from his wordlessness.

> **Brian S:** Worldliness came from wordlessness—great phrase! Is this part of your main idea? What is your main idea?

The tiny house he lived in stood at the far end of our neighborhood. It always smelled of old clothes and forgotten memories. He was a slight man, but his piercing black eyes retained their intensity even after all these years. He must have made one fierce soldier.

> **Sameera K:** You do a good job of showing us why this Vietnam veteran was important to you, but it seems like this draft is more a story about the man and not about you. What do you want readers to understand about you?

"I almost died once," he said, dusting a picture frame. It was one of those rare instances he ever mentioned his life during the war. As he talked, I perched myself on the side of an armchair, rested my head on my tiny hands, and listened intently. I didn't understand much. I just liked hearing his low, humming voice. The concept of war for me was strictly confined to the classroom, and even then, the details of combat were always murky. The teachers just needed us to know that the communist troops enjoyed a glorious victory.

"I was the only survivor of my unit. Twenty guys. All dead within a year. Then they let me go," he said. His voice cracked a little and his eyes misted over as he stared at pictures from his combatant past. "We didn't even live long enough to understand what we were fighting for."

He finished the sentence with a drawn-out sigh, a small set of wrinkles gathering at the end of his eyes. Years later, as I thought about his stories, I started to wonder why he referred to his deceased comrades by the collective pronoun "we." It was as if a little bit of him died on the battlefield with them too.

Three years after my family left the neighborhood, I learned that the man became stricken with cancer. When I came home the next summer, I visited his house and sat by his sickbed. His shoulder-length mop of salt and pepper hair now dwarfed his rail-thin figure. We barely exchanged a word. He just held my hands tightly until my mother called for me to leave, his skeletal fingers leaving a mark on my pale palms. Perhaps he was trying to transmit to me some of his worldliness and his wisdom. Perhaps he was telling me to go out into the world and live the free life he never had.

> **Sameera K:** I'm curious to hear more about you and why this man was so important to you. What did he teach you about writing? What did he see in you?

Some people say that writers are selfish and vain. The truth is, I learned to write because it gave me peace in the much too noisy world of my Vietnamese childhood. In the quiet of the man's house, I gazed out the window, listened to my thoughts, and wrote them down. It all started with a story about a wrinkly Vietnam War veteran who didn't talk much.

> **Alex F:** This sentence is confusing. Your draft doesn't seem to be about the selfishness or vanity of writers.

> **Brian S:** What does "it" refer to? I think you're trying to say something important about silence and noise and literacy, but I'm not sure what it is.

After rereading her draft and considering the feedback from her classmates, Nguyen realized that she had chosen a good direction but hadn't focused her draft to meet the expectations of the assignment. Her classmates offered valuable suggestions about adding a photograph of her Hanoi neighborhood and clarifying her main idea. With her classmates' specific questions and suggestions in mind, and their encouragement to see the undeveloped possibilities in her draft, Nguyen developed some goals for revising.

MICHELLE NGUYEN'S REVISION GOALS

- Add a title.
- Revise the introduction to set the scene more dramatically. Use Sameera's idea to include a photo of my neighborhood.
- Make the story my story, not the man's story. Answer Sameera's question: What did the man see in me and I in him? Delete extra material about the man.
- Answer Brian's question: What is my main idea?
- Follow Brian's suggestion about the connection between wordlessness and worldliness. Maybe I'm trying to say that the surprise was finding writing in silence, not in the noise in my neighborhood.

See 3h for Nguyen's revised draft.

3d Approach global revision in cycles.

Revision is more effective when you approach it in cycles, rather than attempting to change everything all at once. Focus on the big-picture global elements — engaging your audience, sharpening your focus, improving organization, and strengthening content — before revising and editing your sentences. See the next page for questions to ask while revising globally.

3e Revise globally by making a reverse outline.

Outlines are useful before you write a first draft to help you focus and structure your ideas. They are useful, too, *after* you have written a draft to reveal the organization of your essay. Some writers revise globally by making a *reverse outline.*

A reverse outline helps you examine the logical flow of ideas and evaluate each paragraph to see how it supports your thesis. By going through your draft paragraph by paragraph, you can see how the parts work together and determine whether each paragraph has a clear focus. Sometimes a reverse outline reveals that your draft has taken a different direction than you planned and thus you need to revise your thesis. Sometimes it reveals gaps in support or paragraphs that need topic sentences.

CHECKLIST FOR GLOBAL REVISION

Purpose and audience

- Does the draft address a question, a problem, or an issue that readers care about?
- Is the draft appropriate for its audience? Does it account for the audience's knowledge of and possible attitudes toward the subject?

Focus

- Is the thesis clear? Is it prominently placed?
- Does the thesis answer a reader's "So what?" question? (See 1c.)
- If the draft has no thesis, is there a good reason for omitting one?

Organization and paragraphing

- Is each paragraph unified around a main point?
- Does each paragraph support and develop the thesis with evidence?
- Have you stated the main point of each paragraph in a topic sentence?
- Have you presented ideas in a logical order?
- Does each paragraph flow from one to another without gaps or bumps?

Content

- Is the supporting material relevant and persuasive?
- Which ideas need further development? Have you left readers with any unanswered questions?
- Do major ideas receive enough attention?
- Where might you delete redundant or irrelevant information?

Point of view

- Is the dominant point of view — first person (*I* or *we*), second person (*you*), or third person (*he, she, it, one,* or *they*) — appropriate for your purpose and audience?

To make a reverse outline:

- Reread your draft. Write your main points in the margin.
- Number each paragraph or each part of your draft. Make notes in the margin about each paragraph. What is the topic sentence? What is the main idea of the paragraph?
- Ask questions: Is your thesis clear and specific? Have you provided sufficient support for the thesis? Are your paragraphs developed and focused? Did you leave anything out? The answers to these questions will shape your revision plan.

ACADEMIC WRITING When reviewing your draft, carefully consider the language you've used when discussing others. Have you made any assumptions about groups of people that are stereotypical or too general? Have you used any language that might be disrespectful or noninclusive of your readers? See 17e and 17f.

3f Revise and edit sentences.

When you *revise* sentences, you focus on clarity and effectiveness; when you *edit*, you check for correctness. Sentences that are wordy, vague, or rambling may distract readers and make it hard for readers to focus on your purpose or grasp your ideas. Read each sentence slowly to determine whether it communicates your meaning clearly and specifically. You might find it helpful to read your work aloud and trust your ears to detect awkwardness, wordiness, or repetition.

Below is an excerpt from a student draft that included both errors that needed editing (blue comments) and ineffective or unclear sentences that needed revising (black comment). References to relevant handbook sections appear in parentheses.

DRAFT PASSAGE

Wordy sentence (16c, 16d)
Unnecessary comma (34a)
Vague pronoun (23b)

Although some cities have found creative ways to improve access to public transportation for passengers with physical disabilities, and to fund other programs, there have been problems in our city due to the need to address budget constraints and competing problems. This has led citizens to question how funds are distributed?

Wrong punctuation for a statement (39a)

REVISED AND EDITED PASSAGE

Although some cities have found creative ways to improve access to public transportation for passengers with physical disabilities, our city has struggled with budget constraints and competing priorities. The budget crunch has led citizens to question how funds are distributed.

The revised and edited passage is clearer, easier to read, and correct.

HOW TO

Improve your writing with an editing log

An important aspect of becoming a college writer is learning how to identify the grammar, punctuation, and spelling errors that you make frequently and that may make your writing hard to read. You can use an editing log to keep a list of your common errors, anticipate patterns, and learn the rules needed to make corrections or changes. When you receive a draft with feedback, take the following steps.

1 **Review any errors** that your instructor or tutor has identified.

2 **Note which editing problems you commonly have.** For example, have you seen "run-on sentence" or "need a transition" marked in other drafts?

3 **Identify the advice in the handbook** that will help you correct the errors.

4 **Make an entry in your editing log.** A suggested format appears on the next page.

Sample editing log page

ORIGINAL SENTENCE

Athletes who use any type of biotechnology give themselves an unfair advantage they should be banned from competition.

EDITED SENTENCE

Athletes who use any type of biotechnology give themselves an unfair advantage, and they should be banned from competition.

RULE OR PATTERN APPLIED

To edit a run-on sentence, use a comma and a coordinating conjunction (and, but, or). Rules for Writers, section 20a

3g Proofread and format the final manuscript.

Proofreading is a special kind of reading: a slow and methodical search for misspellings, typos, and omitted words or word endings. Such errors can be difficult to spot in your own work because you may read what you intended to write, not what is actually on the page.

A carefully proofread essay sends a positive message: It shows that you value your writing and respect your readers. Try one or more of the following strategies.

PROOFREADING TIPS

- Remove distractions and allow yourself ten to fifteen minutes of pure concentration — without your cell phone.
- Proofread out loud, articulating each word as it is actually written.
- Proofread your sentences in reverse order.
- Don't rely too heavily on spell checkers and grammar checkers. Before accepting their changes, consider the accuracy and appropriateness of the suggestions.
- Ask a volunteer (a friend, roommate, or co-worker) to proofread after you. A second reader may catch something you didn't.

Before turning in your essay, make sure that it is formatted correctly. Use the manuscript format recommended by your instructor or for your academic discipline. For MLA style, see the guidelines in 58a and the sample papers in 4e and 58b. For APA style, see the guidelines and sample paper in 63.

3h Sample student revision: Literacy narrative

In 3c, you'll find Michelle Nguyen's first draft, along with the highlights of her peer review process. Comments from reviewers helped Nguyen develop a revision plan (see p. 41). One reviewer asked, "What is your main idea?" Another reviewer asked, "What do you want readers to understand about you?" As she revised, Nguyen made both global revisions and sentence-level revisions to clarify her main idea and to delete material that might distract readers from her story. Here is Nguyen's final draft, "A Place to Begin."

Nguyen 1

Michelle Nguyen

Professor Wilson

English 101

24 September 2019

A Place to Begin

I grew up in the heart of Hanoi, Vietnam—Nhà Dầu—a small but busy neighborhood swamped with crime. Houses, wedged in among cafés and other local businesses (see fig. 1), measured uniformly about two hundred square feet, and the walls were so thin that we could hear every heated debate and impassioned disagreement. Drug addicts scoured the vicinity and stole the most mundane things—old clothes, worn slippers, even license plates of motorbikes. It was a neighborhood where dogs howled and kids ran amok and where the earth was always moist and marked with stains. It was the 1990s Vietnam in miniature, with all the turmoil and growing pains of a newly reborn nation.

In a city perpetually inundated with screaming children and slimy criminals, I found my place in the home of a Vietnam War veteran. My parents were away a lot, so

Marginal annotations:
- Nguyen formats her final draft using MLA guidelines.
- Nguyen revises her introduction to engage readers with vivid details.
- Sentences are revised for clarity and specificity.

Marginal annotations indicate MLA-style formatting and effective writing.

Nguyen 2

As her peer reviewers suggested, Nguyen adds a photograph to help readers visualize Hanoi.

Fig. 1. Photo of the Nhà Dầu neighborhood in Hanoi. By the author, 6 June 2010.

the older man became like a grandfather to me. He was a slight man who didn't talk much. His vocal cords had been damaged during the war, and it caused him pain to speak. In his quiet home, I could read and write in the presence of someone whose worldliness grew from his wordlessness.

Nguyen's revisions clarify her main idea.

His tiny house stood at the far end of our neighborhood and always smelled of old clothes and forgotten memories. His wall was plastered with pictures from his combatant past, pictures that told his life story when his own voice couldn't. "I almost died once," he said, dusting a picture frame. It was one of those rare instances he ever mentioned his life during the war.

Nguyen focuses on one key story in response to reviewers' questions.

I perched myself on the side of the armchair, rested my head on my tiny hands, and listened intently. I didn't understand much. I just liked hearing his low, raspy voice.

"I was the only survivor of my unit. Twenty guys. All dead within a year. Then they let me go."

Nguyen develops her narrative with dialogue.

He finished the sentence with a drawn-out sigh, a small set of wrinkles gathering at the corner of his eye.

I wanted to hear the details of that story yet was too afraid to ask. But the bits and pieces I did hear, I wrote down

Nguyen 3

in a notebook. I wanted to make sure that there were not only photos but also written words to bear witness to the veteran's existence.

Once, I caught him looking at the jumbled mess of sentences I'd written. I ran to the table and snatched my notebook, my cheeks warmed with a bright tinge of pink. I was embarrassed. But mostly, I was terrified that he'd hate me for stealing his life story and turning it into a collection of words and characters and ambivalent feelings.

"I'm sorry," I muttered, my gaze drilling a hole into the tiled floor.

Quietly, he peeled the notebook from my fingers and placed it back on the table.

In his muted way, with his mouth barely twisted in a smile, he seemed to be granting me permission and encouraging me to keep writing. Maybe he saw a storyteller and a writer in me, a little girl with a pencil and too much free time.

The last time I visited Nhà Dầu was for the veteran's funeral two years ago. It was a cold November afternoon, but the weather didn't dampen the usual tumultuous spirit of the neighborhood. I could hear the jumble of shouting voices and howling dogs, yet it didn't bother me. For a minute I closed my eyes, remembering myself as a little girl with a big pencil, gazing out a window and scribbling words in my first notebook.

Many people think that words emerge from words and from the exchange of voices. Perhaps this is true. But the surprising paradox of writing for me is that I started to write in the presence of silence. It was only in the utter stillness of a Vietnam War veteran's house that I could hear my thoughts for the first time, appreciate language, and find the confidence to put words on a page. With one notebook and a pencil, and with the encouragement of a wordless man to tell his story, I began to write. Sometimes that's all a writer needs, a quiet place to begin.

Marginal notes:

Nguyen revises to keep the focus on her story and not the man's, as her peer reviewers suggested.

Nguyen circles back to the scene from the introduction, giving the narrative coherence.

Nguyen revises the final paragraph to show readers the significance of her narrative.

Following a peer reviewer's advice, Nguyen chooses words from her final sentence for her title.

WRITING GUIDE

How to write a literacy narrative

A **literacy narrative** allows you to reflect on key reading or writing experiences and to ask: How have my experiences shaped who I am as a reader or writer? A sample literacy narrative begins on page 46.

Key features

- **A well-told narrative** shows readers what happened. Lively details present the sights, sounds, and smells of the world in which the story takes place. Dialogue and action add interest and energy.

- **A main idea or insight** about reading or writing gives a literacy narrative its significance and transforms it from a personal story to one with larger, universal interest.

- **A well-organized narrative**, like all essays, has a beginning, a middle, and an ending and is focused around a thesis or main idea. Narratives can be written in chronological order, in reverse chronological order, or with a series of flashbacks.

- **First-person point of view (I)** gives a narrative immediacy and authenticity. Your voice may be serious or humorous, but it should be appropriate for your main idea.

Thinking ahead: Presenting or publishing

You may have some flexibility in how you present or publish your literacy narrative. If you have the opportunity to submit it as a podcast, a video, or another genre, leave time in your schedule for recording or filming. Also, in seeking feedback, ask reviewers to comment on your plans for using sounds or images.

Writing your literacy narrative

1 **Explore**

What story will you tell? You can't write about every reading or writing experience or every influential person. Find one interesting experience to focus your narrative. Generate ideas with questions such as these:

- What challenges have you confronted as a reader or a writer?

HOW TO WRITE A LITERACY NARRATIVE *(Continued)*

- Who were the people who nurtured (or delayed) your reading or writing development?

- What are your childhood memories of reading or writing?

- What images do you associate with learning to read or write?

- What is significant about the story you want to tell? What larger point do you want readers to take away from your narrative?

2 Draft

Figure out the best way to tell your story. A narrative isn't a list of "this happened" and then "that happened." It is a focused story with its own logic and order. You don't need to start chronologically. Experiment: What happens if you start in the middle of the story or work in reverse? Try to come up with a tentative organization, and then start to draft.

3 Revise

Ask reviewers for specific feedback. Here are some questions to guide their comments:

- What main idea do readers take away from your story? Ask them to summarize this idea in one sentence.

- Is the narrative focused around the main idea?

- Are the details vivid? Sufficient? Where might you convey your story more clearly? Would it help to add dialogue? Would visuals deepen the impact of your story?

- Does your introduction bring readers into the world of your story?

- Does your conclusion provide a sense of the story's importance?

3i Reflect on your writing; prepare a portfolio.

Reflection — the process of stepping back to examine your preferences, strengths, and challenges as a writer — helps you recognize your progress as a writer. Thinking about what you've learned about writing makes it possible for you to transfer your learning from one writing assignment to the next. When you complete a piece of writing, reflect on questions such as the following:

- What have you learned about yourself as a writer?
- What parts of the writing process are easy for you? What parts are challenging?
- What do you want to do differently the next time you write?
- Can you identify two or three decisions you made that were successful?
- Can you identify specific feedback that helped you revise? What did you learn from the feedback?

At the end of the semester, your instructor may ask you to reflect on your progress as a writer by submitting a portfolio, or collection, of your writing. A writing portfolio often consists of drafts, revisions, and reflections that demonstrate your thinking and learning processes or that showcase your best work. Assembling a portfolio gives you an opportunity to look back at the writing you've done in the course, identify your favorite pieces, examine the feedback you've received, and evaluate your writing progress. It also gives you an opportunity to look forward, reflecting on how you will transfer your writing skills to the next assignment.

Academic Reading and Writing

4 Reading and writing critically

One of the best ways to become a successful college writer is to become a critical reader. When you read critically, you read with an open, curious mind, trying to understand not only what is written but also why and how it is written. When you write analytically, you respond to a text and its author with your observations and insights. The more you take from your reading, the more you have to give as a writer.

4a Read actively.

Reading, like writing, is an active process that happens in steps. For most texts, such as the ones assigned in college, a single quick reading is often a missed opportunity. Many such texts require you to read and reread to comprehend their ideas and the evidence used to support their claims.

When you read actively, you ask questions about a text and pay attention to details you would miss if you just skimmed the text. Active readers preview a text, annotate it, and then converse with it.

Previewing a text

Start by previewing a text to help you understand its basic features and structure. A text's title, for example, may reveal the author's purpose; a text's style and format, either print or digital, may reveal what kind of text it is — a book, a report, a scholarly article, a memo, or something else. The more you know about a text before you read it, the easier it will be to dig deeper into it.

Annotating a text

Annotating a text helps you read actively and deeply to understand what the text says and why it was written. Think of annotating as an exchange you have with the text's author. Your role in the exchange is to respond as a reader, inserting and adding your observations, questions, responses, and reactions. As you read, you note the strengths and limitations of the text, comment on what's clear and what's confusing, and answer the basic question "What is this text about?" These guidelines will help you annotate a text effectively.

HOW TO

Annotate a text effectively

The more you annotate a text with your words, symbols, and responses, the more you make the text your own—and the easier it is for you to start writing about it. The following strategies will help you annotate a text.

1. **Circle, underline, or bracket the text's thesis, key words, and major pieces of evidence** to help you distinguish the main idea from the supporting ideas.

2. **Use the text's margins to ask questions** about the author's purpose and argument.

3. **Note what surprises or puzzles you** about the text, or where you agree or disagree with the author's points.

4. **Use symbols to visualize your responses,** such as asterisks (*) for important ideas, exclamation points (!) for information that surprises you, and question marks (?) for points that confuse you.

For additional tips on annotating digital sources, see page 58.

The following example shows how one student, Emilia Sanchez, annotated an article from *CQ Researcher*, a newsletter about social and political issues.

ANNOTATED ARTICLE

Big Box Stores Are (Bad) for Main Street

BETSY TAYLOR

Title gives away Taylor's position.

There is plenty of reason to be concerned about the proliferation of Wal-Marts and other so-called "big box" stores. The question, however, is not whether or not these types of stores create jobs (although several studies claim they produce a net job loss in local communities) or whether they ultimately save consumers money. The real *concern about having a 25-acre slab of concrete with a 100,000 square foot box of stuff land on a town is whether it's good for a community's soul.

Assumes readers are concerned.

*Main point of article. But what does she mean by "community's soul"?

The worst thing about "big boxes" is that they have a tendency to produce Ross Perot's famous "big sucking sound" — sucking the life out of cities and small towns across the country. On the other hand, small businesses are great for a community. They offer more personal service; they won't threaten to pack up and leave town if they don't get tax breaks, free roads and other blandishments; and small-business owners are much more responsive to a customer's needs. (Ever try to complain about bad service or poor quality products to the president of Home Depot?)

Lumps all big boxes together.

Assumes all small businesses are attentive.

"Either/or" argument— Main Street is good, big boxes are bad.

Yet, if big boxes are so bad, why are they so successful? One glaring reason is that we've become a nation of hyper-consumers, and the big-box boys know this. Downtown shopping districts comprised of small businesses take some of the efficiency out of overconsumption. There's all that hassle of having to travel from store to store, and having to pull out your credit card so many times. Occasionally, we even find ourselves chatting with the shopkeeper, wandering into a coffee shop to visit with a friend or otherwise wasting precious time that could be spent on acquiring more stuff.!

True?

Word choice makes author seem sentimental.

Author's argument seems one-sided and makes assumptions about consumers.

But let's face it—bustling, thriving city centers are fun. They breathe life into a community. They allow cities and towns to stand out from each other. They provide an atmosphere for people to interact with each other that *just cannot be found at Target, or Wal-Mart or Home Depot.

*Shopping at Target to save money—is that bad?

Is it anti-American to be against having a retail giant set up shop in one's community? Some people would say so. On the other hand, if you board up Main Street, <u>what's left of America?</u>

Ends with emotional appeal. Seems too simplistic!

Conversing with a text

Conversing with a text—that is, responding to a text and its author—helps you move beyond your initial notes to draw conclusions about what you've read. Perhaps you ask additional questions, examine the author's assumptions, point out something that doesn't make sense, or explain how the author's ideas suggest wider implications. As you talk back to a text, you look more closely and skeptically at how the author works through a topic, and you analyze the author's evidence and conclusions.

Conversing takes your annotations to the next level. You might begin your conversation with a text and its author by using sentence starters such as these:

But what about _____?

Have you considered _____?

What's missing here is _____.

I find this point so important because _____.

Couldn't we also see it this way: _____.

What if we conclude _____ instead of _____?

Using a double-entry notebook

Many writers use a double-entry notebook to converse with a text and its author and to generate ideas. To create one, draw a line down the center of a notebook page or create a two-column table in a Word or Google document. On the left side, record what the author says; include quotations, sentences, and key terms from the text. On the right side, record your observations and questions. A double-entry notebook allows you to visualize the conversation between you and the author as it develops.

READING AND ANNOTATING DIGITAL TEXTS

For most assignments, you will be asked to read online sources. It is tempting to skim online texts rather than read them carefully. When you skim a text, you are less likely to remember what you have read and less inclined to reread to grasp layers of meaning. However, when you annotate a text, you slow down your reading, noticing details and observing what is interesting and important about a text.

The purpose of annotating—to better understand what you are reading—stays the same across print and digital texts. What changes are the available tools. In both print and digital texts, you can highlight or underline key passages, write notes in the margins of the text, and insert your reactions and questions. Highlighting works best when it is accompanied by your own observations about the text and your responses to the words and sentences you have highlighted.

11:30 🔒 stopbullying.gov

The psychological effects of bullying include depression, anxiety, low self-esteem, self-harming behavior (especially for girls), alcohol and drug use and dependence, aggression, and involvement in violence or crime (especially for boys). While bullying can lead to mental health problems for any child, those who already have mental health difficulties are even more likely to be bullied and to experience its negative effects.

Surprising notes about gender!

Cyberbullying – bullying that happens with computers or mobile devices – has also been linked to mental health

U.S. DEPARTMENT OF HEALTH AND HUMAN SERVICES

Here are some strategies for reading and annotating online sources:

Experiment with annotation tools. If you prefer working with printed texts, you can print out and annotate hard copies of online sources. But annotating digitally can be just as effective. Adobe Reader, for example, is a free program that offers annotation tools for PDFs, such as sticky notes, a highlighter, and other commenting features. Smartphones have built-in annotation tools for text and images. Try different methods to find which ones work for you.

Save your sources. Make sure you have copies of your sources and annotations so that you can return to them when writing your assignment. Most web browsers allow you to save web pages as PDFs or to print hard copies; you can take screenshots of web pages or other sources that you view on your smartphone.

Read slowly. Instead of sweeping your eyes across the screen, slow the pace of your reading so you can focus on the meaning of each sentence.

Avoid multitasking. Close other applications, especially messaging and social media apps, to avoid distractions. If you follow a link for background information or the definition of a term, return immediately to the original source when you are done.

The guidelines for active reading on page 60 will also help you read online sources effectively.

Here is an excerpt from student writer Emilia Sanchez's double-entry notebook (with sentence starters highlighted).

IDEAS FROM THE TEXT	MY RESPONSES
"The question, however, is not whether or not these types of stores create jobs (although several studies claim they produce a net job loss in local communities) or whether they ultimately save consumers money."	*Why are big-box stores bad if they create jobs or save people money? Taylor dismisses these possibilities without acknowledging their importance. But what about my family? We need to save money and we need jobs more than "chatting with the shopkeeper."*
"The real concern . . . is whether [big-box stores are] good for a community's soul." "[S]mall businesses are great for a community."	*Taylor is missing something here. Are all big-box stores bad? Are all small businesses great? Has Taylor considered that getting rid of big-box stores won't necessarily save the "soul" of America? Taylor assumes that small businesses are always better for consumers. But couldn't we conclude that some big-box stores are better for consumers because they save them time and money?*

★ **Using sources responsibly** To avoid plagiarizing, put quotation marks around words you copy from the text and keep an accurate record of page numbers for quotations.

Asking "So what?"

As you read and annotate a text, make sure you understand its thesis, or central idea. Ask yourself: What is the author's thesis? Then put the author's thesis to the "So what?" test: Why does this thesis matter? Why does it need to be argued? What's at stake? Try using language like the following to evaluate the author's argument:

The author overlooks this important point: _____.

The author's argument is convincing because _____.

Perhaps you'll conclude that the thesis is too obvious and doesn't matter at all — or that it matters so much that you believe the author stopped short and overlooked key details or asked the wrong questions. Or perhaps you'll see many strengths in the author's argument but feel that a reasonable person might draw different conclusions about the issue.

GUIDELINES FOR ACTIVE READING

Preview a written text.

- Who is the author? What are the author's credentials?
- What is the author's purpose: To inform? To persuade? To call to action?
- Who is the expected audience?
- When was the text written? Where was it published or posted?
- What kind of text is it: A book? A scholarly article? An online news report? A public service video?

Annotate a written text.

- What surprises, puzzles, or intrigues you about the text?
- What words or terms do you need to look up?
- What question does the text attempt to answer, or what problem does it attempt to solve?
- What is the author's thesis, or main idea? What does the author want you to believe or do?
- What type of evidence does the author provide to support the thesis?
- How persuasive is this evidence?
- If the text includes sound or images, what purpose do they serve?
- What do you notice about design details?

Converse with a written text.

- What are the strengths and limitations of the text?
- Has the author drawn conclusions that you question?
- Do you have a different interpretation of the evidence?
- Does the text raise questions that it does not answer?
- Does the author consider opposing points of view? Does the author treat sources fairly?
- If the text is multimodal, has the author chosen the best combinations of modes (video, audio, etc.) for the message?

Ask "So what?"

- Why does the author's thesis need to be argued or explained? What's at stake?
- What has the author overlooked in presenting this thesis or message? What's missing?
- Could a reasonable person draw different conclusions?

Read like a writer

Reading like a writer helps you identify the techniques writers use so that you can use them, too. To read like a writer is to pay attention to *how* a text is written and *how* it creates an effect on you. The following strategies will help you develop and strengthen your own reading and writing skills.

1 **Review any notes you've made on a text.** What passages do you find effective? What words or sentences did you underline? If you think the text is powerful or well written, figure out *why* and *how* the text works.

2 **Ask *what, why,* and *how* questions about the techniques writers use.** *What* techniques do writers use in their introductions, for instance, to hook readers? *How* does a writer's use of a surprising statistic or a provocative question capture your attention? Or *how* does a writer find common ground among differing positions to establish trust with readers? Identify the specific techniques you appreciate as a reader—and name them—so that they may become part of your repertoire as a writer.

3 **Observe how writers use specific academic writing techniques you want to learn.** For instance, if you're interested in learning how writers introduce and respond to counterarguments or how they quote and paraphrase sources, pay attention to these academic writing techniques when you read.

4 **Use your experiences as a reader to plan the effect you want to create for your readers.** As you draft and revise your writing, make deliberate choices to create this effect.

4b Outline a text to identify main ideas.

You are probably familiar with using an outline as a planning tool to help organize your ideas. An outline is a useful tool for reading, too. Outlining a text — identifying its main idea and major parts — can be an important step in your reading process and can help you prepare to write about the text.

As you outline, look closely for a text's thesis statement (main idea) and topic sentences, because they serve as important signposts for readers. A thesis statement often appears in the introduction, usually in the first or second paragraph. Put the author's thesis and key points in your own words to show that you understand the text. Here, for example, are the points Emilia Sanchez identified as she prepared to write her analysis of the text by Betsy Taylor in 4a. Notice that Sanchez does not simply trace the author's ideas paragraph by paragraph; instead, she sums up the article's central points.

OUTLINE OF "BIG BOX STORES ARE BAD FOR MAIN STREET"

Thesis: Whether or not they take jobs away from a community or offer low prices to consumers, we should be worried about "big-box" stores like Wal-Mart, Target, and Home Depot because they harm communities by taking the life out of downtown shopping districts.

I.   Small businesses are better for cities and towns than big-box stores are.

    A. Small businesses offer personal service; big-box stores do not.

    B. Small businesses don't make demands on community resources as big-box stores do.

    C. Small businesses respond to customer concerns; big-box stores do not.

II. Big-box stores are successful because they cater to consumption at the expense of benefits to the community.

    A. Buying everything in one place is convenient.

    B. Shopping at small businesses may be inefficient, but it provides opportunities for socializing.

    C. Downtown shopping districts give each city or town a special identity.

Conclusion: Although some people say that it's anti-American to oppose big-box stores, actually these stores threaten the communities that make up America by encouraging buying at the expense of the traditional interactions of Main Street.

4c Summarize to deepen your understanding.

When you summarize, you test your understanding of a text by putting the main ideas in your own words — concisely, objectively, and accurately — and distinguishing between the text's major and minor points. You'll find advice for summarizing effectively on the next page.

Here is Emilia Sanchez's summary of the article in 4a. Notice how Sanchez uses a neutral, objective tone and third-person point of view to keep the focus on the text (as in the highlighted phrases).

Presents Taylor's ideas with signal phrases and in the third person, present tense.

In her essay "Big Box Stores Are Bad for Main Street," Betsy Taylor argues that chain stores harm communities by taking the life out of downtown shopping districts. Explaining that a community's "soul" is more important than low prices or consumer convenience, she argues that small businesses are better than stores like Home Depot and Target because they emphasize personal interactions and don't place demands on a community's resources. Taylor asserts that big-box stores are successful because "we've become a nation of hyper-consumers," although the convenience of shopping in these stores comes at the expense of benefits to the community. She concludes by suggesting that it's not "anti-American" to oppose big-box stores because the damage they inflict on downtown shopping districts extends to America itself.

Represents Taylor's article accurately and fairly.

Summarizes Taylor's article accurately and precisely.

Puts Taylor's words in quotation marks.

— Emilia Sanchez, student

HOW TO

Summarize effectively

1 **Mention the title of the text, the name of the author, and the author's thesis** in the first sentence.

2 **Maintain a neutral tone;** be objective and avoid adding your own views to the summary.

3 **Keep your focus on the text.** Don't state the author's ideas as if they were your own.

4 **Use the third-person point of view and the present tense** to present the author's ideas: *Taylor argues . . .* , *Taylor explains . . .* (If you are writing in APA style, see 61c.) Because the ideas are the author's, avoid writing sentences that begin with *The article says . . .*

5 **Put all or most of your summary in your own words.** If you borrow a phrase or a sentence from the text, put it in quotation marks and give the page number in parentheses. Use a signal phrase to introduce any borrowed language: *According to Singh, immigration data "reflect a slow move away from . . ."*

6 **Limit yourself to presenting the text's key points,** not every detail.

4d Analyze to demonstrate your critical reading.

Whereas a summary most often answers the question of *what* a text says, an analysis looks closely at the parts of a text to examine *how* the text conveys its main idea. Looking at the parts — an author's thesis, evidence, arguments, assumptions, biases, etc. — allows you to offer your insights about how the parts and the whole work together.

Start with questions and observations you have about the text:

- What puzzles you or doesn't make sense about the text?
- What are the strengths of the text?

- What part of the text stands out and needs close examination?
- Is there a contradiction or misguided assumption in the text?
- Do you have any questions about the author's thesis or use of evidence?
- What insights might you offer your readers to help them see the text from your perspective?

WRITING FOR AN AUDIENCE

A good strategy for academic writing is to keep your audience in mind as you develop an analysis. Remember that readers are eager to hear what you take from a text; they want to hear your observations, questions, and ideas. Some readers won't necessarily interpret a text as you do or draw the same conclusions. Through your careful reading of a text, you show your audience something that they might not have seen or understood about it.

Balancing summary with analysis

Summary and analysis need each other in an analytical essay; you can't have one without the other. Your readers may not be familiar with the text you are analyzing, so you should briefly summarize the text to orient readers and help them understand the basis of your analysis. To balance summary with analysis, try the following strategies:

- Pose *why* and *how* questions that lead to an interpretation or a judgment of the text rather than to a summary (*Why is the author's argument unconvincing?*).
- Formulate a strong position (thesis) to answer your questions about the text.
- Make sure your summary sentences serve a purpose and provide a context for analysis.
- Focus your analysis on the text's main ideas or some prominent feature of the reading.
- Pay attention to your topic sentences to make sure they signal analysis.

Here is an example of how student writer Emilia Sanchez balances summary with analysis in her essay about Betsy Taylor's article (see 4a). Notice how Sanchez begins her summary sentences by mentioning the title of the text and the name of the author. Before stating her thesis, she summarizes the author's purpose and central idea for readers who may not be familiar with Taylor's article.

SAMPLE PARAGRAPH BALANCING SUMMARY AND ANALYSIS

Summary

[In her essay "Big Box Stores Are Bad for Main Street," Betsy Taylor focuses not on the economic effects of large chain stores but on the effects these stores have on the "soul" of America. She argues that stores like Home Depot, Target, and Wal-Mart are bad for America because they draw people out of downtown shopping districts and cause them to focus on consumption. In contrast, she believes that small businesses are good for America because they provide personal attention, encourage community interaction, and make each city and town unique.] [But Taylor's argument

Analysis

is unconvincing because it is based on sentimentality—on idealized images of a quaint Main Street—rather than on the roles that businesses play in consumers' lives and communities.]

Drafting an analytical thesis statement

An effective thesis statement for analytical writing responds to a question about a text or tries to resolve a problem in the text. Remember that your thesis isn't the same as the author's thesis or main idea. Your thesis presents your judgment of the author's argument.

If student writer Emilia Sanchez had started her analysis of "Big Box Stores Are Bad for Main Street" (4a) with the following draft thesis statement, she merely would have repeated the main idea of the article.

INEFFECTIVE THESIS STATEMENT (REPEATS AUTHOR'S ARGUMENT)

Big-box stores such as Wal-Mart and Home Depot promote consumerism by offering endless goods at low prices, but they do nothing to promote community.

Instead, Sanchez wrote this analytical thesis statement, which offers her judgment of Taylor's argument.

REVISED THESIS STATEMENT (WRITER'S JUDGMENT OF AUTHOR'S ARGUMENT)

By ignoring the complex economic relationship between large chain stores and their communities, Taylor incorrectly assumes that simply getting rid of big-box stores would have a positive effect on America's communities.

HOW TO

Draft an analytical thesis statement

Analysis begins with asking questions about a text. As you draft your thesis, your questions will help you form a judgment about the text. Let these steps guide you as you develop an analytical thesis statement.

1 **Review your notes to remind yourself of the author's main idea,** supporting evidence, and, if possible, the author's purpose (reason for writing) and audience (intended reader).

2 **Ask *what*, *why*, or *how* questions to show readers what in the text needs to be questioned and is open to debate.** How do the author's perspective and thesis clarify or complicate your understanding of the subject? Why might a reasonable person agree or disagree with the author? Look for patterns among your questions and annotations to help you discover what interests you about the text.

3 **Write your thesis as an answer to the questions** you have posed or as the resolution of a problem you have identified in the text. Remember that your thesis isn't the same as the author's thesis. Your thesis is your position and presents your judgment of the text.

4 **Test your thesis.** An analytical thesis is arguable, one with which readers might disagree, and not a summary of the text. Is your position clear? Is your position debatable? Does your thesis offer a clear judgment of the text? The answer to each question should be yes.

5 **Revise your thesis.** Examine your thesis to make sure you state your position specifically and clearly. Why does your position matter? Put your working thesis to the "So what?" test (see 1c). Consider adding a *because* clause to your thesis to answer a reader's "So what?" question.

4e Sample student writing: Analysis of an article

Following is Emilia Sanchez's analysis of the article by Betsy Taylor (see 4a). Sanchez used MLA (Modern Language Association) style to format her paper and cite the source.

Sanchez 1

Emilia Sanchez

Professor Goodwin

English 10

22 October 2018

Rethinking Big-Box Stores

In her essay "Big Box Stores Are Bad for Main Street," Betsy Taylor focuses not on the economic effects of large chain stores but on the effects these stores have on the "soul" of America. She argues that stores like Home Depot, Target, and Wal-Mart are bad for America because they draw people out of downtown shopping districts and cause them to focus on consumption. In contrast, she believes that small businesses are good for America because they provide personal attention, encourage community interaction, and make each city and town unique. But Taylor's argument is unconvincing because it is based on sentimentality—on idealized images of a quaint Main Street—rather than on the roles that businesses play in consumers' lives and communities. By ignoring the complex economic relationship between large chain stores and their communities, Taylor incorrectly assumes that simply getting rid of big-box stores would have a positive effect on America's communities.

Taylor's use of colorful language reveals that she has a sentimental view of American society and does not understand economic realities. In her first paragraph, Taylor refers to a big-box store as a "25-acre slab of concrete

Marginal annotations:

Summary of the article's thesis orients readers and prepares them for analysis.

Sanchez begins to analyze Taylor's argument.

Thesis expresses Sanchez's judgment of Taylor's article.

Signal phrase introduces quotations from the source.

Marginal annotations indicate MLA-style formatting and effective writing.

Sanchez 2

with a 100,000 square foot box of stuff" that "land[s] on a town," evoking images of a powerful monster crushing the American way of life. But she oversimplifies a complex issue. Taylor does not consider that many downtown business districts failed long before chain stores moved in, when factories and mills closed and workers lost their jobs. In cities with struggling economies, big-box stores can actually provide much-needed jobs. Similarly, while Taylor blames big-box stores for harming local economies by asking for tax breaks, free roads, and other perks, she doesn't acknowledge that these stores also enter into economic partnerships with the surrounding communities by offering financial benefits to schools and hospitals.

> In MLA style, no page number is needed in an in-text citation for a one-page source.

> Sanchez identifies and challenges Taylor's assumptions.

Taylor's assumption that shopping in small businesses is always better for the customer also seems driven by nostalgia for an old-fashioned Main Street rather than by the facts. While she may be right that many small businesses offer personal service and are responsive to customer complaints, she does not consider that many customers appreciate the service at big-box stores. Just as customer service is better at some small businesses than at others, it is impossible to generalize about service at all big-box stores. For example, customers depend on the lenient return policies and the wide variety of products at stores like Target and Home Depot.

> Clear topic sentence announces a shift to a new topic.

> Sanchez refutes Taylor's claim.

Taylor blames big-box stores for encouraging American "hyper-consumerism," but she oversimplifies by equating big-box stores with bad values and small businesses with good values. Like her other points, this claim ignores the economic and social realities of American society today. Big-box stores do not force Americans to buy more. By offering

Sanchez 3

however, they allow consumers to save time and purchase goods they might not be able to afford from small businesses. The existence of more small businesses would not change what most Americans can afford, nor would it reduce their desire to buy affordable merchandise.

Taylor may be right that some big-box stores have a negative impact on communities and that small businesses offer certain advantages. But she ignores the economic conditions that support big-box stores as well as the fact that Main Street was in decline before the big-box store arrived. Getting rid of big-box stores will not bring back a simpler America populated by thriving, unique Main Streets; in reality, Main Street will not survive if consumers cannot afford to shop there.

Sanchez treats the author fairly.

Conclusion returns to the thesis and shows the wider significance of Sanchez's analysis.

Sanchez 4

Work Cited

Taylor, Betsy. "Big Box Stores Are Bad for Main Street." *CQ Researcher,* vol. 9, no. 44, 1999, p. 1011.

Work cited page is in MLA style.

WRITING GUIDE

How to write an analytical essay

An **analysis** of a text allows you to examine the parts of a text to understand *what* it means and *how* it makes its meaning. Your goal is to offer your judgment of the text and to persuade readers to see it through your analytical perspective. You explain to your readers your observations and insights about the text, what you have discovered about what it means, and why it matters. Sample analytical essays appear in 4e and 5d.

Key features

- **A careful and critical reading** of a text reveals what the text says, how it works, and what it means. In an analytical essay, you pay attention to the details of the text, especially its thesis and evidence, and—in the case of a multimodal text—its visual or audio presentation.

- **A thesis that offers a clear judgment** of the text anchors your analysis. Your thesis might be the answer to a question you have posed about the text or the resolution of a problem you have identified in the text.

- **Support for the thesis** comes from evidence in the text. You summarize, paraphrase, and quote passages that support the claims you make about the text.

- **A balance of summary and analysis** helps readers who are not familiar with the text you are analyzing. Summary answers the question of *what* a text says; analysis looks at *how* a text makes its point.

Thinking ahead: Presenting and publishing

You may have the opportunity to present or publish your analysis in the form of a multimodal text such as a slide show or a video. Consider how adding images or sound might strengthen your analysis or help you to better reach your audience. (See section 5.)

Writing your analytical essay

1 **Explore**

Generate ideas for your analysis by responding to questions such as the following:

- What is the text about?
- What do you find interesting, surprising, or puzzling about this text?

HOW TO WRITE AN ANALYTICAL ESSAY (Continued)

- What do you see as the strengths of the text? How does the text clarify or add to your understanding of the subject?
- What is the author's purpose, thesis, or central idea? Put the author's thesis to the "So what?" test.
- What do your annotations of the text reveal about your response to it?

2 Draft

- Draft a working thesis to focus your analysis. Remember that your thesis is not the same as the author's thesis or message. Your thesis presents *your* judgment of the text.
- Draft a plan to organize your paragraphs. Your introductory paragraph will briefly summarize the text and offer your thesis. Your body paragraphs will support your thesis with evidence from the text. Your conclusion will pull together the major points and show the significance of your analysis. (See 1d.)
- Identify specific words, phrases, and sentences from the text as evidence to support your thesis.

3 Revise

Ask your reviewers to give you specific comments. You can use the following questions both to guide their feedback and to guide your own revision plan.

- Is the introduction effective and engaging?
- Is summary balanced with analysis?
- Does the thesis offer a clear judgment of the text?
- What objections might your readers have to your analysis?
- Is the analysis well organized? Are there clear topic sentences and transitions?
- Have you provided sufficient evidence? Have you analyzed the evidence?
- Have you cited words, phrases, or sentences that are summarized or quoted?

5 Reading and writing about multimodal texts

Multimodal texts combine two or more of the following modes: words, static images, moving images, and sound. In many of your college classes, you'll have the opportunity to read and write about multimodal texts, such as advertisements, podcasts, videos, or websites. Like a print text, a multimodal text can be read carefully to understand *what* it says and *how* it communicates its purpose and reaches its audience. Use the guidelines for active reading on page 60 to help you preview, annotate, and converse with a multimodal text.

5a Read actively.

When you read a multimodal text, you are not only reading words; you might also be examining a text's design and composition, and perhaps even its pace and volume. Your work as a reader involves understanding the modes — words, images, and sound — separately and then analyzing how the modes work together.

One student, Ren Yoshida, annotated an advertisement for fairly traded coffee. In his annotations, which appear alongside the ad on the next page, you'll see how Yoshida jotted down his observations of the ad's design features and questioned some of the ad's language. He used his annotations to help him converse with the text, questioning what seemed puzzling and contradictory, as he worked to understand the advertisement's message and his response to it. Yoshida's annotations provided a basis for the analysis that appears in 5d.

5b Summarize a multimodal text to deepen your understanding.

Your goal in summarizing a multimodal text is to state the work's central idea and key points objectively and accurately, in your own words, and usually in paragraph form. Since a summary should be fairly short, you must decide what is most important. Here is the summary Ren Yoshida drafted as he prepared to write an analysis of the advertisement on the next page.

> The Equal Exchange advertisement is selling the message that together farmers and consumers hold the future of the planet in their hands. At the center of the ad is a farmer whose outstretched hands, full of raw coffee, offer the fruit of her labor and a partnership with consumers. The ad suggests that in a global world producers and consumers are bound together. A cup of coffee is more than just a morning ritual. A cup of coffee is part of an equal exchange that empowers farmers to stay on their land and empowers consumers to do the right thing.
>
> — Ren Yoshida, student

For advice on summarizing a source effectively, see the box on page 64.

Annotated Advertisement

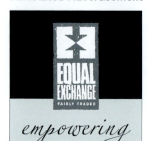

When you choose Equal Exchange fairly traded coffee, tea or chocolate, you join a network that empowers farmers in Latin America, Africa, and Asia to:

- Stay on their land
- Care for the environment
- Farm organically
- Support their family
- Plan for the future

www.equalexchange.coop

Photo: Jesus Choqueheranca de Quevero, Coffee farmer & CEPICAFE Cooperative member, Peru

What is being exchanged?

Why is "fairly traded" so hard to read?

"Empowering" — why in an elegant font? Who is empowering farmers?

"Farmers" in all capital letters — shows strength?

Straightforward design and not much text.

Outstretched hands. Is she giving a gift? Inviting partnership?

Hands: heart-shaped, foregrounded.

Raw coffee beans are red: earthy, natural, warm.

Positive verbs: consumers choose, join, empower; farmers stay, care, farm, support, plan.

How do consumers know their money helps farmers stay on their land?

5c Analyze a multimodal text to demonstrate your critical reading.

When you analyze a multimodal text, you explain to readers your reading of the text — what it means and why it matters. Analysis begins with asking questions about how the text conveys its main idea or message.

GUIDELINES FOR ANALYZING A MULTIMODAL TEXT

- What is your first impression of the text? What details in the text create this response?
- When and why was the text created? Where did the text appear?
- What clues suggest the text's intended audience? What assumptions are being made about the audience?
- What is the thesis, central idea, or message of the text?
- Does this text tell a story? How would you sum up the story?
- What modes are used, and why? How do the modes work together?
- How does the arrangement of sounds or design details help convey the text's meaning or serve its purpose?

Drafting an analytical thesis statement

An effective thesis statement responds to a question about the text or tries to resolve a problem in the text. Remember that your thesis isn't the same as the text's thesis or main idea. Your thesis presents *your judgment* of the multimodal text's message or argument. The following draft thesis summarizes the advertisement shown in 5a; it doesn't present an analysis.

DRAFT THESIS STATEMENT (RESTATES MESSAGE OF TEXT)

Consumers who purchase coffee from farmers in the Equal Exchange network are helping farmers stay on their land.

Student writer Ren Yoshida revised his thesis statement by questioning a single detail.

WRITER'S QUESTIONS

The ad promises an equal exchange, but is the exchange equal between consumers and farmers? Do the words *equal exchange* and *empowering farmers* appeal to consumers' emotions?

REVISED THESIS STATEMENT (PRESENTS WRITER'S JUDGMENT OF TEXT)

Although the ad works successfully on an emotional level, it is less successful on a logical level because of its promise for an equal exchange between consumers and farmers.

5d Sample student writing: Analysis of an advertisement

In analyzing the Equal Exchange advertisement in 5a, Ren Yoshida asked questions about the ad's design details and its emotional and logical appeals. He focused his thesis by questioning a single detail in the ad. Here is the analysis Yoshida wrote.

Yoshida 1

Ren Yoshida

Professor Marcotte

English 101

4 November 2019

Sometimes a Cup of Coffee Is Just a Cup of Coffee

A farmer, her hardworking hands full of coffee

beans, reaches out from an Equal Exchange advertisement

(Advertisement). The hands, in the shape of a heart,

offer to consumers the fruit of the farmer's labor. The ad's

message is straightforward: in choosing Equal Exchange,

consumers become global citizens, partnering with farmers

to help save the planet. Suddenly, a cup of coffee is more

than just a morning ritual; a cup of coffee is a moral

choice that empowers both consumers and farmers. This

simple exchange appeals to a consumer's desire to be a

good person — to protect the environment and do the right

thing. Yet the ad is more complicated than it first seems,

and its design raises some logical questions about such an

exchange. Although the ad works on an emotional level, it

Source is cited in the text. No page number is available for the online source.

Yoshida summarizes the content of the ad.

Marginal annotations indicate MLA-style formatting and effective writing.

Yoshida 2

is less successful on a logical level because of its promise for an equal exchange between consumers and farmers.

The focus of the ad is a farmer, Jesus Choqueheranca de Quevero, and, more specifically, her outstretched, cupped hands. Her hands are full of red, raw coffee, her life's work. The ad successfully appeals to consumers' emotions, assuming they will find the farmer's welcoming face and hands, caked with dirt, more appealing than startling statistics about the state of the environment or the number of farmers who lose their land each year. It seems almost rude not to accept the farmer's generous offering since we know her name and, as the ad implies, have the choice to "empower" her. In fact, how can a consumer resist helping the farmer "[c]are for the environment" and "[p]lan for the future," when it is a simple matter of choosing the right coffee? The ad sends the message that our future is a global future in which producers and consumers are bound together.

First impressions play a major role in the success of an advertisement. Consumers are pulled toward a product, or pushed away, by an ad's initial visual and emotional appeal. Here, the intended audience is busy people, so the ad tries to catch viewers' attention and make a strong impression immediately. Yet with a second or third viewing, consumers might start to ask some logical questions about Equal Exchange before buying their morning coffee. Although the farmer extends her heart-shaped hands to consumers, they are not actually buying a cup of coffee or the raw coffee directly from her. In reality, consumers are buying from Equal Exchange, even if the ad substitutes the more positive word *choose* for *buy*. Furthermore, consumers aren't actually

Thesis expresses Yoshida's analysis of the ad.

Details show how the ad appeals to consumers' emotions.

Yoshida interprets details such as the farmer's hands.

Yoshida begins to challenge the logic of the ad.

Yoshida 3

Words from the ad serve as evidence.

empowering the farmer; they are joining "a network that empowers farmers." The idea of a network makes a simple transaction more complicated. How do consumers know their money helps farmers "[s]tay on their land" and "[p]lan for the future" as the ad promises? They don't.

Clear topic sentence announces a shift.

Summary of the ad's key features serves Yoshida's analysis.

The ad's design elements raise questions about the use of the key terms *equal exchange* and *empowering farmers.* The Equal Exchange logo suggests symmetry and equality, with two red arrows facing each other, but the words of the logo appear almost like an eye exam poster, with each line decreasing in font size and clarity. The words *fairly traded* are tiny. Below the logo, the words *empowering farmers* are presented in contradictory fonts. *Empowering* is written in a flowing, cursive font, almost the opposite of what might be considered empowering, whereas *farmers* is written in a plain, sturdy font. The ad's varying fonts communicate differently and make it hard to know exactly what is being exchanged and who is becoming empowered.

What is being exchanged? The logic of the ad suggests that consumers will improve the future by choosing Equal Exchange. The first exchange is economic: consumers give one thing — dollars — and receive something in return — a cup of coffee — and the farmer stays on her land. The second exchange is more complicated because it involves a moral exchange. The ad suggests that if consumers don't choose "fairly traded" products, farmers will be forced off their land and the environment destroyed. This exchange, when put into motion by consumers choosing to purchase products not "fairly traded," has negative consequences for both consumers and farmers. The message of the ad is that the actual exchange taking place is not economic but moral;

Yoshida 4

after all, nothing is being bought, only chosen. Yet the logic of this exchange quickly falls apart. Consumers aren't empowered to become global citizens simply by choosing Equal Exchange, and farmers aren't empowered to plan for the future by consumers' choices. And even if all this empowerment magically happened, there is nothing equal about such an exchange.

Advertisements are themselves about empowerment—encouraging viewers to believe they can become someone or do something by identifying, emotionally or logically, with a product. In the Equal Exchange ad, consumers are emotionally persuaded to identify with a farmer whose face is not easily forgotten and whose heart-shaped hands hold a collective future. On a logical level, though, the ad raises questions because empowerment, although a good concept to choose, is not easily or equally exchanged. Sometimes a cup of coffee is just a cup of coffee.

> Yoshida shows why his thesis matters.

> Conclusion includes a detail from the introduction.

> Conclusion returns to Yoshida's thesis.

Yoshida 5

Work Cited

Advertisement for Equal Exchange. *Equal Exchange*, equalexchange .coop. Accessed 14 Oct. 2019.

6   Reading arguments

Many of your college assignments will ask you to read and write arguments about debatable issues. The questions being debated might be matters of public policy (*Should law enforcement officers be allowed to seek no-knock warrants?*), or they might be scholarly issues (*What role does social responsibility play in determining behavior in a pandemic?*). On such questions, reasonable people may disagree.

You'll find the critical reading strategies introduced in section 4 — previewing, annotating, and conversing with texts — to be useful as you read an argument and ask questions about its logic, evidence, and use of appeals.

6a Read with an open mind and a critical eye.

As you read arguments across the disciplines and enter into academic or public policy debates, keep an open mind about opposing viewpoints. Be curious about the wide range of positions in the arguments you are reading. Examine an author's assumptions (ideas the author accepts as true), assess the evidence, and weigh conclusions. The following strategies will help you read with an open mind and a critical eye:

- **Read carefully.** Read to understand an author's argument and point of view. Ask questions: What is the author's thesis? What evidence does the author use to support the thesis? How does the author's argument contribute to your understanding of the subject?

- **Read skeptically.** Read to test the strengths and weaknesses of an author's argument. Ask questions: Are any of the author's assumptions or conclusions problematic? Is the author's evidence persuasive and sufficient? How does the author handle opposing views?

- **Read evaluatively.** Read to evaluate the usefulness and significance of an author's argument. Put the argument to the "So what?" test (see 1c). Why does the thesis matter? Why does it need to be argued?

RECOGNIZING LOGICAL FALLACIES

When you evaluate an argument, look closely at the reasoning behind it. Some arguments use unreasonable tactics known as *logical fallacies*.

A **hasty generalization** is a conclusion based on insufficient or unrepresentative evidence.

> *In a single year, scores on standardized tests in California's public schools rose by ten points. Therefore, more children than ever are succeeding in America's public school systems.*

Stereotypes are hasty generalizations about a group.

> *All politicians are corrupt.*

A **false analogy** is a comparison that points out a similarity between two things that are unrelated.

> *If we can send a spacecraft to Mars, we should be able to find a cure for the common cold.*

***Post hoc* fallacy** assumes that because one event follows another, the first is the cause of the second.

> *Since Governor Cho took office, unemployment within communities of color has decreased by seven percent. Governor Cho should be applauded for reducing unemployment.*

Either/or fallacy oversimplifies an argument by suggesting that there are only two alternatives when in fact there are more.

> *Many attempted solutions to opioid addiction have not worked. Either we should stop manufacturing opioid drugs or give everyone access to naloxone, the overdose-preventing drug.*

Non sequitur is Latin for "It does not follow." When a statement or conclusion is an assertion that does not logically follow what came before it, we call it a non sequitur.

> *State governments should not require vaccines in schools because the flu is not usually fatal.*

ACADEMIC WRITING Many hasty generalizations contain words such as *all*, *ever*, *always*, and *never*, when qualifiers such as *most*, *many*, *usually*, and *seldom* would be more accurate.

6b Evaluate ethical, logical, and emotional appeals as a reader.

Ancient Greek rhetoricians distinguished among three kinds of appeals used to influence readers: ethical, logical, and emotional. As you evaluate arguments, identify these appeals and question their effectiveness. Are they appropriate for the audience and the argument? Are they balanced and legitimate or lopsided and misleading?

EVALUATING ETHICAL, LOGICAL, AND EMOTIONAL APPEALS AS A READER

Ethical appeals (*ethos*)

Ethical arguments, also known as *credibility arguments*, call upon a writer's character, knowledge, and authority. Ask questions such as the following when you evaluate the ethical appeal of an argument.

- Is the writer informed and trustworthy? How does the writer establish authority?
- Does the writer use sources knowledgeably and responsibly?
- How does the writer describe the views of others and deal with opposing views?

Logical appeals (*logos*)

Reasonable arguments appeal to readers' sense of logic, rely on evidence, and use inductive and deductive reasoning. Ask questions such as the following to evaluate the logical appeal of an argument.

- Is the evidence sufficient, representative, and relevant?
- Is the reasoning sound?
- Does the argument contain any logical fallacies or unwarranted assumptions?
- Are there any missing or mistaken premises?

Emotional appeals (*pathos*)

Emotional arguments appeal to readers' beliefs and values. Ask questions such as the following to evaluate the emotional appeal of an argument.

- What values or beliefs does the writer address, either directly or indirectly?
- Are the emotional appeals legitimate and fair?
- Does the writer oversimplify or dramatize an issue?
- Do the emotional arguments highlight or shift attention away from the evidence?

Advertising makes use of ethical, logical, and emotional appeals to persuade consumers to buy a product or embrace a brand. This Patagonia ad uses *ethos*; it makes an ethical appeal with its copy that invites customers to rethink their purchasing practices.

EXERCISE 6–1   In the following paragraph, identify the type of appeal used in each sentence that ends with three choices: *ethos* (ethical appeal), *logos* (logical appeal), or *pathos* (emotional appeal).

Elderspeak, the use of pet names such as "dear" and "sweetie" directed toward older adults, is generally intended as an endearment. However, the use of such language suggests a view of seniors as childlike or cognitively impaired. It should be no surprise, then, that older adults find these pet names condescending and demeaning (*ethos / logos / pathos*). Unfortunately, the effects of elderspeak go far beyond insulting older adults. Health care professionals have found that residents in nursing facilities, even those with dementia, respond to patronizing language by becoming uncooperative, aggressive, or depressed. In a study published in the *American Journal of Alzheimer's Disease and Other Dementias*, Ruth Herman and Kristine L. Williams reported that older adults responded to elderspeak by resisting care, yelling, or crying ("Elderspeak's Influence") (*ethos / logos / pathos*). Surprisingly, despite widely published research on the negative effects of elderspeak, the worst offenders are health care workers, the very people we trust to treat our elderly family members with respect and dignity — and the very people who are old enough to know better (*ethos / logos / pathos*).

6c Evaluate the evidence behind an argument.

Writers draw on facts, statistics, examples, expert opinion, and appeals to support their arguments. As you read an argument, look closely at the evidence behind the argument. Ask the following questions:

- Is the evidence **accurate** and fair?
- Is the evidence **sufficient**?
- Is the evidence **representative**?
- Is the evidence **relevant**?

As you read, take time to reflect on the author's use of evidence. Pose counterarguments to test the strength of the author's argument and to consider alternative interpretations of the evidence. Try using these sentence starters to analyze the evidence and the author's argument:

> X's evidence is relevant/no longer relevant because
> _____.
>
> X's evidence is biased and/or insufficient because _____.
>
> Looking at X's evidence, couldn't we also conclude that _____?
>
> X argues _____, but what she hasn't taken into interpretation is _____.
>
> X's argument rests on this faulty assumption: _____.

6d Identify underlying assumptions.

An assumption is a claim that is taken to be true without the need for proof. As you read and evaluate an argument, identify the underlying assumptions on which the argument is based. Look closely at the ideas, values, and beliefs the writer assumes they share with their readers to determine whether those assumptions need to be stated and supported rather than merely accepted as true.

Writers often assume that they share values and beliefs with readers and don't make their assumptions explicit. For example, if you read an argument about limiting population growth in developing nations and the writer assumes that readers agree with

QUESTIONING THE EVIDENCE BEHIND A CONCLUSION

When authors construct an argument, they often use *inductive reasoning* — drawing a conclusion based on a piece of evidence. You can test the evidence and the conclusion an author has made with the following questions.

CONCLUSION   The majority of students on our campus would volunteer at least five hours a week in a community organization if the school provided a placement service for volunteers.

EVIDENCE   In a recent survey, 723 of 1,215 students questioned said they would volunteer at least five hours a week in a community organization if the school provided a placement service for volunteers.

1. *Is the evidence accurate and fair?* The evidence is trustworthy if the survey was conducted fairly and objectively. In weighing the accuracy of survey evidence, ask questions about who conducted the survey and the methods used to collect and analyze data.

2. *Is the evidence sufficient?* That depends. On a small campus (say, 3,000 students), the pool of students surveyed would be sufficient for research, but on a large campus (say, 30,000 students), 1,215 students would be only 4 percent of the population. If those 4 percent were known to be truly **representative** of the other 96 percent, however, even such a small sample would be sufficient (see question 3).

3. *Is the evidence representative?* The evidence is representative if those responding to the survey reflect the entire student population with respect to the characteristics of age, gender, race, field of study, number of extracurricular commitments, and so on. If most of those surveyed are majors in a field such as social work, question the survey's conclusion.

4. *Is the evidence relevant?* Yes. The survey results are directly linked to the conclusion. A survey about the number of hours students work for pay, by contrast, would not be relevant because it would not be about *choosing to volunteer*.

this goal, you might want to question the assumption by asking, "What evidence shows that limiting population growth is always desirable?" Or if a writer argues that everyone agrees that violent crime is increasing because the death penalty isn't widely used, you might want to question the writer's assumptions by asking, "What evidence shows that the death penalty deters violent criminals and that it is a fair punishment?" Perhaps the unstated assumptions are the ones that the writer needs to state as claims and support with evidence.

6e Evaluate how fairly a writer handles opposing views.

The way in which a writer deals with opposing views is telling. Some writers address the arguments of the opposition fairly, conceding points when necessary and countering others, all in a civil spirit. Other writers will do almost anything to win an argument: either ignoring opposing views altogether or misrepresenting such views and attacking their proponents.

Writers build credibility — *ethos* — by addressing opposing arguments fairly. As you read arguments, evaluate how writers deal with views that don't line up with their own. Credible writers deal with opposing arguments by

- respectfully acknowledging alternative positions
- incorporating elements of the opposition into their arguments
- using precise language to describe opposing views
- quoting opposing views accurately and fairly
- not misrepresenting a source by taking it out of context
- finding common ground among differing positions

CHECKLIST FOR READING AND EVALUATING ARGUMENTS

- What is the writer's purpose and thesis?
- Are there any gaps in reasoning? Does the argument contain any logical fallacies (see 6a)?
- On what assumptions does the argument rest? Are any of the assumptions unstated?
- What appeals — ethical, logical, or emotional — does the writer make? Are these appeals effective?
- What evidence does the writer use? Could there be alternative interpretations of the evidence?
- How does the writer handle opposing views?
- If you are not persuaded by the writer's argument, what counterarguments would you make to the writer?

EXERCISE 6–2 Explain what is illogical in each of the following brief arguments. It may be helpful to identify the logical fallacy or fallacies by name. Answers appear in the back of the book.

a. My roommate, who is an engineering major, is taking a course called Structures of Tall Buildings. All engineers have to know how to design tall buildings.

b. If you're old enough to vote, you're old enough to drink alcohol. Therefore, the drinking age should be lowered to eighteen.

c. If you're not part of the solution, you're part of the problem.

d. Every K-12 student in America could have access to the technology they need for successful online learning if it weren't for the outdated, behind-the-times thinking of most school administrators.

e. Charging a fee for curbside trash pickup will encourage everyone to recycle more because no one in my town likes to spend extra money.

7 Writing arguments

Writing an argument gives you the opportunity to take a position on a debatable issue and contribute to the ongoing conversation around the issue. You say to your readers, "Here is my position in the debate, here is the evidence that supports that position, and here is my response to opposing positions on the issue."

Remember that writing is a process. Your position may change from draft to draft as you learn more about your topic. Throughout this chapter, you will see the work of one student writer, Julia Riew. When Riew was given the assignment to write a researched argument, she quickly focused on a topic that mattered to her — zoos. As a supporter of animal rights, she felt passionately that it is unethical to cage animals. Her original position treated the debate as either right or wrong. However, as you'll see in this chapter and in Riew's final paper, her argument became more complex and her writing became more open minded as she developed her essay.

You'll find Julia Riew's argument paper in 7h.

7a Identify your purpose and context.

Your purpose in constructing an argument is to support your position and persuade your readers. As you consider possible topics, start by informing yourself about the debate or conversation around a subject, sometimes called its *context*. Read sources that will help you understand the issues, approaches, and research methods — the ongoing conversation — about a topic.

As you do research, you may find that assumptions you'd held about your topic are untrue, or that the conversation around your topic is more complicated than you'd thought. For example, when student writer Julia Riew chose to write about zoos, she began with the position that zoos are unethical because they cage and exploit animals. However, as she researched the fierce debates around zoos, she learned from experts with differing points of view. Many of her sources emphasized the dramatic rate at which animals are becoming extinct and the success some zoos have had in creating safe habitats for endangered animals. These sources presented evidence and counterarguments that influenced her thinking about the role of zoos in protecting and saving vulnerable species. As she increased her understanding of the topic, she quickly learned how — and why — the debates around zoos were much more complex and interesting than she first imagined. She moved from her original position — zoos are unethical — to a new position: It would be unethical for zoos not to save endangered animals.

7b View your audience as a panel of jurors.

As you build your argument, think about how you will appeal to your audience. It is useful to envision your audience as skeptical readers who, like a panel of jurors, will make up their minds after listening to all sides of the argument. To construct a convincing argument, you need to establish your credibility (*ethos*) and appeal to your readers' sense of logic and reason (*logos*) as well as to their values and beliefs (*pathos*). The box on the next page will help you do so.

USING ETHICAL, LOGICAL, AND EMOTIONAL APPEALS AS A WRITER

Ethical appeals (*ethos*)

To accept your argument, a reader must see you as trustworthy, fair, and reasonable. When you acknowledge alternative positions, you build common ground with readers and gain their trust by showing that you are knowledgeable. And when you use sources responsibly and respectfully, you inspire readers' confidence in your judgment.

> However, not everyone agrees. Critics point out, rightly so, that eliminating grades in academic environments would require massive system-wide rethinking.

Logical appeals (*logos*)

To persuade readers, you need to appeal to their sense of logic and reason. When you provide evidence, you offer readers logical support for your argument. And when you clarify assumptions and avoid logical fallacies, you appeal to readers' desire for reason.

> A recent study showed that an overemphasis on grades — and not learning — has led eighty-seven percent of the study participants to cheat on or consider cheating on an exam.

Emotional appeals (*pathos*)

To establish common ground with readers, you need to appeal to their beliefs and values as well as to their minds. When you offer vivid examples, surprising statistics, or compelling visuals, you engage readers in your argument. And when you balance emotional appeals with logical appeals, you highlight the human dimension of an issue to show readers why they should care about your argument.

> Why continue to promote a culture of fear and intimidation with *report-card Fridays,* days when American students are concerned less with what they've learned than they are with how they've scored?

> **ACADEMIC WRITING** Academic audiences expect your writing to be
> assertive and confident. You can create an assertive tone by acknowledging
> different positions and supporting your ideas with specific evidence.
>
> | **TOO AGGRESSIVE** | Of course only registered organ donors should be eligible for organ transplants. It's selfish and shortsighted to think otherwise. |
> | --- | --- |
> | **TOO PASSIVE** | I might be wrong, but I think that maybe people should have to register as organ donors if they want to be considered for a transplant. |
> | **ASSERTIVE** | If only registered organ donors are eligible for transplants, more people will register as donors. |

7c Build common ground with your audience.

As you construct your argument and counter opposing arguments, try to establish common ground with your readers by
finding one or two assumptions you might share with them. If
you can show that you share their concerns, your audience will
be more likely to accept your argument. By establishing common
ground, you show readers, both those who do not initially agree
with your views and those who already agree with you, that you
are well-informed and reasonable, not one-sided or biased.

To convince readers of the important role zoos play in protecting and saving endangered species, Julia Riew asked herself "So
what?"—why should readers care about the issue of endangered
species? She reasoned that some readers might not care about saving animals, but most readers care about saving themselves from extinction. Through her research, she learned about the connections
between the rapid rate of extinctions and the threat to humans' access
to food, medicine, and clean water. By asking "So what?" she found her
shared concerns with readers, leading her to argue that, in saving animals from extinction, we are also saving ourselves and our ecosystem.

7d In your introduction, establish credibility and state your position.

When you construct an argument, make sure your introduction
includes a thesis statement, a signpost that lets readers know your
position on the issue you have chosen to debate. In the sentences
leading up to the thesis, establish your credibility (*ethos*) with
readers by showing that you are fair-minded and knowledgeable

about the various positions in a debate. By building common ground with readers who at first may not agree with your views, you show them why they should consider your thesis.

In her own introduction, Julia Riew builds credibility by introducing both sides of the debate around zoos and endangered animals, defining important terms (*captivity* versus *custody*), and presenting herself as a fair-minded writer, someone worth listening to. She connects with readers by emphasizing the severity of the extinction rate and establishing the common ground she discovered — that humans are also harmed by animal extinctions. To read Julia's introduction, see 7h.

HOW TO

Draft a thesis statement for an argument

1 **Identify the various positions in the debate you're writing about.** At the heart of a good argument are debate and disagreement. An argumentative thesis takes a clear position on a debatable issue and is supported by evidence. Identify the points in the debate on which there is disagreement. Consider your own questions and thoughts about the topic.

2 **Ask a question that doesn't have an easy yes or no answer.** An open-ended question that doesn't have just one correct answer will lead you to developing a stronger thesis. If your question can be answered with a yes or no response, add *why* or *how* to the question to provide an argumentative edge.

3 **Determine where you stand on the issue.** Consider how the sources you have read provide support for your position. Also consider how the sources make you question your position.

4 **Write your thesis as an answer to your question.** Your thesis should be arguable, one with which readers might disagree. Ask: Is your position debatable? Does your thesis state your position specifically and clearly? Will readers understand why your thesis matters?

5 **Test your thesis with a counterargument.** View your argument through the eyes of readers who disagree with you. Try to imagine a reader's counterargument to your argument.

6 **Revise your thesis.** Why does your position matter? Put your working thesis to the "So what?" test (see 1c). Consider adding *because* or *although* to your thesis to show readers the importance of your position or to set it in the context of an opposing view.

Responding to an argument

Many college assignments ask you to write an argument in response to an argument. You will build your argument around a thesis statement that answers your questions about the argument, takes a position, and shows readers what to expect when they read your essay. The following strategies show the process of drafting a thesis statement about a multimodal text, such as this World Wildlife Fund ad. Use the strategies offered here when you respond to a written argument or to a visual argument such as the public service ad below.

1 **Annotate the text with questions and observations.**

Be an active reader by recording your questions and observations about the text.

2 **Ask *what, why, who,* or *how* questions to explore your thinking and to help you determine what position you want to take.**

- **How** do the words and images work together?
- **Why** is there graffiti on the polar bears?
- **How** does the single line "What will it take before we respect the planet?" play on viewers' emotions?

- **Who** is the "we" being addressed in the ad?
- **How** does the ad accomplish its purposes of speaking out on behalf of vulnerable animals and sparking action?

3 **Test possible working thesis statements.**

The World Wildlife Fund advertisement presents a picture of animals and nature defaced.	This sentence is descriptive and factual. There's no position here.
How does the ad encourage action and advocacy on the part of the viewers?	This is a question. There's no position here.
This is a great ad that makes us all aware of endangered polar bears.	This is an opinion, not a position that suggests why the thesis matters.

4 **Pose a *why* or *how* question that is open to debate.**
How does the combination of the image of the defaced polar bears and the line "What will it take before we respect the planet?" play on viewers' emotions? How is emotion related to action?

5 **Draft a thesis that takes a position and imagines a counterargument.**
If the purpose of the World Wildlife Fund ad is to startle, the ad is successful, but if the purpose of the ad is to urge action, it is unsuccessful.

6 **Try adding a *because* clause to suggest why this thesis matters.**
If the purpose of the World Wildlife Fund ad is to startle, the ad is successful, but if the purpose of the ad is to urge action, it is unsuccessful because it will take more than an emotional appeal to motivate humans to act on behalf of endangered species.

7e Back up your thesis with persuasive lines of argument.

Arguments of any complexity contain lines of argument that, when taken together, might reasonably persuade readers that the thesis has merit. You can think of lines of argument as your *reasons.* The following, for example, are the main lines of argument that student writer Julia Riew uses in her paper about the role of zoos in saving endangered species (see 7h).

THESIS: CENTRAL CLAIM

When zoos protect animals with compassion and consideration for their needs, they encourage concern for the environment and increase financial support for conservation projects — saving not only endangered species but also the planet and humankind in turn.

SUPPORTING CLAIMS

- While some critics believe all zoos are inhumane, zoos can treat animals humanely — keeping animals in *custody* rather than in *captivity* — with oversight and regulations.
- Zoos protect endangered species by providing safe alternatives to their natural habitats, which may no longer exist.
- Although these animals may no longer be able to survive in the wild, zoos help the conservation effort by educating society about the dangers of extinction and humanity's own hand in causing it.
- Zoos also raise money for the conservation effort through sales and donations.

If you sum up your main lines of argument, as Riew did, you will have a rough outline of your essay. In your paper, you will provide evidence for each of these claims.

7f Support your thesis with specific evidence.

You will support your thesis with evidence: facts and statistics, examples and illustrations, visuals, expert opinion, and so on.

★ **Using sources responsibly**   Whether your sources provide facts or statistics, examples, visuals, or expert opinion, remember that you must cite them. Doing so gives credit to authors and shows readers how to locate a source in case they want to assess its credibility or explore the issue. See 57 (MLA) and 62 (APA) for more help.

Using facts and statistics

A fact is something that is known with certainty because it has been objectively verified: Carbon has an atomic weight of 12. Georgia congressman John Lewis died on July 17, 2020. Statistics are based on data and might or might not be factual, depending on the source of the data. If you choose to use statistics, look closely at the source of the statistics. Ask questions: Where do the statistics come from? Can they be verified? Facts can't be manipulated, but statistics can easily be manipulated so that they are unreliable and unrepresentative.

Most arguments are supported, at least to some extent, by facts and statistics. For example, in the following passage, student writer Julia Riew uses statistics — and cites her source — to show how often captive animals cannot survive in the wild.

> Indeed, research indicates that the majority of captive species fail to flourish once reintroduced into their natural habitats: one particularly devastating reintroduction study revealed that "only 16 out of 145 reintroduction projects using captive-born animals were successful" (Keulartz 341).

Writers often use statistics in selective ways to bolster their own positions. If you suspect that a writer's handling of statistics is not fair, track down the original sources for those statistics or read authors with opposing views, as they may give you a fuller understanding of the numbers.

Using examples

Examples rarely prove a point by themselves, but when used in combination with other forms of evidence, they add detail to an argument and bring it to life. Because examples are often concrete and sometimes vivid, they can reach readers in ways that statistics and abstract ideas cannot.

In her essay on zoos' role in protecting endangered species, Riew describes how one zoo in particular raised money for conservation projects.

> Not only can their educational efforts lead visitors to donate to conservation organizations, but zoos also can raise funds with ticket, food, and souvenir sales that they then pass onto conservation

projects. For example, each year the Oakland Zoo donates a portion of every ticket to conservation organizations through an ongoing program called Quarters for Conservation. In 2018, Quarters for Conservation raised $332,000 to help save at-risk species ("Oakland Zoo").

Using visuals

Visuals can support your argument by providing vivid and detailed evidence and by capturing your readers' attention. Bar or line graphs, for instance, describe and organize complex statistical data; photographs can convey abstract ideas; maps can illustrate geography. As you consider using visual evidence, ask whether the evidence will appeal to readers logically, ethically, or emotionally. For examples of eight types of visuals to support your argument, see 1f.

In her essay, Riew uses a graph to show readers the dramatic increase in extinction rates of vertebrates, supporting her argument that the "current extinction rate is an unprecedented crisis that impacts all creatures." To see the visual in Riew's paper, see page 102.

Citing expert opinion

Although they are no substitute for careful reasoning of your own, the views of an expert can contribute to the force of your argument. To help readers recognize the expert, provide credentials showing why the source is worth listening to — why the expert is, in fact, an expert — perhaps by listing their title or expertise. For example, Riew cites a geological expert who studies ecosystems, Paul B. Wignall, and provides his credentials.

> Geologist and environmental researcher Paul B. Wignall designates "human activities" such as poaching, climate change, "habitat destruction, the introduction of invasive species . . . , and the general over-exploitation of natural resources" as the primary causes of this increase (17).

7g Anticipate objections; counter opposing arguments.

No argument is complete without anticipating, acknowledging, and countering opposing arguments. It might seem at first that drawing attention to an opposing point of view or contradictory evidence would weaken your argument. But if you don't acknowledge counterarguments, your readers may ask, "Have you thought about this other point of view?" or "How could that be the only answer?" By acknowledging that not everyone draws the same conclusion or holds the same point of view, you show your *ethos* as a reasonable, fair, and well-informed writer who wants to establish common ground with readers.

There is no best place in an essay to deal with opposing views. Often it is useful to summarize the opposing position early in your essay. After stating your thesis but before developing your own arguments, you might include a paragraph that addresses the most important counterargument. Or you can anticipate objections paragraph by paragraph as you build your case. Wherever you decide to address opposing arguments, you will enhance your credibility if you explain the views of others accurately and fairly.

ANTICIPATING AND COUNTERING OPPOSING ARGUMENTS

As you build your argument, focus on the strengths of your position and the reasons a reader might object to your argument. To **anticipate a possible objection** to your argument, consider the following questions.

- Could a reasonable person draw a different conclusion from your facts or examples?
- Might a reader question any of your assumptions or offer an alternative explanation?
- Is there any evidence that might weaken your position?

The following questions may help you **respond to a potential objection**.

- Can you concede the point to the opposition but challenge the point's importance or usefulness?
- Can you explain why readers should consider a new perspective or question a piece of evidence?
- Should you explain how your position responds to contradictory evidence?
- Can you suggest a different interpretation of the evidence?

Use sentence starters to signal that you're about to **present an objection**.

- Critics of this view argue that _____.
- Some readers might point out that _____.
- Researchers challenge these claims by _____.
- Not everyone accepts this conclusion, however, because _____.

7h Sample student writing: Argument

In the following paper, student writer Julia Riew argues that zoos have an important mission to offer safe, compassionate custody to shelter and save endangered species and protect our ecosystem. Notice how Riew appeals to readers by presenting opposing views fairly before providing her own arguments.

When Riew quotes, summarizes, or paraphrases information from a source, she cites the source with an in-text citation formatted in MLA style. Citations in the paper refer readers to the list of works cited at the end of the paper. (For more details about citing sources in MLA style, see 55.)

A guide to writing an argument essay appears on pages 105–106.

Riew 1

Julia Riew

Professor Pine

Composition I

28 April 2020

From Captors to Custodians: How Zoos Protect Animals,

People, and the Planet

The Tasmanian tiger: extinct. The Japanese sea lion:
extinct. The Pyrenean ibex: extinct. The roster of extinct
species goes on: the Saudi gazelle, the Cape Verde giant
skink, the passenger pigeon, and countless others. The
rate of extinction has risen rapidly within the last three
centuries, and it signifies a crisis known as Earth's sixth
mass extinction (Wignall 19–20). This crisis threatens not
only animals but also our ecosystem as a whole, which in
turn threatens our access to clean water, clean air, food,
and medicine. In response, many zoos have shifted their
mission from pure entertainment to conservation.

> Riew introduces a problem and explains why it matters.

Riew 2

Supporters of the conservation mission claim that zoos possess enormous potential to save endangered species. Critics claim that zoos should have no role in conservation, arguing that animals should be free to roam in their natural habitats, not captive or caged. In this debate, the word *captivity* often conjures images of fear-stricken animals behind bars, gawked at by tourists and eager to escape. However, what if we shift our understanding of *captivity* from imprisonment to compassionate protection, or *custody*? When zoos protect animals with compassion and consideration for their needs, they encourage concern for the environment and increase financial support for conservation projects — saving not only endangered species but also the planet and humankind in turn.

> Riew summarizes the debate.

> Riew defines two key terms, *captivity* and *custody*.

> Thesis takes a position in the debate.

Despite the intentions of zoo conservation programs to protect animals, some animal rights advocates object to any form of captivity, arguing that zoos have a long history of animal abuse and mistreatment. In 2019, hundreds of zoos affiliated with the World Association of Zoos and Aquariums (WAZA) faced criticism for mistreating animals, reportedly using training methods such as "premature separation from mothers, physical restraint, and pain- and fear-based conditioning" in order to allow humans to feed, pet, and even ride the animals (Fobar). Such treatment — "inherently stressful," according to one director at the Animal Welfare Institute — harms the animals both physically and psychologically (Fobar). With a legacy of animal rights violations, zoos have earned their poor reputation among many animal rights activists.

> Riew presents a counterargument fairly.

> Sources are cited in MLA style.

However, captivity does not have to be — and should not be — inhumane. Rather than thinking of housing endangered

> Transition moves from introducing the counterargument to addressing it.

Riew 3

species in zoos as harmful *captivity*, we might instead think
of zookeeping as *custody*—raising, protecting, and caring
for animals with no place to go. A new level of care can
be the reality of all zoos with the help of strict regulations
provided by animal welfare programs. The American Humane
Conservation program, developed by experts in animal welfare
and conservation, evaluates and certifies leading zoos all over
the world based on several criteria, including "excellent health
and housing; positive social interactions . . . ; [and] safe and
stimulating environments" (American Humane). Regulations
are a step in the right direction.

     With animal welfare regulations, zoos will protect
animals at a higher standard than they have in the past—
sometimes at a higher standard than animals can find in
the wild if their habitat has been disrupted. Ron Kagan,
CEO of the Detroit Zoological Society, points to the success
of the Arctic Ring of Life, the largest polar bear facility in
the United States. The facility provides chilled seawater
and a safe environment for bears whose polar habitats
have been destroyed by climate change (00:07:40–08:36).
Kagan argues that by putting the needs of the animals first,
regulated zoos create living environments that can be both
safe and comfortable for animals, giving them access to
shelter and space that they may no longer find in the wild.

     To some critics, capturing and breeding endangered
animals in such situations—when the animals may no
longer be able to survive in their natural habitats—is
pointless. These critics argue that breeding and captive
protection can be permissible only if zoos eventually
release the animals. However, research indicates that
the majority of captive species fail to flourish once
reintroduced into their natural habitats: one particularly
devastating reintroduction study revealed that "only 16 out

Riew backs up her argument with a specific example.

Riew acknowledges a second counterargument.

Riew 4

of 145 reintroduction projects using captive-born animals were successful" (Keulartz 341). Once in captivity, animals tend to remain in captivity for life.

Why, then, do zoos keep these animals? Despite critics' claims, zoo animals help environmentalists achieve a key goal: to educate the general public about the importance of wildlife and the dangers of extinction. Although some level of extinction is natural, the current extinction rate is an unprecedented crisis that impacts all creatures, including humans—and we are largely to blame. Figure 1 demonstrates the dramatic increase in the extinction rates of vertebrates after the start of the Industrial Revolution. Geologist and environmental researcher Paul B. Wignall designates "human activities" such as poaching, climate change, "habitat destruction, the introduction of invasive species . . . , and the general over-exploitation of natural resources" as the primary causes of this increase (17). Animal extinction disrupts the overall ecosystem and directly impacts us in ways we might not realize. For example, anthropologist Thom Van Dooren notes that predators such as vultures play "an important role in containing disease of various kinds" and their decline "may lead to rises in . . . scavengers and in the incidence of diseases." Furthermore, each time a species goes extinct, the event lowers the overall biodiversity of the region and contributes to "an unraveling of cultural and social relationships that ripples out into the world"—an environmental effect that impacts us all (Van Dooren).

To reduce future losses of endangered species, people must gain a better understanding of the environment and animals' roles in it, and zoos help with that education. In 2015, a team researching the educational impacts of zoos surveyed more than six thousand visitors to thirty institutions around the globe. Their study found that "biodiversity understanding and knowledge of

Riew refutes the counterargument and develops the thesis.

Riew calls out and describes a figure, located at the top of the next page.

Riew supports her argument's "So what?" factor—why readers should care.

Visual presents
specific data
that back up
Riew's point.

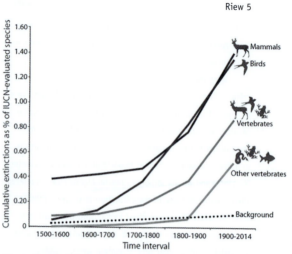

Fig. 1. Gerardo Ceballos et al. Fig. 1A, "Accelerated Modern Human-Induced Species Losses: Entering the Sixth Mass Extinction." *Science Advances*, vol. 1, no. 5, 19 June 2015, https://doi.org/10.1126/sciadv.1400253.

Because
full source
information
is provided in
the caption
and the source
is not cited
elsewhere
in the essay,
no entry for
the source is
needed in the
works cited list.

actions to help protect biodiversity both significantly increased over the course of single zoo and aquarium visits. In other words, zoos and aquariums can and do make a positive contribution" (Moss et al.). By exposing people to different animals and educating people about the negative impacts of extinction, zoos can prompt visitors to care more for wildlife.

Zoos can also directly increase financial support for conservation efforts. Not only can their educational efforts lead visitors to donate to conservation organizations, but zoos also can raise funds with ticket, food, and souvenir sales that they then pass on to conservation projects. For example, each year the Oakland Zoo donates a portion of every ticket to

Riew 6

conservation organizations through a program called Quarters for Conservation. In 2018, Quarters for Conservation raised $332,000 to help save at-risk species ("Oakland Zoo"). As environmental philosopher Jozef Keulartz points out, "to reach the aim of species conservation, [zoos] need to attract visitors"; thus zoos often house not only animals that need protection but also those that will make people want to buy tickets (347). Traditionally, large "charismatic mammals" can "act as flagship species" to attract visitors, while a variety of species and "imaginative displays" can also increase attendance (Keulartz 347). Higher attendance and ticket sales mean zoos can donate more of their proceeds to a range of conservation initiatives.

> Riew uses specific evidence for support.

    By raising animals in regulated and certified habitats, zoos can play a critical role in the conservation cause and can help shift our impressions of zookeepers from captors to custodians. Opponents worry about the necessity of zoos and the health of animals within them. However, with an informed understanding of animal welfare needs, such establishments not only provide animals with humane habitats that no longer exist in the wild but also promote empathy and financial support for conservation. Each day, as the threat of mass extinction continues to sweep the globe and irreversibly damage the worldwide ecosystem, it becomes increasingly urgent for humans to understand the importance of wildlife. With the help of zoos, we can take action to protect animals—and thus ourselves. Perhaps our action today will keep us off the EXTINCT roster tomorrow.

> Conclusion echoes the introduction without repeating it.

> Riew ends by emphasizing why the argument matters.

Riew 7

Works Cited

Works cited list is in MLA style.

American Humane. "Twenty-Five Leading Zoological Facilities Receive Coveted American Humane Conservation Certification for Humane Animal Care in Inaugural Year." *PR Newswire*, Cision, 2 Oct. 2017, www .prnewswire.com/news-releases/twenty-five-leading -zoological-facilities-receive-coveted-american -humane-conservation-certification-for-humane-animal -care-in-inaugural-year-300529156.html. Press release.

Fobar, Rachel. "Hundreds of Zoos and Aquariums Accused of Mistreating Animals." *National Geographic*, 15 Aug. 2019, www.nationalgeographic.com/animals/2019/08 /waza-zoos-accused-of-mistreating-animals-wap -report/.

Kagan, Ron. "Animal Welfare and the Future of Zoos, Ron Kagan, TEDxOaklandUniversity." *YouTube*, uploaded by TEDx Talks, 30 Nov. 2015, www.youtube.com /watch?v=h_FRY4FIkws.

Keulartz, Jozef. "Captivity for Conservation? Zoos at a Crossroads." *Journal of Agricultural and Environmental Ethics*, vol. 28, no. 2, Apr. 2015, pp. 335–51. *SpringerLink*, https://doi.org/10.1007 /s10806-015-9537-z.

Moss, Andrew, et al. "Impact of a Global Biodiversity Education Campaign on Zoo and Aquarium Visitors." *Frontiers in Ecology and the Environment*, vol. 15, no. 5, June 2017, pp. 243–47. *Ecological Society of America*, https://doi.org/10.1002/fee.1493.

"Oakland Zoo Raises Record-Breaking $332,000 for Wildlife Conservation." *Oakland Zoo*, 30 Oct. 2018, www .oaklandzoo.org/news/oakland-zoo-raises-record -breaking-332-000-for-wildlife-conservation. Press release.

List is alphabetized by authors' last names (or by title when a work has no author).

Van Dooren, Thom. "How the Current Mass Extinction
     of Animals Threatens Humans." Interview by Simon
     Worrall. *National Geographic*, 20 Aug. 2014, www
     .nationalgeographic.com/news/2014/8/140820
     -extinction-crows-penguins-dinosaurs-asteroid-sydney
     -booktalk/.

Wignall, Paul B. *Extinction: A Very Short Introduction*. Oxford
     UP, 2019. Very Short Introductions.

WRITING GUIDE

How to write an argument essay

When you compose an **argument**, you take a position on a debatable issue. You state your position, provide evidence to support it, and respond to opposing views on the issue. A sample argument essay begins on page 98.

Key features

- **A thesis, stated as a clear position on a debatable issue**, frames an argument essay. The issue is debatable because reasonable people disagree about it.

- **An examination of the issue's context** indicates why the issue is important, why readers should care about it, or how your position fits into the debates surrounding the topic.

- **Sufficient, representative, and relevant evidence** supports the argument's claims. Evidence needs to be specific and persuasive; quoted, summarized, or paraphrased fairly and accurately; and cited correctly.

- **Opposing positions are summarized and countered.** By anticipating and countering objections to your position, you establish common ground with readers and show yourself to be a reasonable and well-informed writer.

Thinking ahead: Presenting or publishing

You may have some flexibility in how you present or publish your argument. If you submit your argument as an audio or video essay, make sure you understand the genre's conventions and think through →

HOW TO WRITE AN ARGUMENT ESSAY (Continued)

how your voice or a combination of sounds and images can help you establish your credibility. If you are taking a position on a local issue, consider publishing your argument in the form of a newspaper opinion piece or letter to the editor to provide a real-world audience.

Writing your argument

1 Explore

Generate ideas by brainstorming responses to questions such as the following:

- What is the debate around your issue? What sources will help you learn more about your issue?
- What position will you take? Why does your position need to be argued?
- How will you establish common ground with your readers?
- What evidence supports your position? What evidence makes you question your position?
- What types of appeals—*ethos, logos, pathos*—might you use to persuade readers?

2 Draft

Try to figure out the best way to structure your argument. A typical approach might include the following steps: Capture readers' attention; state your thesis; give background information; support your major claims with specific evidence; recognize and respond to opposing points of view; and end by reinforcing your thesis and reminding readers why it matters.

3 Revise

Ask your reviewers for specific feedback. Here are some questions to guide their comments.

- Is the thesis clear? Is the issue debatable?
- Is the evidence persuasive? Is more needed?
- Is your argument organized logically?
- Are there any flaws in your reasoning or assumptions that weaken the argument?
- Have you presented yourself as a knowledgeable, trustworthy writer?
- Does the conclusion pull together your entire argument? How might the conclusion be more effective?

Clarity

8   Prefer active verbs.

Choose an active verb whenever possible. Active verbs express meaning more vigorously than forms of the verb *be* or verbs in the passive voice. Forms of *be* (*be, am, is, are, was, were, being, been*) lack vigor because they convey no action. Passive verbs lack strength because their subjects receive the action instead of doing it.

PASSIVE	The pumps *were destroyed* by a surge of power.
BE VERB	A surge of power *was* responsible for the destruction of the pumps.
ACTIVE	A surge of power *destroyed* the pumps.

Even among active verbs, some are more vigorous and color-ful than others. Carefully selected verbs can energize a piece of writing.

▶ The goalie crouched low, ~~reached~~ out his stick, and ~~sent~~ the

swept   *hooked*

rebound away from the mouth of the net.

> **ACADEMIC WRITING**   Although you may be tempted to avoid the passive voice completely, keep in mind that some situations call for it, including some scientific writing. For appropriate uses of the passive voice, see 8a; for advice about forming the passive voice, see 28b.

8a Choose the active voice or the passive voice, depending on your writing situation.

In the active voice, the subject does the action; in the passive voice, the subject receives the action. Although both voices are grammatically correct, the active voice is usually more effective because it is clearer and more direct.

ACTIVE	Hernando *caught* the fly ball.
PASSIVE	The fly ball *was caught* by Hernando.

In passive sentences, the actor (in this case, *Hernando*) frequently does not appear: *The fly ball was caught.*

Most of the time, you will want to emphasize the actor, so you should use the active voice. To replace a passive verb with an active one, make the actor the subject of the sentence.

▶ *The settlers stripped the land of timber before realizing* ~~The land was stripped of timber before the settlers realized~~ the
^
consequences of their actions.

The revision emphasizes the actors (*settlers*) by naming them in the subject.

Appropriate uses of the passive voice

The passive voice is appropriate if you want to emphasize the receiver of the action or to minimize the importance of the actor. The writer of the following sentence, for example, wished to emphasize the people affected by the earthquake.

Many Hawaiians *were forced* to leave their homes after the earthquake.

In much scientific writing, the passive voice properly emphasizes the experiment or process being described, not the researcher. Check with your instructor for the preference in your discipline.

Just before harvest, the tobacco plants *are sprayed* with a chemical to prevent the growth of suckers.

8b Replace *be* verbs that result in dull or wordy sentences.

Not every *be* verb needs replacing. The forms of *be* (*be, am, is, are, was, were, being, been*) work well when you want to link a subject to a noun that clearly renames it or to an adjective that describes it: *Orchard House was the home of Louisa May Alcott. The harvest will be bountiful this summer.*

If using a *be* verb makes a sentence needlessly wordy, consider replacing it. Often a phrase following the verb contains a noun or an adjective (such as *violation* or *resistant*) that suggests a more vigorous active verb (*violate, resist*).

▶ **Burying nuclear waste in Antarctica would** *violate* ~~be in violation of~~ **an**
^
international treaty.

► When Rosa Parks ~~was resistant to~~ giving up her seat on the bus,

resisted
^

she became a civil rights hero.

8c As a rule, choose a subject that names the person or thing doing the action.

In weak, unemphatic writing, both the actor and the action may be buried in sentence elements other than the subject and the verb. In the following weak sentence, for example, both the actor and the action appear in prepositional phrases, word groups that do not receive much attention from readers.

WEAK   The institution of the New Deal had the effect of reversing some of the economic inequalities of the Great Depression.

EMPHATIC   The New Deal reversed some of the economic inequalities of the Great Depression.

Consider the subjects and verbs of the two versions — *institution had* versus *New Deal reversed*. The second version expresses the writer's point more emphatically.

► ~~The use of~~ pure oxygen can ~~cause~~ healing ~~in~~ wounds that are

P
^

otherwise untreatable.

In the original sentence, the subject and verb — *use can cause* — express the point blandly. *Pure oxygen can heal* makes the point more directly.

EXERCISE 8–1   Revise any weak, unemphatic sentences by replacing passive verbs or *be* verbs with active alternatives. If a sentence is emphatic, do not change it. Possible revisions appear in the back of the book.

The ranger doused the campfire before giving us
► ~~The campfire was doused by the ranger before we were given~~ a

^

ticket for unauthorized use of a campsite.

a. The Saxons were defeated by the Prussians in 1745.
b. The entire operation is managed by Ahmed, the producer.
c. The sea kayaks were expertly paddled by the tour guides.

d. At the crack of rocket and mortar blasts, I jumped from the top bunk and landed on my buddy below, who was crawling on the floor looking for his boots.

e. The protesters' shouts were heard by the senator as she walked up the Capitol steps.

EXERCISE 8–2   For each writing situation below, decide whether it is more appropriate to use the active voice or the passive voice. Answers appear in the back of the book.

a. You are writing a research paper explaining the effects of a deadly bacterial outbreak in a remote Chilean village. (active / passive)

b. You are writing a letter to the editor, praising an emergency medical technician whose quick action saved an injured motorist. (active / passive)

c. You are writing a summary of the procedure you used in an experiment for your biology class. (active / passive)

d. To accompany your résumé, you must write a cover letter explaining your recent accomplishments. (active / passive)

e. You must fill out an incident report, explaining in detail how your actions led to a collision between the forklift you were operating and a wall of fully stocked shelves. (active / passive)

9 Balance parallel ideas.

If two or more ideas are parallel, they should be expressed in parallel grammatical form. Single words should be balanced with single words, phrases with phrases, clauses with clauses.

> There is more work to be done, more justice to be had, more barriers to break.   — Barack Obama

> This novel is not to be tossed lightly aside, but to be hurled with great force.   — Dorothy Parker

9a Balance parallel ideas in a series.

Balance all items in a series by presenting them in parallel grammatical form.

▶ Children who study music also learn confidence, discipline,
  creativity.
  and ~~they are creative.~~
       ^

The revision presents all the items in the series as nouns: *confidence,*
discipline, and *creativity.*

▶ Impressionist painters believed in focusing on ordinary subjects,
                                                         using
  capturing the effects of light on those subjects, and ~~to use~~ short
                                                          ^
  brushstrokes.

The revision uses *-ing* forms for all the items in the series: *focusing, capturing,* and *using.*

Headings

Headings on the same level of organization should be written in parallel form — as single words, phrases, or clauses.

PHRASES AS HEADINGS

Safeguarding Earth's atmosphere

Charting the path to sustainable energy

Conserving global forests

INDEPENDENT CLAUSES AS HEADINGS

Ask the patient to describe current symptoms.

Take a detailed medical history.

Record the patient's vital signs.

Lists

Lists are usually introduced with an independent clause followed by a colon. They are most readable when they are presented in parallel grammatical form. Like headings, lists might consist of single words, phrases, or clauses. The list in the following sentence consists of parallel noun phrases.

Renewable energy technologies include the following: hydroelectric power, solar power, wind energy, and geothermal energy.

9b Balance parallel ideas presented as pairs.

When pairing ideas, underscore their connection by expressing them in similar grammatical form. Paired ideas are usually connected with coordinating conjunctions, with correlative conjunctions, or with *than* or *as*.

Parallel ideas linked with coordinating conjunctions

Coordinating conjunctions (*and*, *but*, *or*, *nor*, *for*, *so*, and *yet*) link ideas of equal importance. When those ideas are closely parallel in content, they should be expressed in parallel grammatical form.

▶ Emily Dickinson's poetry features the use of dashes and

the capitalization of
~~capitalizing~~ common words.
^

The revision balances the nouns *use* and *capitalization*.

▶ Many colleges are making SAT scores optional and ~~encourage~~
encouraging
^

alternative application materials.

The revision balances the verb *making* with the verb *encouraging*.

Parallel ideas linked with correlative conjunctions

Correlative conjunctions come in pairs: *either . . . or*, *neither . . . nor*, *not only . . . but also*, *both . . . and*, *whether . . . or*. Make sure that the grammatical structure following the second half of the pair is the same as that following the first half.

▶ Thomas Edison was not only a prolific inventor but also ~~was~~ a

successful entrepreneur.

The words *a prolific inventor* follow *not only*, so *a successful entrepreneur* should follow *but also*.

▶ The clerk told me either to change my flight or *to* take the train.
^

To change my flight, which follows *either*, should be balanced with *to take the train*, which follows *or*.

Comparisons linked with *than* or *as*

In comparisons linked with *than* or *as*, the elements being compared should be expressed in parallel grammatical structure.

▶ For some situations, it is easier to talk on the phone than ~~texting.~~ to text.

To talk is balanced with *to text*.

Comparisons should also be logical and complete. (See 10c.)

9c Repeat function words to clarify parallels.

Function words such as prepositions (*by, to*) and subordinating
conjunctions (*that, because*) signal the grammatical nature of the
word groups to follow. Although you can sometimes omit function words, be sure to include them whenever they signal parallel
structures that readers might otherwise miss.

▶ Our study revealed that left-handed students were more likely

to have trouble with classroom desks and that rearranging desks for

exam periods was useful.

A second subordinating conjunction helps readers sort out the two
parallel ideas: *that* left-handed students have trouble with classroom
desks and *that* rearranging desks was useful.

EXERCISE 9–1 Edit the following sentences to correct faulty paral-
lelism. Possible revisions appear in the back of the book.

Rowena began her workday by refilling the hand sanitizer

setting
stations and ~~set~~ up the cash registers.

a. Bluetooth technology is used with personal computers, mobile
phones, and listening to audio devices.

b. Hannah told her rock-climbing partner that she bought a new
harness and of her desire to climb Otter Cliffs.

c. It is more difficult to sustain an exercise program than starting
one.

d. During basic training, I was not only told what to do but also what to think.

e. Jan wanted to drive to the wine country or at least Sausalito.

EXERCISE 9–2   Revise the following paragraph to balance parallel ideas.

Community service can provide tremendous benefits not only for the organization receiving the help but the volunteer providing the help, too. This dual benefit idea is behind a recent move to make community service hours a graduation requirement in high schools across the country. For many nonprofit organizations, seeking volunteers is often smarter financially than to hire additional employees. For many young people, community service positions can help develop empathy, being committed, and leadership. Opponents of the trend argue that volunteerism should not be mandatory, but research shows that community service requirements are keeping students engaged in school and lower dropout rates dramatically. Parents, school administrators, and people who are leaders in the community all seem to favor the new initiatives.

10 Add needed words.

Sometimes writers leave out words without affecting the meaning of the sentence. But often the result is confusing or ungrammatical. Readers need to see at a glance how the parts of a sentence are connected.

> **FOR MULTILINGUAL WRITERS**
> Languages sometimes differ in the need for certain words. In particular, be alert for missing articles, verbs, subjects, or expletives. See 29, 30a, and 30b.

10a Add words needed to complete compound structures.

In compound structures, words are often left out for economy: *Horatio is a man who means what he says and [who] says what he means.* Such omissions are acceptable as long as the omitted words are common to both parts of the compound structure.

If omitting a word from a sentence would make the sentence ungrammatical because the word is not common to both parts of the compound structure, the word must be left in.

▶ Advertisers target customers whom they identify through

                    who

  demographic research or have purchased their product in the

                 ^

  past.

  The word *who* must be included because *whom . . . have purchased* is not grammatically correct.

                  accepted

▶ Mayor Davis never has and never will accept a bribe.

                ^

  Has . . . accept is not grammatically correct.

10b Add the word *that* if there is any danger of misreading without it.

If there is no danger of misreading, the word *that* may be omitted when it introduces a subordinate clause: *The value of a principle is the number of things* [*that*] *it will explain.* When a sentence might be misread without *that,* however, include the word.

▶ In his famous obedience experiments, psychologist Stanley

                that

  Milgram discovered ordinary people were willing to inflict

            ^

  physical pain on strangers.

  Milgram didn't discover ordinary people; he discovered that ordinary people were willing to inflict pain on strangers. The word *that* tells readers to expect a clause, not just *ordinary people,* as the direct object of *discovered.*

10c Add words needed to make comparisons logical and complete.

Comparisons should be made between items that are alike. To compare unlike items is illogical and distracting.

▶ The forests of North America are much more extensive than
those of
Europe.
^
Forests must be compared with forests, not with all of Europe.

▶ Some music critics argue that Beyoncé's music videos are better
singer's.
than any other ~~singer.~~
^
Beyoncé's music videos cannot logically be compared with a singer. The revision uses the possessive form *singer's*, with the words *music videos* being implied.

Sometimes the word *other* must be inserted to make a comparison logical.

other
▶ Jupiter is larger than any planet in our solar system.
^
Jupiter is a planet, and it cannot be larger than itself.

Sometimes the word *as* must be inserted to make a comparison grammatically complete.

as
▶ The city of Lowell is as old, if not older than, the neighboring
^
city of Lawrence.

The construction *as old* is not complete without a second *as*: *as old as . . . the neighboring city of Lawrence.*

Comparisons should be complete enough to ensure clarity. The reader should understand what is being compared.

INCOMPLETE	Depression is more common in adolescent girls.
COMPLETE	Depression is more common in adolescent girls than in adolescent boys.

Finally, comparisons should leave no ambiguity for readers. If a sentence lends itself to more than one interpretation, revise the sentence to state clearly which interpretation you intend.

AMBIGUOUS	Ken helped me more than my roommate.
CLEAR	Ken helped me more than *he helped* my roommate.
CLEAR	Ken helped me more than my roommate *did*.

10d Add the articles *a*, *an*, and *the* where necessary for grammatical completeness.

It is not always necessary to repeat articles with paired items: *We bought a laptop and printer.* However, if one of the items requires *a* and the other requires *an*, both articles must be included.

▶ We bought a laptop and ^an^ e-reader.

> **FOR MULTILINGUAL WRITERS**
>
> Choosing and using articles can be challenging for some writers. See 29.

EXERCISE 10–1   Add any words needed for grammatical or logical completeness in the following sentences. Possible revisions appear in the back of the book.

> The plumber feared ^that^ the pipes were completely rusted through.

a. A grapefruit or orange is a good source of vitamin C.

b. The golden eagle's wingspan is nearly as wide as the bald eagle.

c. Looking out the family room window, Sarah saw her favorite tree, which she had climbed as a child, was gone.

d. The graphic designers are interested and knowledgeable about producing posters for the balloon race.

e. The Great Barrier Reef is larger than any coral reef in the world.

11 Untangle mixed constructions.

A mixed construction contains sentence parts that do not sensibly fit together. The mismatch may be a matter of grammar or of logic.

11a Untangle the grammatical structure.

Do not begin a sentence with one grammatical plan and switch without warning to another. Often you must rethink the purpose of the sentence and revise.

MIXED   For most drivers who have a blood alcohol content of .05 percent double their risk of causing an accident.

The writer begins the sentence with a long prepositional phrase and makes it the subject of the verb *double*. But a prepositional phrase can serve only as a modifier; it cannot be the subject of a sentence.

REVISED   For most drivers who have a blood alcohol content of .05 percent, the risk of causing an accident is doubled.

REVISED   Most drivers who have a blood alcohol content of .05 percent double their risk of causing an accident.

In the first revision, the writer begins with the prepositional phrase and finishes the sentence with a proper subject and verb (*risk . . . is doubled*). In the second revision, the writer stays with the original verb (*double*) and begins the sentence another way, making *drivers* the subject of *double*.

▸ ~~When the country elects~~ Electing a president is the most important

responsibility in a democracy.

The adverb clause *When the country elects a president* cannot serve as the subject of the verb *is*. The revision replaces the adverb clause with a gerund phrase, a word group that can function as a subject. (See 49b and 49e.)

▸ Although Luxembourg is a small nation, ~~but~~ it has a rich cultural

history.

The coordinating conjunction *but* cannot link a subordinate clause (*Although Luxembourg. . .*) with an independent clause (*it has a rich cultural history*).

> **FOR MULTILINGUAL WRITERS**
>
> When writing in English, watch out for double subjects, which can happen when a noun and pronoun try to serve the same grammatical function in a sentence. See 30c.
>
> ▶ My father ~~he~~ moved to Peru before he met my mother.
>
> Also take care not to repeat an object or adverb in an adjective clause. See 30d.

11b Straighten out the logical connections.

A subject and its verb should make sense together; when they don't, the error is known as *faulty predication*.

▶ Under the revised plan, first-generation college students~~, who~~ ^financial-aid benefits for^ ~~now receive financial aid benefits,~~ will increase.

The benefits, not the students, will increase.

An appositive is a noun that renames a nearby noun. When an appositive and the noun it renames are not logically equivalent, the error is known as *faulty apposition*. (See 49c.)

▶ ^Tax accounting,^ ~~The tax accountant,~~ a very lucrative profession, requires intelligence, patience, and attention to mathematical detail.

The tax accountant is a person, not a profession.

11c Avoid *is when, is where,* and *reason . . . is because* constructions.

Sentences with *is when, is where,* and *reason . . . is because* constructions are often ungrammatical or illogical and should be avoided. Grammatically, the verb *is* (as well as *are, was,* and *were*) should be followed by a noun or an adjective, not by an adverb clause beginning with *when, where,* or *because.*

Logically, the words *when*, *where*, and *because* suggest relations of time, place, and cause — relations that do not always make sense with *is*, *are*, *was*, or *were*.

▶ Anorexia nervosa is ~~where people~~ think they are overweight and
   a disorder suffered by people who

diet to the point of starvation.

Where refers to places. Anorexia nervosa is a disorder, not a place.

▶ The ~~reason the~~ experiment failed ~~is~~ because conditions in the lab

were not sterile.

The adverb clause beginning with *because* properly modifies the verb *failed*.

EXERCISE 11–1 Edit the following sentences to untangle mixed constructions. Possible revisions appear in the back of the book.

   Taking
   ~~By taking~~ the oath of allegiance made Ling a US citizen.

a. Using surgical gloves is a precaution now worn by dentists to prevent contact with patients' blood and saliva.
b. A physician, the career my brother is pursuing, requires at least ten years of challenging work.
c. The reason the pharaohs had bad teeth was because tiny particles of sand found their way into Egyptian bread.
d. Recurring bouts of flu among team members set a record for number of games forfeited.
e. In this box contains the key to your future.

12 Repair misplaced and dangling modifiers.

Modifiers should point clearly to the words they modify. As a rule, related words should be kept together.

12a Put limiting modifiers in front of the words they modify.

Limiting modifiers such as *only*, *even*, *almost*, *nearly*, and *just* should appear in front of a verb only if they modify the verb:

At first, I couldn't even touch my toes, much less grasp them. If they limit the meaning of some other word in the sentence, they should be placed in front of that word.

▶ Research shows that students ~~only~~ learn new vocabulary words
  only
  when they are encouraged to read.
  ^

  Only limits the meaning of the *when* clause.

▶ If you ~~just~~ interview chemistry majors, your understanding of
        just
        ^
  the student response to the new policies will be incomplete.

  The adverb *just* limits the meaning of *chemistry majors*, not *interview*.

When the limiting modifier *not* is misplaced, the sentence usually suggests a meaning the writer did not intend.

▶ In the United States in 1860, all Black southerners were ~~not~~
                                  not
                                  ^
  enslaved.

  The original sentence says that no Black southerners were enslaved. The revision is clear and accurate.

12b Place phrases and clauses so that readers can see what they modify.

Although phrases and clauses can appear at some distance from the words they modify, make sure your meaning is clear. When phrases or clauses are oddly placed, absurd misreadings can result.

MISPLACED	The soccer player returned to the clinic where he had undergone emergency surgery in 2019 in a limousine sent by Adidas.
REVISED	Traveling in a limousine sent by Adidas, the soccer player returned to the clinic where he had undergone emergency surgery in 2019.

The revision corrects the false impression that the soccer player underwent emergency surgery in a limousine.

Occasionally the placement of a modifier leads to an ambiguity — a *squinting modifier*. In such a case, two revisions will be possible, depending on the writer's intended meaning.

AMBIGUOUS   The animal shelter at which we volunteered occasionally held adoption events on Saturdays.

It's not clear what happened occasionally, the volunteering or the adoption events. Both revisions eliminate the ambiguity.

CLEAR   The animal shelter at which we occasionally volunteered held adoption events on Saturdays.

CLEAR   The animal shelter at which we volunteered held adoption events occasionally on Saturdays.

12c Move awkwardly placed modifiers.

A sentence should flow from subject to verb to object, without lengthy detours along the way. When a long adverbial word group separates a subject from its verb, a verb from its object, or a helping verb from its main verb, the result is often awkward.

▶ ~~Jamaica,~~ after more than 300 years of British rule, gained its ^Jamaica

independence in 1962.

There is no reason to separate the subject, *Jamaica*, from the verb, *gained*, with a long phrase.

FOR MULTILINGUAL WRITERS

When writing in English, take care not to place an adverb between a verb and its object. See 30e.

▶ Yolanda lifted ~~easily~~ the fifty-pound weight.
^easily

12d Avoid split infinitives when they are awkward.

An infinitive consists of *to* plus the base form of a verb: *to think, to breathe, to dance.* When a modifier appears between *to* and the verb, an infinitive is said to be "split": *to carefully balance, to completely understand.* If a split infinitive is awkward, move the modifier.

► The patient should try to ~~if possible~~ avoid going up and down stairs.

If possible, the ^

Attempts to avoid split infinitives can sometimes result in equally awkward sentences. When alternative phrasing sounds unnatural, split the infinitive.

AWKWARD   We decided actually to enforce the law.

BETTER   We decided to actually enforce the law.

EXERCISE 12–1   Edit the following sentences to correct misplaced or awkwardly placed modifiers. Possible revisions appear in the back of the book.

Answering questions can be annoying. ~~in a phone survey.~~

in a phone survey ^   ^

a. The manager asked her employees to if they had time submit their reports on Friday.

b. Many students graduate with debt from college totaling more than fifty thousand dollars.

c. It is a myth that humans only use 10 percent of their brains.

d. Daria found the old nightgown she used to wear to sleep in the closet.

e. All geese do not fly beyond Narragansett for the winter.

12e Repair dangling modifiers.

A dangling modifier fails to refer logically to any word in the sentence. Dangling modifiers are easy to repair, but they can be hard to recognize, especially in your own writing.

Recognizing dangling modifiers

Dangling modifiers are usually word groups (such as verbal phrases) that suggest but do not name an actor. When a sentence opens with such a modifier, readers expect the subject of the next clause to name the actor. If it doesn't, the modifier dangles.

Although most readers will understand the writer's intended meaning in such sentences, the unintended humor can be distracting.

The following sentences illustrate four common kinds of dangling modifiers.

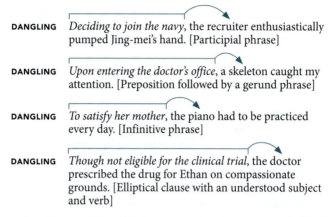

DANGLING *Deciding to join the navy*, the recruiter enthusiastically pumped Jing-mei's hand. [Participial phrase]

DANGLING *Upon entering the doctor's office*, a skeleton caught my attention. [Preposition followed by a gerund phrase]

DANGLING *To satisfy her mother*, the piano had to be practiced every day. [Infinitive phrase]

DANGLING *Though not eligible for the clinical trial*, the doctor prescribed the drug for Ethan on compassionate grounds. [Elliptical clause with an understood subject and verb]

These dangling modifiers falsely suggest that the recruiter decided to join the navy, that the skeleton entered the doctor's office, that the piano intended to satisfy the mother, and that the doctor was not eligible for the clinical trial.

Check your writing for dangling modifiers using the chart below.

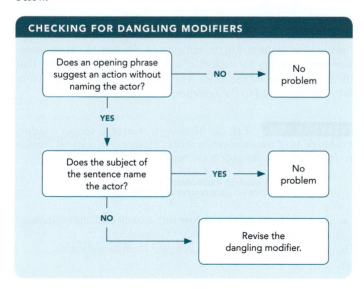

CHECKING FOR DANGLING MODIFIERS

Does an opening phrase suggest an action without naming the actor? — **NO** → No problem

YES

Does the subject of the sentence name the actor? — **YES** → No problem

NO

Revise the dangling modifier.

Repairing dangling modifiers

To repair a dangling modifier, you can revise the sentence in one of two ways: by naming the actor in the subject of the sentence, or by naming the actor in the modifier. Depending on your sentence, one of these revision strategies may be more appropriate than the other.

ACTOR NAMED IN SUBJECT

▶ Upon entering the doctor's office, a skeleton. I noticed ~~caught my attention.~~

▶ To satisfy her mother, the piano Jo had to practice ~~had to be practiced~~ every day.

ACTOR NAMED IN MODIFIER

▶ When Jing-mei decided ~~Deciding~~ to join the navy, the recruiter enthusiastically pumped her ~~Jing-mei's~~ hand.

▶ Ethan was Though not eligible for the clinical trial, the doctor prescribed the drug for him ~~Ethan~~ on compassionate grounds.

NOTE: You cannot repair a dangling modifier just by moving it. Consider, for example, the sentence about the skeleton. If you put the modifier at the end of the sentence (*A skeleton caught my attention upon entering the doctor's office*), you are still suggesting that the skeleton entered the office. The only way to avoid the problem is to put the word *I* in the sentence, as shown in the revision.

EXERCISE 12–2   Edit the following sentences to correct dangling modifiers. Most sentences can be revised in more than one way. Possible revisions appear in the back of the book.

a student must complete
To graduate, two science courses. ~~must be completed.~~

a. To complete an online purchase with a credit card, the expiration date and the security code must be entered.

b. Though only sixteen, UCLA accepted Martha's application.

c. Settled in the cockpit, the pounding of the engine was muffled only slightly by my helmet.

d. After studying polymer chemistry, computer games seemed less complex to Letitia.

e. When a young man, my mother enrolled me in ballet and tap dance classes.

13 Eliminate distracting shifts.

Shifts in point of view, in verb tense, in mood or voice, or from indirect to direct questions or quotations can distract or confuse readers.

13a Make the point of view consistent in person and number.

The point of view in a piece of writing is the perspective from which it is written: first person (*I* or *we*), second person (*you*), or third person (*he*, *she*, *it*, *one*, *they*, or any noun).

The *I* (or *we*) point of view, which emphasizes the writer, is a good choice for informal letters and writing based on personal experience. The *you* point of view, which emphasizes the reader, works well for giving advice or explaining how to do something. The third-person point of view, which emphasizes the subject, is appropriate in academic and professional writing.

Once you have settled on a point of view, stick with it. Shifting points of view within a piece of writing confuses readers.

▶ Our class practiced rescuing a victim trapped in a wrecked car.

We learned to dismantle the car with the essential tools. ~~You~~ ^We^

were graded on ~~your~~ speed and ~~your~~ skill in freeing the victim. ^our^ ^our^

The writer should have stayed with the *we* point of view. *You* is inappropriate because the writer is not addressing readers directly. *You* should not be used in a vague sense meaning "anyone." (See 23d.)

You need
▶ ~~One needs~~ a password and a credit card number to access the
database. You will be billed at an hourly rate.

You is an appropriate choice for giving advice directly to readers.

EXERCISE 13-1   Edit the following paragraph to eliminate distracting shifts in point of view (person and number). Create two versions. First, rewrite it in the first person (using *I* and *we*). Then rewrite the paragraph in the third person (using *people* and *they*). In what contexts would each version be the best choice?

When online dating first became available, many people thought that it would simplify romance. We believed that you could type in a list of criteria — sense of humor, college education, green eyes, good job — and a database would select the perfect mate. Thousands of people signed up for services and filled out their profiles, confident that true love was only a few clicks away. As it turns out, however, virtual dating is no easier than traditional dating. I still have to contact the people I find, exchange messages, and meet him in the real world. Although a dating app might produce a list of possibilities and screen out obviously undesirable people, you can't predict chemistry. More often than not, people who seem perfect online just don't click in person. Dating apps and social media do help a single person expand their pool of potential dates, but they're no substitute for the hard work of romance.

13b Maintain consistent verb tenses.

Consistent verb tenses clearly establish the time of the actions being described. When a passage begins in one tense and then shifts to another for no reason, readers are distracted and confused.

▶ Our candidate struggled in the debate. Just as we gave up hope,
soared
she ~~soars~~ ahead in the polls.

The writer thought that the present tense (*soars*) would convey excitement. But having begun in the past tense (*struggled*, *gave up*), the writer should follow through in the past tense.

Writers often encounter difficulty with verb tenses when writing about literature. Because fictional events occur outside the time frames of real life, the past tense and the present tense may seem equally appropriate. The literary convention is to describe fictional events consistently in the present tense. (See 27f.)

> ▶ The scarlet letter is a punishment sternly placed on Hester's
>
> breast by the community, and yet it ~~was~~ *is* a fanciful and
>
> imaginative product of Hester's own needlework.

EXERCISE 13–2   Edit the following paragraph to eliminate distracting shifts in tense.

> On Election Day in 2020, Mississippi residents approve a new state flag by an overwhelming majority. The old flag, which originated in 1894, includes the Confederate flag in its design. Black Mississippians speak out against the flag for years. They noted that the Confederate flag represents a time when the state fought to continue enslaving Black Americans. However, propositions to change the flag do not pass in previous years. The fight to update the flag gains strength during the police brutality and racial inequality protests of spring 2020. Led by young activists, Mississippi residents renew the push for a flag that represented all Mississippians. Lawmakers passed a bill removing the state flag in June, and voters make the new flag official in November. The new flag featured a magnolia, the state flower.

13c Make verbs consistent in mood and voice.

Unnecessary shifts in the mood of a verb can be distracting and confusing to readers. There are three moods in English: the *indicative*, used for facts, opinions, and questions; the *imperative*, used for orders or advice; and the *subjunctive*, used to express wishes or conditions contrary to fact (see 27g).

The following passage shifts confusingly from the indicative to the imperative mood.

> ▶ The counselor advised us to spread out our core requirements
>
> over two or three semesters. ~~Also,~~ *She also suggested that we* pay attention to prerequisites
>
> for elective courses.

The writer began by reporting the counselor's advice in the indicative mood (*counselor advised*) and switched to the imperative mood (*pay attention*); the revision puts both sentences in the indicative.

A verb may be in either the active voice (with the subject doing the action) or the passive voice (with the subject receiving the action). (See 8a.) If a writer shifts without warning from one to the other, readers may be left wondering why.

▶ Each student completes a self-assessment~~, The self-assessment is~~ *gives it*

~~then given~~ to the teacher, and a copy ~~is exchanged~~ with a classmate. *exchanges*

Because the passage began in the active voice (*student completes*) and then switched to the passive (*self-assessment is given, copy is exchanged*), readers are left wondering who gives the self-assessment to the teacher and the classmate. The active voice, which is clearer and more direct, leaves no ambiguity.

13d Avoid sudden shifts from indirect to direct questions or quotations.

An indirect question reports a question without asking it: *We asked whether we could visit Miriam.* A direct question asks directly: *Can we visit Miriam?* Sentences containing shifts between the two types of questions are awkward and impossible to punctuate because indirect questions must end with a period and direct questions must end with a question mark. (See 39b.)

▶ LGBTQ business owners wonder whether their businesses are

whether they can

unfairly targeted and ~~can they~~ reverse the trend~~?~~.

The revision poses both questions indirectly. The writer could also ask both questions directly: *Are LGBTQ-owned businesses being unfairly targeted? Can these business owners reverse the trend?*

An indirect quotation reports someone's words without quoting word for word: *Senator Kessel said he wants to see evidence.* A direct quotation presents the exact words of a speaker or writer, set off with quotation marks: *Senator Kessel said, "I want to see evidence."* Unannounced shifts from indirect to direct quotations are distracting and confusing.

▶ The patient said she had been experiencing heart palpitations

and ~~please~~ run as many tests as possible to identify the problem.
   asked me to
   ^

The revision reports the patient's words indirectly. The writer also could quote the words directly: *The patient said, "I have been experiencing heart palpitations. Please run as many tests as possible to identify the problem."*

EXERCISE 13–3   Edit the following sentences to make the verbs consistent in mood and voice and to eliminate distracting shifts from indirect to direct questions or quotations. Possible revisions appear in the back of the book.

As a public relations intern, I wrote press releases, managed the

website, and ~~all phone calls were fielded by me.~~
   fielded all phone calls.
   ^

a. An incredibly talented musician, Ray Charles mastered R&B, soul, and gospel styles. Even country music was performed well by him.

b. Environmentalists point out that shrimp farming in Southeast Asia is polluting water and making farmlands useless. They warn that action must be taken by governments before it is too late.

c. The samples were observed for five days before we detected any growth.

d. In his famous soliloquy, Hamlet contemplates whether death would be preferable to his difficult life and, if so, is he capable of committing suicide?

e. The lawyer told the judge that Miranda Hale was innocent and allow her to prove the allegations false.

EXERCISE 13–4   Edit the following sentences to eliminate distracting shifts. Possible revisions appear in the back of the book.

For many first-year engineering students, adjusting to the course

load can be so challenging that ~~you~~ sometimes feel overwhelmed.
   they
   ^

a. We want to play volleyball this afternoon, but you have to reserve the court through the fitness center before you can use it.

b. The interviewer asked if we had brought our proof of citizenship and did we bring our passports?

c. Experienced reconnaissance scouts know how to make fast decisions and use sophisticated equipment to keep one's team from being detected.

d. After the animators finish their scenes, the production designer arranges the clips according to the storyboard. Synchronization notes must also be made for the sound editor and the composer.

e. Madame Defarge is a sinister figure in Dickens's *A Tale of Two Cities*. On a symbolic level, she represents fate; like the Greek Fates, she knitted the fabric of individual destiny.

14 Emphasize key ideas.

Within each sentence, emphasize your point by expressing it in the subject and verb of an independent clause, the words that receive the most attention from readers (see 14a–14e).

Within longer stretches of writing, you can draw attention to ideas deserving special emphasis by using a variety of techniques (see 14f).

14a Coordinate equal ideas; subordinate minor ideas.

When combining two or more ideas in one sentence, you have two choices: coordination or subordination. Choose coordination to indicate that the ideas are equal or nearly equal in importance. Choose subordination to indicate that one idea is less important than another.

Coordination

Coordination draws attention equally to two or more ideas. To coordinate single words or phrases, join them with a coordinating conjunction (see the list on the next page) or with a pair of correlative conjunctions: *bananas and strawberries*; *not only a lackluster plot but also inferior acting* (see 47g).

To coordinate independent clauses — word groups that express a complete thought and that can stand alone as a sentence — join them with a comma and a coordinating conjunction or with a semicolon. The semicolon is often accompanied by a conjunctive adverb such as *therefore* or *however* or by a transitional phrase such as *for example* or *in other words*. For specific coordination strategies and some examples, see the chart on the next page.

USING COORDINATION TO COMBINE SENTENCES OF EQUAL IMPORTANCE

1. Consider using a comma and a coordinating conjunction. (See 33a.)

, and	, but	, or	, nor
, for	, so	, yet	

▶ In Orthodox Jewish funeral ceremonies, the shroud is a simple

         and the

  linen vestment/. ~~The~~ coffin is plain wood.
         ^

2. Consider using a semicolon with a conjunctive adverb or transitional phrase. (See 35b.)

also	however	next
as a result	in addition	now
besides	in fact	of course
consequently	in other words	otherwise
finally	in the first place	still
for example	meanwhile	then
for instance	moreover	therefore
furthermore	nevertheless	thus

             in addition, she

▶ Alicia scored well on the SAT/; ~~She also~~ had excellent grades and a
                 ^

  record of community service.

3. Consider using a semicolon alone. (See 35a.)

          in

▶ In youth we learn/; ~~In~~ age we understand.
          ^

Subordination

To give unequal emphasis to two or more ideas, express the major idea in an independent clause and place any minor ideas in subordinate clauses or phrases. (For specific subordination strategies and some examples, see the chart on the next page.)

Let your intended meaning determine which idea you emphasize. Thinking about your purpose and your audience often helps you decide which ideas deserve emphasis.

USING SUBORDINATION TO COMBINE SENTENCES OF UNEQUAL IMPORTANCE

1. Consider putting the less important idea in a subordinate clause beginning with one of the following words. (See 49e.)

after	before	that	which
although	even though	unless	while
as	if	until	who
as if	since	when	whom
because	so that	where	whose

▶ *When*
   Elizabeth Cady Stanton proposed a convention to discuss the status
   ^

   of women in America~~.~~, Lucretia Mott agreed.
                        ^

▶ My sister owes much of her recovery to a yoga program~~.~~ *that she*/~~She~~ began
                                                          ^

   ~~the program~~ three years ago.

2. Consider putting the less important idea in an appositive phrase. (See 49c.)

▶ Karate, ~~is~~ a discipline based on the philosophy of nonviolence~~.~~,
          ^   ^

   ~~It~~ teaches the art of self-defense.

3. Consider putting the less important idea in a participial phrase. (See 49b.)

▶ ~~American essayist Cheryl Peck was~~ *E*ncouraged by friends to write
                                    ^
   , American essayist Cheryl Peck
   about her life~~.~~/~~She~~ began combining humor and irony in her essays
                ^

   about being overweight.

EXERCISE 14–1   Use the coordination or subordination technique in brackets to combine each pair of independent clauses. Possible revisions appear in the back of the book.

   Ted Williams was one of the best hitters in the history of
   baseball, but he
   ~~baseball. He~~ never won a World Series ring. [*Use a comma*
                ^

   and a coordinating conjunction.]

a. Williams played for the Boston Red Sox from 1939 to 1960. He managed the Washington Senators and the Texas Rangers for several years after retiring as a player. [*Use a comma and a coordinating conjunction.*]

b. In 1941, Williams finished the season with a batting average of .406. No player has hit over .400 for a season since then. [*Use a semicolon.*]

c. Williams acknowledged that Joe DiMaggio was a better all-around player. Williams felt that he was a better hitter than DiMaggio. [*Use the subordinating conjunction* although.]

d. Williams was a stubborn man. He always refused to tip his cap to the crowd after a home run because he claimed that fans were fickle. [*Use a semicolon and the transitional phrase* for example.]

e. Williams's relationship with the media was unfriendly at best. He sarcastically called baseball writers the "knights of the keyboard" in his memoir. [*Use a semicolon.*]

14b Combine choppy sentences.

Short sentences demand attention, so you should use them primarily for emphasis. Too many short sentences, one after the other, will give your writing a choppy effect.

If an idea is not important enough to deserve its own sentence, try combining it with a sentence close by. Put any minor ideas in subordinate structures such as phrases or subordinate clauses. (See 49.)

▶ Twitter has started to label certain posts by its users/ ~~The~~ *because the*

company is concerned about the spread of misinformation on

its platform.

The writer wanted to emphasize that Twitter has started labeling certain posts, so she put the reason in a subordinate clause beginning with *because*.

▶ The Chesapeake and Ohio Canal, ~~is~~ a 184-mile waterway

constructed in the 1800s/. ~~It~~ was a major source of

transportation for goods during the Civil War.

A minor idea is now expressed in an appositive phrase (*a 184-mile waterway constructed in the 1800s*).

Although subordination is ordinarily the most effective technique for combining short, choppy sentences, coordination is appropriate when the ideas are equal in importance.

> On January 1, lawmakers raised the minimum wage/ ~~Lawmakers~~

and

increased funding for public schools.

Combining two short sentences by joining their predicates (*raised . . . increased*) is an effective coordination technique.

FOR MULTILINGUAL WRITERS

Unlike some other languages, written English does not repeat objects or adverbs in adjective clauses. See 30d.

> The apartment that we rented ~~it~~ needed repairs.

The pronoun *it* cannot repeat the relative pronoun *that*.

EXERCISE 14–2 Combine the following sentences by subordinating minor ideas or by coordinating ideas of equal importance. You must decide which ideas are minor because the sentences are given out of context. Possible revisions appear in the back of the book.

Agnes, ~~was~~ another girl I worked with/. ~~She~~ was a quiet child.

a. The X-Men comic books and Japanese woodcuts of kabuki dancers were part of Marlena's research project on popular culture. They covered the tabletop and the chairs.

b. The students organized a petition. The petition asked to change the school motto. The motto was "A man's greatest strength is his education."

c. Employees can apply for a spot in the leadership program. The program teaches management and communication skills.

d. Shore houses were flooded up to the first floor. Beaches were washed away. Brant's Lighthouse was swallowed by the sea.

e. Laura Thackray was an engineer at Volvo Car Corporation. She addressed women's safety needs. She designed a pregnant crash-test dummy.

14c Avoid ineffective or excessive coordination.

Coordinate structures are appropriate only when you intend to draw readers' attention equally to two or more ideas: *Professor Sakellarios praises loudly, and she criticizes softly.* If one idea is more important than another, or if a coordinating conjunction does not clearly signal the relationship between the ideas, you should subordinate the less important idea.

INEFFECTIVE COORDINATION	Closets were taxed as rooms, and most colonists stored their clothes in chests or clothespresses.
IMPROVED WITH SUBORDINATION	Because closets were taxed as rooms, most colonists stored their clothes in chests or clothespresses.

The revision subordinates the less important idea (*closets were taxed as rooms*) by putting it in a subordinate clause. Notice that the subordinating conjunction *Because* signals the relation between the ideas more clearly than the coordinating conjunction *and*.

Because it is so easy to string ideas together with *and*, writers often rely too heavily on coordination in their rough drafts. Look for opportunities to tuck minor ideas into subordinate clauses or phrases.

► ~~Four hours went by, and~~ After four hours, a rescue truck finally arrived, but by that time we had been evacuated in a helicopter.

Having three independent clauses was excessive. The least important idea has become a prepositional phrase.

EXERCISE 14–3 The following sentences show coordinated ideas (ideas joined with a coordinating conjunction or a semicolon). Restructure the sentences by subordinating minor ideas. You must decide which ideas are minor because the sentences are given out of context. Possible revisions appear in the back of the book.

The rowers returned to shore, ~~and~~ where they had a party on the beach ~~and celebrated~~ to celebrate the start of the season.

a. These particles are known as "stealth liposomes," and they can hide in the body for a long time without detection.

b. Irena is a competitive gymnast and majors in biochemistry; her goal is to apply her athletic experience and her science degree to a career in sports medicine.

c. Students, textile workers, and labor unions have loudly protested sweatshop abuses, so apparel makers have been forced to examine their labor practices.

d. IRC (Internet relay chat) was developed in a European university; it was created as a way for a group of graduate students to talk about projects from their dorm rooms.

e. The cafeteria's new menu has an international flavor, and it includes everything from pizza to pad thai.

14d   Do not subordinate major ideas.

If a sentence buries its major idea in a subordinate construction, readers may not give the idea enough attention. Make sure to express your major idea in an independent clause and to subordinate any minor ideas.

> ▶ *As*
> I was driving home from my new job, heading down Ranchitos
>   ^
> Road, ~~when~~ my car suddenly overheated.

> The writer wanted to emphasize that the car overheated, not the fact of driving home. The revision expresses the major idea in an independent clause and places the less important idea in an adverb clause (*As I was driving home from my new job*).

14e   Do not subordinate excessively.

In attempting to avoid short, choppy sentences, writers sometimes go to the opposite extreme, putting more subordinate ideas into a sentence than its structure can bear. If a sentence contains too many ideas, occasionally it can be restructured. More often, however, such sentences must be divided.

> ▶ Some professional athletes argue that they should not be looked
>   *These athletes*
> on as role models. ~~and that they~~ believe that modeling behavior
>   ^^
> is a parent's responsibility.

> By splitting the original sentence in two, the writer makes it easier for the reader to focus on the main claim, that modeling behavior is a parent's job.

EXERCISE 14-4 In each of the following sentences, the idea that the writer wished to emphasize is buried in a subordinate construction. Restructure each sentence so that the independent clause expresses the major idea, as indicated in brackets, and lesser ideas are subordinated. Possible revisions appear in the back of the book.

> *Although*
> Catherine has weathered many hardships, ~~although~~ she has
> ^
> rarely become discouraged. [*Emphasize that Catherine has rarely*
>
> *become discouraged.*]

a. Gina helped the relief effort, distributing food and medical supplies. [*Emphasize distributing food and medical supplies.*]

b. Janbir spent every Saturday learning tabla drumming, noticing that with each hour of practice his memory for complex patterns was growing stronger. [*Emphasize Janbir's memory.*]

c. The rotor hit, gouging a hole about an eighth of an inch deep in my helmet. [*Emphasize that the rotor gouged a hole in the helmet.*]

d. My grandfather, who raised his daughters the old-fashioned way, was born eighty years ago in Puerto Rico. [*Emphasize how the grandfather raised his daughters.*]

e. The Narcan reversed the depressive effect of the drug, saving the patient's life. [*Emphasize that the patient's life was saved.*]

14f Experiment with techniques for gaining special emphasis.

By experimenting with certain techniques, usually involving some element of surprise, you can draw attention to ideas that deserve special emphasis. Use such techniques sparingly, however, or they will lose their punch. The writer who tries to emphasize everything ends up emphasizing nothing.

Using sentence endings for emphasis

You can highlight an idea simply by withholding it until the end of a sentence. The technique works something like a punch line. In the following example, the sentence's meaning is not revealed until its very last word.

> The only completely consistent people are the dead.
>
> — Aldous Huxley

An inverted sentence reverses the normal subject-verb order, placing the subject at the end, where it receives unusual emphasis.

> In golden pots are hidden the most deadly poisons.
>
> — Thomas Draxe

Using parallel structure for emphasis

Parallel grammatical structure draws attention to paired ideas or to items in a series. (See 9.) When parallel ideas are paired, the emphasis falls on words that underscore comparisons or contrasts, especially when they occur at the end of a phrase or clause.

> We must *stop talking* about the *American dream* and *start listening* to the *dreams of Americans.*
>
> — Reubin Askew

In a parallel series, the emphasis falls at the end, so it is generally best to end with the item in the series you most want to emphasize.

> My uncle often talks about growing up in Sudan — playing soccer, eating goat stew, and dodging bullets.
>
> — Alec Hamza, student

15 Provide some variety.

When a rough draft is filled with too many sentences that begin the same way or have the same structure, try injecting some variety — as long as you can do so without sacrificing clarity or ease of reading.

15a Vary your sentence openings.

Most sentences in English begin with the subject, move to the verb, and continue to the object, with modifiers tucked in along the way or put at the end. For the most part, such sentences are fine. Put too many of them in a row, however, and they become monotonous.

Words, phrases, or clauses modifying the verb can often be inserted ahead of the subject.

Eventually a

▶ A few drops of sap ~~eventually~~ began to trickle into the bucket.

Like most adverbs, *eventually* does not need to appear close to the verb it modifies (*began*).

Just as the sun was coming up, a

▶ A pair of black ducks flew over the pond. ~~just as the sun was coming up.~~

The adverb clause, which modifies the verb *flew*, is as clear at the beginning of the sentence as it is at the end.

Adjectives and participial phrases can frequently be moved to the beginning of a sentence without loss of clarity.

Dejected and down,

▶ Edward, ~~dejected and down,~~ nearly gave up his job search.

NOTE: When beginning a sentence with an adjective or a participial phrase, make sure that the subject of the sentence names the person or thing described in the introductory phrase. If it doesn't, the phrase will dangle. (See 12e.)

15b Use a variety of sentence structures.

A writer should not rely too heavily on simple sentences and compound sentences, as the effect tends to be both monotonous and choppy. (See 14b and 14c.) Too many complex or compound-complex sentences, however, can be equally monotonous. Try to achieve a mix of sentence types.

The major sentence types are illustrated in the following sentences, all taken from Flannery O'Connor's "The King of the Birds," an essay describing the author's pet peafowl.

SIMPLE	Frequently the cock combines the lifting of his tail with the raising of his voice.
COMPOUND	Any chicken's dusting hole is out of place in a flower bed, but the peafowl's hole, being the size of a small crater, is more so.
COMPLEX	The peacock does most of his serious strutting in the spring and summer when he has a full tail to do it with.
COMPOUND-COMPLEX	The cock's plumage requires two years to attain its pattern, and for the rest of his life, this chicken will act as though he designed it himself.

For a fuller discussion of sentence types, see 50a.

15c Try inverting sentences occasionally.

A sentence is inverted if it does not follow the normal subject-verb-object pattern. Many inversions sound artificial and should be avoided, except in the most formal contexts. If an inversion sounds natural, however, it can provide a welcome touch of variety.

> *Set at the top two corners of the stage were huge*
> ► ~~Huge~~ lavender hearts outlined in bright white lights. ~~were set at~~
>   ^   ^
>
> ~~the top two corners of the stage.~~

In the revision, the subject, *hearts*, appears after the verb, *were set*. Notice that the two parts of the verb are also inverted — and separated from each other (*Set . . . were*) — without any awkwardness or loss of meaning.

Inverted sentences are used for emphasis as well as for variety (see 14f).

EXERCISE 15–1   Improve variety in each of the following sentences by using the technique suggested in brackets. Possible revisions appear in the back of the book.

> *To protect endangered marine turtles, fishing*
> ~~Fishing~~ crews place turtle excluder devices in fishing nets.
> ^   ^
>
> ~~to protect endangered marine turtles.~~ [*Begin the sentence with*
>
> *the adverbial infinitive phrase.*]

a. The exhibits for insects and spiders are across the hall from the fossils exhibit. [*Invert the sentence.*]

b. Sayuri becomes a successful geisha after growing up desperately poor. [*Move the adverb clause to the beginning of the sentence.*]

c. Researchers have been studying Mount St. Helens for years. They believe that earthquakes may have caused the 1980 eruption. [*Combine the two sentences into a complex sentence.*]

d. Ice cream typically contains 10 percent milk fat. Premium ice cream may contain up to 16 percent milk fat and has less air in it. [*Combine the two sentences as a compound sentence.*]

e. The economy may recover quickly if home values climb. [*Move the adverb clause to the beginning of the sentence.*]

EXERCISE 15–2 Edit the following paragraph to increase sentence variety.

Making architectural models is a skill that requires patience and precision. It is an art that illuminates a design. Architects come up with a grand and intricate vision. Draftspersons convert that vision into blueprints. The model maker follows the blueprints. The model maker builds a miniature version of the structure. Modelers can work in traditional materials like wood and clay and paint. Modelers can work in newer materials like Styrofoam and liquid polymers. Some modelers still use cardboard, paper, and glue. Other modelers prefer glue guns, deformable plastic, and thin aluminum and brass wire. The modeler may seem to be making a small mess in the early stages of model building. In the end the modeler has completed a small-scale structure. Architect Rem Koolhaas has insisted that plans reveal the logic of a design. He has argued that models expose the architect's vision. The model maker's art makes this vision real.

16 Tighten wordy sentences.

Long sentences are not necessarily wordy, nor are short sentences always concise. A sentence is wordy if it can be tightened without loss of meaning.

16a Eliminate redundancies.

Redundancies such as *cooperate together*, *yellow in color*, or *basic essentials* are a common source of wordiness. There is no need to say the same thing twice.

▶ Daniel ~~is now employed~~ ^{works} at a private rehabilitation center ~~working~~ as a registered physical therapist.

Though modifiers ordinarily add meaning to the words they modify, they are redundant when their meanings are suggested by other words in the sentence.

▶ Martina ~~very quickly~~ scribbled her phone number on a greasy napkin.

The word *scribbled* already suggests that Martina wrote *very quickly*.

16b Avoid unnecessary repetition of words.

Though words may be repeated deliberately for effect, repetitions
will seem awkward if they are clearly unnecessary. When a more
concise version is possible, choose it.

▶ His third speech, delivered in Chicago, was ~~an~~ outstanding.

~~speech.~~

▶ The best teachers help each student ~~become a better student~~ *grow* both

academically and emotionally.

16c Cut empty or inflated phrases.

An empty phrase can be cut with little or no loss of meaning.
Common examples are word groups that weaken the writer's
authority by apologizing or hedging: *in my opinion*, *I think that*,
it seems that, and so on.

▶ ~~In my opinion,~~ *O*ur current immigration policy is misguided.

Readers understand that they are hearing the writer's opinion.

Inflated phrases can be reduced to a word or two without
loss of meaning.

INFLATED	CONCISE
along the lines of	like
as a matter of fact	in fact
at this point in time	now (*or* currently)
due to the fact that	because
for the purpose of	for
in order to	to
in spite of the fact that	although (*or* though)
in the event that	if

16d Simplify the structure.

Simplifying sentences and using stronger verbs can make writing more direct.

▶ The analyst claimed that because of volatile market conditions,

she could not ~~make an~~ estimate ~~of~~ the company's future profits.

The verb *estimate* is more vigorous and concise than *make an estimate of.*

The colorless verbs *is*, *are*, *was*, and *were* often generate excess words.

studied
▶ Investigators ~~were involved in studying~~ the effect of classical
    ^

music on unborn babies.

The action (*studying*), originally appearing in a subordinate structure, has become a strong verb, *studied.*

The expletive constructions *there is* and *there are* (or *there was* and *there were*) can also lead to wordy sentences. The same is true of expletive constructions beginning with *it*.

        A
▶ ~~There is~~ another module ~~that~~ tells the story of Charles Darwin
        ^

and introduces the theory of evolution.

16e Reduce clauses to phrases, phrases to single words.

Word groups functioning as modifiers can often be made more compact. Look for opportunities to reduce clauses to phrases or phrases to single words.

▶ We took a side trip to Monticello, ~~which was~~ the home of

Thomas Jefferson.

EXERCISE 16–1 Edit the following sentences to reduce wordiness. Possible revisions appear in the back of the book.

> The Wilsons moved into the house ~~in spite of the fact that~~ *even though* the
>
> back door was only ten yards from the train tracks.

a. Martin Luther King Jr. was a man who set a high standard for future leaders to meet.
b. Alice has been deeply in love with cooking since she was little and could first peek over the edge of a big kitchen tabletop.
c. In my opinion, Bloom's race for the governorship is a futile exercise.
d. It is pretty important in being a successful graphic designer to have technical knowledge and at the same time an eye for color and balance.
e. Your task will be the delivery of mailed correspondence to all employees in the company.

EXERCISE 16–2 Edit the following business memo to reduce wordiness.

To: District managers
From: Margaret Davenport, Vice President
Subject: Customer database

It has recently been brought to my attention that a percentage of our sales representatives have been failing to log reports of their client calls in our customer database each and every day. I have also learned that some representatives are not checking the database on a routine basis.

Our clients sometimes receive a multiple number of sales calls from us when a sales representative is not cognizant of the fact that the client has been contacted at a previous time. Repeated telephone calls from our representatives annoy our customers. These repeated telephone calls also portray our company as one that is lacking in organization.

Effective as of immediately, direct your representatives to do the following:

• Record each and every customer contact in the customer database at the end of each day, without fail.
• Check the database at the very beginning of each day to ensure that telephone communications will not be initiated with clients who have already been called.

Let me extend my appreciation to you for cooperating in this important matter.

17 Choose appropriate language.

Language is appropriate when it suits your subject, engages your audience, and blends naturally with your voice.

To some extent, your choice of language will be governed by the conventions of the genre in which you are writing. When in doubt about the conventions of a particular genre — lab reports, informal essays, business memos, and so on — consult your instructor or look at models written by experts in the field.

17a Choose an appropriate level of formality.

In deciding on a level of formality, consider both your subject and your audience. For most college and professional writing, some degree of formality is appropriate. In a job application, for example, it is a mistake to sound too breezy and informal.

TOO INFORMAL	I'd like to get that sales job you've got on the website.
MORE FORMAL	I would like to apply for the position of sales manager posted on LinkedIn.

In choosing a level of formality, above all be consistent. When a writer's voice shifts from one level of formality to another, readers receive mixed messages.

▶ Jorge's pitching lesson ~~commenced~~ *began* with his famous curveball, ~~implemented~~ *thrown* by tucking the little finger behind the ball. Next he ~~elucidated~~ *revealed* the mysteries of the sucker pitch, a slow ball coming behind a fast windup.

Words such as *commenced* and *elucidated* are inappropriate for the subject matter, and they clash with informal terms such as *sucker pitch* and *fast windup*.

17b Avoid jargon, except in specialized writing situations.

Jargon is special language used among members of a trade, discipline, or professional group. Sentences with jargon can be hard to read. Use jargon only when readers will be familiar with it and when plain English will not do as well.

> JARGON We outsourced the work to an outfit in Ohio because we didn't have the bandwidth to tackle it in-house.

> REVISED We hired a company in Ohio because we had too few employees to do the work.

The following are common examples of jargon from business, government, higher education, and the military, with plain English alternatives in parentheses.

ameliorate (improve)	optimal (best, most favorable)
commence (begin)	parameters (boundaries, limits)
components (parts)	peruse (read, look over)
endeavor (try)	prior to (before)
facilitate (help)	utilize (use)
indicator (sign)	viable (workable)

17c Avoid most euphemisms and doublespeak.

Euphemisms — words or phrases substituted for words thought to sound harsh or ugly — are sometimes appropriate. We may use euphemisms out of concern for someone's feelings. Telling parents, for example, that their daughter is "unmotivated" is more sensitive than saying she's lazy. Tact or politeness, then, can occasionally justify euphemisms, but use them sparingly. Many euphemisms are needlessly evasive or even deceitful.

EUPHEMISM	PLAIN ENGLISH
correctional facility	prison
economically deprived	poor
preowned automobile	used car
revenue enhancers	taxes

The term *doublespeak* applies to any deliberately evasive or deceptive language, including euphemisms. Doublespeak is especially common in politics and business. Torture is described as *enhanced interrogation*, for example, and *downsizing* really means firing or laying off employees.

EXERCISE 17–1   Edit the following sentences to eliminate jargon, euphemisms, and doublespeak. You may need to make substantial changes in some sentences. Possible revisions appear in the back of the book.

> After two weeks in the legal department, Kala has ~~worked~~ *mastered*
> ~~into~~ the routine*, of the office,* and her ~~functional and self-~~ *office* *performance has*
> ~~management skills have~~ exceeded all expectations.

a. In my youth, my family was under the constraints of difficult financial circumstances.

b. In order that I may increase my expertise in the area of delivery of services to clients, I feel that participation in this conference will be beneficial.

c. I am between jobs because my company downsized last fall.

d. Government-sanctioned investigations into the continued value of after-school programs indicate a perceived need in the public realm at large.

e. Let's do a deep dive into the numbers and notify all stakeholders of our findings.

EXERCISE 17–2   Edit the following email message to eliminate jargon.

Dear Ms. Jackson:

We members of the Nakamura Reyes team value our external partnering arrangements with Creative Software, and I look forward to seeing you next week at the trade show in Fresno. Per Mr. Reyes, please let me know when you'll have some downtime there so that he and I can conduct a strategizing session with you concerning our production schedule. It's crucial that we all be on the same page re our 2023–2024 product release dates.

Before we have some face time, however, I have some findings to share. Our customer-centric approach to the new products will necessitate that user testing periods trend upward. The enclosed data should help you effectuate any adjustments to your timeline; let me know ASAP if you require any additional information to facilitate the above.

Before we convene in Fresno, Mr. Reyes and I will agendize any further talking points. Thanks for your help.

Sincerely,

Sylvia Nakamura

17d In most contexts, avoid slang.

Slang is an informal and sometimes private vocabulary that expresses the solidarity of a group such as rock musicians or sports fans. Slang changes rapidly. For example, the slang teenagers use to express approval changes every few years; *cool*, *groovy*, *neat*, *awesome*, *sick*, and *dope* have replaced one another within the last several decades.

Although slang has a certain vitality, it is an informal code that not everyone understands. Avoid using it in academic writing, unless you have a specific purpose for doing so.

▶ Without ~~the receipts,~~ evidence, we can't move forward with our proposal.

17e Avoid sexist and noninclusive language.

Sexist and noninclusive language stereotypes or demeans people and should be avoided. Using inclusive language and recognizing individuals' chosen pronoun usage shows awareness of others. As you write for different audiences, keep in mind that words matter, and always select words that show respect for your readers.

Recognizing sexist and noninclusive language

Some sexist language is easy to recognize because it reflects genuine contempt for women: referring to a woman as a "babe," for example, or calling a lawyer a "lady lawyer."

Other forms of sexist and noninclusive language are less blatant. The following practices reflect stereotypical thinking: referring to members of one profession as exclusively one gender (teachers as women or computer engineers as men, for instance) or using different conventions when naming or identifying people of different genders.

> **STEREOTYPICAL LANGUAGE**
>
> After a nursing student graduates, *she* must face a difficult state board examination. [Not all nursing students are women.]
>
> Running for city council are Boris Stotsky, an attorney, and *Mrs.* Cynthia Jones, a professor of English *and mother of three.* [The title *Mrs.* and the phrase *and mother of three* are irrelevant.]

Sometimes noninclusive language arises from the practice of using gendered pronouns to refer generically to persons of all genders, or from using the incorrect pronouns to refer to individuals.

GENDERED PRONOUNS

A journalist is motivated by *his* deadline. [Not all journalists are men.]

A good interior designer treats *her* clients' ideas respectfully. [Not all interior designers are women.]

When a student applies for federal financial aid, *he or she* is given an FSA ID. [Not all students identify as *he* or *she*.]

Similarly, terms including *man* and *men* were once used to refer generically to all people of that profession or group. Current usage demands gender-neutral terms.

INAPPROPRIATE	APPROPRIATE
chairman	chairperson, moderator, chair, head
congressman	member of Congress, representative, legislator
fireman	firefighter
mailman	mail carrier, postal worker, letter carrier
to man	to operate, to staff
mankind	people, humans
manpower	personnel, staff
weatherman	forecaster, meteorologist

Revising sexist and noninclusive language

When revising sexist language, some writers substitute *he or she* and *his or her*. Others alternate female pronouns with male pronouns. These strategies are wordy, can become awkward or confusing, and are not inclusive of all individuals. Instead, use the plural or revise the sentence. You may also use the singular gender-neutral pronouns *they* and *them* to refer to individuals inclusively.

USING THE PLURAL

Journalists are motivated by *their* deadlines.

REVISING THE SENTENCE

A journalist is motivated by *a* deadline.

USING SINGULAR *THEY*

A journalist is motivated by *their* deadline.

For more examples of these revision strategies, see section 22.

NOTE: When using pronouns to refer to people, choose the pronouns that the individuals themselves would use. Some transgender, nonbinary, and gender-fluid people refer to themselves by new pronouns (*ze/hir*, for example), but if you are unfamiliar with an individual's pronouns, *they* and *them* are acceptable gender-neutral options.

> **EXERCISE 17–3**   Edit the following sentences to eliminate noninclusive language or sexist assumptions. Possible revisions appear in the back of the book.

> Scholarship athletes
> ~~A scholarship athlete~~ must be as concerned about ~~his~~ their academic
> performance as ~~he is~~ they are about ~~his~~ their athletic performance.

a. Mrs. Geralyn Farmer, who is the mayor's wife, is the chief surgeon at University Hospital. Dr. Paul Green is her assistant.
b. Every applicant wants to know how much he will earn.
c. An elementary school teacher should understand the concept of nurturing if she intends to be effective.
d. Our company is going to hire a new I.T. guy. He will update the server and set up remote desktops.
e. If man does not stop polluting his environment, mankind will perish.

17f Avoid biased language.

Your writing should be respectful and free of stereotypical, biased, or other harmful language. Be especially careful when describing groups of people. Avoid outdated labels and generalizations; instead, consider how people identify, and use the language that they themselves would use. You may need to research current terms, but working to use the right identifying language is an important step in recognizing and respecting your audience.

> ▶ Harriet Tubman was an abolitionist who worked to free enslaved Black Americans.
> ~~colored slaves.~~

> ▶ The Supreme Court ruled that ~~gays~~ same-sex couples had the right to marry in all 50 states in 2015.

▶ At every building entrance, our school installed ramps accessible

      people who use wheelchairs.
to ~~the handicapped.~~
  ^

▶ North Dakota takes its name from the *Lakota* ~~Indian~~ word meaning
                                 ^

"friend" or "ally."

Negative stereotypes (such as "drives like an old lady") are of course hurtful. But even if you believe your generalization to be positive, it is harmful to make assumptions based on a person's or group's characteristics.

▶ It was no surprise that Greer, *an excellent math and science student,* ~~a Chinese American,~~ was selected
                                        ^

for the honors chemistry program.

18   Find the exact words.

Two reference works (or their online equivalents) will help you find words to express your meaning exactly: a good dictionary, such as *The American Heritage Dictionary* or *Merriam-Webster* online, and a collection of synonyms and antonyms, such as *Roget's International Thesaurus*.

NOTE: Do not turn to a thesaurus in search of impressive words. Look for words that express your meaning exactly.

18a Select words with appropriate connotations.

In addition to their strict dictionary meanings (or *denotations*), words have *connotations*, emotional colorings that affect how readers respond to them. The word *steel* denotes "commercial iron that contains carbon," but it also calls up images associated with steel. These associations give the word its connotations — cold, hard, smooth, unbending.

    If the connotation of a word does not seem appropriate for your purpose, your audience, or your subject matter, you should change the word. When a more appropriate synonym does not come quickly to mind, consult a dictionary or a thesaurus.

► When American soldiers returned home after World War II,
   ~~abandoned~~ *left*
   many women abandoned their jobs in favor of marriage.

The word *abandoned* is too negative for the context.

EXERCISE 18–1 Use a dictionary and a thesaurus to find at least four synonyms for each of the following words. Be prepared to explain any slight differences in meaning.

1. decay (verb)
2. difficult (adjective)
3. hurry (verb)
4. pleasure (noun)
5. secret (adjective)
6. talent (noun)

18b Prefer specific, concrete nouns.

Unlike general nouns, which refer to broad classes of things, specific nouns point to particular items. *Film*, for example, names a general class, *animated film* names a narrower class, and *Coco* is more specific still. Other examples: *team, football team, Denver Broncos; music, symphony, Beethoven's Ninth*.

Unlike abstract nouns, which refer to qualities and ideas (*justice, beauty, realism*), concrete nouns point to immediate, often sensory experience and to physical objects (*steeple, lilac, stone*).

Specific, concrete nouns express meaning more vividly than general or abstract ones. Although general and abstract language is sometimes necessary to convey your meaning, use specific, concrete words when possible.

► The senator spoke about the challenges of the future:
   climate change, dwindling resources, and domestic extremism.
   ~~the environment and world peace.~~

Nouns such as *thing, area, aspect,* and *factor* are especially dull and imprecise.

►   *motherhood, and memory.*
   Toni Morrison's *Beloved* is about slavery, ~~among other things.~~

18c Take care with idioms.

Idioms are speech forms that follow no easily specified rules. The English say "Bernice went *to hospital*," an idiom strange to American ears, which are accustomed to hearing *the* in front of *hospital*. Idioms with prepositions (such as *with*, *to*, *at*, and *of*) sometimes cause trouble, especially when they follow certain verbs and adjectives. When in doubt, consult a dictionary.

UNIDIOMATIC	IDIOMATIC
agree to (an idea)	agree with (an idea)
angry at (a person)	angry with (a person)
different than (a person or thing)	different from (a person or thing)
off of	off
plan on doing	plan to do
sure and	sure to
try and	try to

FOR MULTILINGUAL WRITERS

Because idioms follow no particular rules, you must learn them individually. You may find it helpful to keep a list of idioms that you frequently encounter in conversation and in reading.

EXERCISE 18–2   Edit the following sentences to eliminate errors in the use of idiomatic expressions. If a sentence is correct, write "correct" after it. Revisions appear in the back of the book.

> We agreed to abide ~~with~~ the decision of the judge.
> ^by^

a. Queen Anne was so angry at Sarah Churchill that she refused to see her again.
b. Jean-Pierre is going to try and finish his sociology project this weekend.
c. The parade moved off of the street and onto the beach.
d. The experienced hikers plan on making the dangerous trek across the mountains.
e. Be sure to fill out the necessary forms before going to the DMV.

18d Do not rely heavily on clichés.

The pioneer who first announced that he had "slept like a log" no doubt amused his companions with a fresh and unlikely comparison. Today, however, that comparison is a cliché, a saying that can no longer add emphasis or surprise.

To see just how predictable clichés are, put your hand over the right-hand column in the following list and then finish the phrases on the left.

busy as a	bee, beaver
cool as a	cucumber
dead as a	doornail
light as a	feather
avoid clichés like the	plague

The solution for clichés is simple: Delete them.

▶ When I received a full scholarship from my second-choice
     felt pressured to settle for second best.
school, I ~~found myself between a rock and a hard place.~~
     ^

Sometimes you can write around a cliché by adding an element of surprise. For example, one student who had written that she had butterflies in her stomach revised her cliché like this:

> If all of the action in my stomach is caused by butterflies, there must be a horde of them, with horseshoes on.

The image of butterflies wearing horseshoes is fresh and unlikely, not predictable like the original cliché.

18e Use figures of speech with care.

A figure of speech is an expression that uses words imaginatively (rather than literally) to make abstract ideas concrete. Most often, figures of speech compare two seemingly unlike things to reveal surprising similarities.

In a *simile*, the writer makes the comparison explicitly, usually by introducing it with *like* or *as*: *By the time cotton had to be picked, Grandfather's neck was as red as the clay he plowed.*

In a *metaphor*, the *like* or *as* is omitted, and the comparison is implied. Historians, economists, and politicians, for example, use metaphors when they describe the future as a rocky path forward, compare the economy to a rigged game, describe a historical moment as a new chapter, or debate whether America is a melting pot.

Although figures of speech are useful devices, writers sometimes misuse them if they don't think about the images they evoke. The result is often a *mixed metaphor*, the use of two or more images that don't make sense together.

▶ Our manager decided to put all controversial issues

~~in a holding pattern~~ on a back burner until after the

annual meeting.

Here the writer is mixing airplanes and stoves. Simply deleting one of the images corrects the problem.

EXERCISE 18–3   Edit the following sentences to replace worn-out expressions and clarify mixed figures of speech. Possible revisions appear in the back of the book.

When he heard about the accident, ~~he turned white as a sheet.~~ *the color drained from his face.*

a. John stormed into the room like a bull in a china shop.

b. Some people insist that they'll always be there for you, even when they haven't been before.

c. The Cubs easily beat the Mets, who were in over their heads early in the game today at Wrigley Field.

d. We ironed out the sticky spots in our relationship.

e. My mother accused me of beating around the bush when in fact I was just talking off the top of my head.

18f Use the right words. (Glossary of usage)

This glossary includes words commonly confused (such as *accept* and *except*), words commonly misused (such as *anxious*), and words and phrases that are used informally (such as *irregardless*). It also lists words that are often appropriate in speech but may be inappropriate in academic writing.

accept, except   *Accept* is a verb meaning "to receive." *Except* is usually a preposition meaning "excluding." *I will accept all the packages except that one. Except* is also a verb meaning "to exclude." *Please except that item from the list.*

advice, advise *Advice* is a noun, *advise* a verb. *We advise you to follow Hector's advice.*

affect, effect *Affect* is usually a verb meaning "to influence." *Effect* is usually a noun meaning "result." *The drug did not affect the disease, and it had adverse side effects. Effect* can also be a verb meaning "to bring about." *Only the president can effect such a dramatic change.*

agree to, agree with *Agree to* means "to give consent to." *Agree with* means "to be in accord with" or "to come to an understanding with." *He agrees with me about the need for change, but he won't agree to my plan.*

all ready, already *All ready* means "completely prepared." *Already* means "previously." *Susan was all ready for the concert, but her friends had already left.*

all together, altogether *All together* means "everyone or everything in one place." *Altogether* means "entirely." *We were not altogether certain that we could bring the family all together for the reunion.*

allude To *allude* to something is to make an indirect reference to it. Do not use *allude* to mean "to refer directly." *In his lecture, the professor referred* (not *alluded*) *to several pre-Socratic philosophers.*

allusion, illusion An *allusion* is an indirect reference. An *illusion* is a misconception or false impression. *Did you catch my allusion to Shakespeare? Mirrors give the room an illusion of depth.*

a lot *A lot* is two words. Do not write *alot*. *Sam lost a lot of weight.* See also *lots, lots of.*

among, between See *between, among.*

amount, number Use *amount* with quantities that cannot be counted; use *number* with those that can. *This recipe calls for a large amount of sugar. We have a large number of toads in our garden.*

anyone, any one *Anyone*, an indefinite pronoun, means "any person at all." *Any one*, the pronoun *one* preceded by the adjective *any*, refers to a particular person or thing in a group. *Anyone from the winning team may choose any one of the prizes on display.*

anyplace *Anyplace* is informal. In formal writing, use *anywhere.*

as Do not use *as* to mean "because" if there is any chance of ambiguity. *We canceled the picnic because* (not *as*) *it began raining. As* here could mean either "because" or "when."

awhile, a while *Awhile* is an adverb; it can modify a verb, but it cannot be the object of a preposition such as *for*. The two-word form *a while* is a noun preceded by an article and therefore can be the object of a preposition. *Stay awhile. Stay for a while.*

being as, being that *Being as* and *being that* are informal expressions. Write *because* instead. *Because* (not *Being as*) *I slept late, I had to skip breakfast.*

beside, besides *Beside* is a preposition meaning "at the side of" or "next to." *Annie sleeps with a flashlight beside her bed. Besides* is a preposition meaning "except" or "in addition to." *No one besides Terrie can have that ice cream. Besides* is also an adverb meaning "in addition." *I'm not hungry; besides, I don't like ice cream.*

between, among Ordinarily, use *among* with three or more entities, *between* with two. *The prize was divided among several contestants. You have a choice between carrots and beans.*

bring, take Use *bring* when an object is being transported toward you, *take* when it is being moved away. *Please bring me a glass of water. Please take these forms to Mr. Scott.*

can, may *Can* is traditionally reserved for ability, *may* for permission. *Can you speak French? May I help you?*

capital, capitol *Capital* refers to a city, *capitol* to a building where lawmakers meet. *Capital* also refers to wealth or resources. *The residents of the state capital protested plans to close the streets surrounding the capitol.*

cite, site *Cite* means "to quote as an authority or example." *Site* is usually a noun meaning "a particular place." *He cited the zoning law in his argument against the proposed site of the gas station.* Locations on the Internet are usually referred to as *sites* (short for *websites*). *The library's site now includes a chat feature.*

compare to, compare with *Compare to* means "to represent as similar." *She compared him to a wild stallion. Compare with* means "to examine similarities and differences." *The study compared the language ability of apes with that of dolphins.*

complement, compliment *Complement* is a verb meaning "to go with or complete" or a noun meaning "something that completes." As a verb, *compliment* means "to flatter"; as a noun, it means "flattering remark." *Her skill at rushing the net complements his skill at volleying. Min's flower arrangements receive many compliments.*

conscience, conscious *Conscience* is a noun meaning "moral principles." *Conscious* is an adjective meaning "aware or alert." *Let your conscience be your guide. Were you conscious of his love for you?*

continual, continuous *Continual* means "repeated regularly and frequently." *She grew weary of the continual telephone calls. Continuous* means "extended or prolonged without interruption." *The broken siren made a continuous wail.*

council, counsel A *council* is a deliberative body, and a *councilor* is a member of such a body. *Counsel* usually means "advice" and can also mean "lawyer"; a *counselor* is one who gives advice or guidance. *The councilors met to draft the council's position paper. The pastor offered wise counsel to the troubled teenager.*

data *Data* is a plural noun technically meaning "facts or propositions." But *data* is increasingly being accepted as a singular noun. *The new data suggest* (or *suggests*) *that our theory is correct.* (The singular *datum* is rarely used.)

different from, different than Ordinarily, write *different from. Your sense of style is different from Jim's.* However, *different than* is acceptable to avoid an awkward construction. *Please let me know if your plans are different than* (to avoid *from what*) *they were six weeks ago.*

disinterested, uninterested *Disinterested* means "impartial, objective"; *uninterested* means "not interested." *We sought the advice of a disinterested counselor to help us solve our problem. Mark was uninterested in anyone's opinion but his own.*

e.g. When writing sentences, replace the Latin abbreviation *e.g.* with its English equivalent: *for example* or *for instance.*

emigrate from, immigrate to *Emigrate* means "to leave one country or region to settle in another." *In 1903, my great-grandfather emigrated from Russia to escape the religious pogroms. Immigrate* means "to enter another country and reside there." *More than fifty thousand Bosnians immigrated to the United States in the 1990s.*

etc. Avoid ending a list with *etc.* It is more emphatic to end with an example, and in most contexts readers will understand that the list is not exhaustive. When you don't wish to end with an example, *and so on* is more graceful than *etc.*

everyone, every one *Everyone* is an indefinite pronoun. *Every one*, the pronoun *one* preceded by the adjective *every*, means "each individual or thing in a particular group." *Every one* is usually followed by *of. Everyone wanted to go. Every one of the missing books was found.*

except See *accept, except.*

explicit, implicit *Explicit* means "expressed directly" or "clearly defined"; *implicit* means "implied, unstated." *I gave him explicit instructions not to go swimming. My mother's silence indicated her implicit approval.*

farther, further *Farther* usually describes distances. *Further* usually suggests quantity or degree. *Chicago is farther from Miami than I thought. I would be grateful for further suggestions.*

fewer, less Use *fewer* for items that can be counted; use *less* for items that cannot be counted. *Fewer people are living in the city. Please put less sugar in my tea.*

firstly *Firstly* sounds pretentious, and it leads to the ungainly series *firstly, secondly, thirdly*, and so on. Write *first, second, third* instead.

further See *farther, further.*

good, well *Good* is an adjective, *well* an adverb. (See 26a, 26b, and 26c.) *He hasn't felt good about his game since he sprained his wrist last season. She performed well on the uneven parallel bars.*

hanged, hung *Hanged* is the past-tense and past-participle form of the verb *hang* meaning "to execute." *The prisoner was hanged at dawn. Hung* is the past-tense and past-participle form of the verb *hang* meaning "to fasten or suspend." *The stockings were hung by the chimney with care.*

hopefully *Hopefully* means "in a hopeful manner." *We looked hopefully to the future.* Some usage experts object to the use of *hopefully* as a sentence adverb on grounds of clarity. To be safe, avoid using *hopefully* in sentences such as the following: *Hopefully, your son will recover soon.* Instead, indicate who is doing the hoping: *I hope that your son will recover soon.*

however It is acceptable to start a sentence with the conjunctive adverb *however,* but be careful to place the word in your sentence according to your intended meaning and emphasis. All of the following sentences are correct. *Pam decided, however, to attend the lecture. However, Pam decided to attend the lecture.* (She had been considering other activities.) *Pam, however, decided to attend the lecture.* (Unlike someone else, Pam chose to attend the lecture.) (See 33f.)

hung See *hanged, hung.*

i.e. When writing sentences, use *in other words* or *that is* rather than the Latin abbreviation *i.e.* to introduce a clarifying statement. *Exposure to borax usually causes only mild skin irritation; in other words* (not *i.e.*), *it's not usually toxic.*

if, whether Use *if* to express a condition and *whether* to express alternatives. *If you go on a trip, whether to Idaho or Italy, remember to bring identification.*

illusion See *allusion, illusion.*

immigrate See *emigrate from, immigrate to.*

imply, infer *Imply* means "to suggest or state indirectly"; *infer* means "to draw a conclusion." *Jonathan implied that he knew all about databases, but the interviewer inferred that John was inexperienced.*

in, into *In* indicates location or condition; *into* indicates movement or a change in condition. *They found the lost letters in a box after moving into the house.*

irregardless *Irregardless* is incorrect. Use *regardless.*

kind of, sort of Avoid using *kind of* or *sort of* to mean "somewhat." *The movie was somewhat* (not *sort of*) *boring.* Do not put *a* after either phrase. *That kind of* (not *kind of a*) *movie bores me.*

lay, lie See *lie, lay.*

lead, led *Lead* is a metallic element; it is a noun. *Led* is the past tense of the verb *lead*. *He led me to the treasure.*

less See *fewer, less.*

lie, lay *Lie* is an intransitive verb meaning "to recline or rest on a surface." Its forms are *lie, lay, lain. Lay* is a transitive verb meaning "to put or place." Its forms are *lay, laid, laid. I'm going to lay my phone on the picnic table and lie in the hammock.*

like, as *Like* is a preposition, not a subordinating conjunction. It can be followed only by a noun or a noun phrase. *As* is a subordinating conjunction that introduces a subordinate clause. In casual speech, you may say *She looks like she hasn't slept.* But in academic writing, use *as. She looks as if she hasn't slept.* (See also 47f and 47g.)

loose, lose *Loose* is an adjective meaning "not securely fastened." *Lose* is a verb meaning "to misplace" or "to not win." *Did you lose all your loose change?*

lots, lots of *Lots* and *lots of* are informal substitutes for *many, much,* or *a lot.* Avoid using them in formal writing.

may See *can, may.*

maybe, may be *Maybe* is an adverb meaning "possibly." *Maybe the sun will shine tomorrow. May be* is a verb phrase. *Tomorrow may be brighter.*

number See *amount, number.*

of Use the verb *have,* not the preposition *of,* after the verbs *could, should, would, may, might,* and *must. They must have* (not *must of*) *left early.*

off of *Off* is sufficient. Omit *of. The ball rolled off* (not *off of*) *the table.*

passed, past *Passed* is the past tense of the verb *pass. Ann passed me another slice of cake. Past* usually means "belonging to a former time" or "beyond a time or place." *Our past president spoke until past midnight. The hotel is just past the next intersection.*

precede, proceed *Precede* means "to come before." *Proceed* means "to go forward." *As we proceeded up the mountain path, we noticed fresh tracks in the mud, evidence that a group of hikers had preceded us.*

principal, principle *Principal* is a noun meaning "the head of a school or an organization" or "a sum of money." It is also an adjective meaning "most important." *Principle* is a noun meaning "a basic truth or law." *The principal expelled her for three principal reasons. We believe in the principle of equal justice for all.*

quotation, quote *Quotation* is a noun; *quote* is a verb. Avoid using *quote* as a shortened form of *quotation. Her quotations* (not *Her quotes*) *are appearing in various social media channels.*

raise, rise *Raise* is a transitive verb meaning "to move or cause to move upward." It takes a direct object. *I raised the shades. Rise* is an intransitive verb meaning "to go up." *Heat rises.*

real, really *Real* is an adjective; *really* is an adverb. *Real* is sometimes used informally as an adverb, but avoid this use in formal writing. *She was really* (not *real*) *angry.*

reason why The expression *reason why* is redundant. *The reason* (not *The reason why*) *Jones lost the election is clear.*

respectfully, respectively *Respectfully* means "showing or marked by respect." *Respectively* means "each in the order given." *He respectfully submitted his opinion to the judge. Sofia, Henry, and Jesse were a butcher, a baker, and a lawyer, respectively.*

set, sit *Set* is a transitive verb meaning "to put" or "to place." Its past tense is *set. Sit* is an intransitive verb meaning "to be seated." Its past tense is *sat. She set the dough in a warm corner of the kitchen. The cat sat in the doorway.*

since Do not use *since* to mean "because" if there is any chance of ambiguity. *Because* (not *Since*) *we won the game, we have been celebrating with pizza. Since* here could mean either "because" or "from the time that."

site See *cite, site.*

sometime, some time, sometimes *Sometime* is an adverb meaning "at an indefinite time." *Some time* is the adjective *some* modifying the noun *time* and means "a period of time." *Sometimes* is an adverb meaning "at times, now and then." *I'll see you sometime soon. I haven't lived there for some time. Sometimes I see him at work.*

suppose to *Suppose to* is an informal version of *supposed to. I am supposed to* (not *suppose to*) *be there by noon.*

sure and Write *sure to. We were all taught to be sure to* (not *sure and*) *look both ways before crossing a street.*

take See *bring, take.*

than, then *Than* is a conjunction used in comparisons; *then* is an adverb denoting time. *That pizza is more than I can eat. Tom laughed, and then we recognized him.*

that See *who, which, that.*

that, which Many writers reserve *that* for restrictive clauses, *which* for nonrestrictive clauses. *Restaurants that allow pets are few in number. Restaurants, which generally don't allow pets, must follow strict health codes.* (See 33e.)

there, their, they're *There* is an adverb specifying place; it is also an expletive (placeholder). Adverb: *Sylvia is sitting there patiently.* Expletive: *There are* *two plums left. Their is a possessive pronoun. Fred and Jane finally washed their car. They're is a contraction of they are. They're later than usual today.*

to, too, two *To* is a preposition; *too* is an adverb; *two* is a number. *Too many of your shots slice to the left, but the last two were just right.*

toward, towards *Toward* and *towards* are generally interchangeable, although *toward* is preferred in American English.

try and *Try and* is an informal version of *try to*. *The teacher asked us all to try to (not try and) write an original haiku.*

unique Avoid expressions such as *most unique, more straight, less perfect, very round*. Either something is unique or it isn't. It is illogical to suggest degrees of uniqueness. (See 26d.)

wait for, wait on *Wait for* means "to be in readiness for" or "to await." *Wait on* means "to serve." *We're waiting for (not waiting on) Ruth to take us to the museum.*

weather, whether The noun *weather* refers to the state of the atmosphere. *Whether* is a conjunction referring to a choice between alternatives. *We wondered whether the weather would clear.*

well, good See *good, well*.

which See *that, which* and *who, which, that*.

while Avoid using *while* to mean "although" or "whereas" if there is any chance of ambiguity. *Although (not While) Gloria lost money in the slot machine, Tanya won money at roulette.* Here *While* could mean either "although" or "at the same time that."

who, which, that Do not use *which* to refer to persons. Use *who* instead. *That*, though generally used to refer to things, may be used to refer to a particular group of people. *The player who (not that or which) made the basket at the buzzer was named MVP. The team that scores the most points in this game will win the tournament.*

who, whom *Who* is used for subjects and subject complements; *whom* is used for objects. *Who are the candidates for this year's scholarship? The candidates, whom I met with yesterday, are impressive.* (See 25.)

who's, whose *Who's* is a contraction of *who is*; *whose* is a possessive pronoun. *Who's ready for more popcorn? Whose coat is this?* (See 37b and 37c.)

would of *Would of* is an informal version of *would have*. *She would have (not would of) had a chance to play if she had arrived on time.*

your, you're *Your* is a possessive pronoun; *you're* is a contraction of *you are*. *Is that your new bike? You're in the finals.* (See 37b, 37c, and 47b.)

Grammar

Language is not static. The rules of grammar change over time, and these rules are not always inclusive of how everyone speaks and writes. The guidelines laid out here are meant to help you make your writing as clear as possible to readers. When your purpose or audience calls for it, you may want to consider putting the rules aside.

19 Repair sentence fragments.

A sentence fragment is a word group that pretends to be a sentence. Sentence fragments are easy to recognize when they appear out of context, like these:

> When the cat leaped onto the table.

> Running for the bus.

When fragments appear next to related sentences, however, they are harder to spot.

> We had just sat down to dinner. When the cat leaped onto the table.

> I tripped and twisted my ankle. Running for the bus.

Recognizing sentence fragments

To be a sentence, a word group must consist of at least one independent clause. An independent clause includes a subject and a verb, and it either stands alone or could stand alone.

To test whether a word group is a complete sentence or a fragment, use the flowchart in this section. By using the flowchart, you can see exactly why *When the cat leaped onto the table* is a fragment: It has a subject (*cat*) and a verb (*leaped*), but it begins with a subordinating word (*When*). *Running for the bus* is a fragment because it lacks a subject and a verb (*Running* is a verbal, not a verb). (See also 49b and 49e.)

Repairing sentence fragments

You can repair most fragments in one of two ways:

- Pull the fragment into a nearby sentence.
- Rewrite the fragment as a complete sentence.

▶ We had just sat down to dinner. ~~When~~ the cat leaped onto the table.
   ^{when}

▶ *Running for the bus,* I tripped and twisted my ankle. ~~Running for the bus.~~

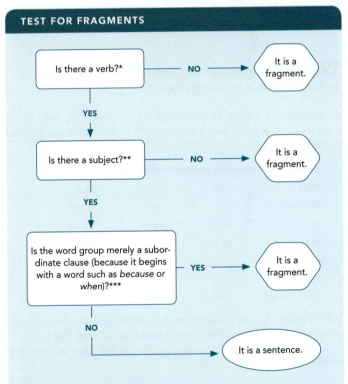

TEST FOR FRAGMENTS

Is there a verb?* — **NO** → It is a fragment.

YES ↓

Is there a subject?** — **NO** → It is a fragment.

YES ↓

Is the word group merely a subordinate clause (because it begins with a word such as *because* or *when*)?*** — **YES** → It is a fragment.

NO ↓

→ It is a sentence.

*Do not mistake verbals for verbs. A verbal is a verb form (such as *walking* or *to act*) that does not function as a verb of a clause. (See 49b.)

**The subject of a sentence may be *you,* understood but not present in the sentence. (See 48a.)

***A sentence may open with a subordinate clause, but the sentence must also include an independent clause. (See 19a and 50a.)

FOR MULTILINGUAL WRITERS

Unlike some other languages, English sentences always have a subject and a verb (except in commands, where the subject *you* is understood but not present: *Sit down*). See 30a and 30b.

▶ *It is*
~~Is~~ often hot and humid during the summer.
  ^

▶ *are*
Students usually very busy at the end of the semester writing
         ^

papers and taking exams.

19a Attach fragmented subordinate clauses or turn them into sentences.

A subordinate clause is patterned like a sentence, with both a subject and a verb, but it begins with a word that marks it as subordinate.

WORDS THAT INTRODUCE SUBORDINATE CLAUSES

after	how	unless	who
although	if	until	whom
as	since	when	whose
as if	so that	where	why
because	than	whether	
before	that	which	
even though	though	while	

Subordinate clauses function within sentences as adjectives, as adverbs, or as nouns. They cannot stand alone. (See 49e.)

Most fragmented clauses can be pulled into a sentence nearby.

▶ *because*
Americans have come to fear the Zika virus/~~Because~~ it is
                                                ^

transmitted by the common mosquito.

Because introduces a subordinate clause, so it cannot stand alone. (For punctuation of subordinate clauses appearing at the end of a sentence, see 34f.)

▶ Although psychiatrist Peter Kramer expresses concerns

about Prozac/, ~~Many~~ *many* other doctors believe that the

benefits of antidepressants outweigh the risks.

Although introduces a subordinate clause, which cannot stand alone.
(For punctuation of subordinate clauses at the beginning of a sentence,
see 33b.)

If a fragmented clause cannot be attached to a nearby sentence or if attaching it would be awkward, try turning the clause into a sentence. The simplest way to do this is to delete the opening word or words that mark it as subordinate.

▶ Uncontrolled development is taking a toll on the environment.

~~So that across~~ *Across* the globe, fragile ecosystems are collapsing.

19b Attach fragmented phrases or turn them into sentences.

Like subordinate clauses, phrases function within sentences as adjectives, as adverbs, or as nouns. They cannot stand alone. Fragmented phrases are often prepositional or verbal phrases; sometimes they are appositives, words or word groups that rename nouns or pronouns. (See 49a, 49b, and 49c.)

Often a fragmented phrase may simply be pulled into a nearby sentence.

▶ The archaeologists worked slowly/, ~~Examining~~ *examining* and labeling every

pottery shard they uncovered.

The word group beginning with *Examining* is a verbal phrase, so it cannot stand alone.

▶ The patient displayed symptoms of ALS/, ~~A~~ *a* neurodegenerative

disease.

A neurodegenerative disease is an appositive renaming the noun *ALS*.
(For punctuation of appositives, see 33e.)

If a fragmented phrase cannot be pulled into a nearby sentence effectively, turn the phrase into a sentence. You may need to add a subject, a verb, or both.

▶ Jamie explained how to access our new database. ~~Also~~ how to

She also taught us

submit expense reports and request vendor payments.

The revision turns the phrase into a sentence by adding a subject and a verb.

19c Attach other fragmented word groups or turn them into sentences.

Other word groups that are commonly fragmented include parts of compound predicates, lists, and examples introduced by *for example*, *in addition*, or similar expressions.

Parts of compound predicates

A predicate consists of a verb and its objects, complements, and modifiers (see 48b). A compound predicate includes two or more predicates joined with a coordinating conjunction such as *and*, *but*, or *or*. Because the parts of a compound predicate have the same subject, they should appear in the same sentence.

▶ The woodpecker finch carefully selects a twig of a certain size

and

and shape. ~~And~~ then uses this tool to pry grubs from trees.

The subject is *finch*, and the compound predicate is *selects . . . and . . . uses*. (For punctuation of compound predicates, see 34a.)

Lists

To correct a fragmented list, often you can attach it to a nearby sentence with a colon or a dash. (See 36a and 40a.)

▶ It has been said that there are only three indigenous American

musical

art forms. : ~~Musical~~ comedy, jazz, and soap opera.

Sometimes terms like *especially*, *namely*, *like*, and *such as* introduce lists that are fragments. Such fragments can usually be attached to the preceding sentence.

▶ In the twentieth century, the South produced some great

American writers/ ~~Such~~ as Flannery O'Connor, William

            such

Faulkner, Zora Neale Hurston, and Tennessee Williams.

Examples introduced by *for example, in addition,* or similar expressions

Other expressions that introduce examples or explanations can lead to unintentional fragments. Although you may begin a sentence with some of the following words or phrases, make sure that what follows has a subject and a verb.

also	for example	mainly
and	for instance	or
but	in addition	that is

Often the easiest solution is to turn the fragment into a sentence.

▶ In his memoir, Primo Levi describes the horrors of living in a

                              he worked

concentration camp. For example, ~~working~~ without food and

suffered

~~suffering~~ emotional abuse.

The writer corrected this fragment by adding a subject — *he* — and substituting verbs for the verbals *working* and *suffering*.

19d Exception: A fragment may be used for effect.

Writers occasionally use sentence fragments for special purposes.

FOR EMPHASIS   Following the dramatic Americanization of their children, even my parents grew more publicly confident. *Especially my mother.*

                                            — Richard Rodriguez

TO ANSWER A QUESTION	Are these new drug tests 100 percent reliable? *Not in the opinion of most experts.*
TRANSITIONS	*And now the opposing arguments.*
EXCLAMATIONS	*Not again!*
IN ADVERTISING	*Fewer carbs. Improved taste.*

Although fragments are sometimes appropriate, writers and readers do not always agree on when they are appropriate. Writing in complete sentences is always a sensible choice.

EXERCISE 19–1   Repair any fragment by attaching it to a nearby sentence or by rewriting it as a complete sentence. If a word group is correct, write "correct" after it. Possible revisions appear in the back of the book.

> One Greek island that should not be missed is Mykonos. A vacation
>
> spot for Europeans and a playground for the rich and famous.

a. Listening to the playlist her sister had created, Blanca was overcome with a mix of emotions. Happiness, homesickness, and nostalgia.

b. Cortés and his soldiers were astonished when they looked down from the mountains and saw Tenochtitlán. The magnificent capital of the Aztecs.

c. Although my spoken Spanish is not very good. I can read the language with ease.

d. There are several reasons for not eating meat. One reason being that dangerous chemicals are used throughout the various stages of meat production.

e. To learn how to sculpt beauty from everyday life. This is my intention in studying art and archaeology.

EXERCISE 19–2   Repair each fragment in the following passage by attaching it to a nearby sentence or by rewriting it as a complete sentence.

Digital technology has revolutionized information delivery. Forever blurring the lines between information and entertainment. Yesterday's readers of books and newspapers are today's readers of e-books and news sites. Countless readers have moved on from print information entirely. Choosing instead to scroll their way through a text online or on an e-reader. Once a nation of people spoon-fed television commercials and the six o'clock evening news. We are now seemingly addicted to YouTube and social media. On family road trips, Dad or Mom used to wrestle with a road map.

On the way to St. Louis or Seattle. No wrestling is required when every smartphone comes with a GPS navigator. Unless it's Mom and Dad wrestling over who can enter the address into their phone first. Accessing information now seems to be America's favorite pastime. In 2019, the Pew Research Center reported that 81 percent of Americans went online daily. With that number likely increasing in 2020 and 2021 when the pandemic forced so many of us to live virtually. As a country, we embrace information and communication technologies. Which now include smartphones, videoconferences, tablets, and AI assistants. Children rely on devices and the Internet from an early age. For everything from attending classes and doing homework to socializing and gaming.

20 Revise run-on sentences.

▶ How to revise a run-on sentence **175**

Run-on sentences are independent clauses that have not been joined correctly. An independent clause is a word group that can stand alone as a sentence. (See 50a.) When two independent clauses appear in one sentence, they must be joined in one of these ways:

- with a comma and a coordinating conjunction (*and, but, or, nor, for, so, yet*)
- with a semicolon (or occasionally with a colon or a dash)

The chart on the next page will help you recognize run-on sentences in your writing. The box on page 175 will help you revise them.

Recognizing run-on sentences

There are two types of run-on sentences. When a writer puts no mark of punctuation and no coordinating conjunction between independent clauses, the result is called a *fused sentence.*

FUSED ┌─────── INDEPENDENT CLAUSE ───────┐ ┌──────
Air pollution poses risks to all humans it can be

── INDEPENDENT CLAUSE ──┐
deadly for asthma sufferers.

A far more common type of run-on sentence is the *comma splice* — two or more independent clauses joined with a comma but without a coordinating conjunction. In some comma splices, the comma appears alone.

> **COMMA SPLICE** Air pollution poses risks to all humans, it can be deadly for asthma sufferers.

In other comma splices, the comma is accompanied by a joining word that is *not* a coordinating conjunction. There are only seven coordinating conjunctions in English: *and, but, or, nor, for, so,* and *yet.*

> **COMMA SPLICE** Air pollution poses risks to all humans, however, it can be deadly for asthma sufferers.

However is a transitional expression and cannot be used with only a comma to join two independent clauses (see 20b).

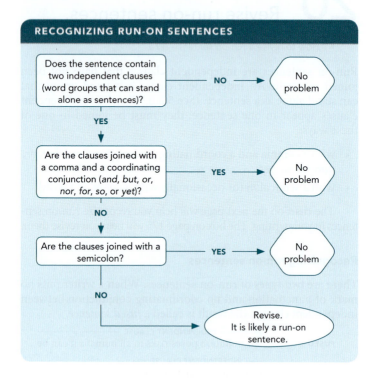

RECOGNIZING RUN-ON SENTENCES

Does the sentence contain two independent clauses (word groups that can stand alone as sentences)? — NO → No problem

YES ↓

Are the clauses joined with a comma and a coordinating conjunction (*and, but, or, nor, for, so,* or *yet*)? — YES → No problem

NO ↓

Are the clauses joined with a semicolon? — YES → No problem

NO ↓

Revise. It is likely a run-on sentence.

HOW TO

Revise a run-on sentence

To revise a run-on sentence, you have four choices.

1 **Use a comma and a coordinating conjunction (*and*, *but*, *or*, *nor*, *for*, *so*, *yet*).**

> ► Air pollution poses risks to all humans, ^{but} it can be deadly for
>
> people with asthma.

2 **Use a semicolon (or, if appropriate, a colon or a dash).**
A semicolon may be used alone; it can also be accompanied by a transitional expression.

> ► Air pollution poses risks to all humans/; it can be deadly for
>
> people with asthma.

> ► Air pollution poses risks to all humans/; ^{however,} it can be deadly for
>
> people with asthma.

3 **Make the clauses into separate sentences.**

> ► Air pollution poses risks to all humans/. ^{It} ~~it~~ can be deadly for
>
> people with asthma.

4 **Restructure the sentence; try subordinating a clause.**

> ► ^{Although air} ~~Air~~ pollution poses risks to all humans, it can be deadly for
>
> people with asthma.

One of these revision techniques usually works better than the others for a particular sentence. The fourth technique, the one requiring the most extensive revision, is often the most effective.

20a Consider separating the clauses with a comma and a coordinating conjunction.

There are seven coordinating conjunctions in English: *and*, *but*, *or*, *nor*, *for*, *so*, and *yet*. When a coordinating conjunction joins independent clauses, it is usually preceded by a comma. (See 33a.)

▶ Some lesson plans include exercises, *but* completing them should not

be the focus of all class periods.

▶ Many law enforcement officials admit that the polygraph is

unreliable, ~~however,~~ *yet* they still use it as an assessment tool.

20b Consider separating the clauses with a semicolon, colon, or dash.

When the independent clauses are closely related and their relation is clear without a coordinating conjunction, a semicolon is one acceptable method of revision. (See 35a.)

▶ Tragedy depicts the individual confronted with the fact of

death/; comedy depicts the adaptability of human society.

A semicolon is required between independent clauses that have been linked with a transitional expression (such as *however*, *therefore*, *moreover*, *in fact*, or *for example*). For a longer list, see 35b.

▶ In his film adaptation, the director changed key details of the

plot/; in fact, he added whole scenes that do not appear in the story.

A colon or a dash may be more appropriate if the first independent clause introduces the second or if the second clause summarizes or explains the first. (See 36a and 40a.) In formal writing, the colon is usually preferred to the dash.

▶ Nuclear waste is hazardous: this is an indisputable fact.

▶ The female black widow spider is often a widow of her own

making/ she has been known to eat her partner after mating.

A colon is an appropriate method of revision if the first independent clause introduces a quoted sentence.

▶ Nobel Peace Prize winner Al Gore had this to say about climate

change/: "The truth is that our circumstances are not only new;

they are completely different than they have ever been in all of

human history."

20c Consider making the clauses into separate sentences.

▶ Why should we spend money on expensive space

exploration/? <del>we</del> *We* have enough underfunded programs here

on Earth.

A question and a statement should be separate sentences.

NOTE: When two quoted independent clauses are divided by explanatory words, make each clause its own sentence.

▶ "It's always smart to learn from your mistakes," quipped my

supervisor/. <del>"it's</del> *"It's* even smarter to learn from the mistakes of

others."

20d Consider restructuring the sentence, perhaps by subordinating one of the clauses.

If one of the independent clauses is less important than the other, turn the less important clause into a subordinate clause or phrase. (For more about subordination, see the chart in 14a.)

▶ One of the most famous advertising slogans is Wheaties cereal's

"Breakfast of Champions," ~~it~~ ^{which} associated the product with

successful athletes.

▶ Mary McLeod Bethune, ~~was~~ the seventeenth child of enslaved

Africans, ~~she~~ founded the National Council of Negro Women.

Minor ideas in these sentences are now expressed in subordinate clauses or phrases.

EXERCISE 20–1 Revise the following run-on sentences using the method of revision suggested in brackets. Possible revisions appear in the back of the book.

 When a
~~A~~ critic commented on Michael Chabon's use of first-person

perspective, the author was inspired to write his next novels in

the third person. [*Restructure the sentence.*]

a. Martina recently started working at a new company, it designs and manufactures educational toys. [*Restructure the sentence.*]

b. The building is being renovated, therefore at times we have no heat, water, or electricity. [*Use a comma and a coordinating conjunction.*]

c. I don't think I will buy the new model of smartphone, why spend the money when my current phone works perfectly?

d. Walker's coming-of-age novel is set against a gloomy scientific backdrop, the earth's rotation has begun to slow down. [*Use a semicolon.*]

e. City officials had good reason to fear a major earthquake, most of the business district was built on landfill. [*Use a colon.*]

EXERCISE 20-2   Revise any run-on sentences using a technique that you find effective. If a sentence is correct, write "correct" after it. Possible revisions appear in the back of the book.

> but
> Running laps in my backyard wasn't very exciting, ~~however,~~ I
>
> wanted to keep up my exercise routine while I couldn't use the
>
> track at the campus gym.

a. Wind power for the home is a supplementary source of energy, it can be combined with electricity, gas, or solar energy.

b. Aidan viewed Sofia Coppola's *Lost in Translation* three times and then wrote a paper describing the film as the work of a mysterious modern painter.

c. In the Middle Ages, the streets of London were dangerous places, it was safer to travel by boat along the Thames.

d. "He's not drunk," I said, "he's in a state of diabetic shock."

e. Are you able to endure extreme angle turns, high speeds, frequent jumps, and occasional crashes, then supermoto racing may be a sport for you.

EXERCISE 20-3   In the following rough draft, revise any run-on sentences.

We may blame television for the number of products based on children's TV show characters from Big Bird to SpongeBob, in fact merchandising that capitalizes on a character's popularity started long before television. Raggedy Ann began as a child's rag doll, a few years later books about she and her brother, Raggedy Andy, were published. A cartoonist named Johnny Gruelle painted a cloth face on a family doll and applied for a patent in 1915. Later Gruelle began writing and illustrating stories about Raggedy Ann, then in 1918 he and a publisher teamed up to publish the books and sell the dolls. He was not the only one to try to sell products linked to children's stories. Beatrix Potter published the first of many Peter Rabbit picture books in 1902, no one was better at making a living from spin-offs. Peter Rabbit and Benjamin Bunny became popular, at that point Potter began putting pictures of them and their little animal friends on merchandise. Potter understood that her fans wanted to see her characters not only in books but also on teapots and plates and lamps, therefore her merchandise was successful. Potter and Gruelle, like countless others before and since, knew that entertaining children could be a profitable business.

21 Make subjects and verbs agree.

In the present tense, verbs agree with their subjects in number (singular or plural) and in person (first, second, third): *I sing, you sing, he sings, she sings, we sing, they sing.* Even if your ear recognizes the subject-verb combinations presented in 21a, you will no doubt encounter tricky situations such as those described in 21b–21k.

21a Learn to recognize subject-verb combinations.

This section describes the basic guidelines for making present-tense verbs agree with their subjects. The present-tense ending *-s* (or *-es*) is used on a verb if its subject is third-person singular (*he, she, it,* and singular nouns); otherwise, the verb takes no ending. Consider, for example, the present-tense forms of the verbs *love* and *try,* given at the beginning of the chart on page 182.

The verb *be* varies from this pattern; it has special forms in both the present and the past tense. These forms appear at the end of the chart.

If you aren't sure which forms to use, use the charts on pages 182 and 183 as you proofread your work for subject-verb agreement. You may also want to look at 27c on *-s* endings of regular and irregular verbs.

21b Make the verb agree with its subject, not with a word that comes between.

Word groups often come between the subject and the verb. Such word groups, usually modifying the subject, may contain a noun that appears to be the subject. By mentally stripping away such modifiers, you can isolate the noun that is in fact the subject.

The *samples* on the tray in the lab *need* testing.

► High levels of air pollution cause~~s~~ damage to the respiratory

tract.

> The subject is *levels*, not *pollution*. Strip away the phrase *of air pollution* to hear the correct verb: *levels cause*.

                                             has

► The slaughter of pandas for their pelts ~~have~~ caused the panda

population to decline drastically.

> The subject is *slaughter*, not *pandas* or *pelts*.

NOTE: Phrases beginning with the prepositions *as well as, in addition to, accompanied by,* and *along with* do not make a singular subject plural.

                                      was

► The governor as well as his press secretary ~~were~~ on the plane.

> To emphasize that two people were on the plane, the writer could use *and* instead: *The governor and his press secretary were on the plane.*

21c Treat most subjects joined with *and* as plural.

A subject with two or more parts is said to be compound. If the parts are connected with *and*, the subject is nearly always plural.

Leon and Jan often *jog* together.

► The Supreme Court's willingness to hear the case and its

                                  have

affirmation of the original decision ~~has~~ set a new precedent.

EXCEPTION 1: When the parts of the subject form a single unit or when they refer to the same person or thing, treat the subject as singular.

> Fish and chips is always on the menu.
> Ali's friend and adviser was surprised by her decision.

SUBJECT-VERB AGREEMENT

Present-tense forms of *love* and *try* (typical verbs)

	SINGULAR		PLURAL	
FIRST PERSON	I	love	we	love
SECOND PERSON	you	love	you	love
THIRD PERSON	he/she/it*	loves	they**	love

	SINGULAR		PLURAL	
FIRST PERSON	I	try	we	try
SECOND PERSON	you	try	you	try
THIRD PERSON	he/she/it*	tries	they**	try

Present-tense forms of *have*

	SINGULAR		PLURAL	
FIRST PERSON	I	have	we	have
SECOND PERSON	you	have	you	have
THIRD PERSON	he/she/it*	has	they**	have

Present-tense forms of *do* (including negative forms)

	SINGULAR		PLURAL	
FIRST PERSON	I	do/don't	we	do/don't
SECOND PERSON	you	do/don't	you	do/don't
THIRD PERSON	he/she/it*	does/doesn't	they**	do/don't

Present-tense and past-tense forms of *be*

	SINGULAR		PLURAL	
FIRST PERSON	I	am/was	we	are/were
SECOND PERSON	you	are/were	you	are/were
THIRD PERSON	he/she/it*	is/was	they**	are/were

*And singular nouns (*child*, *Roger*)
**And plural nouns (*children*, *the Mannings*), or when used as a gender-neutral singular pronoun

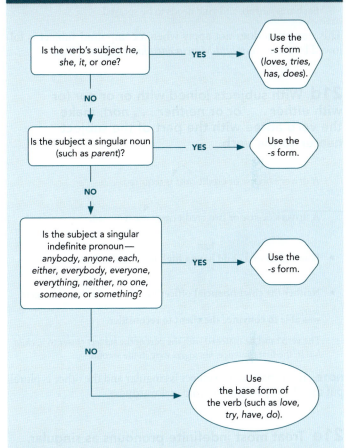

WHEN TO USE THE -*S* (OR -*ES*) FORM OF A PRESENT-TENSE VERB

Is the verb's subject *he, she, it,* or *one*? — **YES** → Use the -*s* form (*loves, tries, has, does*).

NO ↓

Is the subject a singular noun (such as *parent*)? — **YES** → Use the -*s* form.

NO ↓

Is the subject a singular indefinite pronoun— *anybody, anyone, each, either, everybody, everyone, everything, neither, no one, someone,* or *something*? — **YES** → Use the -*s* form.

NO ↓

Use the base form of the verb (such as *love, try, have, do*).

EXCEPTION: Choosing the correct present-tense form of *be* (*am, is,* or *are*) is not quite so simple. See the chart on the previous page for both present- and past-tense forms of *be*.

NOTE: Do not use the -*s* form of a verb if it follows a modal verb such as *can, must,* or *should* or another helping verb. (See 28c.)

EXCEPTION 2: When a compound subject is preceded by *each* or *every*, treat it as singular.

> Each tree, shrub, and vine needs to be sprayed.

This exception does not apply when a compound subject is followed by *each*: *Alan and Marcia each have different ideas.*

21d With subjects joined with *or* or *nor* (or with *either . . . or* or *neither . . . nor*), make the verb agree with the part of the subject nearer to the verb.

A driver's *license* or credit *card is* required.

A driver's *license* or two credit *cards are* required.

> has
▸ If an infant or a child ~~have~~ a high fever, call a doctor.

▸ Neither the chief financial officer nor the marketing managers

> were
~~was~~ able to convince the client to reconsider.

The verb must be matched with the part of the subject closer to it: *child has* in the first sentence, *managers were* in the second.

NOTE: If one part of the subject is singular and the other is plural, put the plural part last to avoid awkwardness.

21e Treat most indefinite pronouns as singular.

Indefinite pronouns, those that do not refer to specific persons or things, are singular.

COMMONLY USED INDEFINITE PRONOUNS

anybody	each	everyone	nobody	somebody
anyone	either	everything	no one	someone
anything	everybody	neither	nothing	something

Many of these words appear to have plural meanings, and they are often treated as plural in casual speech. In formal written English, however, they are nearly always treated as singular.

Everyone on the team *supports* the coach.

has
▶ Each of the essays ~~have~~ been graded.

was
▶ Nobody who participated in the clinical trials ~~were~~ given a

placebo.

> The subjects of these sentences are *Each* and *Nobody.* These indefinite pronouns are third-person singular, so the verbs must be *has* and *was.*

A few indefinite pronouns (*all, any, none, some*) may be singular or plural depending on the noun or pronoun they refer to.

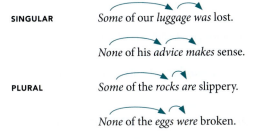

SINGULAR *Some* of our *luggage was* lost.

None of his *advice makes* sense.

PLURAL *Some* of the *rocks are* slippery.

None of the *eggs were* broken.

NOTE: When the meaning of *none* is emphatically "not one," *none* may be treated as singular: *None* [meaning "Not one"] *of the eggs was broken.* Using *not one* instead is sometimes clearer: *Not one of the eggs was broken.*

21f Treat collective nouns as singular unless the meaning is clearly plural.

Collective nouns such as *jury, committee, audience, crowd, troop, family,* and *couple* name a class or a group. Collective nouns are nearly always treated as singular to emphasize the group as a unit. Occasionally, when there is some reason to draw attention to the individual members of the group, a collective noun may be treated as plural. (See also 22b.)

SINGULAR   The *class respects* the teacher.

PLURAL   The *class are* debating among themselves.

To underscore the notion of individuality in the second sentence, many writers would add a clearly plural noun.

PLURAL   The class *members are* debating among themselves.

▶ The board of trustees ~~meet~~ in Denver twice a year.
meets

The board as a whole meets; there is no reason to draw attention to its individual members.

▶ A young couple ~~was~~ arguing about politics while holding
were

hands.

The meaning is clearly plural. Only separate individuals can argue and hold hands.

NOTE: The phrase *the number* is treated as singular, *a number* as plural.

SINGULAR   *The number* of school-age children *is* declining.

PLURAL   *A number* of children *are* attending the wedding.

NOTE: In general, when a fraction or a unit of measurement is used with a singular noun, treat it as singular; when it is used with a plural noun, treat it as plural.

SINGULAR   Twenty *inches* of wallboard *was* covered with mud.

PLURAL   Two *pounds* of blueberries *were* used to make the pie.

21g Make the verb agree with its subject even when the subject follows the verb.

Verbs ordinarily follow subjects. When this order is reversed, it is easy to become confused. Sentences beginning with *there is* or *there are* (or *there was* or *there were*) are inverted; the subject follows the verb.

There *are* surprisingly few *honeybees* left in southern China.

► There ~~was~~ *were* a social worker and a journalist at the meeting.

> The subject, *worker and journalist*, is plural, so the verb must be *were*.

Occasionally, you may decide to invert a sentence for variety or effect. When you do so, check to make sure that your subject and verb agree.

► Of particular concern ~~is~~ *are* penicillin and tetracycline, antibiotics

used to make animals more resistant to disease.

> The subject, *penicillin and tetracycline*, is plural, so the verb must be *are*.

21h Make the verb agree with its subject, not with a subject complement.

One basic sentence pattern in English consists of a subject, a linking verb, and a subject complement: *Amir is a lawyer.* Because the subject complement (*lawyer*) names or describes the subject (*Amir*), it is sometimes mistaken for the subject. (See 48b on subject complements.)

These *exercises are* a way to test your ability to perform under pressure.

► A tent and a sleeping bag ~~is~~ *are* the required equipment.

> *Tent and bag* is the subject, not *equipment*.

▶ A major force in today's economy ~~are~~ ^{is} children — as consumers,

decision makers, and trend spotters.

Force is the subject, not *children*. If the corrected version seems too awkward, make *children* the subject: *Children are a major force in today's economy — as consumers, decision makers, and trend spotters.*

21i Ensure that *who, which,* and *that* take verbs that agree with their antecedents.

Like most pronouns, the relative pronouns *who, which,* and *that* have antecedents, nouns or pronouns to which they refer. A relative pronoun used as the subject of a subordinate clause takes a verb that agrees with its antecedent.

ANT PN   V

Take a *course that prepares* you for classroom management.

One of the

Constructions such as *one of the students who* [or *one of the things that*] cause problems for writers. Do not assume that the antecedent must be *one.* Instead, consider the logic of the sentence.

▶ Our ability to use language is one of the things that sets us apart

from animals.

The antecedent of *that* is *things,* not *one.* Several things set us apart from animals.

Only one of the

When the phrase *the only* comes before *one,* you are safe in assuming that *one* is the antecedent of the relative pronoun.

▶ Veronica was the only one of the first-year Spanish students

who ~~were~~ ^{was} fluent enough to apply for the exchange program.

The antecedent of *who* is *one,* not *students.* Only one student was fluent enough.

21j Treat words such as *athletics, economics, mathematics,* and *news* as singular, despite their plural form.

>   *is*
> ► Politics ~~are~~ among my mother's favorite pastimes.

EXCEPTION: Occasionally some of these words, especially *economics, mathematics, politics,* and *statistics,* have plural meanings: *Office politics often sway decisions about hiring and promotion. The economics of the building plan are prohibitive.*

21k Treat titles of works, company names, words mentioned as words, and gerund phrases as singular.

>   *describes*
> ► *Lost Cities* ~~describe~~ the discoveries of fifty ancient civilizations.

>   *specializes*
> ► Delmonico Brothers ~~specialize~~ in organic produce.

>   *is*
> ► *Controlled substances* ~~are~~ a euphemism for illegal drugs.

A gerund phrase consists of an *-ing* verb form followed by any objects, complements, or modifiers (see 49b). Treat gerund phrases as singular.

>   *makes*
> ► Encountering long wait times ~~make~~ customers impatient.

EXERCISE 21–1   Edit the following sentences to eliminate problems with subject-verb agreement. If a sentence is correct, write "correct" after it. Answers appear in the back of the book.

>   *were*
> Jack's first days in the infantry ~~was~~ grueling.

a. One of the main reasons for elephant poaching are the profits received from selling the ivory tusks.

b. Not until my interview with Dr. Hwang were other possibilities opened to me.

c. A number of students in the seminar was aware of the importance of joining the discussion.

d. Batik cloth from Bali, blue and white ceramics from Delft, and a bocce ball from Turin has made Angelie's room the talk of the dorm.

e. The board of directors, ignoring the wishes of the neighborhood, has voted to allow further development.

EXERCISE 21–2 For each sentence in the following passage, underline the subject (or compound subject) and then select the verb that agrees with it. (If you have trouble identifying the subject, consult 48a.)

Loggerhead sea turtles (migrate / migrates) thousands of miles before returning to their nesting location every two to three years. The nesting season for loggerhead turtles (span / spans) the hottest months of the summer. Although the habitat of Atlantic loggerheads (range / ranges) from Newfoundland to Argentina, nesting for these turtles (take / takes) place primarily along the southeastern coast of the United States. Female turtles that have reached sexual maturity (crawl / crawls) ashore at night to lay their eggs. The cavity that serves as a nest for the eggs (is / are) dug out with the female's strong flippers. Deposited into each nest (is / are) anywhere from fifty to two hundred spherical eggs, also known as a *clutch*. After a two-month incubation period, all eggs in the clutch (begin / begins) to hatch, and within a few days the young turtles attempt to make their way into the ocean. A major cause of the loggerhead's decreasing numbers (is / are) natural predators such as raccoons, birds, and crabs. Beach erosion and coastal development also (threaten / threatens) the turtles' survival. For example, a crowd of curious humans or lights from beachfront residences (is / are) enough to make the female abandon her nesting plans and return to the ocean. Since only one in one thousand loggerheads (survive / survives) to adulthood, special care should be taken to protect this threatened species.

22 Make pronouns and antecedents agree.

A pronoun is a word that substitutes for a noun. Many pronouns have antecedents, nouns or pronouns to which they refer. A pronoun and its antecedent agree when they are both singular or both plural.

SINGULAR   *Dr. Ava Berto* finished *her* rounds.

PLURAL   The hospital *interns* finished *their* rounds.

FOR MULTILINGUAL WRITERS

The pronouns *he, his, she, her, it, its, they,* and *their* should agree in gender (masculine, feminine, or neutral) with their antecedents, not with the words they modify.

Steve visited *his* [not *her*] sister in Seattle.

22a Take care with indefinite pronouns (*anybody, everyone*) and generic nouns.

Writers are frequently tempted to use plural pronouns to refer to two kinds of singular antecedents: indefinite pronouns and generic nouns.

Indefinite pronouns

Indefinite pronouns refer to nonspecific persons or things.

anybody	each	everyone	nobody	somebody
anyone	either	everything	no one	someone
anything	everybody	neither	nothing	something

In the past, indefinite pronouns have been treated as singular. However, using a singular pronoun to refer to an indefinite pronoun can result in a sentence that is sexist, and the traditional alternatives (*he or she, he/she*) are wordy and noninclusive. (See 17e.)

SEXIST   *Everyone* performs at *his* own fitness level.

NONINCLUSIVE   *Everyone* performs at *his or her* own fitness level.

It is increasingly acceptable to use the gender-neutral pronoun *they* to refer to indefinite pronouns.

Everyone performs at *their* own fitness level.

The following are your options for revision.

1. Make the antecedent plural.

2. Rewrite the sentence so that no problem of agreement exists.

3. Use the gender-neutral pronoun *they* to refer to the singular antecedent.

▶ If ~~anyone wants~~ to audition, ~~he or she~~ should sign up.
any singers want *they*

▶ ~~If anyone~~ wants to audition, ~~he or she~~ should sign up.
Anyone who

▶ If anyone wants to audition, ~~he or she~~ should sign up.
they

If you change a pronoun in a sentence, check to be sure that the verb agrees with the new pronoun (see 21e).

Generic nouns

A generic noun represents a typical member of a group, such as a typical student, or any member of a group, such as a lawyer. Like indefinite pronouns, generic nouns have previously been considered singular. However, the singular use of *they* is increasingly acceptable with generic nouns. Avoid using *he* to refer to generic nouns, as in *A runner must train if he wants to excel.*

When revising sentences with generic nouns, you will usually have the same three options as for indefinite pronouns.

▶ ~~A medical student~~ must study hard if ~~he wants~~ to succeed.
Medical students *they want*

▶ A medical student must study hard ~~if he wants~~ to succeed.

▶ A medical student must study hard if ~~he wants~~ to succeed.
they want

22b Treat collective nouns as singular unless the meaning is clearly plural.

Collective nouns such as *jury*, *committee*, *audience*, *crowd*, *class*, *troop*, *family*, *team*, and *couple* name a group. Ordinarily the group functions as a unit, so the noun should be treated as singular; if the members of the group function as individuals, however, the noun should be treated as plural. (See also 21f.)

AS A UNIT The *committee* granted *its* permission to build.

AS INDIVIDUALS The *committee* put *their* signatures on the document.

When treating a collective noun as plural, many writers prefer to add a clearly plural antecedent such as *members* to the sentence: *The members of the committee put their signatures on the document.*

▶ After only an hour of deliberation, the jury returned ~~their~~ its

verdict.

There is no reason to draw attention to the individual members of the jury, so *jury* should be treated as singular.

22c Take care with compound antecedents.

Treat most compound antecedents joined with *and* as plural.

President Obama and President Xi held a meeting at which *they* formally signed the 2016 Paris climate agreement.

With compound antecedents joined with *or* or *nor* (or with *either . . . or* or *neither . . . nor*), make the pronoun agree with the nearer antecedent.

Either *Bruce* or *Tom* should receive first prize for *his* poem.

Neither the *mouse* nor the *rats* could find *their* way through the maze.

NOTE: If one of the antecedents is singular and the other plural, as in the second example, put the plural antecedent last to avoid awkwardness.

EXCEPTION: If the two antecedents are people of different genders, do not follow the traditional rule. The sentence *Either Bruce or Elizabeth should receive first prize for her poem* makes no sense. The best solution is to recast the sentence: *The prize for best poem should go to either Bruce or Elizabeth.*

> **EXERCISE 22–1**   Edit the following sentences to eliminate problems with pronoun-antecedent agreement. Most of the sentences can be revised in more than one way, so experiment before choosing a solution. If a sentence is correct, write "correct" after it. Possible revisions appear in the back of the book.

>   *they choose*
> **Recruiters may tell the truth, but there is much that ~~he chooses~~**
>   ^
>
> **not to tell.**

a. Every presidential candidate must appeal to a wide variety of ethnic and social groups if he wants to win the election.

b. Either Tom Hanks or Denzel Washington will win an award for their lifetime achievement in cinema.

c. The aerobics teacher motioned for everyone to move his or her arms in wide, slow circles.

d. The parade committee was unanimous in its decision to allow all groups and organizations to join the festivities.

e. The applicant should be bilingual if she wants to qualify for this position.

23   Make pronoun references clear.

Pronouns substitute for nouns; they are a kind of shorthand. In the sentence *When Andrew returned home, he took a nap*, the noun *Andrew* is the antecedent of the pronoun *he*. A pronoun should refer clearly to its antecedent.

23a   Avoid ambiguous or remote pronoun reference.

Ambiguous pronoun reference occurs when a pronoun could refer to two possible antecedents.

>   *The pitcher broke when Gloria set it*
> ▶ **~~When Gloria set the pitcher~~ on the glass-topped table/. ~~it broke.~~**
>   ^   ^

> "You have
> ► Tom told James, ~~that he had~~ won the lottery."

What broke — the pitcher or the table? Who won the lottery — Tom or James? The revisions eliminate the ambiguity.

Remote pronoun reference occurs when a pronoun is too far away from its antecedent for easy reading.

► My ex-husband refused to pay child support. Eight

months later, the judge ordered him to make payments

directly to the court, which would in turn pay me.

my ex-husband
After six months, payments stopped. Again ~~he~~ was

summoned to appear in court.

The pronoun *he* was too distant from its antecedent, *ex-husband*, which appeared several sentences earlier.

23b Avoid making broad references with *this*, *that*, *which*, and *it*.

For clarity, the pronouns *this*, *that*, *which*, and *it* should ordinarily refer to specific antecedents rather than to whole ideas or sentences. When a pronoun's reference is needlessly broad, either replace the pronoun with a noun or supply an antecedent to which the pronoun clearly refers.

► By advertising on TV, pharmaceutical companies gain exposure for

the ads
their prescription drugs. Patients respond to ~~this~~ by requesting

drugs they might not need.

The writer substituted the noun *ads* for the pronoun *this*, which referred broadly to the idea expressed in the preceding sentence.

► Romeo and Juliet were both too young to have acquired much

a fact
wisdom, ~~and~~ that accounts for their rash actions.

The writer added an antecedent (*fact*) that the pronoun *that* clearly refers to.

23c Do not use a pronoun to refer to an implied antecedent.

A pronoun should refer to a specific antecedent, not to a word that is implied but not present in the sentence.

> *the braids*
> ► After braiding Ann's hair, Sue decorated ~~them~~ with ribbons.

The pronoun *them* referred to Ann's braids (implied by the term *braiding*), but the word *braids* did not appear in the sentence.

Modifiers, such as possessives, cannot serve as antecedents. A modifier may strongly imply the noun that a pronoun might logically refer to, but it is not itself that noun.

> *Jamaica Kincaid*
> ► In ~~Jamaica Kincaid's~~ "Girl," she describes the advice a mother
>
> gives her daughter, including the mysterious warning not
>
> to be "the kind of woman who the baker won't let near the
>
> bread" (454).

Using the possessive form of an author's name to introduce a source leads to a problem later in this sentence: The pronoun *she* cannot refer logically to a possessive modifier (*Jamaica Kincaid's*). The revision substitutes the noun *Jamaica Kincaid* for the pronoun *she*, thereby eliminating the problem. (For more on writing with sources in MLA style, see 56.)

23d Avoid the indefinite use of *they*, *it*, and *you*.

Do not use the pronoun *they* to refer indefinitely to persons who have not been specifically mentioned. *They* should always refer to a specific antecedent.

> *the school board*
> ► In June, ~~they~~ voted to charge a fee for students to participate in
>
> sports and music programs.

The word *it* should not be used indefinitely in constructions such as *It is said on television . . .* or *In the book, it says that . . .*

> *The*
> ► ~~In the~~ article ~~it~~ states that male moths can smell female moths
>
> from several miles away.

The pronoun *you* is appropriate only when the writer is addressing the reader directly: *Once you have signed the form, return it to your adviser.* Except in informal contexts, *you* should not be used to mean "anyone in general." Use a noun instead.

▶ Ms. Pickersgill's *Guide to Etiquette* stipulates that ~~you~~ a guest should not

arrive at a party too early or leave too late.

23e To refer to persons, use *who, whom,* or *whose,* not *which* or *that.*

In most contexts, use *who, whom,* or *whose* to refer to persons and *which* or *that* to refer to animals or things.

▶ During the two-day festival El Día de los Muertos (Day of the

Dead), Mexican families celebrate loved ones ~~that~~ who have died.

EXERCISE 23–1   Edit the following sentences to correct errors in pronoun reference. In some cases, you will need to decide on an antecedent that the pronoun might logically refer to. Possible revisions appear in the back of the book.

Although Apple makes the most widely recognized

smartphone, other companies have gained a share of the

market. ~~This~~ The competition has kept prices from skyrocketing.

a. They say that engineering students should have hands-on experience with dismantling and reassembling machines.
b. She had decorated her bedroom wall with posters from chamber music festivals. This led her virtual classmates to believe that she was interested in classical music. Actually, she preferred rock.
c. In my high school, you didn't need to get all A's to be considered a success; you just needed to work to your ability.
d. Marianne told Jenny that she was worried about her mother's illness.
e. Though Lewis cried for several minutes after scraping his knee, eventually it subsided.

24 Distinguish between pronouns such as *I* and *me*.

The personal pronouns in the following chart change what is known as *case form* according to their grammatical function in a sentence. Pronouns functioning as subjects or subject complements appear in the *subjective* case; those functioning as objects appear in the *objective* case; and those showing ownership appear in the *possessive* case.

	SUBJECTIVE CASE	OBJECTIVE CASE	POSSESSIVE CASE
SINGULAR	I	me	my
	you	you	your
	he/she/it	him/her/it	his/her/its
PLURAL	we	us	our
	you	you	your
	they	them	their

Pronouns in the subjective and objective cases are frequently confused. Most of the rules in this section specify when to use one or the other of these cases. Section 24f explains a special use of pronouns and nouns in the possessive case.

24a Use the subjective case (*I, you, he, she, it, we, they*) for subjects and subject complements.

When personal pronouns are used as subjects, ordinarily your ear will tell you the correct pronoun. Problems sometimes arise, however, with compound word groups containing a pronoun.

▶ Joel left because his stepfather and ~~him~~ ^{he} had argued.

His stepfather and he is the subject of the verb *had argued*. If we strip away the words *his stepfather and*, the correct pronoun becomes clear: *he had argued* (not *him had argued*).

When a pronoun is used as a subject complement (a word following a linking verb), your ear may mislead you, since the incorrect form is frequently heard in casual speech. (See "Linking verbs and subject complements," 48b.)

▶ During the trial, the defendant repeatedly denied that the

he
kidnapper was ~~him~~.
       ^

> If *kidnapper was he* seems awkward, rewrite the sentence: *During the trial, the defendant repeatedly denied that he was the kidnapper.*

24b Use the objective case (*me, you, him, her, it, us, them*) for all objects.

When a personal pronoun is used as a direct object, an indirect object, or the object of a preposition, it must be in the objective case.

DIRECT OBJECT	Lin found Tony and brought *him* home.
INDIRECT OBJECT	Alice threw *me* a surprise party.
OBJECT OF A PREPOSITION	Keisha wondered if the call was for *her*.

When in doubt about the correct pronoun, some writers try to avoid making the choice by using a reflexive pronoun such as *myself.* Instead, use the objective case.

me
▶ Nidra gave my cousin and ~~myself~~ some good tips on traveling in
                           ^

New Delhi.

> *My cousin and me* is the indirect object of the verb *gave.* For correct uses of *myself*, see the glossary of usage in the appendixes.

24c Put an appositive and the word to which it refers in the same case.

Appositives are noun phrases that rename nouns or pronouns. A pronoun used as an appositive has the same function (usually subject or object) as the word(s) it renames.

▶ The managers, Dr. Bell and ~~me,~~ *I,* could not agree on a plan.

> The appositive *Dr. Bell and I* renames the subject, *managers.* Test: *I could not agree* (not *me could not agree*).

▶ The reporter interviewed only two witnesses, the bicyclist and ~~I.~~ *me.*

> The appositive *the bicyclist and me* renames the direct object, *witnesses.* Test: *interviewed me* (not *interviewed I*).

24d Following *than* or *as*, choose the pronoun that expresses your meaning.

When a comparison begins with *than* or *as*, your choice of a pronoun will depend on your intended meaning. To test for the correct pronoun, mentally complete the sentence: *My roommate likes football more than I [do].*

▶ In our report on nationalized health care in the United States, we

argued that Canadians are much better off than ~~us.~~ *we.*

> *We* is the subject of the verb *are*, which is understood: *Canadians are much better off than we [are]*. If the sentence seems too formal, you can always add the verb.

24e Use the objective case for subjects and objects of infinitives.

An infinitive is the word *to* followed by the base form of a verb. (See 49b.) Both subjects and objects of infinitives take the objective case.

▶ Harriet asked Tamara and ~~I~~ *me* to drive the senator and ~~she~~ *her*

to the airport.

> *Tamara and me* is the subject of the infinitive *to drive*; *senator and her* is the direct object of the infinitive.

24f Use the possessive case to modify a gerund.

A pronoun that modifies a gerund or a gerund phrase should be in the possessive case (*my, our, your, his, her, its, their*). A gerund is a verb form ending in *-ing* that functions as a noun.

> ► The chances of ~~you~~ **your** being hit by lightning are slim.

Your modifies the gerund phrase *being hit by lightning.*

Nouns as well as pronouns may modify gerunds. To form the possessive case of a noun, use an apostrophe and an *-s* (*victim's*) or just an apostrophe (*victims'*). (See 37a.)

> ► The old order in France paid a high price for the ~~aristocracy~~ **aristocracy's**
>
> exploiting the lower classes.

The possessive noun aristocracy's *modifies the gerund phrase* exploiting the lower classes.

EXERCISE 24–1   Edit the following sentences to eliminate errors in pronoun case. If a sentence is correct, write "correct" after it. Answers appear in the back of the book.

> Grandpa mows lawns for neighbors much younger than ~~him.~~ **he.**

a. Rick applied for the job even though he heard that other candidates were more experienced than he.

b. The volleyball team could not believe that the coach was she.

c. She appreciated him telling the truth in such a difficult situation.

d. The director has asked you and I to draft a proposal for a new recycling plan.

e. My roommate and myself dreamed of renting a station wagon, packing it with food, and driving two hundred miles to Mardi Gras.

25 Distinguish between *who* and *whom*.

The choice between *who* and *whom* (or *whoever* and *whomever*) occurs primarily in subordinate clauses and in questions. *Who* and *whoever*, subjective-case pronouns, are used for subjects and subject complements. *Whom* and *whomever*, objective-case pronouns, are used for objects. (See 25a and 25b.)

An exception to this general rule occurs when the pronoun functions as the subject of an infinitive. (See 25c; see also 24e.)

25a Use *who* and *whom* correctly in subordinate clauses.

When *who* and *whom* (or *whoever* and *whomever*) introduce subordinate clauses, their case is determined by their function *within the clause they introduce.*

In the following two examples, the pronouns *who* and *whoever* function as the subjects of the clauses they introduce.

▶ First prize goes to the runner ~~whom~~ who earns the most points.

> The subordinate clause is *who earns the most points.* The verb of the clause is *earns*, and its subject is *who.*

▶ Maya Angelou's *I Know Why the Caged Bird Sings* should be read by ~~whomever~~ whoever is interested in the effects of racism on children.

> The writer selected the pronoun *whomever*, thinking that it was the object of the preposition *by.* However, the object of the preposition is the entire subordinate clause *whoever is interested in the effects of racial prejudice on children.* The verb of the clause is *is*, and the subject of the verb is *whoever.*

When functioning as an object in a subordinate clause, *whom* (or *whomever*) also appears out of order, before the subject and verb. To choose the correct pronoun, you can mentally restructure the clause.

whom
▶ You will work with our senior traders, ~~who~~ you will meet later.
                                          ^

> The subordinate clause is *whom you will meet later*. The subject of the
> clause is *you*, and the verb is *will meet*. *Whom* is the direct object of the
> verb. The correct choice becomes clear if you mentally restructure the
> clause: *you will meet whom later*.

When functioning as the object of a preposition in a subordinate clause, *whom* is often separated from its preposition.

whom
▶ The tutor ~~who~~ I was assigned to was very supportive.
            ^

> *Whom* is the object of the preposition *to*. In this sentence, the writer
> might choose to drop *whom*: *The tutor I was assigned to was very
> supportive*.

25b Use *who* and *whom* correctly in questions.

When *who* and *whom* (or *whoever* and *whomever*) are used to
open questions, their case is determined by their function within
the question. In the following example, *who* functions as the subject of the question.

Who
▶ ~~Whom~~ was responsible for creating that computer virus?
  ^

> *Who* is the subject of the verb *was*.

When *whom* functions as the object of a verb or the object
of a preposition in a question, it appears out of normal order. To
choose the correct pronoun, you can mentally restructure the
question.

Whom
▶ ~~Who~~ did the Democratic Party nominate in 2004?
  ^

> *Whom* is the direct object of the verb *did nominate*. This becomes clear
> if you restructure the question: *The Democratic Party did nominate
> whom in 2004?*

25c Use *whom* for subjects or objects of infinitives.

An infinitive is the word *to* followed by the base form of a verb.
(See 49b.) Subjects of infinitives are an exception to the rule that

subjects must be in the subjective case. The subject of an infinitive must be in the objective case. Objects of infinitives also are in the objective case.

> whom
> ▶ **When it comes to money, I know ~~who~~ to believe.**
>   ^

The infinitive phrase *whom to believe* is the direct object of the verb *know*, and *whom* is the subject of the infinitive *to believe*.

EXERCISE 25–1   Edit the following sentences to eliminate errors in the use of *who* and *whom* (or *whoever* and *whomever*). If a sentence is correct, write "correct" after it. Answers appear in the back of the book.

> whom
> **What is the address of the artist ~~who~~ Antonio hired?**
>   ^

a. Arriving late for rehearsal, we had no idea who was supposed to dance with whom.

b. The environmental policy conference featured scholars who I had never heard of.

c. Whom did you support in last month's election for student government president?

d. Kartik always gives a holiday donation to whomever needs it.

e. So many singers came to the audition that Natalia had trouble deciding who to select for the choir.

26   Choose adjectives and adverbs with care.

Adjectives modify nouns or pronouns. They usually come before the word they modify; occasionally they function as complements following the word they modify. Adverbs modify verbs, adjectives, or other adverbs. (See 47d and 47e.)

Many adverbs are formed by adding *-ly* to adjectives (*normal, normally; smooth, smoothly*). But don't assume that all words ending in *-ly* are adverbs or that all adverbs end in *-ly*. Some adjectives end in *-ly* (*lovely, friendly*), and some adverbs don't (*always, here, there*). When in doubt, consult a dictionary.

FOR MULTILINGUAL WRITERS

Placement of adjectives and adverbs can be a challenge for multilingual writers. See 30e and 30g.

26a Use adjectives to modify nouns.

Adjectives ordinarily precede the nouns they modify. But they can also function as subject complements or object complements, following the nouns they modify.

FOR MULTILINGUAL WRITERS

In English, adjectives are not pluralized to agree with the words they modify:

> red
> ► The ~~reds~~ roses were a surprise.
>   ^

Subject complements

A subject complement follows a linking verb and completes the meaning of the subject. (See 48b.) When an adjective functions as a subject complement, it describes the subject.

Justice is *blind.*

Verbs such as *smell*, *taste*, *look*, and *feel* may be linking verbs. If the word following one of these verbs describes the subject, use an adjective; if the word following the verb modifies the verb, use an adverb.

ADJECTIVE	The detective looked *cautious*.
ADVERB	The detective looked *cautiously* for fingerprints.

The adjective *cautious* describes the detective; the adverb *cautiously* modifies the verb *looked*.

Linking verbs suggest states of being, not actions. Notice, for example, the different meanings of *looked* in the preceding examples. To look cautious suggests the state of being cautious; to look cautiously is to perform an action in a cautious way.

▶ The lilacs in our backyard smell especially ~~sweetly~~ *sweet* this year.

The verb *smell* suggests a state of being, not an action. Therefore, it should be followed by an adjective, not an adverb.

▶ The drawings looked ~~well~~ *good* after the architect made changes.

The verb *looked* is a linking verb suggesting a state of being, not an action. The adjective *good* is appropriate following the linking verb to describe *drawings*. (See also 26c.)

Object complements

An object complement follows a direct object and completes its meaning. (See 48b.) When an adjective functions as an object complement, it describes the direct object.

Sorrow makes *us wise.*

Object complements occur with verbs such as *call, consider, create, find, keep,* and *make.* When a modifier follows the direct object of one of these verbs, use an adjective to describe the direct object; use an adverb to modify the verb.

ADJECTIVE	The referee called the plays *perfect.*
ADVERB	The referee called the plays *perfectly.*

The first sentence means that the referee considered the plays to be perfect; the second means that the referee did an excellent job of calling the plays.

26b Use adverbs to modify verbs, adjectives, and other adverbs.

When adverbs modify verbs (or verbals), they nearly always answer the question When? Where? How? Why? Under what conditions? How often? or To what degree? When adverbs modify adjectives or other adverbs, they usually qualify or intensify the meaning of the word they modify. (See 47e.)

   Adjectives are often used incorrectly in place of adverbs in casual speech.

> *perfectly*
> ► The travel arrangement worked out ~~perfect~~ for everyone.
>
> The adverb *perfectly* modifies the verb *worked out*.

> *really*
> ► The chance of recovering any lost property looks ~~real~~ slim.
>
> Only adverbs can modify adjectives or other adverbs. *Really* intensifies the meaning of the adjective *slim*.

26c Distinguish between *good* and *well*, *bad* and *badly*.

Good is an adjective (*good performance*). *Well* is an adverb when it modifies a verb (*speak well*).

> *well*
> ► We were glad that Sanya had done ~~good~~ on the CPA exam.
>
> The adverb *well* modifies the verb *had done*.

   Confusion can arise because *well* is an adjective when it modifies a noun or pronoun and means "healthy" or "satisfactory" (*The babies were well and warm*).

> *well,*
> ► Adrienne did not feel ~~good,~~ but she performed anyway.
>
> As an adjective following the linking verb *did feel*, *well* describes Adrienne's health.

   Bad is always an adjective and should be used to modify a noun; *badly* is always an adverb and should be used to modify a verb. The adverb *badly* is often used inappropriately to describe a noun, especially following a linking verb.

> *bad*
> ► The sisters felt ~~badly~~ when they realized they had left their
>
> brother out of the planning.
>
> The adjective *bad* is used after the linking verb *felt* to describe the noun *sisters*.

26d Use comparatives and superlatives with care.

Most adjectives and adverbs have three forms: the positive, the comparative, and the superlative.

POSITIVE	COMPARATIVE	SUPERLATIVE
fast	faster	fastest
careful	more careful	most careful
bad	worse	worst
good	better	best

Comparative versus superlative

Use the comparative to compare two things, the superlative to compare three or more.

▶ Which of these two protein shakes is ~~best?~~ better?

▶ Zhao is the ~~more~~ most qualified of the three candidates running

for mayor.

Forming comparatives and superlatives

To form comparatives and superlatives of most one- and two-syllable adjectives, use the endings *-er* and *-est*: *smooth, smoother, smoothest*; *easy, easier, easiest*. With longer adjectives, use *more* and *most* (or *less* and *least* for downward comparisons): *exciting, more exciting, most exciting*; *helpful, less helpful, least helpful*.

Some one-syllable adverbs take the endings *-er* and *-est* (*fast, faster, fastest*), but longer adverbs and all of those ending in *-ly* form the comparative and superlative with *more* and *most* (or *less* and *least*).

The comparative and superlative forms of some adjectives and adverbs are irregular: *good, better, best*; *well, better, best*; *bad, worse, worst*; *badly, worse, worst*.

▶ The Kirov is the ~~talentedest~~ most talented ballet company we have seen.

▶ According to our projections, sales at local businesses will be

~~worser~~ worse than those at the chain stores this winter.

Double comparatives or superlatives

Do not use double comparatives or superlatives. When you have added *-er* or *-est* to an adjective or adverb, do not also use *more* or *most* (or *less* or *least*).

▶ Of all her family, Julia is the ~~most~~ happiest about the move.

▶ All the polls indicated that Gore was more ~~likelier~~ to win than Bush.
  (likely)

Absolute concepts

Avoid expressions such as *less perfect*, *very round*, and *most unique*. Either something is unique or it isn't. It is illogical to suggest that absolute concepts come in degrees.

▶ That is the most ~~unique~~ wedding gown I have ever seen.
  (unusual)

▶ The painting is even more ~~priceless~~ because it is signed.
  (valuable)

26e Avoid double negatives.

Use two negatives only if a positive meaning is intended: *The orchestra was not unhappy with its performance* (meaning that the orchestra was happy). Using a double negative to emphasize a negative meaning creates an illogical sentence.

Negative modifiers such as *never*, *no*, and *not* should not be paired with other negative modifiers or with negative words such as *neither*, *none*, *no one*, *nobody*, and *nothing*.

▶ The county is not doing ~~nothing~~ to see that the trash is collected.
  (anything)

Not doing nothing suggests that the county is doing something — the opposite of the writer's intended meaning.

EXERCISE 26–1   Edit the following sentences to eliminate errors in the use of adjectives and adverbs. If a sentence is correct, write "correct" after it. Answers appear in the back of the book.

We weren't surprised by how ~~good~~ the sidecar racing team
  (well)

flowed through the tricky course.

a. Do you expect to perform good on the exam next week?
b. With the budget deadline approaching, our office hasn't hardly had time to handle routine correspondence.
c. When I worked in a flower shop, I learned that some flowers smell surprisingly bad.
d. The customer complained that he hadn't been treated nice by the agent on the phone.
e. Of all the smart people in my family, Aunt Ida is the most cleverest.

27 Choose appropriate verb forms, tenses, and moods.

Except for the verb *be*, all verbs in English have five forms. The following list shows the five forms and provides a sample sentence in which each might appear.

BASE FORM	Usually I (*walk*, *ride*).
PAST TENSE	Yesterday I (*walked*, *rode*).
PAST PARTICIPLE	I have (*walked*, *ridden*) many times before.
PRESENT PARTICIPLE	I am (*walking*, *riding*) right now.
-S FORM	He/she/it (*walks*, *rides*) regularly.

The verb *be* has eight forms instead of the usual five: *be, am, is, are, was, were, being, been.*

27a Choose correct forms of irregular verbs.

For all regular verbs, the past-tense and past-participle forms are the same (ending in *-ed* or *-d*), so there is no danger of confusion. This is not true, however, for irregular verbs, such as the following.

BASE FORM	PAST TENSE	PAST PARTICIPLE
go	went	gone
break	broke	broken
fly	flew	flown
sing	sang	sung

The past-tense form always occurs alone, without a helping verb. It expresses action that occurred entirely in the past: *I rode to work yesterday. I walked to work last Tuesday.* The past participle is used with a helping verb. It forms the perfect tenses with *has, have,* or *had;* it forms the passive voice with *be, am, is, are, was, were, being,* or *been.* (See 47c for a complete list of helping verbs and 27f for a survey of tenses.)

PAST TENSE   Last July, we *went* to Tokyo.

HELPING VERB + PAST PARTICIPLE   We *have gone* to Tokyo twice.

The list of common irregular verbs below will help you distinguish between the past tense and the past participle. Choose the past-participle form if the verb in your sentence requires a helping verb; choose the past-tense form if the verb does not require a helping verb. (See verb tenses in 27f.)

▶ Yesterday we ~~seen~~ a documentary about Isabel Allende.
  saw

  The past-tense *saw* is required because there is no helping verb.

▶ The truck was apparently ~~stole~~ while the driver ate lunch.
  stolen

▶ By Friday, the stock market had ~~fell~~ two hundred points.
  fallen

  Because of the helping verbs *was* and *had,* the past-participle forms are required: *was stolen, had fallen.*

Common irregular verbs

BASE FORM	PAST TENSE	PAST PARTICIPLE
be	was, were	been
begin	began	begun
bring	brought	brought
buy	bought	bought
catch	caught	caught
choose	chose	chosen
come	came	come
do	did	done
drink	drank	drunk
drive	drove	driven

eat	ate	eaten
fall	fell	fallen
find	found	found
get	got	gotten, got
give	gave	given
hang (execute)	hanged	hanged
hang (suspend)	hung	hung
have	had	had
hear	heard	heard
keep	kept	kept
know	knew	known
lead	led	led
let (allow)	let	let
lose	lost	lost
make	made	made
ride	rode	ridden
rise (get up)	rose	risen
run	ran	run
say	said	said
see	saw	seen
send	sent	sent
set (place)	set	set
sit (be seated)	sat	sat
speak	spoke	spoken
stand	stood	stood
steal	stole	stolen
sting	stung	stung
swear	swore	sworn
take	took	taken
teach	taught	taught
throw	threw	thrown
wake	woke, waked	waked, woken
wear	wore	worn
write	wrote	written

27b Distinguish among the forms of *lie* and *lay*.

Writers and speakers frequently confuse the various forms of *lie* (meaning "to recline or rest on a surface") and *lay* (meaning "to put or place something"). *Lie* is an intransitive verb; it does not take a direct object: *The forms lie on the table.* The verb *lay* is transitive; it takes a direct object: *Please lay the forms on the table.* (See 48b.)

BASE FORM	PAST TENSE	PAST PARTICIPLE	PRESENT PARTICIPLE
lie (recline)	lay	lain	lying
lay (put)	laid	laid	laying

▶ Niko was so exhausted that she ~~laid~~ **lay** down for a nap.

   The past-tense form of *lie* ("to recline") is *lay.*

▶ The patient had ~~laid~~ **lain** in an uncomfortable position all night.

   The past-participle form of *lie* ("to recline") is *lain.* If the correct English seems too stilted, recast the sentence: *The patient had been lying in an uncomfortable position all night.*

▶ The customer gently ~~lay~~ **laid** the tablet on the help desk counter.

▶ Letters dating from 1915 were ~~laying~~ **lying** in a corner of the chest.

   The present participle of *lie* ("to rest on a surface") is *lying.*

EXERCISE 27–1   Edit the following sentences to eliminate problems with irregular verbs. If a sentence is correct, write "correct" after it. Answers appear in the back of the book.

The ranger ~~seen~~ **saw** the forest fire ten miles away.

a. When I get the urge to exercise, I lay down until it passes.

b. Grandmother had drove our new hybrid to the sunrise church service, so we were left with the station wagon.

c. A pile of dirty rags was laying at the bottom of the stairs.

d. How did the game know that the player had went from the room with the blue ogre to the hall where the gold was heaped?

e. Abraham Lincoln took good care of his legal clients; the contracts he drew for the Illinois Central Railroad could never be broke.

27c Use -s or -es endings on present-tense verbs that have third-person singular subjects.

All singular nouns (*child, tree*) and the pronouns *he*, *she*, and *it* are third-person singular; indefinite pronouns such as *everyone* and *neither* are also third-person singular. When the subject of a sentence is third-person singular, its verb takes an *-s* or *-es* ending in the present tense. (See also 21.)

	SINGULAR		PLURAL	
FIRST PERSON	I	know	we	know
SECOND PERSON	you	know	you	know
THIRD PERSON	he/she/it	knows	they	know
	child	knows	parents	know
	everyone	knows		

> My neighbor ~~drive~~ *drives* to Marco Island every weekend.

> Sulfur dioxide ~~turn~~ *turns* leaves yellow, ~~dissolve~~ *dissolves* marble, and ~~eat~~ *eats* away iron and steel.

The subjects *neighbor* and *sulfur dioxide* are third-person singular, so the verbs must end in *-s*.

NOTE: Do not add the *-s* ending to the verb if the subject is not third-person singular. The writers of the following sentences added –*s* endings where they don't belong.

> I prepares system specifications for every installation.

The pronoun *I* is first-person singular, so its verb does not require the *-s*.

> The tile floors requires continual sweeping.

The *-s* form is used only for present-tense verbs with third-person *singular* subjects.

Has versus have

In the present tense, use *has* with third-person singular subjects; all other subjects require *have*.

▶ This respected musician almost always ~~have~~ ^{has} a message to convey

in his work.

The subject *musician* is third-person singular, so the verb should be *has*.

▶ My law classes ~~has~~ ^{have} helped me understand contracts.

The subject of this sentence — *classes* — is third-person plural, so the verb should be *have*.

Does versus *do* and *doesn't* versus *don't*

In the present tense, use *does* and *doesn't* with third-person singular subjects; all other subjects require *do* and *don't*.

▶ Grandfather really ~~don't~~ ^{doesn't} have a place to call home.

Grandfather is third-person singular, so the verb should be *doesn't*.

Am, *is*, and *are*; *was* and *were*

The verb *be* has three forms in the present tense (*am*, *is*, *are*) and two in the past tense (*was*, *were*).

	SINGULAR		**PLURAL**	
FIRST PERSON	I	am/was	we	are/were
SECOND PERSON	you	are/were	you	are/were
THIRD PERSON	he/she/it	is/was	they	are/were

▶ Did you think you ~~was~~ ^{were} going to drown?

The subject *you* is second-person singular, so the verb should be *were*.

27d Do not omit -*ed* endings on verbs.

The verb ending -*ed* is sometimes not fully pronounced with words and phrases such as *asked*, *fixed*, *pronounced*, *supposed to*, and *used to*. While the meaning of such words is often clear while speaking, include -*ed* endings in academic writing to avoid confusion.

Past tense

Use the ending *-ed* or *-d* to express the past tense of regular verbs. The past tense is used when the action occurred entirely in the past.

▶ In 2020, author Colson Whitehead ~~receive~~ received the Pulitzer Prize for

his novel *The Nickel Boys.*

▶ Last summer, my counselor ~~advise~~ advised me to ask my graphic arts

instructor for a recommendation.

Past participles

Past participles are used in three ways: (1) following *have, has,* or *had* to form one of the perfect tenses; (2) following *be, am, is, are, was, were, being,* or *been* to form the passive voice; and (3) as adjectives modifying nouns or pronouns. The perfect tenses are listed in 27f, and the passive voice is discussed in 8a. For a discussion of participles as adjectives, see 49b.

▶ Robin has ~~ask~~ asked for more housing staff for next year.

Has asked is present perfect tense (*have* or *has* followed by a past participle).

▶ Though it is not a new phenomenon, domestic violence is now
~~publicize~~ publicized more than ever.

Is publicized is a verb in the passive voice (a form of *be* followed by a past participle).

▶ All kickboxing classes end in a cool-down period to stretch
~~tighten~~ tightened muscles.

The past participle *tightened* functions as an adjective modifying the noun *muscles.*

27e Do not omit needed verbs.

Linking verbs, used to link subjects to subject complements, are frequently a form of *be*: *be, am, is, are, was, were, being, been.* (See 48b.) While some of these forms may be contracted (*I'm, she's, we're, you're, they're*), avoid omitting them altogether in academic writing.

▶ The city of Venice ^{is} better protected from flooding thanks to its

new system of dams and gates called MOSE.

Helping verbs, used with main verbs, include forms of *be, do,* and *have* and the modal verbs *can, will, shall, could, would, should, may, might,* and *must.* (See 47c.) Like linking verbs, helping verbs may be contracted (*he's leaving, we'll celebrate, they've been told*), but avoid omitting them altogether in your writing.

▶ Astronomers ^{have} been studying the skies with the Hubble Telescope

since 1990.

FOR MULTILINGUAL WRITERS

Some languages do not require a linking verb between a subject and its complement. However, written English sentences always contain a verb. See 30a.

▶ Every night, I read to my daughter. When I ^{am} too busy, her older

brother reads to her.

EXERCISE 27–2 Edit the following sentences to eliminate problems with *-s* and *-ed* verb forms and with omitted verbs. If a sentence is correct, write "correct" after it. Answers appear in the back of the book.

The Pell Grant sometimes ~~cover~~ ^{covers} the student's full tuition.

a. The glass sculptures of the Swan Boats was prominent in the brightly lit lobby.
b. Visitors to the glass museum were not suppose to touch the exhibits.

c. The electrician went to the security office to repair the close circuit TV.

d. Christos didn't know about Marlo's promotion because he never listens. He always talking.

e. Most psychologists agree that no one performs well under stress.

27f Choose the appropriate verb tense.

Tenses indicate the time of an action in relation to the time of the speaking or writing about that action.

The most common problem with tenses, shifting confusingly from one tense to another, is discussed in section 13. Other problems with tenses are detailed in this section, after the following survey of tenses.

Survey of tenses

Tenses are classified as present, past, and future, with simple, perfect, and progressive forms for each.

Simple tenses (base form or -s form) *For general facts, states of being, and habitual actions*

SIMPLE PRESENT

SINGULAR		PLURAL	
I	walk, ride, am	we	walk, ride, are
you	walk, ride, are	you	walk, ride, are
he/she/it	walks, rides, is	they	walk, ride, are

SIMPLE PAST

SINGULAR		PLURAL	
I	walked, rode, was	we	walked, rode, were
you	walked, rode, were	you	walked, rode, were
he/she/it	walked, rode, was	they	walked, rode, were

SIMPLE FUTURE

I, you, he/she/it, we, they   will walk, ride, be

Perfect tenses (a form of *have* plus past participle) *For actions that were or will be completed at the time of another action*

PRESENT PERFECT

I, you, we, they	have walked, ridden, been
he/she/it	has walked, ridden, been

PAST PERFECT

I, you, he/she/it, we, they   had walked, ridden, been

FUTURE PERFECT

I, you, he/she/it, we, they   will have walked, ridden, been

Progressive forms (a form of *have* plus present participle) *For actions in progress*

PRESENT PROGRESSIVE

I   am walking, riding, being

he/she/it   is walking, riding, being

you, we, they   are walking, riding, being

PAST PROGRESSIVE

I, he/she/it   was walking, riding, being

you, we, they   were walking, riding, being

FUTURE PROGRESSIVE

I, you, he/she/it, we, they   will be walking, riding, being

PRESENT PERFECT PROGRESSIVE

I, you, we, they   have been walking, riding, being

he/she/it   has been walking, riding, being

PAST PERFECT PROGRESSIVE

I, you, he/she/it, we, they   had been walking, riding, being

FUTURE PERFECT PROGRESSIVE

I, you, he/she/it, we, they   will have been walking, riding, being

NOTE: The progressive forms are not normally used with certain verbs, such as *believe*, *know*, and *seem*.

FOR MULTILINGUAL WRITERS

See 28a for more specific examples of verb tenses that can be challenging for multilingual writers.

Special uses of the present tense

Use the present tense when expressing general truths, when writing about literature, and when quoting, summarizing, or paraphrasing an author's views.

General truths or scientific principles should appear in the present tense unless such principles have been disproved.

▶ Galileo taught that the earth ~~revolved~~ *revolves* around the sun.

> Because Galileo's teaching has not been discredited, the verb should be in the present tense. The following sentence, however, is acceptable: *Ptolemy taught that the sun revolved around the earth.*

When writing about a work of literature, you may be tempted to use the past tense. The convention, however, is to describe fictional events in the present tense.

▶ In Masuji Ibuse's *Black Rain*, a child ~~reached~~ *reaches* for a pomegranate in his mother's garden, and a moment later he ~~was~~ *is* dead, killed by the blast of the atomic bomb.

When you are quoting, summarizing, or paraphrasing the author of a nonliterary work, use present-tense verbs such as *writes*, *reports*, *asserts*, and so on to introduce the source. This convention is usually followed even when the author is dead (unless a date or the context specifies the time of writing).

▶ Dr. Jerome Groopman ~~argued~~ *argues* that doctors are "susceptible to the subtle and not so subtle efforts of the pharmaceutical industry to sculpt our thinking" (9).

> In MLA style, signal phrases are written in the present tense, not the past tense. (See also 56c.)

EXCEPTION: When you are documenting a paper with the APA (American Psychological Association) style of in-text citations, use past tense verbs such as *argued* or present perfect verbs such as *has argued* to introduce the source. (See also 61c.)

The past perfect tense

The past perfect tense (*had* plus past participle) is used for an action already completed by the time of another past action or for an action already completed at some specific past time.

> Everyone *had spoken* by the time I arrived.
>
> I pleaded my case, but Paula *had made up* her mind.

Writers sometimes use the simple past tense when they should use the past perfect.

>   *had*
> ▶ **By the time dinner was served, the guest of honor ^ left.**

The past perfect tense is needed because the action of leaving was already completed at a specific past time (when dinner was served).

Some writers overuse the past perfect tense. Do not use the past perfect if two past actions occurred at the same time.

>   *wrote*
> ▶ **When Ernest Hemingway lived in Cuba, he ~~had written~~ *For*
>
> *Whom the Bell Tolls.***

Sequence of tenses with infinitives and participles

An infinitive is the base form of a verb preceded by *to*. (See 49b.) Use the present infinitive to show action at the same time as or later than the action of the verb in the sentence.

>   *pay*
> ▶ **Sonia had hoped to ~~have paid~~ the bill by May 1.**

The action expressed in the infinitive (*to pay*) occurred later than the action of the sentence's verb (*had hoped*).

Use the perfect form of an infinitive (*to have* followed by the past participle) for an action occurring earlier than that of the verb in the sentence.

>   *have joined*
> ▶ **Dan would like to ~~join~~ the Coast Guard, but he could not swim.**

The liking occurs in the present; the joining would have occurred in the past.

Like the tense of an infinitive, the tense of a participle is governed by the tense of the sentence's verb. Use the present participle (ending in *-ing*) for an action occurring at the same time as that of the sentence's verb.

Hiking the Appalachian Trail, we spotted many wildflowers.

Use the past participle (such as *given* or *helped*) or the present perfect participle (*having* plus the past participle) for an action occurring before that of the verb.

Discovered off the coast of Florida, the Spanish galleon yielded many treasures.

Having worked her way through college, Lee graduated debt-free.

27g Use the subjunctive mood in the few contexts that require it.

There are three moods in English: the *indicative*, used for facts, opinions, and questions; the *imperative*, used for orders or advice; and the *subjunctive*, used in certain contexts to express wishes, requests, or conditions contrary to fact. For many writers, the subjunctive causes the most problems.

Forms of the subjunctive

In the subjunctive mood, present-tense verbs do not change form to indicate the number and person of the subject (see 21). Instead, the subjunctive uses the base form of the verb (*be, drive, employ*) with all subjects. Also, in the subjunctive mood, there is only one past-tense form of *be*: *were* (never *was*).

It is important that you *be* [not *are*] prepared for the interview.

We asked that she *drive* [not *drives*] more slowly.

If I *were* [not *was*] you, I'd try a new strategy.

Uses of the subjunctive

The subjunctive mood appears only in a few contexts, outlined below.

In contrary-to-fact clauses beginning with *if* When a subordinate clause beginning with *if* expresses a condition contrary to fact, use the subjunctive *were* in place of *was*.

> ► If I ~~was~~ *were* a member of Congress, I would vote for that bill.

> ► The astronomers would be able to see the moons of Jupiter tonight if the weather ~~was~~ *were* clearer.

The verbs in these sentences express conditions that do not exist; the writer is not in Congress, and the weather is not clear.

Do not use the subjunctive mood in *if* clauses expressing conditions that exist or may exist.

If Dana *wins* the contest, she will leave for Barcelona in June.

In clauses expressing a wish In formal English, use the subjunctive *were* in clauses expressing a wish or desire.

INFORMAL   I wish that Dr. Vaughn *was* my professor.

FORMAL   I wish that Dr. Vaughn *were* my professor.

In *that* clauses following verbs such as *ask*, *insist*, *request*, and *suggest* Because requests have not yet become reality, they are expressed in the subjunctive mood.

> ► Professor Moore insists that her students ~~are~~ *be* on time for every class.

> ► We recommend that Lambert ~~files~~ *file* form 1050 soon.

In certain set expressions The subjunctive mood, once more widely used, remains in certain set expressions, including *be that as it may*, *as it were*, and *far be it from me*.

EXERCISE 27–3 Edit the following sentences to eliminate errors in verb tense or mood. If a sentence is correct, write "correct" after it. Answers appear in the back of the book.

> had been
> After the path ~~was~~ plowed, we were able to walk in the park.

a. The palace of Knossos in Crete is believed to have been destroyed by fire around 1375 BCE.

b. Discovered in 1930, Pluto was an icy dwarf planet that exists at the edge of our solar system.

c. When city planners proposed rezoning the waterfront, did they know that the mayor promised to curb development in that neighborhood?

d. Tonight's lecture begins at 7:30. If it was earlier, I'd consider attending.

e. The math position was filled by the instructor who had been running the tutoring center.

Multilingual Writers and ESL Topics

This section of *Rules for Writers* is primarily for multilingual writers. You may find this section helpful if you learned English as a second language (ESL) or if you speak a language other than English with your friends and family.

28 Verbs

All speakers of English encounter challenges with verbs. This chapter focuses on specific challenges that multilingual writers sometimes face when they write in English. You can find more help with verbs in other sections in the book:

> making subjects and verbs agree (21)
>
> using irregular verb forms (27a, 27b)
>
> using correct verb endings (27c, 27d)
>
> choosing the correct verb tense (27f)
>
> avoiding inappropriate uses of the passive voice (8a)

28a Use effective verb forms and tenses.

This section offers a brief review of English verb forms and tenses. For additional help, see 27 and 47c.

BASIC VERB FORMS

	REGULAR VERB *HELP*	IRREGULAR VERB *GIVE*	IRREGULAR VERB *BE**
BASE FORM	help	give	be
PAST TENSE	helped	gave	was, were
PAST PARTICIPLE	helped	given	been
PRESENT PARTICIPLE	helping	giving	being
-*S* FORM	helps	gives	is

*Be also has the forms *am* and *are*, which are used in the present tense.

Basic verb forms

Every main verb in English has five forms, which are used to create all of the verb tenses. The chart on the previous page shows these forms for the regular verb *help* and the irregular verbs *give* and *be*. See 27a for the forms of other common irregular verbs.

Verb tenses

Section 27f describes all the verb tenses in English, showing the forms of a regular verb, an irregular verb, and the verb *be* in each tense. The following chart provides more details about the tenses commonly used in the active voice in writing; the chart on page 230 gives details about tenses commonly used in the passive voice.

VERB TENSES COMMONLY USED IN THE ACTIVE VOICE

For descriptions and examples of all verb tenses, see 27f.

Simple tenses
For general facts, states of being, habitual actions

Simple present   **Base form or -s form**

- general facts   College students often *study* late at night.
- states of being   Water *becomes* steam at 100 degrees centigrade.
- habitual, repetitive actions   We *donate* to a different charity each year.
- scheduled future events   The train *arrives* tomorrow at 6:30 p.m.

NOTE: For uses of the present tense in writing about literature, see page 220.

Simple past   **Base form + -ed or -d or irregular form**

- completed actions at a specific time in the past   The storm *destroyed* their property. She *drove* to Montana three years ago.
- facts or states of being in the past   When I *was* young, I *walked* to school with my sister.

Simple future   ***will* + base form**

- future actions, promises, or predictions   I *will exercise* tomorrow. The snowfall *will begin* around midnight.

VERB TENSES COMMONLY USED IN THE ACTIVE VOICE, continued

Simple progressive forms
For continuing actions

Present progressive   *am, is, are* + present participle

- actions in progress at the present time, not continuing indefinitely
- future actions (with *leave, go, come, move,* etc.)

The students *are taking* an exam in Room 105.

The valet *is parking* the car.

I *am leaving* tomorrow morning.

Past progressive   *was, were* + present participle

- actions in progress at a specific time in the past
- *was going to, were going to* for past plans that did not happen

They *were swimming* when the storm struck.

We *were going to* submit a proposal, but the funding was canceled.

NOTE: Some verbs are not normally used in the progressive: *appear, believe, belong, contain, have, hear, know, like, need, see, seem, taste, understand,* and *want.*

      want
▶ I ~~am wanting~~ to see August Wilson's *Ma Rainey's Black Bottom.*
     ^

Perfect tenses
For actions that happened or will happen before another time

Present perfect   *has, have* + past participle

- repetitive or constant actions that began in the past and continue to the present
- actions that happened at an unknown or unspecific past time

I *have loved* cats since I was a child. Alicia *has worked* in Kenya for ten years.

Stephen *has visited* Wales three times.

Past perfect   *had* + past participle

- actions that began or occurred before another time in the past

She *had* just *crossed* the street when the runaway car crashed into the building.

NOTE: For more discussion of uses of the past perfect, see 27f. For uses of the past perfect in conditional sentences, see 28e.

> **VERB TENSES COMMONLY USED IN THE ACTIVE VOICE,** continued
>
> **Perfect progressive forms**
> *For continuous past actions before another time*
>
> | **Present perfect progressive** | ***has, have + been + present participle*** |
> |---|---|
> | • continuous actions that began in the past and continue to the present | Yolanda *has been trying* to get a job in Boston for five years. |
> | **Past perfect progressive** | ***had + been + present participle*** |
> | • actions that began and continued in the past until another past action | By the time I moved to Georgia, I *had been supporting* myself for five years. |

28b To write a verb in the passive voice, use a form of *be* with the past participle.

When a sentence is written in the passive voice, the subject receives the action instead of doing it.

> The solution *was heated* to 80 degrees Celsius.

To form the passive voice, use a form of *be* — *am, is, are, was, were, being, be,* or *been* — followed by the past participle of the main verb: *was chosen, are remembered.* (Sometimes a form of *be* follows another helping verb: *will be considered, could have been broken.*)

> written
> ► *Dreaming in Cuban* was ~~writing~~ by Cristina García.
>   ^
>
> In the passive voice, the past participle *written,* not the present participle *writing,* must follow *was* (the past tense of *be*).

> tested.
> ► The child is being ~~test.~~
>   ^
>
> The past participle *tested,* not the base form *test,* must be used with *is being* to form the passive voice.

For details on forming the passive in various tenses, consult the chart on the next page. (For appropriate uses of the passive voice, see 8a.)

VERB TENSES COMMONLY USED IN THE PASSIVE VOICE

Simple tenses (passive voice)

Simple present   *am, is, are* + past participle

- general facts   Breakfast is *served* daily.
- habitual, repetitive actions   The receipts are *counted* every night.

Simple past   *was, were* + past participle

- completed past actions   He *was rewarded* for being on time.

Simple future   *will be* + past participle

- future actions, promises, or predictions   The decision *will be made* by the committee next week.

Simple progressive forms (passive voice)

Present progressive   *am, is, are* + *being* + past participle

- actions in progress at the present time   The new stadium *is being built* with private money.
- future actions   Jo *is being promoted* to a new job next month.

Past progressive   *was, were* + *being* + past participle

- actions in progress at a specific time in the past   We thought we *were being followed*.

Perfect tenses (passive voice)

Present perfect   *has, have* + *been* + past participle

- actions that began in the past and continue to the present   The store *has been closed* while the owners remodel the building.
- actions that happened at an unknown or unspecific time in the past   Wars *have been fought* throughout history.

Past perfect   *had* + *been* + past participle

- actions that began or occurred before another time in the past   He *had been given* all the hints he needed to complete the puzzle.

NOTE: Future progressive, future perfect, and perfect progressive forms are not used in the passive voice.

NOTE: Only transitive verbs, those that take direct objects, may be used in the passive voice. Intransitive verbs such as *occur*, *happen*, *sleep*, *die*, *become*, and *fall* are not used in the passive. (See 48b.)

▶ The accident ~~was~~ happened suddenly.

EXERCISE 28–1   Revise the following sentences to correct errors in verb forms and tenses in the active and the passive voice. You may need to look at 27a for the correct form of some irregular verbs and at 27f for help with tenses. Answers appear in the back of the book.

> begins
> The meeting ~~begin~~ tonight at 7:30.
> ⌃

a. In the past, tobacco companies deny any connection between smoking and health problems.

b. The volunteer's compassion has touch many lives.

c. I am wanting to register for a summer tutoring session.

d. By the end of the year, the state will have open a dozen career and employment centers.

e. The golfers were prepare for all weather conditions.

28c Use the base form of the verb after a modal.

The modal verbs are *can*, *could*, *may*, *might*, *must*, *should*, *will*, and *would*. (*Ought to* is also considered a modal verb.) The modals are used with the base form of a verb to show ability, certainty, necessity, permission, obligation, or possibility.

Modals and the verbs that follow them do not change form to indicate tense. For a summary of modals and their meanings, see the chart in this section. (See also 27e.)

> launch
> ▶ The art museum will ~~launches~~ its fundraising campaign
> ⌃
> next month.

> The modal *will* must be followed by the base form *launch*, not the present tense *launches*.

MODALS AND THEIR MEANINGS

can

- general ability (present)

  Ants *can survive* anywhere, even in space. Jorge *can run* a marathon faster than his brother.

- informal requests or permission

  Can you *tell* me where the light is? Sandy *can borrow* my calculator.

could

- general ability (past)

  Lea *could read* when she was only three years old.

- polite, informal requests or permission

  Could you *give* me that pen?

may

- formal requests or permission

  May I *see* the report? Students *may park* only in the yellow zone.

- possibility

  I *may try* to finish my homework tonight, or I *may wake up* early and *finish* it tomorrow.

might

- possibility

  Funding for the language lab *might double* by 2025.

NOTE: *Might* usually expresses a stronger possibility than *may*.

must

- necessity (present or future)

  To be effective, welfare-to-work programs *must provide* access to job training.

- strong probability

  Amy *must be* nervous. [She is probably nervous.]

- near certainty (present or past)

  I *must have left* my wallet at home. [I almost certainly left my wallet at home.]

should

- suggestions or advice

  Diabetics *should drink* plenty of water every day.

- obligations or duties

  The government *should protect* citizens' rights.

- expectations

  The books *should arrive* soon. [We expect the books to arrive soon.]

MODALS AND THEIR MEANINGS, continued	
will	
• certainty	If you don't leave now, you *will be* late for your rehearsal.
• requests	*Will* you *help* me study for my psychology exam?
• promises and offers	Jonah *will arrange* the carpool.
would	
• polite requests	*Would* you *help* me carry these books? I *would like* some coffee. [*Would like* is more polite than *want*.]
• habitual or repeated actions (past)	Whenever Elena needed help with sewing, she *would call* her aunt.

^{speak}
▶ The translator could ~~spoke~~ many languages, so the ambassador

hirer her for the European tour.

The modal *could* must be followed by the base form *speak*, not the past tense *spoke*.

For the use of modals in conditional sentences, see 28e.

EXERCISE 28–2   Edit the following sentences to correct errors in the use of verb forms with modals. You may find it helpful to consult the chart in section 28c. If a sentence is correct, write "correct" after it. Answers appear in the back of the book.

We should ~~to~~ order pizza for dinner.

a. A major league pitcher can to throw a baseball more than ninety-five miles per hour.
b. The writing center tutor will helps you revise your essay.
c. A reptile must adjusted its body temperature to its environment.
d. In some states, individuals may renew a driver's license online.
e. My uncle, a cartoonist, could sketched a face in less than two minutes.

28d To make negative verb forms, add *not*.

If the verb is the simple present or past tense of *be* (*am, is, are, was, were*), add *not* after the verb to form a negative statement.

> Gianna *is not* a member of the club.

For simple present-tense verbs other than *be*, use *do* or *does* plus *not* before the base form of the verb. (For the correct forms of *do* and *does*, see the subject-verb agreement chart on page 182.)

> ▶ Mariko ~~no~~ want more dessert.
>   ^ does not

> ▶ Mariko does not wants more dessert.

For simple past-tense verbs other than *be*, use *did* plus *not* before the base form of the verb.

> ▶ They did not ~~planted~~ corn this year.
>   ^ plant

In a verb phrase consisting of one or more helping verbs and a present or past participle (*is watching, were living, has played, could have been driven*), use the word *not* after the first helping verb.

> ▶ Inna should have ~~not~~ gone dancing last night.
>   ^ not

> ▶ Bonnie is ~~no~~ singing this weekend.
>   ^ not

NOTE: English uses only one negative in an independent clause to express a negative idea; using more than one is an error known as a *double negative* (see 26e).

> ▶ We could not find ~~no~~ books about the history of our school.
>   ^ any

28e In a conditional sentence, choose verb tenses according to the type of condition expressed in the sentence.

Conditional sentences contain two clauses: a subordinate clause (usually starting with *if, when,* or *unless*) and an independent clause. The subordinate clause (sometimes called the *if* or *unless* clause) states the condition or cause; the independent clause states the result or effect. In each example in this section, the subordinate clause (*if* clause) is marked SUB, and the independent clause is marked IND. (See 49e on subordinate clauses.)

Factual

Factual conditional sentences express relationships based on facts. If the relationship is a scientific truth, use the present tense in both clauses.

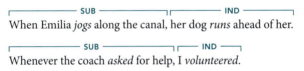

If water *cools* to 32 degrees Fahrenheit, it *freezes*.

If the sentence describes a condition that is (or was) habitually true, use the same tense in both clauses.

┌──────────── SUB ────────────┐┌──────────── IND ────────────┐
When Emilia *jogs* along the canal, her dog *runs* ahead of her.

┌──────────── SUB ────────────┐┌──────── IND ────────┐
Whenever the coach *asked* for help, I *volunteered*.

Predictive

Predictive conditional sentences are used to predict the future or to express future plans or possibilities. To form a predictive sentence, use a present-tense verb in the subordinate clause; in the independent clause, use the modal *will*, *can*, *may*, *should*, or *might* plus the base form of the verb.

┌──────── SUB ────────┐┌──────────── IND ────────────┐
If you *practice* regularly, your tennis game *should improve*.

┌──────────── IND ────────────┐┌──────── SUB ────────┐
We *will lose* our remaining wetlands unless we *act* now.

NOTE: In all types of conditional sentences (factual, predictive, and speculative), *if* or *unless* clauses do not use the modal verb *will*.

▶ If Jenna ~~will pass~~ her history test, she will graduate this year.

Speculative

Speculative conditional sentences express unlikely, contrary-to-fact, or impossible conditions. English uses the past or past perfect tense in the *if* clause, even for conditions in the present or the future.

Unlikely possibilities If the condition is possible but unlikely in the present or the future, use the past tense in the subordinate clause; in the independent clause, use *would*, *could*, or *might* plus the base form of the verb.

┌──── SUB ────┐ ┌──── IND ────┐
If I *won* the lottery, I *would buy* a home.

The writer does not expect to win the lottery. Because this is a possible but unlikely present or future situation, the past tense is used in the subordinate clause.

Conditions contrary to fact For conditions that are currently unreal or contrary to fact, use the past-tense verb *were* (not *was*) in the *if* clause for all subjects. (See also 27g on the subjunctive mood.)

▸ If I ~~was~~ *were* president, I would make student loan debt a priority.

The writer is not president, so *were* is correct in the *if* clause.

Events that did not happen In a conditional sentence that speculates about an event that did not happen or was impossible in the past, use the past perfect tense in the *if* clause; in the independent clause, use *would have*, *could have*, or *might have* with the past participle. (See also "past perfect tense" on p. 228.)

┌──── SUB ────┐ ┌──── IND ────┐
If I *had saved* more money, I *would have moved* last year.

The writer did not save more money and did not move. This sentence shows a possibility that did not happen.

EXERCISE 28–3 Edit the following sentences to correct problems with verbs. In some cases, more than one revision is possible. Possible revisions appear in the back of the book.

If I ~~have~~ *had* time, I would study both French and Russian next

semester.

a. The electrician might have discovered the broken circuit if she inspected the wires thoroughly.
b. If Verena wins a scholarship, she would go to graduate school.
c. Whenever a rainbow appears after a storm, everybody came out to see it.
d. Sarah did not understood the terms of her internship.
e. If I live in Budapest with my cousin Szusza, she would teach me Hungarian cooking.

28f Become familiar with verbs that may be followed by gerunds or infinitives.

A gerund is a verb form that ends in *-ing* and is used as a noun: *sleeping, dreaming*. An infinitive is the word *to* plus the base form of the verb: *to sleep, to dream*. The word *to* is an infinitive marker, not a preposition, in this use. (See 49b.)

A few verbs may be followed by either a gerund or an infinitive; others may be followed by a gerund but not by an infinitive; still others may be followed by an infinitive but not by a gerund.

Verb + gerund or infinitive (no change in meaning)

The following commonly used verbs may be followed by a gerund or an infinitive, with little or no difference in meaning:

begin	hate	love
continue	like	start

I love *skiing*. I love *to ski*.

Verb + gerund or infinitive (change in meaning)

With a few verbs, the choice of a gerund or an infinitive affects the meaning dramatically:

forget	remember	stop	try

She stopped *speaking* to Lucia. [She no longer spoke to Lucia.]
She stopped *to speak* to Lucia. [She paused so that she could speak to Lucia.]

Verb + gerund

These verbs may be followed by a gerund but not by an infinitive:

admit	discuss	imagine	put off	risk
appreciate	enjoy	miss	quit	suggest
avoid	escape	postpone	recall	tolerate
deny	finish	practice	resist	

Bill enjoys *playing* [not *to play*] the piano.
Jun quit *smoking*.

Verb + infinitive

These verbs may be followed by an infinitive but not by a gerund:

agree	decide	manage	plan	wait
ask	expect	mean	pretend	want
beg	help	need	promise	wish
claim	hope	offer	refuse	would like

Jill has offered *to water* [not *watering*] the plants while we are away.
Orlando finally managed *to find* a parking space.

A few of these verbs may be followed either by an infinitive directly or by a noun or pronoun plus an infinitive:

ask	help	promise	would like
expect	need	want	

We asked *to speak* to the congregation.
We asked *Rabbi Abrams to speak* to our congregation.

Verb + noun or pronoun + infinitive

With certain verbs in the active voice, a noun or pronoun must come between the verb and the infinitive that follows it. The noun or pronoun usually names a person who is affected by the action of the verb.

advise	convince	order	tell
allow	encourage	persuade	urge
cause	have (own)	remind	warn
command	instruct	require	

      V   N ⌐ INF ⌐

The class encouraged Luis to tell the story of his escape.

The counselor *advised Haley to take* four courses instead of five.

Verb + noun or pronoun + unmarked infinitive

An unmarked infinitive is an infinitive without *to*. A few verbs (often called *causative verbs*) may be followed by a noun or pronoun and an unmarked infinitive.

    have (cause)   let (allow)   make (force)

▶ **Rosa had the attendant ~~to~~ wash the windshield.**

Help can be followed by a noun or pronoun and either an unmarked or a marked infinitive.

Emma *helped Brian wash* the dishes.

Emma *helped Brian to wash* the dishes.

NOTE: The infinitive is used in some typical constructions with *too* and *enough*.

TOO + ADJECTIVE + INFINITIVE	The gift is *too large to wrap*.
ENOUGH + NOUN + INFINITIVE	Our emergency pack has *enough bottled water to last* a week.
ADJECTIVE + ENOUGH + INFINITIVE	Some of the hikers felt *strong enough to climb* another thousand feet.

EXERCISE 28–4   Form sentences by adding gerund or infinitive constructions to the following sentence openings. In some cases, more than one kind of construction is possible. Possible answers appear in the back of the book.

      Please remind   your sister to call me.
                 ^

a. I enjoy

b. The tutor told Samantha

c. The team hopes

d. Ricardo and his brothers miss

e. Jon remembered

29 Articles (*a, an, the*)

Articles (*a, an, the*) are part of a category of words known as *noun markers* or *determiners*.

29a Be familiar with articles and other noun markers.

English uses noun markers to help identify the nouns that follow. In addition to articles (*a, an,* and *the*), noun markers include the following, which are covered in other sections of this book:

- possessive nouns, such as *Elena's* (see 37a)
- possessive pronoun/adjectives: *my, your, his, her, its, our, their* (see 47b)
- demonstrative pronoun/adjectives: *this, that, these, those* (see 47b)
- quantifiers: *all, any, each, either, every, few, many, more, most, much, neither, several, some,* and so on (see 29d)
- numbers: *one, twenty-three,* and so on

Using articles and other noun markers

Articles and other noun markers always appear before nouns; sometimes other modifiers, such as adjectives, come between a noun marker and a noun.

        ART N
Felix is reading a book about mythology.

       ART   ADJ   N
We took an exciting trip to Alaska when I was a child.

NOUN
MARKER ADV   ADJ   N
That very delicious meal was made from her grandmother's recipe.

In most cases, do not use an article with another noun marker.

> ~~The~~ Natalie's older brother lives in Wisconsin.

Expressions like *a few*, *the most*, and *all the* are exceptions: *a few potatoes*, *all the rain*. See also 29d.

Types of articles and types of nouns

To choose an appropriate article for a noun, first determine whether the noun is *common* or *proper*, *count* or *noncount*, *singular* or *plural*, and *specific* or *general*. The chart in 29b describes the types of nouns.

Articles are classified as *indefinite* and *definite*. The indefinite articles, *a* and *an*, are used with general nouns. The definite article, *the*, is used with specific nouns. (The last section of the chart in 29b explains general and specific nouns.)

A and *an* both mean "one" or "one among many." Use *a* before a consonant sound: *a banana*, *a vacation*, *a picture*, *a happy child*, *a united family*. Use *an* before a vowel sound: *an eggplant*, *an occasion*, *an uncle*, *an honorable person*. (See also 10d.)

The shows that a noun is specific; use *the* with one or more than one specific thing: *the newspaper*, *the soldiers*.

29b Use *the* with most specific common nouns.

The definite article, *the*, is used with most nouns — both count and noncount — that the reader can identify specifically. Usually the identity will be clear to the reader for one of the following reasons. (See also the first chart in 29c.)

1. The noun has been previously mentioned.

> A truck cut in front of our van. When ^the^ truck skidded a few
>
> seconds later, we almost crashed into it.

The article *A* is used before *truck* when the noun is first mentioned. When the noun is mentioned again, it needs the article *the* because readers can now identify which truck skidded — the one that cut in front of the van.

2. A phrase or clause following the noun restricts its identity.

► Bryce warned me that ~~the~~ radio in his car was not working.

The phrase *in his car* identifies the specific radio.

NOTE: Descriptive adjectives do not necessarily make a noun specific. A specific noun is one that readers can identify within a group of nouns of the same type.

► If I win the lottery, I will buy ~~the~~ *a* brand-new bright red

sports car.

The reader cannot identify which specific brand-new bright red sports car the writer will buy. Even though *car* has many adjectives in front of it, it is a general noun in this sentence.

3. A superlative adjective such as *best* or *most intelligent* makes the noun's identity specific. (See also 26d.)

► Our petite daughter dated *the* tallest boy in her class.

The superlative *tallest* makes the noun *boy* specific. Although there might be several tall boys, only one boy can be the tallest.

4. The noun describes a unique person, place, or thing.

► During an eclipse, one should not look directly at *the* sun.

There is only one sun in our solar system, so its identity is clear.

5. The context or situation makes the noun's identity clear.

► Please don't slam *the* door when you leave.

Both the speaker and the listener know which door is meant.

6. The noun is singular and refers to a scientific class or category of items (most often animals, musical instruments, and inventions).

► ~~Tin~~ *The tin* whistle is common in traditional Irish music.

The writer is referring to the tin whistle as a class of musical instruments.

TYPES OF NOUNS

Common or proper

Common nouns	**Examples**	
• name general persons, places, things, or ideas	religion	beauty
	knowledge	student
• begin with lowercase letters	rain	country

Proper nouns	**Examples**	
• name specific persons, places, things, or ideas	Hinduism	President Adams
	Philip	Blue Mosque
• begin with capital letters	Vietnam	Renaissance

Count or noncount (common nouns only)

Count nouns	**Examples**
• name persons, places, things, or ideas that can be counted	girl, girls
	city, cities
	goose, geese
• have plural forms	philosophy, philosophies

Noncount nouns	**Examples**	
• name things or abstract ideas that cannot be counted	water	patience
	silver	knowledge
	furniture	air
• cannot be made plural		

NOTE: See the second chart in 29c for commonly used noncount nouns.

Singular or plural (both common and proper)

Singular nouns (count and noncount)	**Examples**	
• represent one person, place, thing, or idea	backpack	rain
	country	beauty
	woman	Nile River
	achievement	Block Island

Plural nouns (count only)	**Examples**	
• represent more than one person, place, thing, or idea	backpacks	Ural Mountains
	countries	Falkland Islands
• must be count nouns	women	achievements

TYPES OF NOUNS, continued

Specific (definite) or general (indefinite) (count and noncount)

Specific nouns	Examples
• name persons, places, things, or ideas that can be identified within a group of the same type	*The students* in Professor Martin's *class* should study. *The airplane* carrying *the senator* was late. *The furniture* in *the truck* was damaged.

General nouns	Examples
• name categories of persons, places, things, or ideas (often plural)	*Students* should study. *Books* bridge *gaps* between *cultures*. *The airplane* has made commuting between *cities* easy.

29c Use *a* (or *an*) with common singular count nouns that refer to "one" or "any."

If a count noun refers to an unspecific item (not a whole category), use the indefinite article, *a* or *an*. *A* and *an* can mean "one among many" or "any one." (See the chart below.)

▶ My English professor asked me to bring ^*a*^ dictionary to class.

  The noun *dictionary* refers to "any dictionary."

▶ We want to rent ^*an*^ apartment close to the lake.

  The noun *apartment* refers to "any apartment close to the lake," not a specific apartment.

CHOOSING ARTICLES FOR COMMON NOUNS

Use *the*

• if the reader has enough information to identify the noun specifically	**COUNT:** Please turn on *the lights*. We're going to *the lake* tomorrow. **NONCOUNT:** *The food* throughout Italy is excellent.

Use *a* or *an*

• if the noun refers to one item *and* • if the item is singular but not specific	**COUNT:** Bring *a pencil* to class. Charles wrote *an essay* about his first job.

NOTE: Do not use *a* or *an* with plural or noncount nouns.

CHOOSING ARTICLES FOR COMMON NOUNS, continued

Use a quantifier (*enough, many, some,* etc.)

- if the noun represents an unspecified amount of something

  COUNT (plural): Amir showed us *some photos* of India. *Many turtles* return to the same nesting site each year.

- if the amount is more than one but not all items in a category

  NONCOUNT: We didn't get *enough rain* this summer.

NOTE: Sometimes no article conveys an unspecified amount: *Amir showed us photos of India.*

Use no article

- if the noun represents all items in a category

  COUNT (plural): *Students* can attend the show for free.

- if the noun represents a category in general

  NONCOUNT: *Coal* is a natural resource.

NOTE: *The* is occasionally used when a singular count noun refers to all items in a class or a specific category: *The bald eagle is no longer endangered in the United States.*

COMMONLY USED NONCOUNT NOUNS

Food and drink

beef, bread, butter, candy, cereal, cheese, cream, meat, milk, pasta, rice, salt, sugar, water, wine

Nonfood substances

air, cement, coal, dirt, gasoline, gold, paper, petroleum, plastic, rain, silver, snow, soap, steel, wood, wool

Abstract nouns

advice, anger, beauty, confidence, courage, employment, fun, happiness, health, honesty, information, intelligence, knowledge, love, poverty, satisfaction, wealth

Use no article

biology (and other areas of study), clothing, equipment, furniture, homework, jewelry, luggage, machinery, mail, money, news, poetry, pollution, research, scenery, traffic, transportation, violence, weather, work

NOTE: A few noncount nouns (such as *love*) can also be used as count nouns: *He had two loves: music and archery.*

29d Use a quantifier, not *a* or *an*, with a noncount noun to express an approximate amount.

Do not use *a* or *an* with noncount nouns. Also do not use numbers or words such as *several* or *many*; they must be used with plural nouns, and noncount nouns do not have plural forms. (See page 245 for a list of commonly used noncount nouns.)

▶ Dr. Snyder gave us ~~an~~ information about the Peace Corps.

▶ Do you have ~~many~~ money with you?

You can use quantifiers such as *enough*, *less*, and *some* to suggest approximate amounts or nonspecific quantities of noncount nouns: *a little salt, any homework, enough wood, less information.*

29e Use no article with nouns that refer to all of something or something in general.

When a noncount noun refers to all of its type or to a concept in general, it is not marked with an article.

Kindness
▶ ~~The kindness~~ is a virtue.
  ^

The noun represents kindness in general; it does not represent a specific type of kindness, such as *the kindness he showed me after my surgery.*

▶ In some parts of the world, ~~the~~ rice is preferred to all other grains.

The noun *rice* represents rice in general. To refer to a specific type or serving of rice, use the definite article: *The rice my husband served last night is the best I've ever tasted.*

In most cases, when you use a count noun to represent a general category, make the noun plural. Do not use unmarked singular count nouns to represent whole categories.

Fountains are
▶ ~~Fountain is~~ an expensive element of landscape design.
  ^

Fountains is a count noun that represents fountains in general.

EXCEPTION: In some cases, *the* can be used with singular count nouns to represent a class or specific category: *The Chinese alligator is smaller than the American alligator.* See number 6 in 29b.

29f Use no article with most singular proper nouns; use *the* with most plural proper nouns.

Since singular proper nouns are already specific, they typically do not need an article: *Chancellor Merkel, Jamaica, Lake Huron, Mount Etna.*

There are, however, many exceptions. In most cases, if the proper noun consists of a common noun with modifiers (adjectives or an *of* phrase), use *the* with the proper noun.

▶ We visited ^the^ Great Wall of China during our honeymoon.

▶ Imelda wants to be a translator for ^the^ Central Intelligence Agency.

The is used with most plural proper nouns: *the McGregors, the Bahamas, the Finger Lakes, the United States.*

Geographic names create problems because there are so many exceptions to the rules. When in doubt, consult the chart below, check a dictionary, or ask a native speaker.

USING *THE* WITH GEOGRAPHIC NOUNS

When to omit *the*

streets, squares, parks	Ivy Street, Union Square, Denali National Park
cities, states, counties	Miami, New Mexico, Bee County
most countries, continents	Italy, Nigeria, China, South America, Africa
bays, single lakes	Tampa Bay, Lake Geneva
single mountains, islands	Mount Everest, Crete

When to use *the*

country names with *of* phrase	the United States (of America), the People's Republic of China
large regions, deserts	the East Coast, the Sahara
peninsulas	the Baja Peninsula, the Sinai Peninsula
oceans, seas, gulfs	the Pacific Ocean, the Dead Sea, the Persian Gulf
canals and rivers	the Panama Canal, the Amazon
mountain ranges	the Rocky Mountains, the Alps
groups of islands	the Solomon Islands

~~The~~ Josefina's dance routine was flawless.

a. Doing volunteer work often brings a satisfaction.
b. Although Gemma now lives on the West Coast, she grew up in the Cape Cod.
c. Melina likes to drink her coffees with lots of cream.
d. Recovering from abdominal surgery requires patience.
e. I completed the my homework assignment quickly.

30 Sentence structure

Although their structure can vary, sentences in English generally flow from subject to verb to object or complement: *Bears eat fish.* This section focuses on the major challenges that multilingual students face when writing sentences in English. For more details on parts of speech and parts of sentences, see sections 47–50.

30a Use a linking verb between a subject and its complement.

Some languages, such as Russian and Turkish, do not use linking verbs (*is*, *are*, *was*, *were*) between subjects and complements (nouns or adjectives that rename or describe the subject). Every English sentence, however, must include a verb. For more on linking verbs, see 27e.

▶ Jim ^is^ intelligent.

▶ Many streets in San Francisco ^are^ very steep.

30b Include a subject in every sentence.

Some languages, such as Spanish and Japanese, do not require a subject in every sentence. Every English sentence, however, needs a subject.

► Your aunt is very energetic. ~~Seems~~ young for her age.
   She seems

Commands are an exception: The subject *you* is understood but not present in the sentence ([*You*] *Give me the book*).

The word *it* is used as the subject of a sentence describing the weather or temperature, stating the time, indicating distance, or suggesting an environmental fact.

► ~~Is~~ raining in the valley and snowing in the mountains.
   It is

► ~~Is~~ 9:15 a.m.
   It is

In most English sentences, the subject appears before the verb. Some sentences, however, are inverted: The subject comes after the verb. In these sentences, a placeholder called an *expletive* (*there* or *it*) often comes before the verb.

EXP V ⌐— S —⌐   ⌐— S —⌐ V
There are many people here today. (Many people are here today.)

► ~~Is~~ an apple pie in the refrigerator.
   There is

► As you know, ⌃ many religious sects in India.
   there are

Notice that the verb agrees with the subject that follows it: *apple pie is, sects are.* (See 21g.)

Sometimes an inverted sentence has an infinitive (*to work*) or a noun clause (*that she is intelligent*) as the subject. In such sentences, the placeholder *it* is needed before the verb. (See also 49b and 49e.)

EXP V   ⌐ S ⌐   ⌐ S ⌐   V
It is important to study daily. (To study daily is important.)

► Because the road is flooded, ⌃ is necessary to change our route.
   it

NOTE: The words *here* and *there* can be used as placeholders. When they mean "in this place" (*here*) or "in that place" (*there*), they are adverbs, which are never subjects.

▶ ~~Here~~ ^{This school} offers a master's degree in physical therapy; ~~there~~ ^{that school} has only a

bachelor's program.

30c Avoid using both a noun and a pronoun to play the same grammatical role in a sentence.

Do not repeat a subject in its own clause.

▶ The doctor ~~she~~ advised me to cut down on salt.

The pronoun *she* cannot repeat the subject, *doctor*.

Do not add a pronoun even when a word group comes between the subject and the verb.

▶ The watch that I lost on vacation ~~it~~ was in my backpack.

The pronoun *it* cannot repeat the subject, *watch*.

Some languages allow "topic fronting," placing a word or phrase (a "topic") at the beginning of a sentence and following it with an independent clause that explains something about the topic. This form is not allowed in English because the sentence seems to start with one subject but then introduces a new subject in an independent clause.

           ┌─ TOPIC ─┐┌──── IND CLAUSE ────┐
INCORRECT   The seeds I planted them last fall.

The sentence can be corrected by bringing the topic (*seeds*) into the independent clause.

▶ ~~The seeds~~ I planted ~~them~~ ^{the seeds} last fall.

30d Avoid repeating a subject, an object, or an adverb in an adjective clause.

Adjective clauses begin with relative pronouns (*who, whom, whose, which, that*) or relative adverbs (*when, where*). Relative pronouns usually serve as subjects or objects in the clauses they introduce; another word in the clause cannot serve the same function. Relative adverbs should not be repeated by other adverbs later in the clause.

———— ADJ CLAUSE ————
The cat ran under the car that was parked on the street.

▶ **The cat ran under the car that it̶ was parked on the street.**

The relative pronoun *that* is the subject of the adjective clause, so the pronoun *it* cannot be added as a subject.

Sometimes the relative pronoun is understood but not present in the sentence. In such cases, do not add another word with the same function as the omitted pronoun.

▶ **Myrna enjoyed the seminars she attended t̶h̶e̶m̶ last week.**

The relative pronoun *that* is understood after *seminars* even though it is not present in the sentence.

EXERCISE 30–1 In the following sentences, add needed subjects or expletives and delete any repeated subjects, objects, or adverbs. Answers appear in the back of the book.

The new geology professor is the one whom we saw h̶i̶m̶ on TV this morning.

a. Are some cartons of ice cream in the freezer.
b. I don't use the subway because am afraid.
c. The prime minister she is the most popular leader in my country.
d. We tried to get in touch with the same manager whom we spoke to him earlier.
e. Recently have been a number of earthquakes in Turkey.

30e Avoid placing an adverb between a verb and its direct object.

Adverbs modifying verbs can appear in various positions: at the beginning or end of a sentence, before or after a verb, or between a helping verb and its main verb.

> *Slowly*, we drove along the rain-slick road.

> Martin handled the teapot very *carefully*.

> Mia *always* wins our tennis matches.

> Christina is *rarely* late for our lunch dates.

However, an adverb cannot appear between a verb and its direct object.

carefully
▶ Mother wrapped ~~carefully~~ the gift.
        ^

The adverb *carefully* cannot appear between the verb, *wrapped*, and its direct object, *the gift*.

30f Distinguish between present participles and past participles used as adjectives.

Both present and past participles may be used as adjectives. The present participle always ends in *-ing*. Past participles usually end in *-ed, -d, -en, -n,* or *-t*. (See 27a.)

PRESENT PARTICIPLES	confusing, speaking, boring
PAST PARTICIPLES	confused, spoken, bored

Like all other adjectives, participles can come before nouns; they also can follow linking verbs, in which case they describe the subject of the sentence. (See 48b.)

Use a present participle to describe a person or thing *causing or stimulating an experience*.

> The *boring lecture* put us to sleep. [The lecture caused boredom.]

Use a past participle to describe a person or thing *undergoing an experience*.

> The *audience* was *bored* by the lecture. [The audience experienced boredom.]

Participles that describe emotions or mental states often cause the most confusion.

annoying/annoyed	exhausting/exhausted
boring/bored	fascinating/fascinated
confusing/confused	frightening/frightened
exciting/excited	surprising/surprised

EXERCISE 30–2   Edit the following sentences for proper use of present and past participles. If a sentence is correct, write "correct" after it. Answers appear in the back of the book.

excited
Danielle and Monica were very ~~exciting~~ to be going to a

Broadway show for their anniversary.

a.   Listening to everyone's complaints all day was irritated.
b.   The all-day online classes were exhausted.
c.   His skill at chess is amazing.
d.   After a great deal of research, the scientist made a fascinated discovery.
e.   Surviving that tornado was one of the most frightened experiences I've ever had.

30g Place cumulative adjectives in an appropriate order.

Adjectives usually come before the nouns they modify; they may also come after linking verbs. (See 47d and 48b.)

ADJ   N   V   ADJ
Janine wore a new necklace. Janine's necklace was new.

Cumulative adjectives are adjectives that build on one another, cannot be joined by the word *and*, and are not separated by commas. These adjectives must be listed in a particular order. If you use cumulative adjectives before a noun, see the chart in this section.

stained red plastic
▶ **My dorm room has only a bed and a ~~plastic red stained~~ chair.**

ORDER OF CUMULATIVE ADJECTIVES

FIRST

ARTICLE OR OTHER NOUN MARKER a, an, the, her, Joe's, two, many, some

EVALUATIVE WORD attractive, dedicated, delicious, ugly, disgusting

SIZE large, enormous, small, little

LENGTH OR SHAPE long, short, round, square

AGE new, old, young, antique

COLOR yellow, blue, crimson

NATIONALITY French, Peruvian, Vietnamese

RELIGION Catholic, Protestant, Jewish, Muslim

MATERIAL silver, walnut, wool, marble

LAST

NOUN/ADJECTIVE tree (as in *tree* house), kitchen (as in *kitchen* table)

THE NOUN MODIFIED house, coat, bicycle, bread, woman, coin

My large blue wool **coat** *is in the attic.*

EXERCISE 30–3   Using the chart in 30g as necessary, arrange the following modifiers and nouns in their proper order. Answers appear in the back of the book.

> two new French racing bicycles
> **new, French, two, bicycles, racing**

a.   sculptor, young, an, Vietnamese, intelligent

b.   dedicated, a, priest, Catholic

c.   old, her, sweater, blue, wool

d.   delicious, Elias's, Scandinavian, bread

e.   many, boxes, jewelry, antique, beautiful

31 | Prepositions and idiomatic expressions

31a Become familiar with prepositions that show time and place.

The most frequently used prepositions in English are *at*, *by*, *for*, *from*, *in*, *of*, *on*, *to*, and *with*. Prepositions can be difficult to master because the differences among them are subtle and idiomatic. The chart in this section is limited to three troublesome prepositions that show time and place: *at*, *on*, and *in*.

AT, ON, AND *IN* TO SHOW TIME AND PLACE

Showing time

AT	*at* a specific time: *at* 7:20, *at* dawn, *at* dinner
ON	*on* a specific day or date: *on* Tuesday, *on* June 4
IN	*in* a part of a 24-hour period: *in* the afternoon, *in* the daytime [but *at* night]
	in a year or month: *in* 2008, *in* July
	in a period of time: finished *in* three hours

Showing place

AT	*at* a meeting place or location: *at* home, *at* the club
	at the edge of something: sitting *at* the desk
	at the corner of something: turning *at* the intersection
	at a target: throwing the snowball *at* Lucy
ON	*on* a surface: placed *on* the table, hanging *on* the wall
	on a street: the house *on* Spring Street
	on an electronic medium: *on* television, *on* the Internet
IN	*in* an enclosed space: *in* the garage, *in* an envelope
	in a geographic location: *in* San Diego, *in* Texas
	in a print medium: *in* a book, *in* a magazine

Not every possible use is listed in the chart, so don't be surprised when you encounter exceptions and idiomatic uses that you must learn one at a time. For example, in English a person rides *in* a car but *on* a bus, plane, train, or subway.

> **EXERCISE 31–1**   In the following sentences, replace prepositions that are not used correctly. You may need to refer to the chart in 31a. If a sentence is correct, write "correct" after it. Answers appear in the back of the book.

>   *at*
> **The play begins ~~on~~ 7:20 p.m.**
>   ^

a. Whenever we eat at the Centerville Café, we sit at a small table on the corner of the patio.

b. In the 1990s, entrepreneurs created new online businesses in record numbers.

c. In Thursday, Nancy will attend her first home repair class at the community center.

d. Alex began looking for her lost mitten in another location.

e. We decided to go to the grocery store because there was no fresh food on the refrigerator.

31b Use nouns (including *-ing* forms) after prepositions.

In a prepositional phrase, use a noun (not a verb) after the preposition. Sometimes the noun will be a gerund, the *-ing* verb form that functions as a noun (see 49b).

>   *saving*
> ▶ **Our student government is good at ~~save~~ money.**
>   ^

Distinguish between the preposition *to* and the infinitive marker *to*. If *to* is a preposition, it should be followed by a noun or a gerund.

>   *helping*
> ▶ **We are dedicated to ~~help~~ our neighbors.**
>   ^

If *to* is an infinitive marker, it should be followed by the base form of the verb.

▶ We want to ~~helping~~ our neighbors.
       help ^

To test whether *to* is a preposition or an infinitive marker, insert a word that you know is a noun after the word *to*. If the noun makes sense in that position, *to* is a preposition. If the noun does not make sense after *to*, then *to* is an infinitive marker.

> Zoe is addicted *to* _____.
> They are planning *to* _____.

In the first sentence, a noun (such as *magazines*) makes sense after *to*, so *to* is a preposition and should be followed by a noun or a gerund: Zoe is addicted *to magazines*. Zoe is addicted *to running*.

In the second sentence, a noun (such as *magazines*) does not make sense after *to*, so *to* is an infinitive marker and must be followed by the base form of the verb: They are planning *to build* a new school.

31c Become familiar with common adjective + preposition combinations.

Some adjectives appear only with certain prepositions. These expressions are idiomatic and may be different from the combinations used in your native language.

▶ Paula is married ~~with~~ Mateo.
             to ^

31d Become familiar with common verb + preposition combinations.

Many verbs and prepositions appear together in idiomatic phrases. Pay special attention to the combinations that are different from the combinations used in your native language.

▶ Your success depends ~~of~~ your effort.
                on ^

ADJECTIVE + PREPOSITION COMBINATIONS

accustomed to	connected to	guilty of	preferable to
addicted to	covered with	interested in	proud of
afraid of	dedicated to	involved in	responsible
angry with	devoted to	involved with	for
ashamed of	different from	known as	satisfied with
aware of	engaged in	known for	scared of
committed to	engaged to	made of (or	similar to
concerned	excited about	made from)	tired of
about	familiar with	married to	worried
concerned with	full of	opposed to	about

NOTE: Check an ESL dictionary for other combinations.

VERB + PREPOSITION COMBINATIONS

agree with	compare with	forget about	speak to (or
apply to	concentrate on	happen to	speak with)
approve of	consist of	hope for	stare at
arrive at	count on	insist on	succeed at
arrive in	decide on	listen to	succeed in
ask for	depend on	participate in	take advantage of
believe in	differ from	rely on	take care of
belong to	disagree with	reply to	think about
care about	dream about	respond to	think of
care for	dream of	result in	wait for
compare to	feel like	search for	wait on

NOTE: Check an ESL dictionary for other combinations.

32 Paraphrasing sources effectively

Effective paraphrasing is an important skill for writing in college. However, learning how to paraphrase can be challenging because some of the vocabulary may be new and unfamiliar to multilingual writers.

The purpose of paraphrasing is to restate an author's ideas in your own words. Most writers find the following process for paraphrasing useful:

1. Read and understand the text.
2. Put the text aside.
3. Express the information in your own words.
4. Compare your paraphrase to the original text to check that you have used different words and different sentence structures but have kept the author's meaning.

This process provides an effective way to paraphrase. However, it requires that the writer have a large vocabulary and well-developed sentence-writing abilities. Sometimes it's hard to find the right words to paraphrase a sentence or to know whether a paraphrase has the same meaning as the original source.

The following sections provide rules of thumb that can help you develop skill with paraphrasing. For more on how to paraphrase effectively, see 52c, 55d, and 56a.

32a Avoid replacing a source's words with synonyms.

Learning to paraphrase will help you communicate the ideas of authors effectively and avoid plagiarism — using another person's ideas or words without giving credit to that person. However, even if you tell your reader that information comes from another author, you still plagiarize if you change only the words but do not make the *presentation* of the information your own.

Some writers misinterpret the instructions to "use your own words"; they simply replace words in the source with synonyms, words that have similar meanings. Such word-by-word paraphrases frequently result in awkward sentence structures and inaccuracy. Meaning in English often comes from phrases and sentences rather than from individual words. Also, synonyms have similar meanings, but they rarely have *identical* meanings. Sometimes a synonym requires a different sentence structure than the original word does.

The following examples illustrate some of the problems that can arise with word-by-word paraphrasing.

Here is a short passage from Rebecca Webber's article "Make Your Own Luck."

ORIGINAL SOURCE

People who spot and seize opportunity are different. They are more open to life's forking paths, so they see possibilities others miss. And if things don't work out the way they'd hoped, they brush off disappointment and launch themselves headlong toward the next fortunate circumstance. As a result, they're happier and more likely to achieve their goals.

— Rebecca Webber, "Make Your Own Luck," p. 64

The following is a word-by-word paraphrase of the highlighted sentences.

INEFFECTIVE PARAPHRASE: MEANING CHANGED

Persons who see and grab chances are diverse. They are further exposed to life's dividing trails, and they view prospects others ignore.

The first problem with this paraphrase is that the student who wrote it used the same sentence structure as in the original passage. Because she did not use her own sentence structure, this paraphrase is plagiarized. Second, the words that the student substituted are not exact synonyms, so the paraphrase has lost some of the meaning of the original passage.

- The word *grab* is an informal synonym of the word *seize* and may not be acceptable in an academic paper.

- *Diverse* and *different* have similar, but not identical, meanings. The word *different* in the original passage implies that people who are open to opportunities are different from people who are not open to opportunities. Using *diverse* in this context implies that people who welcome opportunity are different from one another. Using *diverse* distorts the meaning of the sentence.

- Using *exposed* instead of *open* changes the meaning in a significant way. *Exposed* implies that something negative has happened to these people, while *open* is a positive character trait.

The following paraphrase of the underlined sentence demonstrates another potential problem with word-by-word paraphrases. Using synonyms often requires changing the surrounding sentence structure because the same word can be more than one part of speech. For example, *work* can be either a noun or a verb; in the following paraphrase, the student has substituted the noun *effort* for the verb *work*, which is not an effective substitution.

INEFFECTIVE PARAPHRASE: AWKWARD RESULT

And if everything don't effort out the manner they'd wanted, they rebuff disappointment and throw themselves impulsive toward the next lucky situation.

- When the student changed *things* to *everything*, she also needed to change the verb from the plural form (*don't*) to the singular form (*doesn't*).
- Using *effort* in place of *work* is not effective. *Effort* is a synonym for the noun *work* but not a synonym for the verb *work*. The part of speech of a word is an important consideration when choosing a synonym.
- When the student substituted *manner* for *way*, she should have used a different structure: *in the manner*.
- Although *headlong* has a similar meaning to *impulsive*, in the original passage *headlong* is an adverb modifying the verb *launch*; *impulsive* is an adjective. An adjective cannot replace an adverb in a sentence.

32b Determine the meaning of the original source.

Rather than trying to paraphrase word for word within each sentence, a better approach is to look at an entire passage and try to understand its meaning as well as how the information is organized before you try to present it in your own words. Look at the meaning of each phrase or clause rather than just the meaning of each word.

ORIGINAL SOURCE

People who spot and seize opportunity are different. They are more open to life's forking paths, so they see possibilities others miss. And if things don't work out the way they'd hoped, they brush off disappointment and launch themselves headlong toward the next fortunate circumstance. As a result, they're happier and more likely to achieve their goals.

The topic sentence of a paragraph is important. The topic sentence here (the first sentence in the paragraph) tells you about a particular group of people; from the title of the article, you can tell that Webber is talking about people who create their own luck. Lucky people, according to the author, have different characteristics from people who are not lucky. The rest of the paragraph then describes how lucky people are different.

Here is the original passage as the student writer annotated it. She worked through the original passage, repeatedly asking herself, "What is the author's point here?"

ORIGINAL SOURCE WITH STUDENT ANNOTATIONS

⌐— Lucky people?
People who spot and seize opportunity are different. They are
⌐— More willing to take risks?
more open to life's forking paths, so they see possibilities others

miss. And if things don't work out the way they'd hoped, they
⌐— Don't get discouraged/upset   keep looking? —⌐
brush off disappointment and launch themselves headlong

toward the next fortunate circumstance. As a result, they're
⌐— More positive personalities overall
happier and more likely to achieve their goals.

32c Present the author's meaning in your own words.

If you analyze a paragraph in its entirety rather than look at each word individually, you should be able to organize your information differently from the way the original author did and write a better paraphrase. As you analyze a source, you may still need to figure out the meaning of certain words, but do not focus on word-for-word substitutions. Here is one student's paraphrase of Rebecca Webber's work using her annotations of the text (see 32b).

EFFECTIVE PARAPHRASE

Individuals notice and respond to life's chances in different ways. Some people notice opportunities that other people might not notice, they are more willing to take risks, and they do not get discouraged if their decisions do not work out. Because they do not get discouraged easily, they are able to stay positive and content and to continue to search enthusiastically for the next opportunity (Webber 64).

This paraphrase presents the student's understanding of the author's meaning — without using words or sentence structure from the original. Notice that the paraphrase includes a citation. The idea is still Webber's idea, so a citation is needed, but the student uses her own words to communicate the information from Webber's article.

Punctuation

33 The comma

The comma was invented to help readers. Without it, sentence parts can collide into one another unexpectedly, causing misreadings.

> CONFUSING   If you cook Elmer will do the dishes.
>
> CONFUSING   While we were eating a rattlesnake
>   approached our campsite.

Add commas in the logical places (after *cook* and *eating*), and suddenly all is clear. No longer is Elmer being cooked, the rattlesnake being eaten.

Various rules have evolved to prevent such misreadings and to speed readers along through complex grammatical structures. Those rules are detailed in this section. (Section 34 explains when not to use commas.)

33a Use a comma before a coordinating conjunction joining independent clauses.

When a coordinating conjunction connects two or more independent clauses — word groups that could stand alone as separate sentences — a comma must precede the conjunction. There are seven coordinating conjunctions in English: *and, but, or, nor, for, so,* and *yet.*

A comma tells readers that one independent clause has come to a close and that another is about to begin.

▸ **The department sponsored a seminar on college survival skills**,

  and it also hosted a barbecue for new students.

EXCEPTION: If the two independent clauses are short and there is no danger of misreading, the comma may be omitted: *The plane took off and we were on our way.*

NOTE: Do *not* use a comma with a coordinating conjunction that joins only two words, phrases, or subordinate clauses. (See 34a.)

▶ A good money manager controls expenses/and invests surplus

dollars to meet future needs.

The word group following *and* is not an independent clause; it is the
second half of a compound predicate (*controls . . . and invests*).

33b Use a comma after an introductory clause or phrase.

The most common introductory word groups are clauses and
phrases functioning as adverbs. Such word groups usually tell
when, where, how, why, or under what conditions the main action of the sentence occurred. (See 49a, 49b, and 49e.)

A comma tells readers that the introductory clause or phrase
has come to a close and that the main part of the sentence is
about to begin.

▶ When Irwin was ready to iron, his cat tripped on the cord.
                                  ^

Without the comma, readers may think that Irwin is about to iron his
cat. The comma signals that *his cat* is the subject of a new clause, not
part of the introductory one.

EXCEPTION: The comma may be left out after a short adverb
clause or phrase if there is no danger of misreading: *In no time
we were at 2,800 feet.*

Sentences also frequently begin with participial phrases that
function as adjectives, describing the noun or pronoun immediately following them. The comma tells readers that they are about
to learn the identity of the person or thing described; therefore,
the comma is usually required even when the phrase is short.
(See 49b.)

▶ Buried under layers of younger rocks, the earth's oldest rocks
                                      ^

contain no fossils.

NOTE: Other introductory word groups include transitional
expressions and absolute phrases (see 33f).

EXERCISE 33–1   Add or delete commas where necessary in the following sentences. If a sentence is correct, write "correct" after it. Answers appear in the back of the book.

> **Because we had been saving molding for a few weeks, we had**
>
> **enough wood to frame all thirty paintings.**

a. Alisa brought the injured bird home, and fashioned a splint out of Popsicle sticks for its wing.

b. Considered a classic of early animation *The Adventures of Prince Achmed* used hand-cut silhouettes against colored backgrounds.

c. If you complete the evaluation form and return it within two weeks you will receive a free breakfast during your next stay.

d. After retiring from the New York City Ballet in 1965, legendary dancer Maria Tallchief went on to found the Chicago City Ballet.

e. As an intern, I learned most aspects of the broadcasting industry but I never learned about fundraising.

33c   Use a comma between all items in a series.

When three or more items are presented in a series, those items should be separated from one another with commas. Items in a series may be single words, phrases, or clauses.

> ▶ **Langston Hughes's poetry is concerned with racial pride, social**
>
> **justice, and the diversity of the Black American experience.**

Although some writers view the last comma in a series as optional, most experts advise using the comma because its omission can result in ambiguity or misreading.

> ▶ **The wildfire destroyed all of our property, barns, and farm**
>
> **equipment.**

Did the wildfire destroy the property *and* barns *and* farm equipment — or simply the property, consisting of barns and farm equipment? If the former meaning is intended, a comma is necessary to prevent ambiguity.

33d Use a comma between coordinate adjectives not joined with *and*.

When two or more adjectives each modify a noun separately, they are coordinate.

> Roberto is a *warm, gentle, affectionate* father.

If the adjectives can be joined with *and*, the adjectives are coordinate, so you should use commas: *warm* and *gentle* and *affectionate* (*warm, gentle, affectionate*).

NOTE: Do not use a comma between cumulative adjectives, those that do not each modify the noun separately.

> *Three large gray* shapes moved slowly toward us.

Cumulative adjectives cannot be joined with *and* (not *three* and *large* and *gray shapes*).

EXERCISE 33–2 Add or delete commas where necessary in the following sentences. If a sentence is correct, write "correct" after it. Answers appear in the back of the book.

> We gathered our essentials, took off for the great outdoors, and
>
> ignored the fact that it was Friday the 13th.

a. The cold impersonal atmosphere of the university was unbearable.
b. An ambulance threaded its way through police cars, fire trucks and irate citizens.
c. The *1812 Overture* is a stirring, magnificent piece of music.
d. After two broken arms, three cracked ribs and one concussion, Ken quit the varsity football team.
e. My cat's pupils had constricted to small black shining slits.

33e Use commas to set off nonrestrictive (nonessential) elements, but not restrictive (essential) elements.

Certain word groups that modify nouns or pronouns can be restrictive or nonrestrictive — that is, essential or not essential to the meaning of a sentence. These word groups are usually adjective clauses, adjective phrases, or appositives.

Restrictive (essential) elements

A restrictive element defines or limits the meaning of the word it modifies; it is therefore essential to the meaning of the sentence and is not set off with commas. If you remove a restrictive modifier from a sentence, the meaning changes significantly, becoming more general than you intended.

RESTRICTIVE (NO COMMAS)

The campers need clothes *that are durable.*

Scientists *who study the earth's structure* are called geologists.

The first sentence does not mean that the campers need clothes in general. The intended meaning is more limited: The campers need durable clothes. The second sentence does not mean that scientists in general are called geologists; only those scientists who specifically study the earth's structure are called geologists. The italicized word groups are essential and are therefore not set off with commas.

Nonrestrictive (nonessential) elements

A nonrestrictive modifier describes a noun or pronoun whose meaning has already been clearly defined or limited. Because the modifier contains nonessential or parenthetical information, it is set off with commas. If you remove a nonrestrictive element from a sentence, some meaning may be lost, but the defining characteristics of the person or thing remain the same.

NONRESTRICTIVE (WITH COMMAS)

The campers need sturdy shoes, *which are expensive.*

The computer scientists, *who represented eight different universities*, met to review applications for the Turing Award.

In the first sentence, the campers need sturdy shoes, and the shoes happen to be expensive. In the second sentence, the computer scientists met to review applications for the award; that they represented eight different universities is informative but not critical to the meaning of the sentence. The nonessential information in both sentences is set off with commas.

NOTE: Often it is difficult to tell whether a word group is restrictive or nonrestrictive without seeing it in context and considering the writer's meaning. Both of the following sentences are grammatically correct, but their meaning is slightly different.

> The dessert made with fresh raspberries was delicious.
>
> The dessert, made with fresh raspberries, was delicious.

In the first example, the phrase *made with fresh raspberries* tells readers which of two or more desserts the writer is referring to. In the example with commas, the phrase merely adds information about the dessert.

Adjective clauses

Adjective clauses are patterned like sentences, but they function within sentences as modifiers of nouns or pronouns. They usually follow the word they modify and begin with a relative pronoun (*who, whom, whose, which, that*) or with a relative adverb (*where, when*). (See also 49e.)

Nonrestrictive adjective clauses are set off with commas; restrictive adjective clauses are not.

NONRESTRICTIVE CLAUSE (WITH COMMAS)

▶ Ed's house, which is located on thirteen acres, was completely

furnished with bats in the rafters and mice in the kitchen.

The adjective clause *which is located on thirteen acres* does not restrict the meaning of *Ed's house* and is therefore set off with commas.

RESTRICTIVE CLAUSE (NO COMMAS)

▶ The giant panda/ that was born at the National Zoo in 2013/ was

sent to China in 2017.

Because the adjective clause *that was born at the National Zoo in 2013* identifies one particular panda out of many, the information is not set off with commas.

NOTE: Use *that* only with restrictive (essential) clauses. Many writers prefer to use *which* only with nonrestrictive (nonessential) clauses, but usage varies.

Adjective phrases

Prepositional or verbal phrases functioning as adjectives may be restrictive or nonrestrictive. Nonrestrictive phrases are set off with commas; restrictive phrases are not.

NONRESTRICTIVE PHRASE (WITH COMMAS)

▶ The helicopter, with its million-candlepower spotlight illuminating the area, circled above.

The *with* phrase is nonessential because its purpose is not to specify which of two or more helicopters is being discussed. The phrase is not required for readers to understand the meaning of the sentence.

RESTRICTIVE PHRASE (NO COMMAS)

▶ One corner of the attic was filled with newspapers/ dating from the early 1900s.

Dating from the early 1900s restricts the meaning of *newspapers*, so the comma should be omitted.

Appositives

An appositive is a noun or noun phrase that renames a nearby noun. Nonrestrictive appositives are set off with commas; restrictive appositives are not.

NONRESTRICTIVE APPOSITIVE (WITH COMMAS)

▶ Darwin's most important book, *On the Origin of Species,* was the result of many years of research.

Most important restricts the meaning to one book, so the appositive *On the Origin of Species* is nonrestrictive and should be set off with commas.

RESTRICTIVE APPOSITIVE (NO COMMAS)

▶ The song/ "Formation/" was blasted out of huge amplifiers.

Once they've read *song,* readers still don't know precisely which song the writer means. The appositive following *song* restricts its meaning, so the appositive should not be set off with commas.

EXERCISE 33-3   Add or delete commas where necessary in the following sentences. If a sentence is correct, write "correct" after it. Answers appear in the back of the book.

> My sister, who plays center for the Sparks, now lives at The Sands,
>
> a beach house near Los Angeles. [*The writer has only one sister.*]

a. Choreographer Alvin Ailey's best-known work *Revelations* is more than just a crowd-pleaser.

b. Twyla Tharp's contemporary ballet *Push Comes to Shove* was made famous by the Russian dancer Baryshnikov. [*Tharp has written more than one contemporary ballet.*]

c. The glass sculptor sifting through hot red sand explained her technique to the other glassmakers. [*There is more than one glass sculptor.*]

d. A member of an organization, that provides job training for teens, was also appointed to the education commission.

e. Brian Eno who began his career as a rock musician turned to meditative compositions in the late 1970s.

33f Use commas to set off transitional expressions and other word groups.

Transitional expressions

Transitional expressions serve as bridges between sentences or parts of sentences. They include conjunctive adverbs such as *however*, *therefore*, and *moreover* and transitional phrases such as *for example*, *as a matter of fact*, and *in other words*. (For complete lists of these expressions, see 35b.)

When a transitional expression appears between independent clauses in a compound sentence, it is preceded by a semicolon and is usually followed by a comma. (See 35b.)

> ▶ Minh did not understand the language; moreover, he was
>
> unfamiliar with the customs.

When a transitional expression appears at the beginning of a sentence or in the middle of an independent clause, it is usually set off with commas.

> ▶ Natural foods are not always salt free; celery, for example,
>
> contains more sodium than most people think.

EXCEPTION: If a transitional expression blends smoothly with the rest of the sentence, calling for little or no pause in reading, it does not need to be set off with a comma.

> Aidy's bicycle is broken; *therefore* you will need to borrow Saya's.

Parenthetical expressions

Expressions that provide only supplemental information and interrupt the flow of a sentence should be set off with commas.

> ► Evolution, as far as we know, doesn't work this way.

Absolute phrases

An absolute phrase usually consists of a noun followed by a participle or participial phrase. (See 49d.) These phrases should be set off with commas.

```
┌────────── ABSOLUTE PHRASE ──────────┐
│      N   PARTICIPLE                  │
```
The sun appearing for the first time in a week, we were at last able

to begin the archaeological dig.

> ► Elvis Presley made music industry history in the 1950s, his
>
> records having sold more than ten million copies.

NOTE: Do not insert a comma between the noun and the participle in an absolute construction.

> ► The next contestant⁄being five years old, the host adjusted the
>
> height of the microphone.

Word groups expressing contrast

Sharp contrasts beginning with words such as *not*, *never*, and *unlike* are set off with commas.

> ► Unlike Robert, Celia loves singing competitions.

33g Use commas to set off nouns of direct address, the words *yes* and *no*, interrogative tags, and mild interjections.

> ► Forgive me, Angela, for forgetting your birthday.

▶ Yes, the loan will probably be approved.

▶ The film was faithful to the book, wasn't it?

33h Use commas with expressions such as *he said* to set off direct quotations.

▶ In his "Letter from Birmingham Jail," Martin Luther King Jr.

wrote, "We know through painful experience that freedom is

never voluntarily given by the oppressor; it must be demanded

by the oppressed" (225).

See 38 on the use of quotation marks and pages 413–15 on citing literary sources in MLA style.

33i Use commas with dates, addresses, titles, and numbers.

Dates

In dates, set off the year from the rest of the sentence with a pair of commas.

▶ On December 12, 1890, orders were sent out for the arrest of

Sitting Bull.

EXCEPTIONS: Commas are not needed if the date is inverted or if only the month and year are given: *15 April 2009; January 2021.*

Addresses

The elements of an address or a place name are separated with commas. A zip code, however, is not preceded by a comma.

▶ Please send the package to Greg Tarvin at 708 Spring Street,

Washington, IL 61571.

Titles

If a title follows a name, set off the title with a pair of commas.

▶ Ann Hall, MD, has been appointed to the board of trustees.
         ^   ^

Numbers

In numbers more than four digits long, use commas to separate the numbers into groups of three, starting from the right. In numbers four digits long, a comma is optional.

3,500 [*or* 3500]   100,000   5,000,000

EXCEPTIONS: Do not use commas in street numbers, zip codes, telephone numbers, or years with four or fewer digits.

EXERCISE 33–4   This exercise covers the major uses of the comma described in 33a–33e. Add or delete commas where necessary. If a sentence is correct, write "correct" after it. Answers appear in the back of the book.

Even though our brains actually can't focus on two tasks at a

time, many people believe they can multitask.
    ^

a. Cricket which originated in England is also popular in Australia, South Africa and India.
b. At the sound of the starting pistol the horses surged forward toward the first obstacle, a sharp incline three feet high.
c. After seeing an exhibition of Western art Gerhard Richter escaped from East Berlin, and smuggled out many of his notebooks.
d. Corrie's new wet suit has an intricate, blue pattern.
e. We replaced the rickety, old, spiral staircase with a sturdy, new ladder.

EXERCISE 33–5   This exercise covers the major uses of the comma described in 32a–32e. Edit the following paragraph to correct any comma errors.

Hope for Paws, a nonprofit rescue organization in Los Angeles tells many sad stories of animal abuse and neglect. Most of the stories, however have happy endings. One such story involves Woody, a dog left behind, after his master died. For a long lonely year, Woody took refuge under a neighbor's shed, waiting in vain, for his master's return. He survived on occasional scraps from his neighbors who eventually contacted Hope for Paws. When rescuers reached Woody, they found a malnourished, and frightened dog who had one blind eye and dirty, matted, fur. Gently, Woody was pulled from beneath the shed, and taken to the home of a volunteer, who fosters orphaned pets. There, Woody was fed, shaved, bathed and loved. Woody's story had the happiest of endings, when a family adopted him. Now Woody has a new forever home and he is once again a happy, well-loved dog.

EXERCISE 33–6   This exercise covers all uses of the comma. Add or delete commas where necessary in the following sentences. If a sentence is correct, write "correct" after it. Answers appear in the back of the book.

> "Yes, neighbors, we must work together to save the community
> ^
> center," urged Mr. Owusu.

a. On January 16, 2017 our office moved to 29 Commonwealth Avenue, Mechanicsville VA 23111.

b. The coach having resigned after the big game, we left the locker room in shock.

c. Ms. Carlson you are a valued customer whose satisfaction is very important to us.

d. Mr. Mundy was born on July 22, 1939 in Arkansas, where his family had lived for four generations.

e. Her board poised at the edge of the half-pipe, Shanice waited her turn to drop in.

34 Unnecessary commas

34a Do not use a comma with a coordinating conjunction that joins only two words, phrases, or subordinate clauses.

Though a comma should be used before a coordinating conjunction joining independent clauses (see 33a) or with a series of three or more elements (see 33c), these rules should not be extended to other compound word groups, as shown by the examples on the next page.

▶ Ron discovered a leak/and came back to fix it.

The coordinating conjunction *and* links two verbs in a compound predicate: *discovered* and *came*.

▶ We knew that she had won/but that the election was close.

The coordinating conjunction *but* links two subordinate clauses, each beginning with *that*.

34b Do not use a comma to separate a verb from its subject or object.

Commas may appear between these major sentence elements only when a specific rule calls for them.

▶ Zoos large enough to give the animals freedom to roam/are

becoming more popular.

The comma should not separate the subject, *Zoos*, from the verb, *are becoming*.

34c Do not use a comma before the first or after the last item in a series.

Though commas are required between items in a series (33c), do not place them either before or after the whole series.

▶ Other causes of asthmatic attacks are/stress, change in

temperature, and cold air.

▶ Even novels that focus on horror, evil, and alienation/often have

themes of spiritual renewal and redemption as well.

34d Do not use a comma between cumulative adjectives, between an adjective and a noun, or between an adverb and an adjective.

Commas are required between coordinate adjectives (those that can be joined with *and*), but they do not belong between cumulative adjectives (those that cannot be joined with *and*; see 33d).

▶   In the corner of the closet, we found an old/ maroon hatbox.

A comma should never be used between an adjective and the noun that follows it, nor should it be placed between an adverb and an adjective that follows it.

▶   It was a senseless, dangerous/ mission.

▶   Deer are often responsible for severely/ damaged crops.

34e Do not use commas to set off restrictive (essential) elements.

Because restrictive elements are essential to the meaning of the sentence, they are not set off with commas. (See 33e.)

▶   Drivers/ who think they own the road/ make cycling a

dangerous sport.

> The modifier *who think they own the road* restricts the meaning of *Drivers* and is essential to the meaning of the sentence. Putting commas around the *who* clause falsely suggests that all drivers think they own the road.

34f Do not use a comma to set off a concluding adverb clause that is essential for meaning.

When adverb clauses introduce a sentence, they are nearly always followed by a comma (see 33b). When they conclude a sentence, however, they are not set off by a comma if their content is essential to the meaning of the earlier part of the sentence. Adverb clauses beginning with *after*, *as soon as*, *because*, *before*, *if*, *since*, *unless*, *until*, and *when* are usually essential. See the example on the next page.

► Don't try to visit the botanical garden╱unless you have booked a

tour in advance.

Without the *unless* clause, the meaning of the sentence might at first seem broader than the writer intended.

When a concluding adverb clause is nonessential, it should be preceded by a comma. Clauses beginning with *although*, *even though*, *though*, and *whereas* are usually nonessential.

► The lecture seemed to last only a short time, although the clock
                                                   ^

said it had gone on for more than an hour.

34g Do not use a comma after a phrase that begins an inverted sentence.

Though a comma belongs after most introductory phrases (see 33b), it does not belong after phrases that begin an inverted sentence. In an inverted sentence, the subject follows the verb, and a phrase that ordinarily would follow the verb is moved to the beginning.

► At the bottom of the hill╱sat the stubborn mule.

34h Avoid other common misuses of the comma.

Do not use a comma in the following situations.

AFTER A COORDINATING CONJUNCTION (*AND, BUT, OR, NOR, FOR, SO, YET*)

► Medical schools are beginning to change, but╱traditional

dermatology programs have often ignored Black and brown skin.

AFTER *SUCH AS* OR *LIKE*

► Shade-loving plants such as╱begonias, impatiens, and coleus can

add color to a shady garden.

AFTER *ALTHOUGH*

▶ Although,/the air was balmy, the water was cold.

BEFORE A PARENTHESIS

▶ Sylvia knew that her ACT score was low,/(only 22), but she felt

confident about her application essay.

TO SET OFF AN INDIRECT (REPORTED) QUOTATION

▶ Samuel Goldwyn once said,/that a verbal contract isn't worth the

paper it's written on.

WITH A QUESTION MARK OR AN EXCLAMATION POINT

▶ "Why don't you try it?,/" she coaxed. "You can't do any worse

than the rest of us."

EXERCISE 34–1   Delete any unnecessary commas in the following
sentences. If a sentence is correct, write "correct" after it. Answers appear in the back of the book.

In his Silk Road Project, Yo-Yo Ma incorporates work by

composers such as,/Kayhan Kalhor and Richard Danielpour.

a. After the morning rains cease, the swimmers emerge from their
   cottages.
b. Tricia's first artwork was a bright, blue, clay dolphin.
c. Some modern musicians, (trumpeter Jon Hassell is an example)
   blend several cultural traditions into a particular sound.
d. Myra liked hot, spicy foods such as, chili, kung pao chicken, and
   buffalo wings.
e. On the display screen, was a soothing pattern of light and shadow.

EXERCISE 34–2   Delete unnecessary commas in the following passage.

Each spring since 1970, New Orleans has hosted the Jazz and
Heritage Festival, an event that celebrates the music, food, and
culture, of the region. Although, it is often referred to as "Jazz

Fest," the festival typically includes a wide variety of musical styles such as, gospel, Cajun, blues, zydeco, and, rock and roll. Famous musicians who have appeared regularly at Jazz Fest, include Dr. John, B. B. King, and Aretha Franklin. Large stages are set up throughout the fairgrounds in a way, that allows up to ten bands to play simultaneously without any sound overlap. Food tents are located throughout the festival, and offer popular, local dishes like crawfish Monica, jambalaya, and fried, green tomatoes. Following Hurricane Katrina in 2005, Jazz Fest revived quickly, and attendance has steadily increased each year. Like many festivals and events around the world, the Jazz and Heritage Festival was canceled in 2020, because of the pandemic. Fans, who missed the festival, still enjoyed the music by downloading songs, watching previous years' performances online, and looking forward, to the festival's return in future years.

35   The semicolon

35a Use a semicolon between closely related independent clauses not joined with a coordinating conjunction.

The semicolon is used to connect major sentence elements of equal grammatical rank. When two independent clauses appear in one sentence, they are usually linked with a comma and a coordinating conjunction (*and, but, or, nor, for, so, yet*). If the clauses are closely related and the relation is clear without a conjunction, they may be linked with a semicolon instead.

> In film, a low-angle shot makes the subject look powerful; a high-angle shot does just the opposite.

A semicolon must be used whenever a coordinating conjunction has been omitted between independent clauses. To use merely a comma creates a type of run-on sentence known as a *comma splice*. (See 20.)

▶ In 1800, a traveler needed six weeks to get from New York City to

Chicago,; in 1860, the trip by railroad took only two days.

35b Use a semicolon between independent clauses linked with a transitional expression.

Transitional expressions include conjunctive adverbs and transitional phrases.

CONJUNCTIVE ADVERBS

accordingly	furthermore	moreover	still
also	hence	nevertheless	subsequently
anyway	however	next	then
besides	incidentally	nonetheless	therefore
certainly	indeed	now	thus
consequently	instead	otherwise	
conversely	likewise	similarly	
finally	meanwhile	specifically	

TRANSITIONAL PHRASES

after all	even so	in fact
as a matter of fact	for example	in other words
as a result	for instance	in the first place
at any rate	in addition	on the contrary
at the same time	in conclusion	on the other hand

When a transitional expression appears between independent clauses, it is preceded by a semicolon and usually followed by a comma.

► Many corals grow very gradually; in fact, the creation of a coral

reef can take centuries.

When a transitional expression appears in the middle or at the end of the second independent clause, the semicolon goes between the clauses.

► Biologists have observed laughter in primates other than

humans; chimpanzees, however, sound more like they are

panting than laughing.

Transitional expressions should not be confused with the co-ordinating conjunctions *and*, *but*, *or*, *nor*, *for*, *so*, and *yet*, which are preceded by a comma when they link independent clauses. (See 33a.)

35c Use a semicolon between items in a series containing internal punctuation.

▶ Researchers point to key benefits of positive thinking: It leads to high self-esteem, especially in people who focus on their achievements~~,~~; it helps make social interactions, such as those with co-workers, more enjoyable~~,~~; and, most important, it results in better sleep and overall health.

Without the semicolons, the major word groupings are unclear. Inserting semicolons at the major breaks makes the sentence clear.

35d Avoid common misuses of the semicolon.

Do not use a semicolon in the following situations.

BETWEEN A SUBORDINATE CLAUSE AND THE REST OF THE SENTENCE

▶ Although children's literature was added to the National Book Awards in 1969~~;~~, it has had its own award, the Newbery Medal, since 1922.

BETWEEN AN APPOSITIVE AND THE WORD IT REFERS TO

▶ The scientists were fascinated by the species *Argyroneta aquatica*~~;~~, a spider that lives underwater.

TO INTRODUCE A LIST

▶ Some of my favorite musicians have performed at the Newport Folk Festival~~;~~: Dolly Parton, Kacey Musgraves, and Hozier.

BETWEEN INDEPENDENT CLAUSES JOINED BY *AND, BUT, OR, NOR, FOR, SO,* OR *YET*

▶ Five of the applicants had worked with spreadsheets~~,~~ **;** but only

one was familiar with database management.

EXCEPTIONS: If one or both of the independent clauses contain a comma, you may use a semicolon with a coordinating conjunction between the clauses.

EXERCISE 35–1   Edit the following sentences to correct errors in the use of the comma and the semicolon. If a sentence is correct, write "correct" after it. Answers appear in the back of the book.

> Love is blind~~,~~ **;** envy has its eyes wide open.

a. Strong black coffee will not sober you up, the truth is that time is the only way to get alcohol out of your system.

b. Margaret was not surprised to see hail and vivid lightning, conditions had been right for violent weather all day.

c. There is often a fine line between right and wrong; good and bad; truth and deception.

d. My mom always says that you can't learn common sense; either you're born with it or you're not.

e. Severe, unremitting pain is a ravaging force; especially when the patient tries to hide it from others.

---

36   The colon

36a   Use a colon after an independent clause to direct attention to a list, an appositive, a quotation, or a summary or an explanation.

The colon is used primarily to call attention to the words that follow it, such as in the following situations.

A LIST

The daily routine should include at least the following: ten minutes of stretching, forty abdominal crunches, and a twenty-minute run.

AN APPOSITIVE

My roommate seems to live on two things: sushi and social media.

A QUOTATION

Consider the words of John Lewis: "Never, ever be afraid to make some noise and get in good trouble, necessary trouble."

A SUMMARY OR AN EXPLANATION

Faith is like love: it cannot be forced.

NOTE: When an independent clause follows a colon, beginning with a capital letter is optional. Some disciplines use a lowercase letter (*Faith is like love: it cannot be forced*). See also 46f.

36b Use a colon according to convention.

SALUTATION IN A LETTER   Dear Editor:

HOURS AND MINUTES   5:30 p.m.

PROPORTIONS   The ratio of women to men was 2:1.

TITLE AND SUBTITLE   *The Glory of Hera: Greek Mythology and the Greek Family*

BIBLIOGRAPHIC ENTRIES   Boston: Bedford/St. Martin's, 2021

CHAPTER AND VERSE IN SACRED TEXT   Luke 2:14, Qur'an 67:3

36c Avoid common misuses of the colon.

A colon must be preceded by a full independent clause. Therefore, avoid using it in the following situations.

BETWEEN A VERB AND ITS OBJECT OR COMPLEMENT

▶ Some important vitamins found in vegetables are꞉ vitamin A, thiamine, niacin, and vitamin C.

BETWEEN A PREPOSITION AND ITS OBJECT

▶ The heart's two pumps each consist of꞉ an upper chamber, or atrium, and a lower chamber, or ventricle.

AFTER SUCH AS, INCLUDING, OR FOR EXAMPLE

▶ The NCAA regulates college athletic teams, including~~,~~

basketball, baseball, softball, and football.

EXERCISE 36–1 Edit the following sentences to correct errors in the use of the comma, the semicolon, or the colon. If a sentence is correct, write "correct" after it. Answers appear in the back of the book.

Lifting the cover gently, Luca found the source of the odd

sound~~:~~ a marble in the gears.

a. We always looked forward to Thanksgiving in Vermont: It was our only chance to see our Grady cousins.

b. If we have come to fight, we are far too few, if we have come to die, we are far too many.

c. Each of the gift baskets included: a greeting card, a scarf, and homemade cookies.

d. The news article portrays the land use proposal as reckless; although 62 percent of the town's residents support it.

e. Activist and politician Stacey Abrams asks readers of her book *Lead from the Outside* a powerful question, "How do I banish doubts and get out of my own way?" (xxvii).

37 The apostrophe

37a Use an apostrophe to indicate that a noun is possessive.

Possessive nouns usually indicate ownership, as in *Tim's hat* or *the lawyer's desk*. Frequently, however, ownership is only loosely implied: *the tree's roots, a day's work*. If you are not sure whether a noun is possessive, try turning it into an *of* phrase: *the roots of the tree, the work of a day*. (Pronouns also have possessive forms. See 37b and 37e.)

When to add -'s

1. If the noun does not end in -s, add -'s.

   Luck often propels a rock musician's career.

   The Children's Defense Fund is a nonprofit organization that supports programs for poor children.

2. If the noun is singular and ends in -s or an s sound, add -'s to indicate possession.

   Lois's sister spent a year in India.

   Her article presents an overview of Marx's teachings.

NOTE: To avoid potentially awkward pronunciation, some writers use only the apostrophe with a singular noun ending in -s: *Sophocles'*.

When to add only an apostrophe

If the noun is plural and ends in -s, add only an apostrophe.

   Both diplomats' briefcases were searched by guards.

Joint possession

To show joint possession, use -'s or (-s') with the last noun only; to show individual possession, make all nouns possessive.

   Have you seen Joyce and Greg's new camper?

   Hernando's and Maria's expectations of marriage couldn't have been more different.

Joyce and Greg jointly own one camper. Hernando and Maria individually have different expectations.

Compound nouns

If a noun is compound, use -'s (or -s') with the last element.

   My father-in-law's memoir about his childhood in Sri Lanka was published in September.

37b Use an apostrophe and -s to indicate that an indefinite pronoun is possessive.

Indefinite pronouns refer to no specific person or thing: *everyone, someone, no one, something.* (See 47b.)

> Someone's raincoat has been left behind.

37c Use an apostrophe to mark omissions in contractions and numbers.

In a contraction, the apostrophe takes the place of one or more missing letters. *It's* stands for *it is, can't* for *cannot.*

> It's a shame that Frank can't go on the tour.

The apostrophe is also used to mark the omission of the first two digits of a year (*the class of '20*) or years (*the '80s generation*).

37d Do not use an apostrophe in certain situations.

Plural of numbers and abbreviations

Do not use an apostrophe in the plural of any numbers or abbreviations.

> Oksana skated nearly perfect figure 8s.
>
> The 1920s are known as the Jazz Age.
>
> Marco earned two PhDs before his 30th birthday.

Plural of letters and words mentioned as words

Generally, do not use an apostrophe to form the plural of letters and words mentioned as words. If the letter or word is italicized, the *-s* ending appears in roman (regular) type.

> We've heard enough *maybe*s.
>
> Two large *P*s were painted on the door.

Letters and words mentioned as words may also appear in quotation marks. When you choose this option, use the apostrophe.

> We've heard enough "maybe's."

> Two large "J's" were painted on the door.

EXCEPTION: To avoid misreading, you may use an apostrophe to form the plural of lowercase letters and the capital letters *A* and *I*: *two A's in biology.*

37e Avoid common misuses of the apostrophe.

Do not use an apostrophe with nouns that are not possessive or with the possessive pronouns *its, whose, his, hers, ours, yours,* and *theirs.*

> ▶ Some ~~outpatient's~~ have special parking permits.
> _{outpatients}

> ▶ Each area has ~~it's~~ own conference room.
> _{its}

> *It's* means "it is." The possessive pronoun *its* contains no apostrophe despite the fact that it is possessive.

> ▶ We attended a reading by Richard Blanco, ~~who's~~ poetry focuses
> _{whose}
>
> on the experiences of Cuban immigrants.

> *Who's* means "who is." The possessive pronoun is *whose.*

EXERCISE 37–1   Edit the following sentences to correct errors in the use of the apostrophe. If a sentence is correct, write "correct" after it. Answers appear in the back of the book.

> Our favorite barbecue restaurant is Poor ~~Richards~~ Ribs.
> _{Richard's}

a. This diet will improve almost anyone's health.

b. The innovative shoe fastener was inspired by the designers young son.

c. Each days menu features a different European country's dish.

d. Lottie worked overtime to increase her families earnings.

e. Ms. Jacobs is unwilling to listen to students complaints about computer failures.

EXERCISE 37–2 Edit the following passage to correct errors in the use of the apostrophe.

Its never too soon to start holiday shopping. In fact, some people choose to start shopping as early as January, when last seasons leftover's are priced at their lowest. Many stores try to lure customers in with promise's of savings up to 90 percent. Their main objective, of course, is to make way for next years inventory. The big problem with postholiday shopping, though, is that there isn't much left to choose from. Store's shelves have been picked over by last-minute shoppers desperately searching for gifts. The other problem is that its hard to know what to buy so far in advance. Next year's hot items are anyones guess. But proper timing, mixed with lot's of luck and determination, can lead to good purchases at great price's.

38 Quotation marks

38a Use quotation marks to enclose direct quotations.

Direct quotations of a person's words, whether spoken or written, must be in quotation marks.

> "Twitter," according to social media researcher Jameson Brown, "is the best social network for brand to customer engagement."

In dialogue, begin a new paragraph to mark a change in speaker.

> "Mom, his name is Willie, not William. A thousand times I've told you, it's *Willie*."
> "Willie is a derivative of William, Lester. Surely his birth certificate doesn't have Willie on it, and I like calling people by their proper names."
> "Yes, it does, ma'am. My mother named me Willie K. Mason."
> — Gloria Naylor

If a single speaker utters more than one paragraph, introduce each paragraph with a quotation mark, but do not use a closing quotation mark until the end of the speech.

Exception: Indirect quotations

Do not use quotation marks around indirect quotations, which report someone's ideas without using that person's exact words. In academic writing, indirect quotation is called *paraphrase* or *summary*.

> Researcher Jameson Brown claims that Twitter is the best social media tool for companies that want to reach their consumers.

Exception: Long quotations

Long quotations of prose or poetry are generally set off from the text by indenting. Quotation marks are not used because the indented format tells readers that the quotation is taken word-for-word from the source.

> After making an exhaustive study of the historical record, James Horan evaluates Billy the Kid like this:
>> The portrait that emerges of [the Kid] from the thousands of pages of affidavits, reports, trial transcripts, his letters, and his testimony is neither the mythical Robin Hood nor the stereotyped adenoidal moron and pathological killer. Rather Billy appears as a disturbed, lonely young man, honest, loyal to his friends, dedicated to his beliefs, and betrayed by our institutions and the corrupt, ambitious, and compromising politicians in his time. (158)

The number in parentheses is a citation in MLA style. (See 57a.)

MLA and APA have specific guidelines for what constitutes a long quotation and how it should be indented (see 56b and 61b, respectively).

38b Use single quotation marks to enclose a quotation within a quotation.

> Megan Marshall notes that Elizabeth Peabody's school focused on "not merely 'teaching' but 'educating children morally and spiritually as well as intellectually from the first' " (107).

38c Use quotation marks around the titles of short works.

Short works include newspaper and magazine articles, poems, short stories, songs, episodes of television and radio programs, and chapters or subdivisions of books.

> James Baldwin's story "Sonny's Blues" tells the story of two brothers who come to understand each other's suffering.

NOTE: Titles of long works such as books, films, and magazines appear in italics. (See 43a.)

38d Quotation marks may be used to set off words used as words.

Although words used as words are ordinarily italicized (see 43c), quotation marks are also acceptable. Be consistent throughout your paper.

> The literary terms "simile" and "metaphor" are sometimes confused.

> The literary terms *simile* and *metaphor* are sometimes confused.

38e Use punctuation with quotation marks according to convention.

This section describes the conventions American publishers follow in placing various marks of punctuation inside or outside quotation marks. It also explains how to punctuate when introducing quoted material. (For the use of quotation marks in MLA and APA styles, see 57a and 62a, respectively. The examples in this section show MLA style.)

Periods and commas

Place periods and commas inside quotation marks.

> "I'm here as part of my service-learning project," I told the classroom teacher. "I'm hoping to become a reading specialist."

This rule applies to single quotation marks as well as double quotation marks. (See 38b.) It also applies to all uses of quotation marks: for quoted material, for titles of works, and for words used as words.

NOTE: In MLA and APA styles of parenthetical in-text citations, the period follows the citation in parentheses.

> James M. McPherson comments, approvingly, that the Whigs "were not averse to extending the blessings of American liberty, even to Mexicans and Indians" (48).

Colons and semicolons

Put colons and semicolons outside quotation marks.

> Harold wrote, "I regret that I am unable to attend the fundraiser for diabetes research"; his letter, however, came with a contribution.

Question marks and exclamation points

Put question marks and exclamation points inside quotation marks unless they apply to the whole sentence.

> Dr. Abram's first question was "What three goals do you have for the course?"

> Have you heard the proverb "Do not climb the hill until you reach it"?

In the first sentence, the question mark applies only to the quoted question. In the second sentence, the question mark applies to the whole sentence.

NOTE: For a quotation that ends with a question mark or an exclamation point, the parenthetical citation and a period should follow the entire quotation.

> Rosie Thomas asks, "Is nothing in life ever straight and clear, the way children see it?" (77).

Introducing quoted material

After a word group introducing a quotation, choose a colon, a comma, or no punctuation at all, whichever is appropriate in context.

Formal introduction   If a quotation is formally introduced, a colon is appropriate. A formal introduction is a full independent clause, not just an expression such as *he said.*

> Thomas Friedman provides a challenging yet optimistic view of the future: "We need to get back to work on our country and on our planet. The hour is late, the stakes couldn't be higher, the project couldn't be harder, the payoff couldn't be greater" (25).

Expression such as *she writes*   If a quotation is introduced with an expression such as *he writes* or *she explained* — or if it is followed by such an expression — a comma is needed.

> Mark Twain once declared, "In the spring I have counted one hundred and thirty-six different kinds of weather within four and twenty hours" (55).

Blended quotation   When a quotation is blended into the writer's own sentence, either a comma or no punctuation is appropriate, depending on how the quotation fits into the sentence structure.

> The future champion could, as he put it, "float like a butterfly and sting like a bee."
>
> Virginia Woolf wrote in 1928 that "a woman must have money and a room of her own if she is to write fiction" (4).

Beginning of sentence   If a quotation appears at the beginning of a sentence, use a comma after it unless the quotation ends with a question mark or an exclamation point.

> "I've always thought of myself as a reporter," American poet Gwendolyn Brooks once stated (162).
>
> "What is it?" she asked, bracing herself.

Interrupted quotation   If a quoted sentence is interrupted by explanatory words, use commas to set off the explanatory words.

> "With regard to air travel," Stephen Ambrose notes, "Jefferson was a full century ahead of the curve" (53).

If two successive quoted sentences from the same source are interrupted by explanatory words, use a comma before the explanatory words and a period after them.

> "Everyone agrees journalists must tell the truth," Bill Kovach and Tom Rosenstiel write. "Yet people are befuddled about what 'the truth' means" (37).

38f Avoid common misuses of quotation marks.

Do not use quotation marks to draw attention to familiar slang, to disown trite expressions, or to justify an attempt at humor.

▶ The economist emphasized that 5 percent was a

~~"~~ballpark figure.~~"~~

EXERCISE 38–1   Add or delete quotation marks as needed and make any other necessary changes in punctuation in the following sentences. If a sentence is correct, write "correct" after it. Answers appear in the back of the book.

Gandhi once said, ⌃"An eye for an eye only ends up making the

whole world blind."⌃

a. As for the advertisement "Sailors have more fun", if you consider chipping paint and swabbing decks fun, then you will have plenty of it.

b. Even after forty minutes of discussion, our class could not agree on an interpretation of Robert Frost's poem "The Road Not Taken."

c. After winning the lottery, Juanita said that "she would give half the money to charity."

d. After the movie, Vicki said, "The reviewer called this flick "trash of the first order." I guess you can't believe everything you read."

e. "Cleaning your house while your kids are still growing," said Phyllis Diller, "is like shoveling the walk before it stops snowing."

EXERCISE 38–2   Add or delete quotation marks as needed and make any other necessary changes in punctuation in the following passage. Citations should conform to MLA style (see 55).

In her book "The World Has Curves," Julia Savacool studies global beauty standards. The author describes an article she wrote for *Marie Claire* titled Women's Bodies, Then and Now about "the ways in which women's body shapes have changed around the world" over two centuries (ix). In her book, Savacool goes deeper into the topic by focusing on the idea of globalization. "Distinctions between cultures are being blurred, she writes, so that geographical boundaries no longer determine a population's music tastes, movie idols, and gastronomic preferences." (x) Savacool questions whether this is also true of bodies. "Does the same principle apply to women's appearances", she asks (x)?

Savacool also questions whether such beauty standards are realistic or healthy. She explains:

> "In America, the ideal body for women is increasingly longer and leaner than seems humanly possible — and indeed, is frequently not humanly possible, a realization that has given rise to a booming industry of cosmetic procedures, products, and diet and fitness plans. The exception, or perhaps contradiction, to the skinny-is-beautiful trend in America is our fixation on breasts, the only acceptable fat on an otherwise lean body." (xi)

In some ways, this image is beginning to change — but perhaps not as quickly as it could. Savacool argues that, "Never before has the "perfect" body been at such odds with our true size. (xii)"

(Source of quotations: Julia Savacool, *The World Has Curves*)

39   End punctuation

39a   The period

Use a period to end all sentences except direct questions or genuine exclamations. Also use periods in abbreviations according to convention.

To end sentences

Most sentences should end with a period. A sentence that reports a question instead of asking it directly (an indirect question) should end with a period, not a question mark.

▶ The professor asked whether talk therapy was more beneficial

than antidepressants?.
           ^

In abbreviations

A period is conventionally used in the following abbreviations.

Mr.	i.e.	a.m. (or AM)
Ms.	e.g.	p.m. (or PM)
Dr.	etc.	

NOTE: If a sentence ends with a period marking an abbreviation, do not add a second period.

Do not use a period in abbreviations of organization names, academic degrees, states, and designations for eras.

NATO	UCLA	BS	TX	BC
IRS	NIH	PhD	NY	BCE

39b The question mark

A direct question should be followed by a question mark.

What is the horsepower of a 777 engine?

39c The exclamation point

Use an exclamation point after a word group or sentence to express exceptional feeling or to provide special emphasis.

When Gloria entered the room, I switched on the lights, and we all yelled, "Surprise!"

NOTE: Do not overuse the exclamation point. Let your words be emphatic and specific so that they do not need an exclamation point.

▶ In the fisherman's memory, the fish lives on, increasing in length and weight with each passing year, until at last it is big enough to shade a fishing boat!.

EXERCISE 39–1 Add appropriate end punctuation in the following paragraph.

Although I am generally rational, I am superstitious I never walk under ladders or put shoes on the table If I spill the salt, I go into frenzied calisthenics picking up the grains and tossing them over my left shoulder As a result of these curious activities, I've always wondered whether knowing the roots of superstitions would quell my irrational responses Superstition has it, for example, that one should never place a hat on the bed This superstition arises from a time when head lice were common and placing a guest's hat on the bed stood a good chance of spreading lice through the host's bed Doesn't this make good sense And doesn't it stand to reason that, if I know that my guests don't have lice, I shouldn't care where their hats go Of course it does It is fair to ask, then, whether I have changed my ways and place hats on beds Are you kidding I wouldn't put a hat on a bed if my life depended on it

40 Other punctuation marks

40a The dash

To use a dash while typing, insert what is called an em-dash using your word processor's tools or type two hyphens (--). (Most word processing and messaging programs will convert the two hyphens to a dash.) Do not put a space before or after the dash.

Use a dash to set off parenthetical material that deserves emphasis.

Everything in the classroom — from the pencils on the desks to the books on the shelves — was in perfect order.

Appositives, nouns or noun phrases that rename a nearby noun, are ordinarily set off with commas (see 33e). However, when the appositive itself contains commas, use a pair of dashes instead.

In my hometown, people's basic needs — food, clothing, and shelter — are less costly than in a big city like Los Angeles.

A dash can also be used to introduce a list, a restatement or an amplification, or a dramatic shift in tone or thought.

Along the wall are the bulk liquids — sesame seed oil, honey, safflower oil, and that half-liquid "peanuts only" peanut butter.

In his last semester, Peter tried to pay more attention to his priorities — applying to graduate school and getting financial aid.

Kiere took a few steps back, came running full speed, kicked a mighty kick — and missed the ball.

In the first two examples, the writer could instead use a colon. (See 36a.) The colon is more formal than the dash and not quite as dramatic.

NOTE: Do not overuse the dash. Unnecessary dashes create a choppy effect.

40b Parentheses

Use parentheses to enclose supplemental material, minor digressions, and afterthoughts.

Nurses record patients' vital signs (temperature, pulse, and blood pressure) several times a day.

Use parentheses to enclose letters or numbers labeling items in a series.

Regulations stipulated that only the following equipment could be used on the survival mission: (1) a knife, (2) thirty feet of parachute line, (3) a book of matches, (4) two ponchos, (5) an E tool, and (6) a signal flare.

NOTE: Do not overuse parentheses. As writers draft, they often think of additional details and use parentheses to work them in as best they can. Such sentences usually can be revised to add the details without parentheses.

▶ Researchers have said that seventeen million ~~(estimates run as~~ *from*
~~high as~~ twenty-three million)̶ Americans have diabetes. *to*

40c Brackets

Use brackets to enclose any words or phrases that you have inserted into an otherwise word-for-word quotation.

Audubon reports that "if there are not enough young to balance deaths, the end of the species [California condor] is inevitable" (4).

The sentence quoted from the *Audubon* article did not contain the words *California condor* (since the context of the full article made clear what species was meant), so the writer needed to add the name in brackets.

The Latin word "sic" in brackets indicates that an error in a quoted sentence appears in the original source.

> According to the review, Lizzo's performance was brilliant, "exceding [sic] the expectations of even her most loyal fans."

Instead of using "sic," the writer could have paraphrased the quotation: *According to the review, even Lizzo's biggest fans were surprised by the brilliance of her performance.*

NOTE: For advice on using "sic" in MLA and APA styles, see 56b and 61b, respectively.

40d The ellipsis

The ellipsis consists of three spaced periods. Use an ellipsis to indicate that you have deleted words from an otherwise word-for-word quotation.

> Shute acknowledges that treatment for autism can be expensive: "Sensory integration therapy . . . can cost up to $200 an hour" (82).

If you delete a full sentence or more in the middle of a quoted passage, use a period before the ellipsis.

> "If we don't properly train, teach, or treat our growing prison population," says longtime reform advocate Luis Rodríguez, "somebody else will. . . . This may well be the safety issue of the new century" (16).

NOTE: Ordinarily, do not use the ellipsis at the beginning or at the end of a quotation. Readers will understand that the quoted material is taken from a longer passage. If you have cut some words from the end of the final quoted sentence, however, MLA requires an ellipsis.

In quoted poetry, use a full line of ellipsis dots to indicate that you have dropped a line or more from the poem, as in this example from "To His Coy Mistress" by Andrew Marvell:

> Had we but world enough, and time,
> This coyness, lady, were no crime.
> . . . .
> But at my back I always hear
> Time's wingèd chariot hurrying near; (1–2, 21–22)

40e The slash

Use the slash to separate two or three lines of poetry that have been run into your text. Add a space both before and after the slash.

> In the opening lines of "Jordan," George Herbert pokes gentle fun at popular poems of his time: "Who says that fictions only and false hair / Become a verse? Is there in truth no beauty?" (1–2).

Four or more lines of poetry should be handled as an indented quotation. (See 38a.)

The slash may occasionally be used to separate paired terms such as *pass/fail* and *producer/director*. Be sparing in this use of the slash. In particular, avoid the use of *and/or*, *he/she*, and *his/her*. Opt for more graceful and inclusive alternatives. (See 17e and 22a.)

EXERCISE 40–1   Edit the following sentences to correct errors in punctuation, focusing especially on appropriate use of the dash, parentheses, brackets, the ellipsis, and the slash. If a sentence is correct, write "correct" after it. Answers appear in the back of the book.

> Social insects/—bees, for example,/—are able to communicate complicated messages to one another.

a. A client left his/her cell phone in our conference room after the meeting.

b. The films we made of Kilauea — on our trip to Hawaii Volcanoes National Park — illustrate a typical spatter cone eruption.

c. Although he was confident in his course selections, Greg chose the pass/fail option for Chemistry 101.

d. Of three engineering fields, chemical, mechanical, and materials, Keegan chose materials engineering for its application to toy manufacturing.

e. The writer Chitra Divakaruni explained her work with other Indian American immigrants: "Many women who came to Maitri [a women's support group in San Francisco] needed to know simple things like opening a bank account or getting citizenship. . . . Many women in Maitri spoke English, but their English was functional rather than emotional. They needed someone who understands their problems and speaks their language."

Mechanics

41 Abbreviations

41a Use abbreviations for titles immediately before and after proper names.

TITLES BEFORE PROPER NAMES	TITLES AFTER PROPER NAMES
Mr. Rafael Zabala	William Albert Sr.
Ms. Nancy Linehan	Thomas Hines Jr.
Dr. Shanice Wallace	Juan López, MD
Rev. John Stone	Margaret Chin, LLD

Do not abbreviate a title if it is not used with a proper name.

> ▶ My history ~~prof.~~ is an expert on race relations in South Africa.
>   professor

Avoid redundant titles such as *Dr. Amy Day, MD*. Choose one title or the other.

41b Use abbreviations only when you are sure your readers will understand them.

Familiar abbreviations for the names of organizations, companies, countries, academic degrees, and common terms, written without periods, are generally acceptable.

NBA	CEO	DVD
FBI	NAACP	ESL

Talk show host Conan O'Brien is a Harvard graduate with a BA in history.

When using an unfamiliar abbreviation (such as *NASW* for National Association of Social Workers) or a potentially ambiguous abbreviation (such as *AMA*, which might refer to the American Medical Association or the American Management Association), write the full name followed by the abbreviation in parentheses at the first mention. Then use just the abbreviation throughout the rest of the paper.

41c Use *BCE, CE, a.m., p.m., No.,* and *$* only with specific dates, times, numbers, and amounts.

The abbreviations *BCE* (before the common era) and *CE* (common era) both follow a date. Common alternatives are *BC*, which follows a date, and *AD*, which precedes a date.

40 BCE (or 40 BC)   4:00 a.m. (or AM)   No. 12 (or no. 12)

44 CE (or AD 44)   6:00 p.m. (or PM) $150

Avoid using *a.m., p.m., No.,* or *$* when not accompanied by a specific numeral: *in the morning* (not *in the a.m.*).

41d Abbreviate units of measurement used with numerals.

Generally, use the abbreviations for units when they appear with numerals; spell out the units when they are used alone or when they are used with spelled-out numbers (see also 42a).

METRIC UNITS	US STANDARD UNITS
m, cm, mm	yd, ft, in.
km, kph	mi, mph
kg, g, mg	lb, oz

Results were measured in pounds.

Runners in the 5-km race had to contend with pouring rain.

Use no periods after abbreviations for units of measurement. Only the abbreviation for "inch" (*in.*) takes a period, to distinguish it from the preposition *in.*

41e Be sparing in your use of Latin abbreviations.

Latin abbreviations are acceptable in footnotes and bibliographies.

e.g. (Latin *exempli gratia*, "for example")

et al. (Latin *et alia*, "and others")

etc. (Latin *et cetera*, "and so forth")

i.e. (Latin *id est*, "that is")

In the text of a paper, use the full English phrase.

41f Plural of abbreviations

To form the plural of most abbreviations, add *-s*, without an apostrophe: *PhDs, DVDs*. Do not add *-s* to indicate the plural of units of measurement: *mm* (not *mms*).

EXERCISE 41–1   Edit the following sentences to correct errors in abbreviations. If a sentence is correct, write "correct" after it. Answers appear in the back of the book.

> evening.
> **We will check on the samples before we leave the lab this ~~p.m.~~**
> ^

a. Since its inception, the BBC has maintained a consistently high standard of radio and television broadcasting.
b. All of the students must meet with the prof. to discuss their final projects.
c. Mahatma Gandhi has inspired many modern leaders, including Martin Luther King Jr.
d. A gluten-free diet is not always the best strategy for shedding lbs.
e. The work of Dr. Anand Khan, PhD, has helped practitioners better understand post-traumatic stress.

42 Numbers

42a Follow the conventions in your discipline for spelling out or using numerals to express numbers.

MLA style uses numerals only for specific numbers larger than one hundred: *353, 1,020*. Spell out numbers one hundred and below and large round numbers: *eleven, thirty-five, fifteen million*.

APA style uses numerals for all but the numbers one through nine. Spell out numbers from one to nine even when they are used with related numerals in a passage: *The survey found that nine of the 157 respondents had not taken a course on alcohol use.*

If a sentence begins with a number, spell out the number or rewrite the sentence.

> One hundred fifty-two
> ~~152~~ children in our program need dental treatment.
>   ^

Rewriting the sentence may be less awkward if the number is long: *In our program, 152 children need dental treatment.*

42b Use numerals according to convention in dates, addresses, and so on.

DATES July 4, 1776; 56 BCE; AD 30

ADDRESSES 77 Latches Lane, 519 West 42nd Street

PERCENTAGES 55 percent (or 55%)

FRACTIONS, DECIMALS ⅞, 0.047

SCORES 7 to 3, 21–18

STATISTICS average age 37, average weight 180

SURVEYS 4 out of 5

EXACT AMOUNTS OF MONEY $105.37, $106,000

DIVISIONS OF BOOKS volume 3, chapter 4, page 189

DIVISIONS OF PLAYS act 3, scene 3 (or act III, scene iii)

TIME OF DAY 4:00 p.m., 1:30 a.m.

NOTE: When not using *a.m.* or *p.m.*, write out the time in words (*two o'clock in the afternoon, twelve noon, seven in the morning*).

EXERCISE 42–1   Edit the following sentences to correct errors in the use of numbers. If a sentence is correct, write "correct" after it. Answers appear in the back of the book.

$3.06
By the end of the evening, Ashanti had only ~~three dollars~~
                                                   ^
~~and six cents~~ left.

a. The carpenters located 3 maple timbers, 21 sheets of cherry, and 10 oblongs of polished ebony for the theater set.

b. The program's cost is well over one billion dollars.

c. The score was tied at 5–5 when the momentum shifted and carried the Standards to a decisive 12–5 win.

d. 8 students in the class signed up for tutoring.

e. The Vietnam Veterans Memorial in Washington, DC, had fifty-eight thousand one hundred thirty-two names inscribed on it when it was dedicated in 1982.

43 Italics

43a Italicize the titles of works according to convention.

Titles of the following types of works should be italicized.

TITLES OF BOOKS *The Color Purple, The Round House*

MAGAZINES *Time, Scientific American, Slate*

NEWSPAPERS the *Baltimore Sun*, the *Orlando Sentinel*

LONG POEMS *The Waste Land, Paradise Lost*

PLAYS *The Humans, Hamilton*

FILMS *Casablanca, Moonlight*

TELEVISION PROGRAMS *The Voice, Frontline*

RADIO PROGRAMS *All Things Considered*

PODCAST SERIES *Embedded*

MUSICAL COMPOSITIONS *Porgy and Bess*

WORKS OF VISUAL ART *American Gothic*

DATABASES OR WEBSITES [MLA] *JSTOR, Google*

SOFTWARE OR APPS [MLA] *Photoshop, Instagram*

The titles of other works — including short stories, essays, episodes of radio and television programs, songs, and short poems — are enclosed in quotation marks. (See 38c.)

NOTE: Do not use italics when referring to the Bible, titles of books in the Bible (Genesis, not *Genesis*), or titles of legal documents (the Constitution, not the *Constitution*).

43b Italicize non-English words used in an English sentence.

I wished my German teacher a *gute Reise* before his flight.

EXCEPTION: Do not italicize non-English terms that have become part of the English language — "laissez-faire" and "per diem," for example.

43c Italicize words mentioned as words, letters mentioned as letters, and numbers mentioned as numbers.

> Tomás assured us that the chemicals could probably be safely mixed, but his *probably* stuck in our minds.

> Some toddlers have trouble pronouncing the letters *f* and *s*.

> A big *3* was painted on the stage door.

NOTE: Quotation marks may be used instead of italics to set off words mentioned as words. (See 38d.) In particular, APA style recommends using quotation marks to set off words mentioned as words and letters mentioned as letters. An exception is that italics are used for key terms that are being defined.

> Social scientists use the term *androgyny* to describe a blending of traditionally masculine and feminine traits.

EXERCISE 43–1   Edit the following sentences to correct errors in the use of italics. If a sentence is correct, write "correct" after it. Answers appear in the back of the book.

> **The lecture was about Gini Alhadeff's memoir *The Sun at***
>
> **_Midday._** Correct

a. André De Shields, who starred in Broadway musicals like The Wiz and Hadestown, won his first Tony Award in 2019.

b. The old man *screamed* his anger, *shouting* to all of us, "I will not leave my money to you worthless layabouts!"

c. I learned the Latin term ad infinitum from an old nursery rhyme about fleas: "Great fleas have little fleas upon their backs to bite 'em, / And little fleas have lesser fleas and so ad infinitum."

d. Cinema audiences once gasped at hearing the word *damn* in *Gone with the Wind*.

e. Neve Campbell's lifelong interest in ballet inspired her involvement in the film "The Company," which portrays a season with the Joffrey Ballet.

44 Spelling

You learned to spell from repeated experience with words in both reading and writing. As you proofread, you may be able to tell if a word doesn't look quite right. In such cases, the solution is simple: Look up the word in a dictionary.

44a Become familiar with the major spelling rules.

i before *e* except after *c*

In general, use *i* before *e* except after *c* and except when sounded like *ay*, as in *neighbor* and *weigh*.

I BEFORE E	relieve, believe, sieve, niece, fierce, frieze
E BEFORE I	receive, deceive, sleigh, freight, eight
EXCEPTIONS	seize, either, weird, height, foreign, leisure

Suffixes

Final silent -e Generally, drop a final silent -*e* when adding a suffix that begins with a vowel. Keep the final -*e* if the suffix begins with a consonant.

achieve, achievement	desire, desirable
care, careful	entire, entirety
combine, combination	gentle, gentleness
EXCEPTIONS	changeable, judgment, argument, truly

Final -y When adding -*s* or -*d* to words ending in -*y*, ordinarily change -*y* to -*ie* when the -*y* is preceded by a consonant but not when it is preceded by a vowel.

comedy, comedies	monkey, monkeys
dry, dried	play, played

With proper names ending in *y*, do not change the -*y* to -*ie* even if it is preceded by a consonant: *the Bradys* (*the Brady family*).

Final consonants If a final consonant is preceded by a single vowel *and* the consonant ends a one-syllable word or a stressed syllable, double the consonant when adding a suffix beginning with a vowel.

> bet, betting
>
> commit, committed
>
> occur, occurrence

Plurals

-s or -es Add *-s* to form the plural of most nouns; add *-es* to singular nouns ending in *-s*, *-sh*, *-ch*, or *-x*.

> table, tables   church, churches
>
> paper, papers   dish, dishes

Ordinarily, add *-s* to nouns ending in *-o* when the *-o* is preceded by a vowel. Add *-es* when the *-o* is preceded by a consonant.

> hero, heroes   tomato, tomatoes
>
> radio, radios   video, videos

Other plurals To form the plural of a hyphenated compound word, add *-s* to the chief word even if it does not appear at the end.

> mother-in-law, mothers-in-law

English words derived from other languages such as Latin, Greek, or French sometimes form the plural as they would in their original language.

> chateau, chateaux
>
> criterion, criteria
>
> medium, media

44b Differentiate words that sound alike but have different meanings.

Words that sound alike or nearly alike but have different meanings and spellings are called *homophones*. The list on the next page shows sets of words that are commonly confused. (See also the glossary of usage in 18f.)

COMMON HOMOPHONES

affect (verb: to exert an influence)
effect (verb: to accomplish; noun: result)

its (possessive pronoun: of or belonging to it)
it's (contraction of *it is* or *it has*)

loose (adjective: free, not securely attached)
lose (verb: to fail to keep, to be deprived of)

their (possessive pronoun: belonging to them)
they're (contraction of *they are*)
there (adverb: that place or position)

who's (contraction of *who is* or *who has*)
whose (possessive form of *who*)

your (possessive pronoun: belonging to you)
you're (contraction of *you are*)

EXERCISE 44–1 The following memo has been run through a spell checker. Proofread it carefully, editing the errors that remain.

November 3, 2020
To: Patricia Wise
From: Constance Mayhew
Subject: Express Tours annual report

Thank you for agreeing to draft the annual report for Express Tours. Before you begin you're work, let me outline the initial steps.

First, its essential for you to include brief profiles of top management. Early next week, I'll provide profiles for all manages accept Samuel Heath, who's biographical information is being revised. You should edit these profiles carefully and than format them according to the enclosed instructions. We may ask you to include other employee's profiles at some point.

Second, you should arrange to get complete financial information for fiscal year 2020 from our comptroller, Richard Chang. (Helen Boyes, to, can provide the necessary figures.) When you get this information, precede according to the plans we discuss in yesterday's meeting. By the way, you will notice from the figures that the sale of our Charterhouse division did not significantly effect net profits.

Third, you should email a first draft of the report by December 13. Of coarse, you should proofread you writing.

I am quiet pleased that you can take on this project. If I can answers questions, don't hesitate to call.

45 Hyphenation

45a Consult the dictionary to determine how to treat a compound word.

The dictionary indicates whether to treat a compound word as a hyphenated compound (*water-repellent*), one word (*waterproof*), or two words (*water table*). If the compound word is not in the dictionary, treat it as two words.

▶ The prosecutor chose not to cross-examine any witnesses.

▶ All students are expected to record their data in a small note book.

45b Hyphenate two or more words used together as an adjective before a noun.

▶ Today's teachers depend on both traditional textbook material

and web-delivered content.

▶ Richa Gupta is not yet a well-known candidate.

Generally, do not use a hyphen when such compounds follow the noun.

▶ After our television campaign, Richa Gupta will be well-known.

Do not use a hyphen to connect *-ly* adverbs to the words they modify.

▶ A slowly-moving truck tied up traffic.

45c Hyphenate fractions and certain numbers when they are spelled out.

For numbers written as words, use a hyphen in all fractions (*two-thirds*) and in all forms of compound numbers from twenty-one to ninety-nine (*thirty-five, sixty-seventh*).

▶ One-fourth of my income goes to pay my child-care expenses.
      ^

45d Use a hyphen with the prefixes *all-, ex-* (meaning "former"), and *self-* and with the suffix *-elect.*

▶ The private foundation is funneling more money into self-help
                                                              ^

  projects.

▶ The Student Senate bylaws require the president-elect to attend
                                                       ^

  all senate meetings before the transfer of office.

45e Use a hyphen in certain words to avoid ambiguity.

Without the hyphen, there would be no way to distinguish between words such as *re-creation* and *recreation*.

  Bicycling in the city is my favorite form of recreation.

  The film was praised for its astonishing re-creation of nineteenth-century London.

  Hyphens are sometimes used to separate awkward double or triple letters in compound words (*anti-intellectual, cross-stitch*).

45f Check for correct word breaks when words must be divided at the end of a line.

Only words that already contain a hyphen should be broken at the end of a line of text. If your word processor automatically breaks words at the ends of lines, disable that setting.

Email addresses, URLs, and DOIs need special attention when they break at the end of a line of text or in bibliographic citations. Do not insert a hyphen. Instead, consult the guidelines for URLs and DOIs in MLA style (58a) and APA style (63a). Break an email address after the @ symbol or before a period.

EXERCISE 45–1   Edit the following sentences to correct errors in hyphenation. If a sentence is correct, write "correct" after it. Answers appear in the back of the book.

> **Émile Zola's first readers were scandalized by his slice-of-life**
>
> **novels.**

a. Gold is the seventy-ninth element in the periodic table.
b. The swiftly-moving tugboat pulled alongside the barge and directed it away from the oil spill in the harbor.
c. The ice-encrusted fossil was a major find.
d. Your dog is well-known in our neighborhood.
e. Road-blocks were set up along all the major highways leading out of the city.

46 Capitalization

46a Capitalize proper nouns and words derived from them; do not capitalize common nouns.

Proper nouns are the names of specific persons, places, and things. All other nouns are common nouns. The following types of words are usually capitalized: names of deities, religions, religious followers, sacred books; words of family relationship used as names; particular places; nationalities and their languages, races, tribes; departments, degrees, particular courses at educational institutions; government departments, organizations, political parties; historical movements, periods, events, documents; and trade names. The next page lists examples of proper and common nouns.

PROPER NOUNS	COMMON NOUNS
God (used as a name)	a god
Uncle Pedro	my uncle
Father (used as a name)	my father
the South	a southern state
Environmental Protection Agency	a federal agency
the Democratic Party	a political party
the Enlightenment	the eighteenth century
the Treaty of Versailles	a treaty
Advil	a painkiller

Months, holidays, and days of the week are treated as proper nouns: *May, Memorial Day, Monday.* The seasons and numbers of the days of the month are not: *summer, the seventh of September.*

EXCEPTION: Capitalize Fourth of July (or July Fourth) when referring to the holiday.

Names of school subjects are capitalized only if they are names of languages: *English, Mandarin.* Names of particular courses are capitalized: *Geology 101.*

The term *Internet* is typically capitalized, but other common nouns related to the Internet and computers are not: *home page, website.* Usage varies widely, however, so check the rules of the discipline or style in which you are writing.

46b Capitalize titles of persons when used as part of a proper name but usually not when used alone.

District Attorney Marshall was reprimanded for badgering the witness.

The district attorney was elected for a two-year term.

Usage varies when the title of an important public figure is used alone: *The president* [or *President*] *vetoed the bill.*

46c Capitalize titles according to convention.

In both titles and subtitles of works mentioned in the text of a paper, major words such as nouns, pronouns, verbs, adjectives, and adverbs should be capitalized. Minor words such as articles, prepositions, and coordinating conjunctions are not capitalized unless they are the first or last word of a title or subtitle. (In APA style, capitalize all words of four or more letters. See 63a.)

Capitalize the second part of a hyphenated term in a title if it is a major word but not if it is a minor word. Capitalize chapter titles and the titles of other major divisions of a work.

Seizing the Enigma: The Race to Break the German U-Boat Codes

A River Runs through It

Titles of works are handled differently in the APA reference list. See "Preparing the list of references" in 63a.

46d Capitalize the first word of a sentence.

The first word of a sentence should be capitalized. When a sentence appears within parentheses, capitalize its first word unless the parentheses appear within another sentence.

Early detection of cancer increases survival rates. (See table 2.)

Early detection of cancer increases survival rates (see table 2).

46e Capitalize the first word of a quoted sentence but not a quoted word or phrase.

Loveless writes, "If failing schools are ever to be turned around, much more must be learned about how schools age as institutions" (25).

Steven Pinker has written that one important element of good writing is "attention to the readers' vantage point" (26).

If a quoted sentence is interrupted by explanatory words, do not capitalize the first word after the interruption. (See 38e.)

"When we all think alike," he said, "no one is thinking."

When quoting poetry, copy the poet's capitalization exactly. Many poets capitalize the first word of every line of poetry; a few contemporary poets dismiss capitalization altogether.

it was the week   that

i felt the city's narrow breezes rush about
me   — Don L. Lee

46f Know your options when the first word after a colon begins an independent clause.

When a group of words following a colon can stand on its own as a complete sentence, MLA recommends using lowercase for the first word except in certain situations (such as if the sentence following the colon is a question). APA calls for capitalizing it.

> **MLA STYLE**
> Clinical trials revealed a problem: a high percentage of participants reported severe headaches.

> **APA STYLE**
> Clinical trials revealed a problem: A high percentage of participants reported severe headaches.

Always use lowercase for a list or an appositive that follows a colon (see 36a).

> Students were divided into two groups: residents and commuters.

EXERCISE 46–1   Edit the following sentences to correct errors in capitalization. If a sentence is correct, write "correct" after it. Answers appear in the back of the book.

> On our trip to the West, we visited the grand ͟c͟anyon and the ͟g͟reat ͟s͟alt ͟d͟esert.

a. Assistant dean Shirin Ahmadi recommended offering more world language courses.

b. We went to the Mark Taper Forum to see a production of *Angels in America*.

c. Kalindi has an ambitious semester, studying differential calculus, classical hebrew, brochure design, and greek literature.

d. Lydia's Aunt and Uncle make modular houses as beautiful as modernist works of art.

e. The labs in Ohio began their research in the Spring, and we expect clinical trials to start at our Cleveland lab next Summer.

Grammar Basics

47   Parts of speech

Traditional grammar recognizes eight parts of speech: noun, pronoun, verb, adjective, adverb, preposition, conjunction, and interjection. Many words can function as more than one part of speech. For example, the word *paint* can be a noun (*The paint is wet*) or a verb (*Please paint the ceiling*).

47a   Nouns

A noun is the name of a person, place, thing, or concept.

>   N   N   N
> The *bird* in the *sky* flew down into its *nest*.

Nouns sometimes function as adjectives modifying other nouns. Because of their dual roles, nouns used in this manner may be called *noun/adjectives*.

>   N/ADJ   N/ADJ
> The *leather* notebook was tucked in the *student's* backpack.

Nouns are classified in a variety of ways.

- *Proper* nouns are capitalized, but *common* nouns are not (see 46a).
- For clarity, writers choose between *concrete* and *abstract* nouns (see 18b).
- The distinction between *count* nouns and *noncount* nouns can be helpful to multilingual writers (see 29a).
- Most nouns have *singular* and *plural* forms; *collective* nouns may be either singular or plural, depending on how they are used (see 21f and 22b).
- *Possessive* nouns require an apostrophe (see 37a).

EXERCISE 47–1   Underline the nouns (and noun/adjectives) in the following sentences. Answers appear in the back of the book.

> **The best <u>part</u> of <u>dinner</u> was the <u>chef's</u> newest <u>dessert</u>.**

a. The stage was set for a confrontation of biblical proportions.
b. The courage of the nurses was an inspiration to the community.
c. The need to arrive before the guest of honor motivated us to navigate the thick fog.
d. The defense attorney made a final appeal to the jury.
e. A national museum dedicated to women artists opened in 1987.

47b Pronouns

A pronoun is a word used in place of a noun. Usually the pronoun substitutes for a specific noun, known as its *antecedent*.

ANT   PN
When the *battery* wears down, we recharge *it*.

Although most pronouns function as substitutes for nouns, some can function as adjectives modifying nouns. Such pronouns may be called *pronoun/adjectives*.

PN/ADJ
That bird was at the same window yesterday morning.

Pronouns are classified in the following ways.

Personal pronouns   Personal pronouns refer to specific persons or things. They always function as subsitutes for nouns.

Singular: I, me, you, she, her, he, him, it
Plural: we, us, you, they, them

Possessive pronouns   Possessive pronouns indicate ownership.

Singular: my, mine, your, yours, her, hers, his, its
Plural: our, ours, your, yours, their, theirs

Some of these possessive pronouns function as adjectives modifying nouns: *my, your, his, her, its, our, their.*

Intensive and reflexive pronouns   Intensive pronouns emphasize a noun or another pronoun (The senator *herself* met us at the door). Reflexive pronouns name a receiver of an action identical with the doer of the action (Paula nominated *herself*).

Singular: myself, yourself, himself, herself, itself
Plural: ourselves, yourselves, themselves

Relative pronouns Relative pronouns introduce subordinate clauses functioning as adjectives (The writer *who won the award* refused to accept it). The relative pronoun (in this case *who*) also points back to a noun or pronoun that the clause modifies (*writer*). (See 49e.)

who, whom, whose, which, that

The pronouns *whichever*, *whoever*, *whomever*, *what*, and *whatever* are sometimes considered relative pronouns, but they introduce noun clauses and do not point back to a noun or pronoun. (See "Noun clauses" in 49e.)

Interrogative pronouns Interrogative pronouns introduce questions (*Who* is expected to win the election?).

who, whom, whose, which, what

Demonstrative pronouns Demonstrative pronouns identify or point to nouns. Frequently they function as adjectives (*This* chair is my favorite), but they may also function as substitutes for nouns (*This* is my favorite chair).

this, that, these, those

Indefinite pronouns Indefinite pronouns refer to nonspecific persons or things. Most are always singular (*everyone*, *each*); some are always plural (*both*, *many*); a few may be singular or plural (see 21e). Most indefinite pronouns function as substitutes for nouns (*Something* is burning), but some can also function as adjectives (*All* campers must check in at the lodge).

all	anything	everyone	nobody	several
another	both	everything	none	some
any	each	few	no one	somebody
anybody	either	many	nothing	someone
anyone	everybody	neither	one	something

Reciprocal pronouns Reciprocal pronouns refer to individual parts of a plural antecedent (By turns, the penguins fed *one another*).

each other, one another

NOTE: See also pronoun-antecedent agreement (22), pronoun reference (23), distinguishing between pronouns such as *I* and *me* (24), and distinguishing between *who* and *whom* (25).

EXERCISE 47-2 Underline the pronouns (and pronoun/adjectives) in the following sentences. Answers appear in the back of the book.

<u>We</u> enjoyed the video <u>that</u> the fifth graders produced as

<u>their</u> final project.

a. The governor's loyalty was his most appealing trait.
b. In the fall, the geese that fly south for the winter pass through our town in huge numbers.
c. As Carl Sandburg once said, even he himself did not understand some of his poetry.
d. I appealed my parking ticket, but you did not get one.
e. Angela did not mind gossip as long as no one gossiped about her.

47c Verbs

The verb of a sentence usually expresses action (*jump*, *think*) or being (*is*, *become*). It is composed of a main verb possibly preceded by one or more helping verbs.

> MV
> The horses *exercise* every day.

> HV   MV
> The task force report *was* not *completed* on schedule.

> HV HV   MV
> No one *has been defended* with more passion than our mayor.

Notice that words, usually adverbs, can intervene between the helping verb and the main verb (was *not* completed). (See 47e.)

Helping verbs

There are twenty-three helping verbs in English: forms of *have*, *do*, and *be*, which may also function as main verbs; and nine modals, which function only as helping verbs. *Have*, *do*, and *be* change form to indicate tense; the nine modals do not.

FORMS OF *HAVE, DO,* AND *BE*

have, has, had

do, does, did

be, am, is, are, was, were, being, been

MODALS

can, could, may, might, must, shall, should, will, would

The verb phrase *ought to* is often classified as a modal as well.

Main verbs

The main verb of a sentence is always the kind of word that would change form if put into these test sentences:

BASE FORM	Usually I (*cook*, *drive*).
PAST TENSE	Yesterday I (*cooked*, *drove*).
PAST PARTICIPLE	I have (*cooked*, *driven*) many times before.
PRESENT PARTICIPLE	I am (*cooking*, *driving*) right now.
-S FORM	Usually he/she/it (*cooks*, *drives*).

If a word doesn't change form when slipped into the test sentences, you can be certain that it is not a main verb. For example, the noun *revolution*, though it may seem to suggest an action, can never function as a main verb. Just try to make it behave like one (*Today I revolution . . . Yesterday I revolutioned . . .*) and you'll see why.

When both the past-tense and the past-participle forms of a verb end in *-ed*, the verb is regular (*cooked, cooked*). Otherwise, the verb is irregular (*drove, driven*). (See 27a.)

The verb *be* is highly irregular, having eight forms instead of the usual five: the base form *be*; the present-tense forms *am*, *is*, and *are*; the past-tense forms *was* and *were*; the present participle *being*; and the past participle *been*.

Helping verbs combine with main verbs to create tenses. For a survey of tenses, see 27f.

NOTE: Some verbs are followed by words that look like prepositions but are so closely associated with the verb that they are a part of its meaning. These words are known as *particles*. Common verb-particle combinations include *bring up, call off, drop off, give in, look up, run into,* and *take off*.

> Sharon *packed up* her broken laptop and *sent* it *off* to the repair shop.

TIP: For more information about using verbs, see these sections: active verbs (8), subject-verb agreement (21), verb forms (27), verb tense and mood (27f and 27g), and multilingual/ESL challenges with verbs (28).

EXERCISE 47-3   Underline the verbs in the following sentences, including helping verbs and particles. If a verb is part of a contraction (such as *is* in *isn't* or *would* in *I'd*), underline only the letters that represent the verb. Answers appear in the back of the book.

> **The ground under the pine trees <u>was</u>n't wet from the rain.**

a. My grandmother always told me a soothing story before bed.
b. There were fifty apples on the tree before the frost killed them.
c. Morton brought down the box of letters from the attic.
d. Stay on the main road and you'll arrive at the base camp.
e. The fish struggled vigorously but was trapped in the net.

47d Adjectives

An adjective is a word used to modify, or describe, a noun or pronoun. An adjective usually answers one of these questions: Which one? What kind? How many?

> ADJ
> the *broken* window   **Which window?**
>
> ADJ   ADJ
> *cracked old* plates   **What kind of plates?**
>
> ADJ
> *nine* months   **How many months?**

Adjectives usually come before the words they modify. They may also follow linking verbs, in which case they describe the subject. (See 48b.)

> ADJ
> The decision was *unpopular.*

The definite article *the* and the indefinite articles *a* and *an* are also classified as adjectives.

> ART   ART   ART
> *A* defendant should be judged on *the* evidence provided to *the* jury, not on hearsay.

Some possessive, demonstrative, and indefinite pronouns can function as adjectives: *their*, *its*, *this*, *all* (see 47b). And nouns can function as adjectives when they modify other nouns: *apple pie* (the noun *apple* modifies the noun *pie*; see 47a).

TIP: You can find more details about using adjectives in 26. If you are a multilingual writer, you may find help with articles and specific uses of adjectives in 29, 30f, and 30g.

47e Adverbs

An adverb is a word used to modify, or qualify, a verb (or verbal), an adjective, or another adverb. It usually answers one of these questions: When? Where? How? Why? Under what conditions? To what degree?

> Pull *firmly* on the emergency handle.   Pull how?
> Read the text *first* and *then* complete the exercises.   Read when?
>   Complete when?

Adverbs modifying adjectives or other adverbs usually intensify or limit the intensity of the word they modify.

>   ADV
> Be *extremely* kind, and you will have many friends.

>   ADV
> We proceeded *very* cautiously in the dark house.

The words *not* and *never* are classified as adverbs.

EXERCISE 47–4   Underline the adjectives and circle the adverbs in the following sentences. If a word is a noun or pronoun functioning as an adjective, underline it and mark it as a noun/adjective or pronoun/adjective. Also treat the articles *a*, *an*, and *the* as adjectives. Answers appear in the back of the book.

> **Finding <u>an</u> <u>available</u> room during <u>the</u> convention**
>
> **was ⃝not <u>easy</u>.**

a. Generalizations lead to weak, unfocused essays.

b. The Spanish language is wonderfully flexible.

c. The wildflowers smelled especially fragrant after the steady rain.

d. I'd rather be slightly hot than bitterly cold.

e. The cat slept soundly in its wicker basket.

47f Prepositions

A preposition is a word placed before a noun or pronoun to form a phrase that modifies another word in the sentence. The prepositional phrase nearly always functions as an adjective or as an adverb.

> P   P   P
> The road *to* the summit travels *past* craters *from* an extinct volcano.

To the summit functions as an adjective modifying the noun *road*; *past craters* functions as an adverb modifying the verb *travels*; *from an extinct volcano* functions as an adjective modifying the noun *craters*. (For more on prepositional phrases, see 49a.)

English has a limited number of prepositions. The most common ones are included in the following list.

COMMON PREPOSITIONS

about	beside	from	outside	toward
above	besides	in	over	under
across	between	inside	past	underneath
after	beyond	into	plus	unlike
against	but	like	regarding	until
along	by	near	respecting	unto
among	concerning	next	round	up
around	considering	of	since	upon
as	despite	off	than	with
at	down	on	through	within
before	during	onto	throughout	without
behind	except	opposite	till	
below	for	out	to	

Some prepositions are more than one word long: *along with, as well as, in addition to, next to, rather than.*

TIP: Prepositions are used in idioms such as *capable of* and *dig up* (see 18c). For specific issues for multilingual writers, see 31.

47g Conjunctions

Conjunctions join words, phrases, or clauses, and they indicate the relation between the elements joined.

Coordinating conjunctions A coordinating conjunction is used to connect grammatically equal elements. (See 9b and 14a.) The coordinating conjunctions are *and, but, or, nor, for, so,* and *yet.*

> The sociologist interviewed children *but* not their parents.
>
> Write clearly, *and* your readers will appreciate your efforts.

In the first sentence, *but* connects two noun phrases; in the second, *and* connects two independent clauses.

Correlative conjunctions Correlative conjunctions come in pairs; they connect grammatically equal elements.

> both . . . and   not only . . . but also
>
> either . . . or   whether . . . or
>
> neither . . . nor

Either the painting was brilliant *or* it was a forgery.

Subordinating conjunctions A subordinating conjunction introduces a subordinate clause and indicates the relation of the clause to the rest of the sentence. (See 49e.) The most common subordinating conjunctions are *after, although, as, as if, because, before, even though, if, in order that, once, since, so that, than, that, though, unless, until, when, where, whether,* and *while.*

> *When* the fundraiser ends, we expect to have raised a million dollars.

Conjunctive adverbs Conjunctive adverbs connect independent clauses and indicate the relation between the clauses. They can be used with a semicolon to join two independent clauses in one sentence, or they can be used alone with an independent clause. The most common conjunctive adverbs are *finally, furthermore, however, moreover, nevertheless, similarly, then, therefore,* and *thus.*

> The photographer failed to take a light reading; *therefore,* all the pictures were underexposed.
>
> During the day, the kitten sleeps peacefully. *However,* when night falls, the kitten is wide awake and ready to play.

Conjunctive adverbs can appear at the beginning or in the middle of a clause.

> When night falls, *however*, the kitten is wide awake and ready to play.

TIP: Recognizing conjunctive adverbs and coordinating conjunctions will help you avoid run-on sentences and make punctuation decisions (see 20, 33a, and 33f). Recognizing subordinating conjunctions will help you avoid sentence fragments (see 19).

47h Interjections

An interjection is a word used to express surprise or emotion (*Oh! Hey! Wow!*).

48 Sentence patterns

The vast majority of sentences in English conform to one of these five patterns:

> subject/verb/subject complement
>
> subject/verb/direct object
>
> subject/verb/indirect object/direct object
>
> subject/verb/direct object/object complement
>
> subject/verb

Adverbial modifiers (single words, phrases, or clauses) may be added to any of these patterns, and they may appear nearly anywhere — at the beginning, in the middle, or at the end.

Predicate is the grammatical term given to the verb plus its objects, complements, and adverbial modifiers.

48a Subjects

The subject of a sentence names whom or what the sentence is about. The simple subject is always a noun or pronoun; the complete subject consists of the simple subject and any words or word groups modifying the simple subject.

The complete subject

To find the complete subject, ask Who? or What?, insert the verb, and finish the question. The answer is the complete subject.

> ┌────── COMPLETE SUBJECT ──────┐
> The devastating effects of famine can last for many years.

Who or what can last for many years? *The devastating effects of famine.*

> ┌─────────── COMPLETE SUBJECT ───────────┐
> Adventure novels that contain multiple subplots are often made into successful movies.

Who or what are often made into movies? *Adventure novels that contain multiple subplots.*

> ┌──── COMPLETE SUBJECT ────┐
> In our program, student teachers work full-time for ten months.

Who or what works full-time for ten months? *Student teachers.* Notice that *In our program, student teachers* is not a sensible answer to the question. (It is not safe to assume that the subject must always appear first in a sentence.)

The simple subject

To find the simple subject, strip away all modifiers in the complete subject. This includes single-word modifiers such as *the* and *devastating*, phrases such as *of famine*, and subordinate clauses such as *that contain multiple subplots*.

> ┌ SS ┐
> *The devastating effects of famine* can last for many years.

> ┌ SS ┐
> *Adventure novels that contain multiple subplots* are often made into successful movies.

A sentence may have a compound subject containing two or more simple subjects joined with a coordinating conjunction such as *and*, *but*, or *or*.

┌───── SS ─────┐   ┌ SS ┐
Great commitment and a little luck make a successful actor.

Understood subjects

In imperative sentences, which give advice or issue commands, the subject is understood but not actually present in the sentence. The subject of an imperative sentence is understood to be *you*.

[*You*] Put your hands on the steering wheel.

Subject after the verb

Although the subject ordinarily comes before the verb (*The planes took off*), occasionally it does not. When a sentence begins with *There is* or *There are* (or *There was* or *There were*), the subject follows the verb. In such inverted constructions, the word *There* is an expletive, an empty word serving merely to get the sentence started.

┌─ SS ─┐
There are *eight planes waiting to take off.*

Occasionally a writer will invert a sentence for effect.

┌ SS ┐
Joyful is *the child whose school closes for snow.*

Joyful is an adjective, so it cannot be the subject. Turn this sentence around and its structure becomes obvious.

The *child* whose school closes for snow is joyful.

In questions, the subject frequently appears between the helping verb and the main verb.

HV   ┌───── SS ─────┐ MV
Do *Olympic marathoners* train year-round?

TIP: Recognizing the subject of a sentence will help you edit for fragments (19), subject-verb agreement (21), pronouns such as *I* and *me* (24), missing subjects (30b), and repeated subjects (30c).

EXERCISE 48–1   In the following sentences, underline the complete subject and write *SS* above the simple subject(s). If the subject is an understood *you*, insert *you* in parentheses. Answers appear in the back of the book.

⌐ SS ¬   ⌐ SS ¬
<u>Parents and their children</u> often look alike.

a.   The hills and mountains seemed endless, and the snow glistened.
b.   In foil fencing, points are scored by hitting an electronic target.
c.   Do not stand in the aisles or sit on the stairs.
d.   There were hundreds of fireflies in the open field.
e.   The evidence against the defendant was staggering.

48b   Verbs, objects, and complements

Section 47c explains how to find a sentence's verb. A verb is classified as linking, transitive, or intransitive, depending on the kinds of objects or complements the verb can (or cannot) take.

Linking verbs and subject complements

Linking verbs connect the subject to a subject complement, a word or word group that completes the meaning of the subject by renaming or describing it.

⌐——————— S ———————¬ ⌐ V ¬⌐ SC ¬
An email requesting personal information may be a scam.

⌐——— S ———¬ V   SC
Last month's temperatures were mild.

Whenever they appear as main verbs (rather than helping verbs), the forms of *be* — *be, am, is, are, was, were, being, been* — usually function as linking verbs. In the preceding examples, for instance, the main verbs are *be* and *were*.

Verbs such as *appear, become, feel, grow, look, make, seem, smell, sound,* and *taste* are linking when they are followed by a word or word group that renames or describes the subject.

⌐ S ¬⌐ V ¬   SC
As it thickens, the sauce will look unappealing.

Transitive verbs and direct objects

A transitive verb takes a direct object, a word or word group that names a receiver of the action.

⌐——— S ———¬ V   ⌐——— DO ———¬
The hungry cat clawed the bag of dry food.

The simple direct object is always a noun or pronoun, in this case *bag*. To find it, simply strip away all modifiers.

Transitive verbs usually appear in the active voice, with the subject doing the action and a direct object receiving the action. Active-voice sentences can be transformed into the passive voice, with the subject receiving the action.

Transitive verbs, indirect objects, and direct objects

The direct object of a transitive verb is sometimes preceded by an indirect object, a noun or pronoun telling to whom or for whom the action of the sentence is done.

> S   V   IO ⌐— DO —⌐   S ⌐— V —⌐ IO ⌐ DO ⌐
> You give her some yarn, and she will knit you a scarf.

The simple indirect object is always a noun or pronoun. To test for an indirect object, insert the word *to* or *for* before the word or word group in question. If the sentence makes sense, the word or word group is an indirect object.

> You give [to] *her* some yarn, and she will knit [for] *you* a scarf.

Transitive verbs, direct objects, and object complements

The direct object of a transitive verb is sometimes followed by an object complement, a word or word group that renames or describes the object.

> S   V   DO ⌐——— OC ———⌐
> People often consider chivalry a thing of the past.

> ⌐— S —⌐ V   DO ⌐——— OC ———⌐
> The kiln makes clay firm and strong.

When the object complement renames the direct object, it is a noun or pronoun (such as *thing*). When it describes the direct object, it is an adjective (such as *firm* and *strong*).

Intransitive verbs

Intransitive verbs take no objects or complements.

> ⌐—— S ——⌐ V
> The audience laughed.

> ⌐—— S —⌐   V
> The driver accelerated in the straightaway.

Nothing receives the actions of laughing and accelerating in examples on the previous page, so the verbs are intransitive. Notice that such verbs may or may not be followed by adverbial modifiers. In the second sentence, *in the straightaway* is an adverbial prepositional phrase modifying *accelerated*.

NOTE: The dictionary will tell you whether a verb is transitive or intransitive. Some verbs can have either function depending on context.

TRANSITIVE	Sandra *flew* her small plane over the canyon.
INTRANSITIVE	A flock of migrating geese *flew* overhead.

In the first example, *flew* has a direct object that receives the action: *her small plane.* In the second example, the verb is followed by an adverb (*overhead*), not by a direct object.

EXERCISE 48–2   Label the subject complements and direct objects in the following sentences, using the labels *SC* and *DO*. If a subject complement or direct object consists of more than one word, bracket and label all of it. Answers appear in the back of the book.

┌──── DO ────┐
The sharp right turn confused most drivers.

a. Mangoes are expensive.
b. Samurai warriors never fear death.
c. Successful coaches always praise their players' efforts.
d. St. Petersburg was the capital of the Russian Empire for two centuries.
e. The medicine tasted bitter.

EXERCISE 48–3   Each of the following sentences has either an indirect object followed by a direct object or a direct object followed by an object complement. Label the objects and complements, using the labels *IO*, *DO*, and *OC*. If an object or a complement consists of more than one word, bracket and label all of it. Answers appear in the back of the book.

┌──────── DO ────────┐┌─ OC ─┐
Most people consider their own experience normal.

a. Stress can make adults and children weary.
b. The dining hall offered students healthy meal choices.
c. Consider the work finished.
d. We showed the agent our tickets, and she gave us boarding passes.
e. Zita has made community service her priority this year.

49 Subordinate word groups

Subordinate word groups include phrases and clauses. Phrases are subordinate because they lack a subject and a verb; they are classified as prepositional, verbal, appositive, or absolute (see 49a–49d). Subordinate clauses have a subject and a verb, but they begin with a word (such as *although*, *that*, or *when*) that marks them as subordinate (see 49e).

49a Prepositional phrases

A prepositional phrase begins with a preposition (see 47f) and usually ends with a noun or noun equivalent: *on the table, for him, by sleeping late*. The noun or noun equivalent is known as the *object of the preposition*.

Prepositional phrases function either as adjectives or as adverbs. As an adjective, a prepositional phrase nearly always appears immediately following the noun or pronoun it modifies.

The hut had *walls of mud*.

Adjective phrases usually answer one or both of the questions Which one? and What kind of? If we ask Which walls? or What kind of walls? we get a sensible answer: *walls of mud*.

Adverbial prepositional phrases usually modify the verb, but they can also modify adjectives or other adverbs. When a prepositional phrase modifies the verb, it can appear nearly anywhere in a sentence.

James *walked* his dog *on a leash*.

Sabrina *in time adjusted* to life in Ecuador.

During a mudslide, the terrain *can change* drastically.

If a prepositional phrase is movable, you can be certain that it is adverbial.

In the cave, the explorers found well-preserved prehistoric drawings.

The explorers found well-preserved prehistoric drawings *in the cave*.

Adverbial word groups usually answer one of these questions: When? Where? How? Why? Under what conditions? To what degree?

> James walked his dog *how*? *On a leash.*
>
> Sabrina adjusted to life in Ecuador *when*? *In time.*
>
> The terrain can change drastically *under what conditions*? *During a mudslide.*

In questions and subordinate clauses, a preposition may appear after its object.

> *What* are you afraid *of*?
>
> We avoided the bike trail *that* John had warned us *about*.

EXERCISE 49–1   Underline the prepositional phrases in the following sentences. Tell whether each one is an adjective phrase or an adverb phrase and what it modifies in the sentence. Answers appear in the back of the book.

> **Flecks of mica glittered in the new granite floor.**   (Adjective phrase modifying "Flecks"; adverb phrase modifying "glittered")

a. In northern Italy, we met many people who speak German as their first language.

b. William completed the yoga routine for beginners with ease.

c. To my boss's dismay, I was late for work again.

d. The traveling exhibit of Mayan artifacts gave viewers new insight into pre-Columbian culture.

e. In 2002, the euro became the official currency in twelve European countries.

49b Verbal phrases

A verbal is a verb form that does not function as the verb of a clause. Verbals include infinitives (the word *to* plus the base form of the verb), present participles (the *-ing* form of the verb), and past participles (the verb form usually ending in *-d, -ed, -n, -en,* or *-t*). (See 27a and 47c.)

INFINITIVE	PRESENT PARTICIPLE	PAST PARTICIPLE
to dream	dreaming	dreamed
to choose	choosing	chosen
to build	building	built

Instead of functioning as the verb of a clause, a verbal functions as an adjective, a noun, or an adverb.

ADJECTIVE	*Broken* promises cannot be fixed.
NOUN	Constant *complaining* becomes wearisome.
ADVERB	Can you wait *to celebrate*?

Verbals with objects, complements, or modifiers form verbal phrases.

In my family, *singing loudly* is more appreciated than *singing well*.

Like verbals, verbal phrases function as adjectives, nouns, or adverbs. Verbal phrases are ordinarily classified as participial, gerund, or infinitive.

Participial phrases

Participial phrases always function as adjectives. Their verbals are either present participles (such as *dreaming* or *asking*) or past participles (such as *stolen* or *reached*).

Participial phrases frequently appear immediately following the noun or pronoun they modify.

Congress shall make no *law abridging the freedom of speech or of the press*.

Participial phrases are often movable. They can precede the word they modify.

Being a weight-bearing joint, the *knee* is among the most frequently injured.

They may also appear at some distance from the word they modify.

Last night we saw a *play* that affected us deeply, *written with profound insight into the lives of immigrants*.

Gerund phrases

Gerund phrases are built around present participles (verb forms that end in *-ing*), and they always function as nouns: usually as subjects, subject complements, direct objects, or objects of a preposition.

    ┌────── S ──────┐
Rationalizing a fear can eliminate it.

                           ┌────── SC ──────┐
The key to a good sauce is browning the mushrooms.

                    ┌────── DO ──────┐
Lizards usually enjoy sunning themselves.

The American Heart Association has documented the benefits of
                  ┌────── OBJ OF PREP ──────┐
diet and exercise in reducing the risk of heart attack.

Infinitive phrases

Infinitive phrases, usually constructed around *to* plus the base form of the verb (*to call, to drink*), can function as nouns, as adjectives, or as adverbs. When functioning as a noun, an infinitive phrase may appear in almost any noun slot in a sentence, usually as a subject, subject complement, or direct object.

    ┌────── S ──────┐
To hike without a navigation device is risky.

Infinitive phrases functioning as adjectives usually appear immediately following the noun or pronoun they modify.

The Nineteenth Amendment gave women the *right to vote.*

The infinitive phrase modifies the noun *right.* Which right? *The right to vote.*

Adverbial infinitive phrases usually qualify the meaning of the verb, telling when, where, how, why, under what conditions, or to what degree an action occurred.

Volunteers *rolled up* their pants *to wade through the floodwaters.*

Why did they roll up their pants? *To wade through the floodwaters.*

EXERCISE 49–2   Underline the verbal phrases in the following sentences. Tell whether each phrase is participial, gerund, or infinitive and how each is used in the sentence. Answers appear in the back of the book.

Do you want <u>to watch that documentary?</u> (Infinitive phrase used as direct object of "Do want")

a. Updating your software will fix the computer glitch.
b. The challenge in decreasing the town budget is identifying nonessential services.
c. Cathleen tried to help her mother by raking the lawn.
d. Understanding little, I had no hope of passing my biology final.
e. Working with animals gave Steve a sense of satisfaction.

49c Appositive phrases

Appositive phrases describe nouns or pronouns. Instead of modifying nouns or pronouns, however, appositive phrases rename them. In form they are nouns or noun equivalents.

Podcasts, *the modern equivalent of radio talk shows*, are increasingly easy to record and produce.

49d Absolute phrases

An absolute phrase modifies a whole clause or sentence, not just one word. It consists of a noun or noun equivalent usually followed by a participial phrase.

Her words reverberating in the hushed arena, the senator urged the crowd to support her former opponent.

49e Subordinate clauses

Subordinate clauses are patterned like sentences, having subjects and verbs and sometimes objects or complements. But they function within sentences as adjectives, adverbs, or nouns. They cannot stand alone as complete sentences.

A subordinate clause usually begins with a subordinating conjunction or a relative pronoun. The chart in this section classifies these words according to the kinds of clauses (adjective, adverb, or noun) they introduce.

Adjective clauses

Adjective clauses modify nouns or pronouns, usually answering the question Which one? or What kind of? Most adjective clauses begin with a relative pronoun (*who, whom, whose, which,* or *that*). In addition to introducing the clause, the relative pronoun points back to the noun that the clause modifies.

The coach chose *players who would benefit from intense drills.*

A *book that goes unread* is a writer's worst nightmare.

Relative pronouns are sometimes "understood."

The things [*that*] *we cherish most* are the things [*that*] *we might lose.*

Occasionally an adjective clause is introduced by a relative adverb, usually *when, where,* or *why.*

The aging actor returned to the *stage where he had made his debut as Hamlet half a century earlier.*

The parts of an adjective clause are often arranged as in sentences (subject/verb/object or complement).

                                   S   V   DO

Sometimes it is our closest friends who disappoint us.

Frequently, however, the object or complement appears first, out of the normal order of subject/verb/object.

                            DO   S   V

They can be the very friends whom we disappoint.

TIP: For punctuation of adjective clauses, see 33e and 34e. For advice about avoiding repeated words in adjective clauses, see 30d.

> ### WORDS THAT INTRODUCE SUBORDINATE CLAUSES
>
> #### Words introducing adjective clauses
>
> **RELATIVE PRONOUNS:** that, which, who, whom, whose
> **RELATIVE ADVERBS:** when, where, why
>
> #### Words introducing adverb clauses
>
> **SUBORDINATING CONJUNCTIONS:** after, although, as, as if, because, before, even though, if, in order that, once, since, so that, than, that, though, unless, until, when, where, whether, while
>
> #### Words introducing noun clauses
>
> **RELATIVE PRONOUNS:** that, which, who, whom, whose
> **OTHER PRONOUNS:** what, whatever, whichever, whoever, whomever
> **OTHER SUBORDINATING WORDS:** how, if, when, whenever, where, wherever, whether, why

Adverb clauses

Adverb clauses modify verbs, adjectives, or other adverbs, usually answering one of these questions: When? Where? Why? How? Under what conditions? To what degree? They always begin with a subordinating conjunction (such as *after, although, because, that, though, unless,* or *when*). (For a complete list, see the chart on this page.)

When the sun went down, the bats *hunted* for food.

Kate *would have made* the team *if she hadn't broken her ankle.*

Noun clauses

A noun clause functions just like a single-word noun, usually as a subject, a subject complement, a direct object, or an object of a preposition. It usually begins with one of the following words: *how, if, that, what, whatever, when, whenever, where, whether, which, whichever, who, whoever, whom, whomever, whose, why.*

         S
Whoever leaves the house last must double-lock the door.

         DO
Copernicus argued that the sun is the center of the universe.

The subordinating word introducing the clause may or may not play a significant role in the clause. In the preceding example sentences, *Whoever* is the subject of its clause, but *that* does not perform a function in its clause.

As with adjective clauses, the parts of a noun clause may appear in normal order (subject/verb/object or complement) or out of their normal order.

S   V   ┌─ DO ─┐   OC

Loyalty is what keeps a friendship strong.

DO   S   V

New Mexico is where we live.

EXERCISE 49–3 Underline the subordinate clauses in the following sentences. Tell whether each clause is an adjective, adverb, or noun clause and how it is used in the sentence. Answers appear in the back of the book.

Show the committee the latest draft <u>before you print the</u>

<u>final report</u>. (Adverb clause modifying "Show")

a. The city's electoral commission adjusted the voting process so that every vote would count.

b. A marketing campaign that targets baby boomers may not appeal to young professionals.

c. After the Tambora volcano erupted in the southern Pacific in 1815, no one realized that it would contribute to the "year without a summer" in Europe and North America.

d. The concept of peak oil implies that at a certain point there will be no more oil to extract from the earth.

e. Details are easily overlooked when you are rushing.

50 Sentence types

Sentences are classified in two ways: according to their structure (simple, compound, complex, or compound-complex) and according to their purpose (declarative, imperative, interrogative, or exclamatory).

50a Sentence structures

Depending on the number and the types of clauses they contain, sentences are classified as simple, compound, complex, or compound-complex.

Clauses come in two varieties: independent and subordinate. An independent clause contains a subject and a predicate, and it either stands alone or could stand alone as a sentence. A subordinate clause also contains a subject and a predicate, but it functions within a sentence as an adjective, an adverb, or a noun; it cannot stand alone. (See 49e.)

Simple sentences

A simple sentence is one independent clause with no subordinate clauses.

┌─────────────── INDEPENDENT CLAUSE ───────────────
Without a passport, Eva could not visit her grandparents in
┌──────┐
Hungary.

A simple sentence may contain compound elements—a compound subject, verb, or object, for example—but it does not contain more than one full sentence pattern. The following sentence is simple because its two verbs (*comes in* and *goes out*) share a subject (*Spring*).

┌─────────────── INDEPENDENT CLAUSE ───────────────┐
Spring comes in like a lion and goes out like a lamb.

Compound sentences

A compound sentence is composed of two or more independent clauses with no subordinate clauses. The independent clauses are usually joined with a comma and a coordinating conjunction (*and, but, or, nor, for, so, yet*) or with a semicolon. (See 14a.)

```
      INDEPENDENT                    INDEPENDENT
┌──     CLAUSE     ──┐     ┌───────    CLAUSE    ──────────┐
The car broke down, but a rescue van arrived within minutes.
```

```
┌───── INDEPENDENT CLAUSE ─────┐ ┌─ INDEPENDENT CLAUSE ─┐
A shark was spotted near shore; people left immediately.
```

Complex sentences

A complex sentence is composed of one independent clause with one or more subordinate clauses. (See 49e.)

SUBORDINATE
CLAUSE

ADJECTIVE   The pitcher who won the game is a rookie.

SUBORDINATE
CLAUSE

ADVERB   If you leave late, take a cab home.

SUBORDINATE
CLAUSE

NOUN   What matters most to us is respect for the land.

Compound-complex sentences

A compound-complex sentence contains at least two independent clauses and at least one subordinate clause. The following sentence contains two independent clauses, each of which contains a subordinate clause.

INDEPENDENT CLAUSE   INDEPENDENT CLAUSE
SUB CL

Tell the doctor how you feel, and she will decide whether

SUB CL

you can go home.

50b Sentence purposes

Writers use declarative sentences to make statements, imperative sentences to issue requests or commands, interrogative sentences to ask questions, and exclamatory sentences to make exclamations.

DECLARATIVE	The echo sounded in our ears.
IMPERATIVE	Love your neighbor.
INTERROGATIVE	Did the better team win tonight?
EXCLAMATORY	We're here to save you!

EXERCISE 50–1   Identify the following sentences as simple, compound, complex, or compound-complex. Identify the subordinate clauses and classify them according to their function: adjective, adverb, or noun. (See 49e.) Answers appear in the back of the book.

> **The deli in Courthouse Square was crowded with lawyers at**
>
> **lunchtime.** (Simple)

a. Fires that are ignited in dry areas spread especially quickly.

b. The early Incas were advanced; they used a calendar and developed a decimal system.

c. Elaine's jacket was too thin to block the wintry air.

d. Before we leave for the station, we always check the Amtrak website.

e. Decide when you want to leave, and I will be there to pick you up.

Research

51 Thinking like a researcher; gathering sources

A college research assignment asks you to pose questions worth exploring, read widely in search of possible answers, interpret what you read, draw reasoned conclusions, and support those conclusions with evidence. In short, it asks you to enter a research conversation by being *in* conversation with other writers and thinkers who have explored and studied your topic. As you listen to and learn from the voices already in the conversation, you'll find entry points where you can add your own insights and ideas.

Keep an open mind throughout the research process, and enjoy the detective work of finding answers to questions that matter to you. Take time to discover what has been written about your topic and to uncover what's missing and needs to be questioned and researched.

51a Manage the project.

When you begin a research project, you will need to understand the assignment, choose a direction, and ask questions about your topic. The following tips will help you manage the beginning phase of research.

Managing time

When you receive your assignment, set a realistic schedule of deadlines. Think about how much time you might need for each step of your project. Consider creating a calendar to map out the tasks for your project, keeping in mind that some tasks might overlap or need to be repeated. See the sample research calendar on the next page.

Getting the big picture

As you consider a possible research topic, take time to read a few sources to gain an overview of your topic. Ask yourself questions such as these:

- What aspects of the topic are generating the most debate?
- Why and how do people disagree?
- Which arguments and approaches seem worth exploring?

Keeping a research log

Research is a process. As your topic evolves, you may find yourself asking new questions that require you to create a new search strategy, find additional sources, or revise your initial assumptions. A research log — a hard-copy notebook or a digital file — helps you maintain records of the sources you read and your questions and ideas about those sources.

Sample calendar for a research assignment

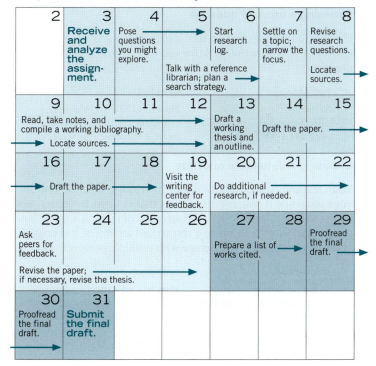

2	3	4	5	6	7	8
	Receive and analyze the assignment.	Pose questions you might explore. →	Talk with a reference librarian; plan a search strategy. →	Start research log.	Settle on a topic; narrow the focus.	Revise research questions. Locate sources. →

9	10	11	12	13	14	15
Read, take notes, and compile a working bibliography. →				Draft a working thesis and an outline.	Draft the paper. →	
→ Locate sources.						

16	17	18	19	20	21	22
→ Draft the paper. →			Visit the writing center for feedback.	Do additional research, if needed. →		

23	24	25	26	27	28	29
Ask peers for feedback.				Prepare a list of works cited. →		Proofread the final draft. →
Revise the paper; if necessary, revise the thesis. →						

30	31					
Proofread the final draft.	Submit the final draft.					

51b Pose questions worth exploring.

Every research project starts with questions. Try using *who*, *what*, *when*, *where*, *how*, and *why* to form research questions for your project.

- **Who** is responsible for the contaminated drinking water in Flint, Michigan?
- **What** happens to the arts without public funding?
- **How** can nutritional food labels be redesigned so that they inform rather than confuse consumers?
- **Why** are boys diagnosed with attention deficit disorder more often than girls are?

See "How to enter a research conversation" on the next page for advice on choosing and developing a research question.

Choosing a focused question

If your initial question is too broad, given the length of the essay you plan to write, look for ways to narrow and focus your question.

TOO BROAD	**NARROWER**
What are the economic effects of a global pandemic such as COVID-19?	**How** has COVID-19 changed economic realities for lower-income women in the U.S.?

Choosing a debatable question

Your research paper will be more interesting to both you and your audience if you ask a question that is open to debate, not a question that leads to a report or a list of facts. A *why* or *how* question most often leads to a researched argument and engages you and your readers in a debate with multiple perspectives.

TOO FACTUAL	**DEBATABLE**
What percentage of state police departments use body cameras?	**How** has the widespread use of body cameras changed encounters between officers and civilians?

Choosing a question grounded in evidence

For most college courses, the central argument of a research paper should be grounded in evidence, not in personal preferences or opinions. Your question should lead you to evidence, not to a defense of your beliefs.

TOO DEPENDENT ON PERSONAL OPINION

Do medical scientists have the right to experiment on animals?

GROUNDED IN EVIDENCE

How have technical breakthroughs made medical experiments on animals increasingly unnecessary?

HOW TO

Enter a research conversation

A college research project asks you to be in conversation with writers and researchers who have studied your topic or with people who have *lived* your topic—responding to their ideas, experiences, and arguments and contributing your own insights to move the conversation forward. As you ask preliminary research questions, you may wonder where and how to step into a research conversation.

1 **Identify the experts and ideas in the conversation.** Ask: Who are the major writers and most influential people researching your topic? What are their credentials? What positions have they taken? How and why do the experts disagree?

2 **Identify any gaps in the conversation.** What is missing? Where are the gaps in the existing research? What questions haven't been asked yet? What positions need to be challenged? What perspectives seem to be missing? (See the box on p. 354 for guidance on widening the research conversation.)

3 **Try using sentence starters** to help you find a point of entry.

- *On one side of the debate is position X, and on the other side is Y, but there is a middle position: _____.*

- *The conventional view about the problem needs to be challenged because _____.*

- *Key details in this debate that have been overlooked are _____.*

- *Researchers have drawn conclusion X from the evidence, but one could also draw a different conclusion: _____.*

> ### WRITING FOR AN AUDIENCE
>
> Follow your curiosity, but think about your readers, too. Ask yourself: How will my research question engage readers? Why will readers think the question is worth asking? How might my research help readers understand a topic they care about? Frame your research question to show readers why it needs to be asked — and why the answer matters to them.

Testing your research question

Once you have a tentative research question, check to see that it is interesting, provocative, and flexible enough to pursue.

- Does your question allow you to research a topic that interests you?
- Does your question give you (and your readers) an opportunity to think about your topic in a new way?
- Is the question debatable and flexible enough to allow for many possible answers?
- Can you answer "So what?" (see 1c) to show why the question needs to be asked and why the answer is worth knowing?

51c Map out a search strategy.

Before you search for sources, think about what kinds of sources will be appropriate for your project. Considering the kinds of sources you need will help you develop a search strategy — a systematic plan for locating sources. Try to cast a wide net in your search strategy to learn about what aspects of your topic are generating the most debate.

No single search strategy works for every topic. For some topics, it may be useful to search for information in newspapers, government publications, films, and websites. For others, the best sources might be scholarly journals and books, research reports, and specialized reference works. Still other topics might be enhanced by field research — interviews, surveys, or observation.

With the help of a librarian, each of the students whose research essays appear in this handbook constructed a search strategy appropriate for her research question.

Researcher: Sophie Harba (See her full paper in 58b.)

Research question: Why should (or why shouldn't) the government enact laws to regulate healthy eating choices?

Search strategy

- Search the web to locate current news, government publications, and information from organizations that focus on government regulation of food.
- Check a library database for current peer reviewed research articles.
- Use the library catalog to search for a recently published book that was cited by a source.

Researcher: April Bo Wang (See her full paper in 63b.)

Research question: How can technology facilitate a shift from teacher-delivered to student-centered learning?

Search strategy

- Search Google Scholar and *CQ Researcher* to see which aspects of the question are generating debate.
- View a TED talk to deepen her understanding of education technology.
- Use specialized databases related to education and technology to search for studies and scholarly articles.

51d Search efficiently; master a few shortcuts to finding good sources.

You can save yourself time by becoming an efficient searcher of library databases and the web.

Using the library

The website hosted by your college library links to databases and other references containing articles, studies, and reports written by key researchers. Use your library's resources, designed for academic researchers, to find the most authoritative sources for your project.

WIDENING THE RESEARCH CONVERSATION

Locating sources involves detective work. As you search for sources to answer your research question, note who is in the research conversation, and ask whose voices haven't been represented — and need to be represented. In many research conversations, perspectives become skewed when all the experts are asking the same questions and sharing the same assumptions. As you research a topic, search for voices that might be underrepresented or excluded from research conversations and mainstream publications, especially voices whose perspectives question and challenge traditional assumptions.

If, for instance, you are researching the intersection of race and public health, ask whether the voices and perspectives of people of color are included in the research conversation — and, if not, why they are absent and where you will locate them. Or if you are researching the effects of bullying on the mental health of adolescents, seeking out the experiences of specific groups — such as LGBTQ youth — will paint a much more complex picture than researching the topic generally. Even when a topic may not seem related to specific marginalized groups, searching for viewpoints from people of varied backgrounds will result in a far more accurate and representative understanding of the conversation.

As you develop your search strategy, ask questions such as these:

- What sources provide a range of viewpoints, including those that counter mainstream perspectives?
- What assumptions do mainstream sources share? Do those assumptions seem accurate? If not, how might someone challenge them?
- Whose voices are missing from the research conversation — and why might that be?
- Where might you seek out underrepresented voices on your topic? Where have they been published?

The following databases feature underrepresented voices and are excellent starting points for finding diverse viewpoints.

Alternative Press Index

HAPI (Hispanic American Periodicals Index)

Ethnic NewsWatch

LGBT Magazine Archive

Oxford African American Studies Center

Using the web

When conducting searches, use terms that are as specific as possible. Your keywords will determine the quality of the results you see. Use clues in what you find (such as websites of organizations or government agencies that seem informative) to refine your search. The box on the next page provides more advice on searching for sources online.

Using bibliographies and citations as shortcuts

Scholarly books and articles list the works the author has cited, usually at the end. Skimming these lists is a useful shortcut for finding additional reliable sources on your topic. Let one source guide you to the next. Following the trail of citations may lead you to helpful sources and a network of relevant research about your topic.

Check URLs for clues about sponsorship

Sometimes a web search brings you to a page that looks useful, but you find it difficult to tell whether it's legitimate. You may find it helpful to shorten a longer URL to its root address — one that ends with .org, .gov, .edu, or .com, for example — so that you can make a better judgment about the usefulness of the content of the website or web page.

DISTINGUISHING BETWEEN PRIMARY AND SECONDARY SOURCES

As you search for sources, determine whether you are looking at a primary or a secondary source.

Primary source	letter, diary, film, legislative bill, laboratory study, field research report, speech, eyewitness account, poem, short story, novel
Secondary source	commentary on or review or interpretation of a primary source by another writer

Although a primary source is not necessarily more reliable than a secondary source, it has the advantage of being a firsthand account. You can better evaluate what a secondary source says if you have read any primary source it discusses.

HOW TO

Go beyond a Google search

You might start with Google to gain an overview of your topic, but relying on the search engine to choose your sources isn't a research strategy. Good research involves going beyond the information available from a quick Google search. To locate reliable, authoritative sources, be strategic about *how* and *where* to search.

1 **Familiarize yourself with the research conversation.** Identify the current debate about the topic you have chosen and the most influential writers and experts in the debate. Where is the research conversation happening? In scholarly sources? Government agencies? The popular media?

2 **Generate keywords to focus your search.** Use specific words and combinations to search. Add words such as *debate*, *disagreements*, *proponents*, or *opponents* to track down the various positions in the research conversation. Use a journalist's questions—Who? When? Where? What? How? Why?—to refine a search.

3 **Search discipline-specific databases available through your school library** to locate carefully chosen scholarly (peer reviewed) content that doesn't appear in search results on the open web. Use databases such as JSTOR and Academic Search Premier, designed for academic researchers, to locate sources in the most influential publications.

4 **If your topic has been in the news, try *CQ Researcher*,** available through most college libraries. Its brief articles provide pro/con arguments on current controversies in criminal justice, law, environment, technology, health, and education.

5 **Explore the Pew Research Center** (pewresearch.org), which sponsors original research and nonpartisan discussions of findings and trends in a wide range of academic fields.

51e Write a research proposal.

One effective way to manage your project and focus your thinking is to write a research proposal. A proposal gives you an opportunity to look back — to remind yourself why you chose your topic — and to look forward — to predict any difficulties or obstacles that might arise during your project.

The following questions will help you organize your proposal.

- **Research question:** What question will you be exploring? Why does this question need to be asked? What do you hope to learn from the project?
- **Research conversation:** What have you learned so far about the debate or the specific research conversation you will enter? What entry point have you found to offer your own insights and ideas?
- **Search strategy:** What kinds of sources will you use to explore your question? What sources will be most useful, and why? How will you locate a variety of sources (primary/ secondary, textual/visual)?
- **Research challenges:** What challenges, if any, do you anticipate (locating sufficient sources, managing the project, finding a position to take)? What resources are available to help you meet these challenges?

51f Conduct field research, if appropriate.

Your own field research can enhance or be the focus of a writing project. For a composition class, for example, you might interview a local politician about a current issue, such as the initiation of a city bike-share program. For a sociology class, you might conduct a survey about campus trends in community service.

NOTE: Colleges and universities often require researchers to submit projects to an institutional review board (IRB) if the research involves human subjects outside a classroom setting. Before administering a survey or conducting other fieldwork, check with your instructor to see whether IRB approval is required.

Interviewing

Interviews can often shed new light on a topic. Look for an expert who has firsthand knowledge of the subject, or seek out an individual whose personal experience will provide a valuable perspective. Ask open questions that lead to facts, anecdotes, and vivid details that will add a meaningful dimension to your paper.

★ **Using sources responsibly** When quoting your source (the interviewee), be accurate and fair. Do not change the meaning of your interviewee's words or take them out of context. Also, don't change the phrasing or dialect of the interviewee's speech. If your interviewee grants permission, record your interview so you can review the accuracy of any quotations and the context in which they were spoken.

Conducting a survey

For some topics, you may find it useful to survey opinions or practices through a written questionnaire, a phone or email poll, or questions posted on a social media site. Many people resist long questionnaires, so for a good response rate, limit your questions with your purpose in mind.

Surveys with yes/no questions or multiple-choice options can be completed quickly, and the results are easy to tally, but you may also want to ask a few open-ended questions to invite more individual responses.

52 Managing information; taking notes responsibly

An effective researcher is a good record keeper. Whether you decide to keep records on paper or on a computer or mobile device, you will need methods for managing information: maintaining a working bibliography (see 52a), keeping track of source materials (see 52b), and taking notes without plagiarizing your sources (see 52c).

52a Maintain a working bibliography.

Keep a record of sources you read, listen to, or view. This record, called a *working bibliography*, will help you keep track of publication information for the sources you might use so that you can easily refer to them as you write and also compile a list of works cited. The box on the next page will guide you through what information is important to collect for your working bibliography. The format of this list depends on the documentation style you are using (for MLA style, see 57b; for APA style, see 62b). See 53d for advice on using your working bibliography as the basis for an annotated bibliography.

52b Keep track of source materials.

Save a copy of each potential source as you conduct your research. Many database services will allow you to email, text, save, or print citations or full texts, and you can easily download, copy, or take screen shots of information from the web. It is always a good idea to use browser bookmarks and make a folder to save sources for your research assignment. (See the box on p. 57 for more advice on working with digital sources.)

Working with hard copies, screen shots, or files — as opposed to relying on memory or hastily written notes — lets you annotate each source as you read. You also reduce the chances of unintentional plagiarism since you will be able to compare your use of a source in your paper with the actual source, not just with your notes.

52c As you take notes, avoid unintentional plagiarism.

Plagiarism, using someone's words or ideas without giving credit, is often accidental. After spending so much time thinking through your topic and reading sources, it's easy to forget where a helpful idea came from or that the idea wasn't yours to begin with. Even if you half-copy an author's sentences — either by mixing the author's phrases with your own without using quotation marks or by plugging your synonyms into an author's sentence structure — you are plagiarizing.

INFORMATION TO COLLECT FOR A WORKING BIBLIOGRAPHY

For an article

- All authors of the article
- Title and subtitle of the article
- Title of the journal, magazine, or newspaper
- Date; volume, issue, and page numbers
- Date you accessed the source (for an online source that lists no publication date)

For an article retrieved from a database (in addition to preceding information)

- Name of the database
- Accession number or other number assigned by the database
- Digital object identifier (DOI), if there is one
- URL of the database home page or of the journal's home page, if there is no DOI

For a web source (including visual, audio, and multimedia sources)

- All authors, editors, or composers of the source
- Title and subtitle of the source
- Title of the longer work, if the source is contained in a longer work
- Title of the website
- Print publication information for the source, if available
- Online page or paragraph numbers or other retrieval information (such as a time stamp or slide number)
- Date of online publication or latest update
- Sponsor or publisher of the site
- Date you accessed the source (for an undated source)
- URL or permalink for the page on which the source appears

For an entire book

- All authors; any editors or translators
- Title and subtitle
- Edition, if not the first
- Publication information: city, publisher, and date
- Date you accessed the source (for an undated online book)

To take notes responsibly, make sure you grasp the ideas in the source. Circle words or terms that you don't understand and look them up. Ask these questions: What is the meaning of the source? What is the argument? What is the evidence? Then, resist the temptation to look at the source as you take notes — except when you are quoting. Keep the source close by so that you can check for accuracy, but don't try to put ideas in your own words with the source's sentences in front of you. When you need to quote a source, make sure you copy the words exactly and put quotation marks around them.

Summarizing or paraphrasing ideas and quoting exact language are three ways of taking notes without unintentionally plagiarizing. See 4c for how to write a summary and 56a for how to paraphrase. Also see section 56 for when to summarize, paraphrase, or quote.

HOW TO

Avoid plagiarizing from the web

1 **Understand what plagiarism is.** When you use another author's intellectual property (language, visuals, or ideas) in your own writing without giving proper credit, you engage in a kind of academic dishonesty called *plagiarism*.

2 **Treat online sources as someone else's intellectual property.** Language, data, or images that you find on the web must be cited, even if the material is publicly accessible on free sites or social media, is on a government website, or is in the public domain (which includes older works no longer protected by copyright law).

3 **Keep track of words and ideas borrowed from sources.** When you copy and paste passages from online sources, put quotation marks around any text that you have copied. Develop a system for distinguishing your words and ideas from anything you've summarized, paraphrased, or quoted.

4 **Create a complete bibliographic entry for each source to keep track of publication information.** From the start of your research project, maintain accurate records for all online sources you read, listen to, or view.

Below is a passage from a National Oceanic and Atmospheric Administration (NOAA) website that Aisha, a student writer, came across while researching marine pollution. Following the passage are Aisha's annotations — in other words, notes and questions that help her figure out meaning — and then examples of a summary, a paraphrase, and a quotation she could use to refer to the original source.

ORIGINAL SOURCE

A question that is often posed to the NOAA Marine Debris Program (MDP) is "How much debris is actually out there?" The MDP has recognized the need for this answer as well as the growing interest and value of citizen science. To that end, the MDP is developing and testing two types of monitoring and assessment protocols: 1) rigorous scientific survey and 2) volunteer at-sea visual survey. These types of monitoring programs are necessary in order to compare marine debris composition, abundance, distribution, movement, and impact data on national and global scales.

> — NOAA Marine Debris Program. "Efforts and Activities Related to the 'Garbage Patches.' " *Marine Debris*, 2012, pm22100.net/docs/pdf/enercoop/pollutions/noaa-plastiques.pdf

ORIGINAL SOURCE WITH STUDENT ANNOTATIONS

⌐ by whom?   ocean ⌐   ⌐ trash

A question that is often posed to the NOAA Marine Debris

Program (MDP) is "How much debris is actually out there?" The

MDP has recognized the need for this answer as well as the

aha

growing interest and value of (citizen) science. To that end, the MDP

is developing and testing two types of monitoring and assessment

ways of gathering information

protocols: 1) rigorous scientific survey and 2) volunteer at-sea visual

survey. These types of monitoring programs are necessary in order

kinds of materials ⌐   ⌐ how much?

to compare marine debris, composition, abundance, distribution,

⌐ why it matters

movement, and impact data on national and global scales.

SUMMARY

Having to field citizens' questions about the size of debris fields in Earth's oceans, the Marine Debris Program, an arm of the US National Oceanic and Atmospheric Administration, is currently implementing methods to monitor and draw conclusions about our oceans' patches of pollution (NOAA).

PARAPHRASE

Citizens concerned and curious about the amount, makeup, and locations of debris patches in our oceans have been pressing NOAA's Marine Debris Program for answers. In response, the organization is preparing to implement plans and standards for expert study and nonexpert observation, both of which will yield results that will be helpful in determining the significance of the pollution problem (NOAA).

QUOTATION

The NOAA Marine Debris Program has noted that, as our oceans become increasingly polluted, surveillance is "necessary in order to compare marine debris composition, abundance, distribution, movement, and impact data on national and global scales."

NOTE: Because the source is from an unpaginated website, the in-text citation includes only the author's name placed either in parentheses (as in the first two examples above) or in a signal phrase (as in the third example).

In a second pass through the source, the student would engage more with the ideas and start to plan next steps for her research. The student might write annotations such as these:

Find out what kind of debris is most harmful

Seems like a good idea to get citizens involved — marine debris is vast

Quote these words from source to show why surveillance is necessary

Take notes responsibly

1 **Understand the ideas in the source.** Start by determining the purpose and meaning of the source. Focus on the overall ideas in the source. Ask: What is the argument? What is the evidence?

2 **Keep the source close by to check for accuracy,** but resist the temptation to look at the source as you take notes—except when you are quoting.

3 **Use quotation marks around any borrowed words or phrases.** Copy the borrowed words exactly and keep complete bibliographic information for each source.

4 **Develop an organized system** to distinguish your insights and ideas from those of the source. Take time to note how you might use a source and what it will contribute to answering your research question.

5 **Create a method to label and identify** when you have summarized a text or its data or paraphrased or quoted an author's words.

6 **Record complete bibliographic information for each source** so you can give credit to the source, cite it accurately, and find it again easily.

53 Evaluating sources

You will often locate far more potential sources on your topic than you will have time to read. Your challenge then is to determine what kinds of sources you need and what you need these sources to do — and to select a reasonable number of trust-worthy sources. This kind of decision making is referred to as *evaluating sources*.

53a Evaluate the reliability and usefulness of a source.

Using reliable sources adds to your credibility and authority as a writer. The following questions will help you judge the reliability and usefulness of sources you might use to support your research project. Ideally, you want to choose sources that are relevant, current, credible, and bias-free.

Relevance Is the source clearly related to your research topic and your argument? Will your readers understand why you've included the source in your paper? What does the source add to your understanding of the research conversation? How does it help you answer your research question?

Currency How recent is the source? Is the information up-to-date? Does your research topic require current information? Will your research benefit from consulting older sources, including primary sources from a historical period?

DETERMINING WHETHER A SOURCE IS SCHOLARLY

Scholarly sources are written by experts for a knowledgeable audience and usually go into more depth than books and articles written for a general audience. Scholarly sources are sometimes called *refereed* or *peer reviewed* because the work is evaluated by experts in the field before publication.

To determine whether a source is scholarly, look for the following:

- Formal language and presentation
- Authors who are academics or scientists
- Footnotes or a bibliography documenting the works cited in the source
- Original research and interpretation (rather than a summary of other people's work)

Credibility Where does the source come from? Who is the author? What are the author's credentials or experience? How accurate and trustworthy is the information? Who published the source? Is it an academic, peer reviewed source? If the source is authored by an organization, what research has the organization done to support its claims? Are the source's ideas and research cited by other writers? For more advice on evaluating a source's credibility, see the box on page 367.

Bias Does the author endorse political or religious views that could affect objectivity? Are evidence and counterevidence presented in a fair and objective way? Is the author engaging in a scholarly debate or giving a personal point of view?

READING LIKE A RESEARCHER

To read like a researcher is to read with an open, curious mind, to find out not only what has been written about a topic but also what is missing from the research conversation.

- **Read carefully.** Read to understand and summarize the main ideas of a source and an author's point of view. Ask questions: What does the source say? What is the author's central claim or thesis? What evidence does the author use to support the thesis? What are the strengths of the source?

- **Read skeptically.** Read to examine an author's assumptions, evidence, and conclusions and to pose counterarguments. Ask questions: Are any of the author's arguments or conclusions problematic? Is the author's evidence persuasive and sufficient? Does the author make leaps in logic? Note *how* and *why* you agree or disagree with an author.

- **Read evaluatively.** Read to judge the usefulness of a source for your research project. You may disagree with an author's argument or use of evidence, but refuting the author's ideas will help you clarify your position. Ask questions: Is the author an expert on the topic? Will the source provide background information, lend authority, explain a concept, or offer counterevidence for your claims?

- **Read responsibly.** Take time to read the entire source and to understand its author's arguments, assumptions, and conclusions. Avoid taking quotations from the first few pages of a source before you understand whether the ideas are representative of the work as a whole.

HOW TO

Detect false and misleading sources

Sources can distort information or spread misinformation by taking information out of context or by promoting opinions as facts. As you evaluate sources, determine authenticity: Can the information be verified? Is the source reliable? You can verify facts and quotations by reading multiple sources and gathering a variety of perspectives. Because information and misinformation live side by side on the web, you need to read critically to determine the truth.

1 **Consider the source.** Is more than one source covering the topic? Is the author anonymous or named? What can you learn about the author's credentials and the mission of a site from checking the "About Us" tab? Does the site present only one side of an issue? Be skeptical if the source is the only one reporting the story.

2 **Examine the source's language.** Is the language informal? Does the source overuse superlatives such as *most, best,* or *worst*? Does it use the second-person pronoun *you*?

3 **Question the seriousness of the source.** Is the source attempting to mimic a reliable source? Is it possible that the source is satirical and humorous and is not intended to be read as factual?

4 **Fact-check the information.** Can the facts be objectively verified? If the conclusions of a research study are cited, find the study to verify; if an authority is quoted, research the original source of the quotation, if possible, to see whether the quotation was taken out of context. Also, be skeptical if a source reports a research study but doesn't quote the study's principal investigator or other respected researchers.

5 **Pay attention to the URL.** Among the more credible sites are those sponsored by higher education (.edu), nonprofit groups (.org), and government agencies (.gov). Established news organizations have standard domain names. Fake sites often use web addresses such as "Newslo" or "com.co" that imitate the addresses of real sites, and they package information with misinformation to make themselves look authentic.

HOW TO DETECT FALSE AND MISLEADING SOURCES *(Continued)*

6 **Note your biases.** If an article makes you angry or challenges your beliefs, or if it confirms your beliefs by ignoring evidence to the contrary, take notice, and try to be as objective as possible. Learn about an issue from reliable sources and from multiple perspectives.

53b Read with an open mind and a critical eye.

As you begin reading the sources you have chosen, keep an open mind. Do not let your personal beliefs or an initial working thesis statement prevent you from listening to new ideas and opposing viewpoints. Be curious about the wide range of positions in the research conversation you are entering. Your research question should guide you as you read your sources (see p. 366).

53c Assess web sources with special care.

Before using a web source in your paper, make sure you know who created the material and for what purpose. Sources with reliable information can stand up to scrutiny. As you evaluate sources, ask questions about their reliability and purpose.

Evaluating a website: Checking reliability

1 This page on Internet monitoring and privacy appears on a website sponsored by the National Conference of State Legislatures (NCSL). The NCSL is a bipartisan group that provides support and information to state lawmakers. The URL ending .org marks this sponsor as a nonprofit organization.

2 A clear date of publication shows currency.

3 An "About Us" page confirms that this is a credible organization whose credentials can be verified.

Evaluating a website: Checking purpose

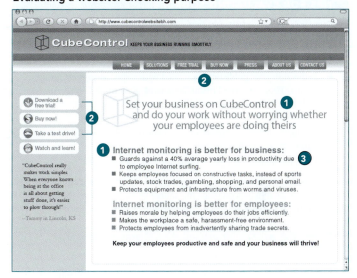

1 The site is sponsored by a company that specializes in employee-monitoring software.

2 Repeated links for trial downloads and purchase suggest the site's intended audience: consumers seeking to purchase software (probably not researchers seeking detailed information about employees' use of the Internet in the workplace).

3 The site appears to provide information and even shows statistics from studies, but ultimately the purpose of the site is to sell a product.

53d Construct an annotated bibliography.

Constructing an annotated bibliography allows you to summarize, evaluate, and record publication information for your sources before drafting your research paper. You summarize each source to understand its main ideas; you evaluate each source to assess how it contributes to your research project; and you record bibliographic information to keep track of publication details for each source.

TIPS FOR EVALUATING SOURCES

Check for signs of bias

- Does the author or publisher endorse political or religious views that could affect objectivity?
- Is the author or publisher associated with a special-interest group, such as People for the Ethical Treatment of Animals (PETA) or the National Rifle Association (NRA), that might emphasize one side of an issue?
- Are alternative views presented and addressed? How fairly does the author treat opposing views?
- Does the author's language show signs of bias?

Bias doesn't always render a source unuseful. Acknowledging bias when you see it helps you place the source in the context of the debate and in the context of your own purpose and audience.

Assess the writer's (or organization's) argument

- What is the author's central claim or thesis?
- How does the author support this claim — with relevant and sufficient evidence or with just a few anecdotes or emotional examples?
- Are statistics consistent with those you encounter in other sources? Does the author explain where the statistics come from?
- Are any of the author's assumptions questionable? Is the logic flawed?
- Does the author consider opposing arguments and refute them persuasively?

You want to find sources that both support your argument and present other arguments, but it helps to try to determine whether a source's argument has merit and is based on evidence.

Constructing an annotated bibliography focuses your attention on the most promising sources you've located, providing you with an opportunity to assess the usefulness of these sources as you reflect on *how* and *why* they will help you answer your research question. Take the following steps for each source in your annotated bibliography.

RECORD   Using whatever style your assignment requires, record the publication information for your source.

SUMMARIZE   Start by identifying the purpose and thesis of the source and the author's credentials. Summarize the source's main ideas and the evidence used to support these ideas. Summarizing gives you an opportunity to test your understanding of the source's meaning.

EVALUATE   Ask yourself what role a source might play and how it will contribute to your argument. Did it shape your thinking? Provide key evidence? Lend authority? Offer a counterargument? Evaluate how and why the source can help you answer your research question and support your position.

SAMPLE ANNOTATED BIBLIOGRAPHY ENTRY (MLA STYLE)

Resnik, David. "Trans Fat Bans and Human

Freedom." *American Journal of Bioethics*,   citation

vol. 10, no. 3, Mar. 2010, pp. 27–32.

Type of source; author's name and credentials

In this scholarly article, bioethicist David Resnik argues that bans on unhealthy foods threaten our personal freedom. He claims that researchers don't have enough evidence to know whether banning trans fats will save lives or money; all we know is that   summary such bans restrict dietary choices.

Summary presents the author's ideas and shows the student's understanding of the main points.

Resnik explains why most Americans oppose food restrictions, noting our multiethnic and regional food traditions as well as our resistance to government limitations on personal freedoms.

SAMPLE ANNOTATED BIBLIOGRAPHY ENTRY (MLA STYLE),
continued

Evaluation judges the source's reliability and shows how the source contributes to the student's research.

Resnik offers a well-reasoned argument, but he goes too far by insisting that all proposed food restrictions will do more harm than good. This article contributes important perspectives on American resistance to government intervention in food choice and counters arguments in other sources that support the idea of food legislation to advance public health.

evaluation

WRITING GUIDE

How to write an annotated bibliography

Creating an **annotated bibliography** gives you an opportunity to summarize, evaluate, and record publication information for your sources before drafting your research paper. You summarize each source to understand its main ideas, and you evaluate each source for accuracy, quality, and relevance. Finally, you reflect, asking yourself how the source will contribute to your research project.

Key features

- **The list of sources, arranged in alphabetical order by author,** includes complete bibliographic information for each source.

- **A brief annotation or note for each source,** typically no longer than one paragraph, contains a summary and an evaluation. The annotation may be written in full sentences or as brief notes; check with your instructor for preferences.

- **The summary** of each source states the work's main ideas and key points briefly and accurately. The summary is written in the present tense, third person, directly and concisely. Summarizing helps you test your understanding of a source and restate its meaning responsibly.

- **The evaluation** of the source's role and usefulness in your project includes an assessment of the source's strengths and limitations, the author's qualifications and expertise, and the function of the source in your project. Evaluating a source helps you analyze how the source fits into your project and separate the source's ideas from your own.

Thinking ahead: Presenting or publishing

You may be asked to submit your annotated bibliography electronically. If this is the case, be sure that any entry for a web source includes a functioning link to the source so that your reader can easily access it, if necessary.

Writing your annotated bibliography

1 Explore

For each source, begin by brainstorming responses to questions such as the following.

- What is the purpose of the source? Who is the author's intended audience?

- What is the author's thesis? What evidence supports the thesis?

- What qualifications and expertise does the author bring? Does the author have any biases or make any questionable assumptions?

- Why do you think this source is useful for your project?

- How does this source relate to the other sources in your bibliography?

2 Draft

The following tips can help you draft one or more entries in your annotated bibliography.

- Arrange the sources in alphabetical order by author (or by title for works with no author).

- Provide consistent bibliographic information for each source. For the exact bibliographic format, see 57b for MLA style or 62b for APA style.

- Start your summary by identifying the thesis and purpose of the source as well as the credentials of the source's author.

- Keep your research question in mind. How does this source contribute to your project? How does it help you take your place in the conversation?

→

HOW TO WRITE AN ANNOTATED BIBLIOGRAPHY (*Continued*)

3 Revise

Ask reviewers for specific feedback. Here are some questions to guide their comments.

- Is each source summarized clearly? Have you identified the author's main idea?

- For each source, have you made a clear judgment about how and why the source is useful for your project?

Writing Papers in MLA Style

Note: An in-text citation is a reference to a source that you place within your paper. A works cited entry is a reference to a source that you include at the end of your paper.

MLA-style papers in this book: See pages 68, 76, 98, and 448.

In English and other humanities courses, you may be asked to use the Modern Language Association (MLA) system for documenting sources. When writing a research paper based on sources, you will follow three important conventions:

1. supporting a thesis statement (54)
2. citing your sources accurately and avoiding plagiarism (55)
3. integrating source material effectively (56)

Examples in sections 54–56 are drawn from one student's research. Sophie Harba's research paper, in which she argues that state governments have the responsibility to set health policies and to regulate healthy eating choices, appears in 58b.

54 Supporting a thesis

Once you have read a range of sources, considered your subject from different perspectives, and chosen an entry point in the research conversation, you are ready to focus your research paper by forming a thesis statement and supporting that thesis with well-organized evidence.

54a Form a working thesis statement.

A thesis statement expresses your informed answer to your research question — an answer about which people might disagree. Start by developing a working thesis statement to help you narrow your ideas and clarify your purpose. As your ideas develop, you'll revise your working thesis to make it more specific and focused.

Here, for example, are student writer Sophie Harba's research question and working thesis statement.

RESEARCH QUESTION

Should the government enact laws to regulate healthy eating choices?

WORKING THESIS STATEMENT

Good start: It provides an answer to the question but doesn't show why the thesis matters.

State governments have the responsibility to regulate healthy eating choices because of the rise of chronic diseases.

After you have written a rough draft and perhaps done more reading, you may decide to revise your thesis, as Harba did, to give it a sharper focus and to offer a "So what?" to show readers why the thesis matters.

REVISED THESIS STATEMENT

This more focused thesis announces a clear position and shows readers why it matters.

In the name of public health and safety, state governments have the responsibility to shape health policies and to regulate healthy eating choices, especially since doing so offers a potentially large social benefit for a relatively small cost.

In a research paper, readers are accustomed to seeing the thesis statement at the end of the introductory paragraph. Here is Harba's thesis in the context of her introduction. (See 58b for the entire MLA paper.)

Introduction opens with a question to engage and hook readers.

Should the government enact laws to regulate healthy eating choices? Many Americans would answer an emphatic "No," arguing that what and how much we eat should be left to individual choice rather than unreasonable laws.

Harba introduces a research conversation to show the debate.

Others might argue that it would be unreasonable for the government not to enact legislation, given the rise of chronic diseases that result from harmful diets. In this debate, both the definition of reasonable regulations and the role of government to legislate food choices are

Thesis answers the opening question and states Harba's position.

at stake. In the name of public health and safety, state governments have the responsibility to shape health policies and to regulate healthy eating choices, especially since doing so offers a potentially large social benefit for a relatively small cost.

TESTING YOUR THESIS STATEMENT

An effective thesis argues for a position in a debate. Keep the following guidelines in mind to develop an effective thesis statement.

- **A thesis should be your answer to a question** and should take a position that needs to be argued and supported. It should not be a statement of fact or a description. Make sure your position is debatable by anticipating opposing viewpoints and counterarguments.

- **A thesis should match the scope of the research project.** If your thesis is too broad, explore a subtopic of your original topic. If your thesis is too narrow, pose a research question that has more than one answer.

- **A thesis should be focused.** Avoid vague words such as *interesting* or *good*. Use concrete language and make sure your thesis lets readers know your position.

- **A thesis should stand up to the "So what?" test** (see 1c). Ask yourself why readers should be interested in your essay and care about your thesis.

54b Organize ideas with an informal plan.

The body of your paper will consist of evidence in support of your thesis. Try sketching an informal plan to focus and organize your ideas. Sophie Harba, for example, used this simple plan to outline the structure of her argument.

INFORMAL OUTLINE

- Debates about the government's role in regulating food have a long history in the United States.

- Some experts argue that we should focus on the dangers of unhealthy eating habits and on preventing chronic diseases linked to diet.

- But food regulations are not a popular solution because many Americans object to government restrictions on personal choice.

- Food regulations designed to prevent chronic disease don't ask Americans to give up their freedom; they ask Americans to see health as a matter of public good.

After you have written a rough draft, a formal outline can help you test and fine-tune the organization of your argument. See 1d to read Harba's formal outline.

To help organize your ideas, you might want to experiment with graphic organizers before and during the drafting of your paper. A fairly typical way for research writers to proceed is shown here, but of course your own assignment, purpose, audience, argument, and sources will determine the most effective way to organize and develop your paper.

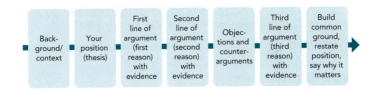

54c Consider how sources will contribute to your research paper.

The source materials you have gathered can play many different roles to support your thesis and develop your argument. As you consider using a source, ask yourself what you learned from the source and how it might function to answer your research question.

Providing context or background information

Readers need some background information and context to anchor their understanding of your topic and the debate around it. Describing a research study or offering statistics can help readers grasp your topic's significance. Student writer Sophie Harba uses a source to give context for her topic, the benefits of laws designed to prevent chronic disease.

> To give just one example, Marion Nestle, New York University professor of nutrition and public health, notes that "a 1% reduction in intake of saturated fat across the population would prevent more than 30,000 cases of coronary heart disease annually and save more than a billion dollars in health care costs" (7).

Explaining terms or concepts

If readers are unfamiliar with a term or concept, you will want to define or explain it. Quoting or paraphrasing a source can help you define terms and concepts in accessible language. Harba defines the term *refined grains* as part of her claim that the typical American diet is getting less healthy over time.

> A diet that is low in nutritional value and high in sugars, fats, and refined grains — grains that have been processed to increase shelf life but that contain little fiber, iron, and B vitamins — can be damaging over time (United States, Department of Agriculture 36).

Supporting your claims

As you develop your argument, back up your assertions with facts, examples, and other evidence from your research. (See also 7f.) Harba, for example, uses factual evidence to support her claim that the typical American diet is damaging.

> Michael Pollan, who has written extensively about Americans' unhealthy eating habits, notes that "[t]he Centers for Disease Control estimates that fully three quarters of US health care spending goes to treat chronic diseases, most of which are preventable and linked to diet: heart disease, stroke, type 2 diabetes, and at least a third of all cancers."

Lending authority to your argument

Expert opinion can add weight and credibility to your argument. (See also 7f.) But don't rely on experts to make your points for you. State your ideas in your own words and, when appropriate, cite the judgment of an authority in the field to support your position, as Harba does below.

> Debates surrounding the government's role in regulating food have a long history in the United States. According to Lorine Goodwin, a food historian, nineteenth-century reformers who sought to purify the food supply were called "fanatics" and "radicals" by critics who argued that consumers should be free to buy and eat what they want (77).

Anticipating and countering objections

Do not ignore sources that seem contrary to your position. Instead, use them to give voice to opposing points of view and to state potential objections to your argument before you counter them (see 7g). By explaining why many Americans oppose laws that limit what they eat, Sophie Harba creates an opportunity to counter that objection and build common ground with her readers.

> Why is the public largely resistant to laws that would limit unhealthy choices or penalize those choices with so-called fat taxes? Many consumers and civil rights advocates find such laws to be an unreasonable restriction on individual freedom of choice. As health policy experts Mello and others point out, opposition to food and beverage regulation is similar to the opposition to early tobacco legislation: the public views the issue as one of personal responsibility rather than one requiring government intervention (2602). In other words, if a person eats unhealthy food and becomes ill as a result, that is his or her choice. But those who favor legislation claim that freedom of choice is a myth because of the strong influence of food and beverage industry marketing on consumers' dietary habits.

55 Citing sources; avoiding plagiarism

▶ How to be a responsible research writer **386**

In a research paper, you draw on the work of other writers, and you must document their contributions by citing your sources. As an academic writer, you'll cite sources for two reasons:

1. to tell readers where your information comes from — so that they can assess its reliability and, if interested, find and read the original source
2. to give credit to the writers from whom you have borrowed words and ideas

You must include a citation when you quote from a source, when you summarize or paraphrase, and when you borrow facts that are not common knowledge. Borrowing another writer's language, sentence structure, or ideas without proper acknowledgment is plagiarism. The only exception is common knowledge — information that your readers may know or could easily locate in any number of general sources.

55a Understand how the MLA system works.

MLA style requires you to acknowledge your sources by using an in-text citation — a citation placed in parentheses within the body of your paper — to indicate the source of a quotation, paraphrase, or summary. The in-text citation points readers to a list of works cited at the end of your paper. There is a direct connection between the in-text citation and the alphabetical entry in your works cited list.

IN-TEXT CITATION

Signal phrase names the author and gives credentials.

In-text citation points readers to the works cited list.

Bioethicist David Resnik emphasizes that such policies "open the door to excessive government control over food, which could restrict dietary choices, interfere with cultural, ethnic, and religious traditions, and exacerbate socioeconomic inequalities" (31).

Material being cited is followed by a page number in parentheses (unless the source is unpaginated) and then a period.

ENTRY IN THE LIST OF WORKS CITED

Resnik, David. "Trans Fat Bans and Human
  Freedom." *The American Journal of
  Bioethics*, vol. 10, no. 3, Mar. 2010,
  pp. 27–32.

Works cited list at the end of the paper gives complete publication information for the source.

NOTE: This basic MLA format varies for different types of sources. For a detailed discussion and other models, see 57.

WRITING FOR AN AUDIENCE

You demonstrate your credibility, your *ethos*, by choosing the most trustworthy and reliable sources and showing readers how to find them. When your citations guide readers quickly to the sources of quoted, paraphrased, and summarized ideas, you show respect for your audience's interest in your research. Ask yourself two questions: How can I make my documentation useful to my readers? What would readers need to know to find each source themselves?

55b Understand what plagiarism is.

To be fair and responsible, you must document the work of others by citing your sources. When you acknowledge and document your sources, you avoid *plagiarism*, a form of academic dishonesty. The only exception to this requirement is common knowledge — but if you are unsure whether something is or isn't common knowledge, acknowledge the source. (See also 52c.)

In general, these three acts are considered plagiarism:

1. failing to cite quotations and borrowed ideas
2. failing to enclose borrowed language in quotation marks
3. failing to put summaries and paraphrases in your own words and sentence structure

Definitions of plagiarism vary; it's a good idea to find out how your school defines academic dishonesty.

55c Use quotation marks around borrowed language.

To indicate that you are using a source's exact phrases or sentences, you must enclose them in quotation marks unless they have been set off from the text by indenting (see 56b). To omit the quotation marks is to claim — falsely — that the language is your own, as in the example that starts on the next page. Such an omission is plagiarism even if you have cited the source.

ORIGINAL SOURCE

Although these policies may have a positive impact on human health, they open the door to excessive government control over food, which could restrict dietary choices, interfere with cultural, ethnic, and religious traditions, and exacerbate socioeconomic inequalities.

— David Resnik, "Trans Fat Bans and Human Freedom," p. 31

PLAGIARISM

Bioethicist David Resnik points out that policies to ban trans fats may protect human health, but they open the door to excessive government control over food, which could restrict dietary choices and interfere with cultural, ethnic, and religious traditions (31).

BORROWED LANGUAGE IN QUOTATION MARKS

Bioethicist David Resnik points out that policies to ban trans fats may protect human health, but they "open the door to excessive government control over food, which could restrict dietary choices [and] interfere with cultural, ethnic, and religious traditions" (31).

55d Put summaries and paraphrases in your own words.

A summary condenses information from a source; a paraphrase conveys the information using roughly the same number of words as the original source. When you summarize or paraphrase, it is not enough to name the source. You must restate the source's meaning using your own words and sentence structure. (See also 52c and 56a.) Half-copying the author's sentences either by using the author's phrases in your own sentences without quotation marks or by plugging synonyms into the author's sentence structure (sometimes called *patchwriting*) is a form of plagiarism.

The first paraphrase of the following source is plagiarism, even though the source is cited, because the paraphrase borrows too much of its language from the original. The highlighted strings of words have been copied exactly (without quotation marks), and the writer has closely echoed the sentence structure of the source, merely substituting some synonyms.

ORIGINAL SOURCE

[A]ntiobesity laws encounter strong opposition from some quarters on the grounds that they constitute paternalistic intervention into lifestyle choices and enfeeble the notion of personal responsibility. Such arguments echo those made in the early days of tobacco regulation.

— Michelle M. Mello et al.,
"Obesity — the New Frontier of Public Health Law," p. 2602

PLAGIARISM: UNACCEPTABLE BORROWING

Health policy experts Mello and others argue that antiobesity laws encounter strong opposition from some quarters because they interfere with lifestyle choices and decrease the feeling of personal responsibility. These arguments mirror those made in the early days of tobacco regulation (2602).

To avoid plagiarizing an author's language, resist the temptation to look at the source while you are summarizing or paraphrasing. After you have read the passage you want to paraphrase, set the source aside. Ask yourself, "What is the author's meaning?" In your own words, state your understanding of the author's ideas. Then return to the source and check that you haven't used the author's language or sentence structure or misrepresented the author's ideas. Following these steps will help you avoid plagiarizing the source.

ACCEPTABLE PARAPHRASE

As health policy experts Mello and others point out, opposition to food and beverage regulation is similar to the opposition to early tobacco legislation: the public views the issue as one of personal responsibility rather than one requiring government intervention (2602).

HOW TO

Be a responsible research writer

Using good citation habits is the best way to avoid plagiarizing sources and to demonstrate that you are a responsible researcher.

1 **Cite your sources as you write drafts.** Don't wait until your final draft is complete to add citations. Include a citation when you quote from a source, when you summarize or paraphrase, and when you borrow facts that are not common knowledge.

2 **Place quotation marks around direct quotations,** both in your notes and in your drafts.

3 **Check each quotation, summary, and paraphrase against the source** to make certain you aren't misrepresenting the source. For a paraphrase, be sure that your language and sentence structure differ from those in the original passage.

4 **Provide a full citation in your works cited list.** It is not sufficient to cite a source only in the body of your paper; you must also provide complete publication information for each source in a list of works cited.

EXERCISE 55–1   Summarize the following passage from a research source. Then paraphrase the same source. Use MLA-style in-text citation.

> Until recently, school-readiness skills weren't high on anyone's agenda, nor was the idea that the youngest learners might be disqualified from moving on to a subsequent stage. But now that kindergarten serves as a gatekeeper, not a welcome mat, to elementary school, concerns about school preparedness kick in earlier and earlier. A child who's supposed to read by the end of kindergarten had better be getting ready in preschool.
>
> — Erika Christakis, "How the New Preschool Is Crushing Kids,"
> *The Atlantic*, Jan.–Feb. 2016, p. 18

56 Integrating sources

Quotations, summaries, paraphrases, and facts will help you develop your argument, but they cannot speak for you. You need to find a balance between the words of your sources and your own voice so that readers always know who is speaking in your paper. You can use several strategies to integrate sources into your paper while maintaining your voice.

- Use sources as concisely as possible so that your own thinking and voice aren't lost (56a and 56b).

- Use signal phrases to avoid dropping quotations into your paper without indicating the boundary between your words and the source's words (56c).

- Use language that shows readers how each source supports your argument and how sources relate to one another (56d).

56a Summarize and paraphrase effectively.

In your academic writing, keep the emphasis on your ideas and your language; use your own words to summarize and paraphrase sources and to explain your points. Whether you choose to summarize or paraphrase a source depends on your purpose.

> ★ **Using sources responsibly**   When you use your own words to summarize or paraphrase, the original idea remains the intellectual property of the author, so you must include a citation. (See 55d.)

Summarizing

When you summarize a source, you express another writer's ideas in your own words, condensing the author's key points and using fewer words than the author.

WHEN TO SUMMARIZE

- When you want to state a source's main ideas simply and briefly in your own words
- When you want to compare arguments or ideas from various sources
- When you want to provide readers with an understanding of a source's argument before you respond to it or launch your own argument

Paraphrasing

When you paraphrase, you express an author's ideas in your own words and sentence structure, using approximately the same number of words and details as in the source.

WHEN TO PARAPHRASE

- When the ideas and information are important but the author's exact words are not needed
- When you want to restate a source's ideas in your own words
- When you need to simplify and explain a technical or complicated source

56b Use quotations effectively.

When you quote a source, you borrow the author's exact words and enclose them in quotation marks. Quotation marks show your readers that both the idea and the words belong to the author.

WHEN TO USE QUOTATIONS

- When language is especially vivid or expressive
- When exact wording is needed for technical accuracy
- When it is important to let the debaters of an issue explain their positions in their own words
- When the words of an authority lend weight to an argument
- When the language of a source is the topic of your discussion

HOW TO

Paraphrase effectively

A paraphrase shows your readers that you understand a source and can explain it to them. When you choose to paraphrase a passage from a source, you use the source's information and ideas for your own purpose—to provide background information, explain a concept, or advance your argument—while maintaining your voice. It is challenging to write a paraphrase that isn't a word-for-word translation of the original source and doesn't imitate the source's sentence structure. The following strategies will help you paraphrase effectively. The examples in this box are in MLA style.

1 **Understand the source.** Identify the source's key points and argument. Test your understanding by asking questions: *What* is being said? *Why* and *how* is it being said? Look up words you don't know to help you understand the ideas, not just the words.

> **ORIGINAL**
>
> People's vision of the world has broadened with the advent of global media such as television and the Internet. Those thinking about going elsewhere can see what the alternatives are and appear to have fewer inhibitions about resettling.
> — Darrell M. West, *Brain Gain: Rethinking US Immigration Policy*, Brookings Institution Press, 2011, p. 5

> **STUDENT'S NOTES**
>
> - TV and Internet have opened our eyes, our minds
> - We can imagine making big moves (country to country) as we never could before; the web offers a preview
> - "resettling" = moving to a new location, out of the familiar region
> - Lessens the anxiety about starting over in a new place

2 **Use your own vocabulary and sentence structure** to convey the source's information. Check to make sure there is no overlap in vocabulary or sentence structure with the original.

> Since TV and the web can offer a preview of life in other places, people feel less uncertainty and anxiety about moving from one area of the world to another.   ➔

HOW TO PARAPHRASE EFFECTIVELY *(Continued)*

3 **Use a signal phrase to identify the source** (*X argues that* _____, or *According to X*, _____).

> West argues that since TV and the web can offer a preview of life in other places, people feel less uncertainty and anxiety about moving from one area of the world to another.

4 **Include a citation to give credit to the source.** Even though the words are yours, you need to give credit for the idea. Here, the author's name and the page number on which the original passage appeared are listed.

> West argues that since TV and the web can offer a preview of life in other places, people feel less uncertainty and anxiety about moving from one area of the world to another (5).

NOTE: If you choose to use exact language from the source in a paraphrase, be sure to put quotation marks around any borrowed words or phrases.

> West argues that since TV and the web can offer a preview of life in other places, people "have fewer inhibitions" about moving from one area of the world to another (5).

Limiting your use of quotations

Keep the emphasis on your own ideas, and, as much as possible, keep your ideas in your own voice. It is not always necessary to quote full sentences from a source. Often you can integrate words and phrases from a source into your own sentence structure quite effectively. (For the use of signal phrases in integrating quotations, see 56c.)

> Resnik acknowledges that his argument relies on "slippery slope" thinking, but he insists that "social and political pressures" regarding food regulation make his concerns valid (31).

Using the ellipsis

To condense a quoted passage, you can use an ellipsis — a series of three spaced periods — to indicate that you have omitted words. What remains must be grammatically complete.

> In Mississippi, legislators passed "a ban on bans—a law that forbids . . . local restrictions on food or drink" (Conly A23).

The writer has omitted the words *municipalities to place* before *local restrictions* in the original source.

If you want to leave out one or more full sentences, use a period before the ellipsis.

> Legal scholars Gostin and Gostin argue that "individuals have limited willpower to defer immediate gratification for longer-term health benefits. . . . A person understands that high-fat foods or a sedentary lifestyle will cause adverse health effects, or that excessive spending or gambling will cause financial hardship, but it is not always easy to refrain" (217).

Ordinarily, do not use an ellipsis at the beginning or at the end of a quotation. Your readers will understand that you have taken the quoted material from a longer passage. The only exception occurs when you have dropped words at the end of the final quoted sentence. In such cases, put an ellipsis before the closing quotation mark and parenthetical citation.

★ **Using sources responsibly** Make sure omissions and ellipses do not distort the meaning of your source.

Using brackets

Brackets allow you to insert your own words into quoted material to clarify a confusing reference or to keep a sentence grammatical in the context of your writing. You also use brackets to indicate that you are changing a letter from capital to lowercase (or vice versa) to fit your sentence. In the following example, the writer inserted words in brackets to clarify the meaning of *help*.

> Neergaard and Agiesta argue that "a new poll finds people are split on how much the government should do to help [find solutions to the national health crisis]—and most draw the line at attempts to force healthier eating."

QUOTATION MARKS WITH OTHER PUNCTUATION

Integrating sources smoothly into your own sentences is easier when you follow guidelines about using periods, commas, and question marks with quotation marks.

Quotation with no page number, author mentioned in sentence

The ban, according to MacMillan, "gave consumers a healthier default option."

The ban "gave consumers a healthier default option," according to MacMillan.

NOTE: Place periods and commas inside quotation marks.

Quotation with no page number, author name in parentheses

The ban "gave consumers a healthier default option" (MacMillan).

Quotation with page number

Fortin notes that instead of a ban, the FDA "took a more moderate approach" (113).

Quotation within a writer's own question

Why did the FDA choose "a more moderate approach" (Fortin 113)?

Quotation that is itself a question

Fortin begins with a key question: "Why do we have food laws?" (3).

Long quotation

Hilts argues that Americans have faith in the FDA:

> The Roper Organization has tracked the FDA and government issues consistently, and found that among all government agencies, the FDA has been among the most popular, and routinely number one among regulatory agencies. (295)

NOTE: For a quotation of more than four typed lines, indent the quoted words, do not use quotation marks, and place the parenthetical citation outside of the final punctuation.

To indicate an error such as a misspelling in a quotation, insert the word "sic" in brackets right after the error.

> "While Americans of every race, gender and ethnicity are affected
> by this disease, diabetes disproportionately effects [sic] Black
> adults in the US."

Setting off long quotations

When you quote more than four typed lines of prose or more than three lines of poetry, set off the quotation by indenting it one-half inch from the left margin, and use the normal right margin.

Long quotations should be introduced by an informative sentence, usually followed by a colon. Quotation marks are unnecessary because the indented format tells readers that the passage is taken word for word from the source.

> In response to critics who claim that laws aimed at stopping us from
> eating whatever we want are an assault on our freedom of choice,
> Conly offers a persuasive counterargument:
>
>> [L]aws aren't designed for each one of us individually. Some of
>> us can drive safely at 90 miles per hour, but we're bound by the
>> same laws as the people who can't, because individual speeding
>> laws aren't practical. Giving up a little liberty is something we
>> agree to when we agree to live in a democratic society that is
>> governed by laws. (A23)

NOTE: At the end of an indented quotation, the parenthetical citation goes outside the final mark of punctuation.

56c Use signal phrases to integrate sources.

When you include a paraphrase, summary, or direct quotation of another writer's work in your paper, prepare your readers for it with introductory words called a *signal phrase*. A signal phrase usually names the author of the source, provides some context for the source material — such as the author's credentials — and helps readers distinguish your ideas from those of the source.

When you write a signal phrase, choose a verb that fits with the way you are using the source. For example, are you using the source to support a claim or to refute an argument? The signal phrase you choose shows readers how you want them to think about the source.

WEAK VERB	Lorine Goodwin, a food historian, says, ". . ."
STRONGER VERB	Lorine Goodwin, a food historian, rejects the claim: ". . ."
WEAK VERB	Bioethicist David Resnik mentions . . .
STRONGER VERB	Bioethicist David Resnik argues . . .

NOTE: MLA style calls for verbs in the present tense or present perfect tense (*argues, has argued*) to introduce source material unless you include a date that specifies the time of the original author's writing.

USING SIGNAL PHRASES IN MLA PAPERS

To avoid monotony, try to vary both the language and the placement of your signal phrases.

Model signal phrases

Michael Pollan, who has written extensively about Americans' unhealthy eating habits, emphasizes ". . ."

As health policy experts Mello and others point out, ". . ."

Marion Nestle, New York University professor of nutrition and public health, notes . . .

Bioethicist David Resnik acknowledges that his argument . . .

In response to critics, Conly offers a persuasive counterargument: ". . ."

Verbs in signal phrases

acknowledges	comments	endorses	points out
adds	compares	explains	reasons
admits	confirms	grants	refutes
agrees	contends	illustrates	rejects
argues	declares	implies	reports
asserts	denies	insists	responds
believes	disputes	notes	suggests
claims	emphasizes	observes	writes

Marking boundaries

Readers need to move smoothly from your words to the words of a source. Avoid dropping a quotation into the text without warning. Provide a clear signal phrase, including at least the author's name, to indicate the boundary between your words and the source's words. The signal phrase is highlighted in the second example.

DROPPED QUOTATION

Laws designed to prevent chronic disease by promoting healthier food and beverage consumption also have potentially enormous economic benefits. "[A] 1% reduction in intake of saturated fat across the population would prevent more than 30,000 cases of coronary heart disease annually and save more than a billion dollars in health care costs" (Nestle 7).

QUOTATION WITH SIGNAL PHRASE

Laws designed to prevent chronic disease by promoting healthier food and beverage consumption also have potentially enormous economic benefits. Marion Nestle, New York University professor of nutrition and public health, notes that "a 1% reduction in intake of saturated fat across the population would prevent more than 30,000 cases of coronary heart disease annually and save more than a billion dollars in health care costs" (7).

Establishing authority

The first time you mention a source, include in the signal phrase the author's title, credentials, or experience to help your readers recognize the source's authority and your own credibility (*ethos*) as a responsible researcher who has located reliable sources. The signal phrases are highlighted in the examples below.

SOURCE WITH NO CREDENTIALS

Michael Pollan notes that "[t]he Centers for Disease Control estimates that fully three quarters of US health care spending goes to treat chronic diseases, most of which are preventable and linked to diet: heart disease, stroke, type 2 diabetes, and at least a third of all cancers."

SOURCE WITH CREDENTIALS

Journalist Michael Pollan, who has written extensively about Americans' unhealthy eating habits, notes that "[t]he Centers for Disease Control estimates that fully three quarters of US health care spending goes to treat chronic diseases, most of which are preventable and linked to diet: heart disease, stroke, type 2 diabetes, and at least a third of all cancers."

Introducing summaries and paraphrases

Introduce most summaries and paraphrases with a signal phrase that names the author and places the material in the context of your argument. Readers will then understand that everything between the signal phrase and the parenthetical citation summarizes or paraphrases the cited source. Without the signal phrase (highlighted) in the following example, readers might think that only the quotation at the end is being cited, when in fact the whole paragraph is based on the source.

To improve public health, advocates such as Bowdoin College philosophy professor Sarah Conly contend that it is the government's duty to prevent people from making harmful choices whenever feasible and whenever public benefits outweigh the costs. In response to critics who claim that laws aimed at stopping us from eating whatever we want are an assault on our freedom of choice, Conly asserts that "laws aren't designed for each one of us individually" (A23).

There are times when a summary or a paraphrase does not require a signal phrase naming the author. When the context makes clear where the cited material begins, you may omit the signal phrase and include the author's last name in parentheses.

According to a nationwide poll, seventy-five percent of Americans are opposed to laws that restrict or put limitations on access to healthy foods (Neergaard and Agiesta).

USING SENTENCE GUIDES TO INTEGRATE SOURCES

You build your credibility (*ethos*) by accurately representing the views of others and by integrating these views into your paper. An important way to present the views of others before agreeing or disagreeing with them is to use sentence guides. These guides act as academic sentence starters; they show you how to use signal phrases in sentences to make clear to your reader whose ideas you're presenting — your own or those you have encountered in a source.

Presenting others' ideas. The following language will help you demonstrate your understanding of a source by summarizing the views or arguments of its author:

X argues that _____.

X and Y emphasize the need for _____.

Presenting direct quotations. To introduce the exact words of a source because their accuracy and authority are important for your argument, you might try phrases like these:

X describes the problem this way: "_____."

Y argues in favor of the policy, pointing out that "_____."

Presenting alternative views. At times you will have to synthesize the views of multiple sources before you introduce your own:

While X and Y have asked an important question, Z suggests that we should be asking a different question: _____?

X has argued that Y's research findings rest upon the questionable assumption that _____.

Presenting your own views by agreeing or extending. You may agree with the author of a source but want to add your own voice to extend the point or go deeper:

X's argument is convincing because _____.

Y claimed that _____. But isn't it also true that _____?

Presenting your own views by disagreeing and questioning. College writing assignments encourage you to show your understanding of a subject but also to question or challenge ideas and conclusions about the subject:

X's claims about _____ are misguided.

Y insists that _____, but perhaps she is asking the wrong question.

> ### USING SENTENCE GUIDES TO INTEGRATE SOURCES, continued
>
> **Presenting and countering objections to your argument.** To anticipate objections that readers might make, try the following sentence guides:
>
> Not everyone will embrace this argument; some may argue instead that _____.
>
> Some will object to this proposal on the grounds that _____.

Integrating statistics and other facts

When you cite a statistic or another specific fact, a signal phrase is often not necessary. Readers usually will understand that the citation refers to the statistic or fact and not the whole paragraph.

> Seat belt use saved an average of more than fourteen thousand lives per year in the United States between 2000 and 2010 (United States, Department of Transportation 231).

There is nothing wrong, however, with using a signal phrase to introduce a statistic or another fact.

Putting source material in context

Readers should not have to guess why source material appears in your paper. A signal phrase can help you connect your own ideas with those of another writer by clarifying how the source will contribute to your paper (see 53a).

If you use another writer's words, you must explain how they relate to your argument. Quotations don't speak for themselves; you must create a context for readers. Sandwich each quotation between sentences of your own, introducing the quotation with a signal phrase and following it with comments that link the quotation to your paper's argument.

> **QUOTATION WITH EFFECTIVE CONTEXT (QUOTATION SANDWICH)**
>
> In response to critics who claim that laws aimed at stopping us from eating whatever we want are an assault on our freedom of choice, Conly offers a persuasive counterargument:

Long
quotation is
set off from
the text.
Quotation
marks are
omitted.

> [L]aws aren't designed for each one of us
> individually. Some of us can drive safely at
> 90 miles per hour, but we're bound by the
> same laws as the people who can't, because
> individual speeding laws aren't practical.
> Giving up a little liberty is something we
> agree to when we agree to live in a democratic
> society that is governed by laws. (A23)

Analysis
connects the
source to
the student's
argument.

As Conly suggests, we need to change our
either/or thinking (either we have complete freedom
of choice *or* we have government regulations and lose
our freedom) and instead need to see health as a
matter of public good, not individual liberty.

56d Synthesize sources.

When you synthesize multiple sources in a research paper, you create a conversation about your research topic. You show readers that your argument is based on your analysis and integration of ideas and is not just a series of quotations and paraphrases strung together. Your synthesis will show how your sources relate to one another; one source may support, extend, or counter the ideas of another. Not every source has to "speak" to another in a research paper, but readers should understand how each source functions in your argument.

Considering how sources relate to your argument

Before you integrate sources and show readers how they relate to one another, consider how each source might contribute to your argument. As student writer Sophie Harba became more informed about her research topic, she asked herself these questions:

- What have I learned from my sources?
- Which sources might support my ideas or illustrate the points I want to make?
- What counterarguments do I need to address to strengthen my position?

She annotated a passage from one of her sources—a nonprofit group's assertion that our choices about food are skewed by marketing messages.

STUDENT NOTES ON THE ORIGINAL SOURCE

The food and beverage industry spends approximately $2 billion per year marketing to children.

— "Facts on Junk Food"

Could use this to counter the point about personal choice in Mello.

Placing sources in conversation

You can show readers how the ideas of one source relate to those of another by connecting and analyzing the ideas in your own voice. After all, you've done the research and thought through the issues, so you should control the conversation. Keep the emphasis on your own writing. The thread of your argument should be easy to identify and to understand, with or without your sources.

SAMPLE SYNTHESIS (MLA STYLE)

Student writer Sophie Harba sets up her synthesis with a question.

> Why is the public largely resistant to laws that would limit unhealthy choices or penalize those choices with so-called fat taxes? Many consumers and civil rights advocates find such laws to be an unreasonable restriction on individual freedom of choice.

Student writer

Signal phrase indicates how the source contributes to Harba's argument and shows that the idea that follows is not her own.

> As health policy experts Mello and others point out, opposition to food and beverage regulation is similar to the opposition to early tobacco legislation: the public views the issue as one of personal responsibility rather than one requiring government intervention (2602).

Source 1

Harba interprets a paraphrased source.

> In other words, if a person eats unhealthy food and becomes ill as a result, that is his or her choice. But those who favor legislation claim that freedom of choice is a myth because of the strong influence of food and beverage industry marketing on consumers' dietary habits.

Student writer

Harba uses a source to support her counter argument.

> According to one nonprofit health advocacy group, food and beverage companies spend roughly two billion

Source 2

dollars per year marketing directly to children. As a result, kids see nearly four thousand ads per year encouraging them to eat unhealthy food and drinks ("Facts"). As was the case with antismoking laws passed in recent decades, taxes and legal restrictions on junk food sales could help to counter the strong marketing messages that promote unhealthy products.

Student writer

Harba extends the argument and follows it with an interpretive comment.

The United States has a history of state and local public health laws that have successfully promoted a particular behavior by punishing an undesirable behavior. The decline in tobacco use as a result of antismoking taxes and laws is perhaps the most obvious example. Another example is legislation requiring the use of seat belts, which have significantly reduced fatalities in car crashes. One government agency reports that seat belt use saved an average of more than fourteen thousand lives per year in the United States between 2000 and 2010 (United States, Department of Transportation 231). Perhaps seat belt laws have public support because the cost of wearing a seat belt is small, especially when compared with the benefit of saving fourteen thousand lives per year.

Source 3

Student writer

In this synthesis, Harba uses her own analysis to shape the conversation among her sources. She does not simply string quotations together or allow them to overwhelm her writing. She guides readers through a conversation about laws that could promote and have promoted public health. She finds points of intersection among her sources, acknowledges the contributions of others, and shows readers, in her voice, how the sources support her argument.

REVIEWING AN MLA PAPER: USE OF SOURCES

When you have completed a draft of your research paper, ensure you have used sources effectively and responsibly by asking the following questions as you review your writing.

Use of quotations

- Have you used quotation marks around quoted material (unless it has been set off from the text)? (See 55c.)
- Have you checked that quoted language is word-for-word accurate? If it is not, do ellipses or brackets indicate the omissions or changes? (See 56b.)
- Does a clear signal phrase (usually naming the author) prepare readers for each quotation and for the purpose the quotation serves? (See 56c.)
- Does a parenthetical citation follow each quotation? (See 57a.)
- Is each quotation put in context? (See 56c.)

Use of summaries and paraphrases

- Are summaries and paraphrases free of plagiarized wording — not copied or half-copied from the source? (See 55d.)
- Are summaries and paraphrases documented with parenthetical citations? (See 57a.)
- Do readers know where the cited material begins? Does a signal phrase mark the boundary between your words and the summary or paraphrase? (See 56c.)
- Does a signal phrase prepare readers for the purpose of the summary or paraphrase in your argument? (See 56c.)

Use of statistics and other facts

- Are statistics and facts (other than common knowledge) documented with parenthetical citations? (See 56c and 57a.)
- If there is no signal phrase, will readers understand exactly which facts are being cited? (See 56c.)

When synthesizing sources, use the following guidelines:

- Be sure your sources address your research question.
- Think about how your sources converse with each other. How do they support, extend, contextualize, or counter each other?

- Be sure that your synthesis is more than a series of quotations and paraphrases strung together. You can do this by connecting and analyzing sources in your own voice.

- Ask: Is my argument easy to identify and to understand, with or without my sources? The answer should be yes.

57 Documenting sources in MLA style

In English and other humanities classes, you may be asked to use the MLA (Modern Language Association) system for documenting sources, which is set forth in the *MLA Handbook*, 9th edition (MLA, 2021).

MLA recommends in-text citations that refer readers to a list of works cited. A typical in-text citation names the author of the source, often in a signal phrase, and gives a page number in parentheses. At the end of the paper, the list of works cited provides publication information for each cited source; the list is alphabetized by authors' last names (or by titles for works without authors). There is a direct connection between the in-text citation and the alphabetical listing. In the following example, that connection is highlighted.

IN-TEXT CITATION

Bioethicist David Resnik emphasizes that such policies, despite their potential to make our society healthier, "open the door to excessive government control over food, which could restrict dietary choices, interfere with cultural, ethnic, and religious traditions, and exacerbate socioeconomic inequalities" (31).

ENTRY IN THE LIST OF WORKS CITED

Resnik, David. "Trans Fat Bans and Human Freedom." *The American Journal of Bioethics*, vol. 10, no. 3, Mar. 2010, pp. 27–32.

For a list of works cited that includes this entry, see 58b.

List of MLA in-text citation models

List of MLA works cited models

List of MLA works cited models, continued

57a MLA in-text citations

MLA in-text citations are made with a combination of signal phrases and parenthetical references. A signal phrase introduces information taken from a source (a quotation, summary, paraphrase, or fact); usually the signal phrase includes the author's name. The parenthetical citation comes after the cited material, often at the end of the sentence. It includes at least a page number (except for unpaginated sources, such as those found on the web). In the models in this section, certain elements of the citation are underlined.

IN-TEXT CITATION

Resnik acknowledges that his argument relies on "slippery slope" thinking, but he insists that "social and political pressures" regarding food regulation make his concerns valid (31).

Readers can look up the author's last name in the alphabetized list of works cited, where they will learn the work's title and other publication information. If readers decide to consult the source, the page number will take them straight to the cited passage.

General guidelines for signal phrases and page numbers

Items 1–5 explain how the MLA system usually works for all sources — in print, on the web, in other media, and with or without authors and page numbers. Items 6–25 give variations on the basic guidelines.

■ **1. Author named in a signal phrase** Ordinarily, introduce the material being cited with a signal phrase that includes the author's name. The first time you cite a source, include the author's first name in the signal phrase. In addition to preparing readers for the source, the signal phrase allows you to keep the parenthetical citation with the quotation's page number brief.

According to Lorine Goodwin, a food historian, nineteenth-century reformers who sought to purify the food supply were called "fanatics" and "radicals" by critics who argued that consumers should be free to buy and eat what they want (77).

Notice that the period follows the parenthetical citation. When a quotation ends with a question mark or an exclamation point, leave the end punctuation inside the quotation mark and add a period at the end of your sentence, after the parenthetical citation.

> <u>Burgess</u> asks a critical question: "How can we think differently about food labeling?" (<u>51</u>).

■ **2. Author named in parentheses** If you do not give the <u>author's name</u> in a signal phrase, put the last name in parentheses with the page number (if the source has one). Use no punctuation between the name and the page number: (Moran 351).

> According to a nationwide poll, seventy-five percent of Americans are opposed to laws that restrict or put limitations on access to unhealthy foods (<u>Neergaard and Agiesta</u>).

■ **3. Author unknown** If a source has no author, the works cited entry will begin with the title. In your in-text citation, either use the complete title in a signal phrase or use a <u>short form of the title</u> in parentheses. Titles of books and other long works are italicized; titles of articles and other short works are put in quotation marks.

> As a result, kids see nearly four thousand ads per year encouraging them to eat unhealthy food and drinks (<u>"Facts"</u>).

NOTE: If the author is a corporation or a government agency, see items 8 and 16.

■ **4. Source with no page numbers** Do not include a page number if a source does not provide page numbers. (When the pages of a web source are stable, as in PDF files, supply a page number in your in-text citation.)

> Michael Pollan points out that "cheap food" actually has "significant costs—to the environment, to public health, to the public purse, even to the culture."

If a source has numbered paragraphs or sections, use "par." (or "pars.") or "sec." (or "secs.") in the parentheses: (Smith, par. 4). Notice that a comma follows the author's name. If you cite an audiovisual source (such as an online video), include a time stamp for the material you have quoted or paraphrased: (00:08:31–40).

■ **5. One-page source** If a source is only one page long, do not include the page number in your in-text citation. You should, however, include the page number in your works cited list entry.

IN-TEXT CITATION FOR ONE-PAGE SOURCE

Sarah Conly uses John Stuart Mill's "harm principle" to argue that citizens need their government to intervene to prevent them from taking harmful actions — such as driving too fast or buying unhealthy foods — out of ignorance of the harm they can do.

ENTRY IN THE WORKS CITED LIST

Conly, Sarah. "Three Cheers for the Nanny State." *The New York Times*, 25 Mar. 2013, p. A23.

Variations on the general guidelines

This section describes the MLA guidelines for handling a variety of situations not covered in items 1–5.

■ **6. Two authors** Name both authors in a signal phrase, as in the following example, or include their last names in the parenthetical citation: (Gostin and Gostin 214).

As legal scholars Gostin and Gostin explain, "[I]nterventions that do not pose a truly significant burden on individual liberty" are justified if they "go a long way towards safeguarding the health and well-being of the populace" (214).

■ **7. Three or more authors** In a parenthetical citation, give the first author's name followed by "et al." (Latin for "and others"). In a signal phrase, give the first author's name followed by a phrase such as "and others."

The clinical trials were extended for two years, and only after results were reviewed by an independent panel did the researchers publish their findings (Blaine et al. 35).

Researchers Blaine and others note that clinical trial results were reviewed by an independent panel (35).

◼ **8. Organization as author**   When the author is a <u>corporation or an organization</u>, name that author either in the signal phrase or in the parenthetical citation. (For a government agency as author, see item 16.)

> The <u>American Diabetes Association</u> estimates that the cost
> of diagnosed diabetes in the United States in 2012 was
> $245 billion.

In the list of works cited, the American Diabetes Association is treated as the author and alphabetized under *A*. When you give the organization name in the text, spell out the name; when you use it in parentheses, shorten the name to the first noun and any preceding adjectives, removing any articles (*A, An, The*).

> The cost of diagnosed diabetes in the United States in 2012 has
> been estimated at $245 billion (<u>American Diabetes</u>).

◼ **9. Authors with the same last name**   If your list of works cited includes works by two or more authors with the same last name, include the author's first name in the signal phrase or <u>first initial</u> in the parentheses.

> One approach to the problem is to introduce nutrition literacy at the
> elementary level in public schools (<u>E.</u> Chen 15).

◼ **10. Two or more works by the same author**   In addition to the <u>author's name</u>, mention the title of the work in the signal phrase or include a <u>short version of the title</u> in the parentheses.

> The <u>American Diabetes Association</u> tracks trends in diabetes
> across age groups. In 2012, more than 200,000 children and
> adolescents had diabetes (<u>"Fast Facts"</u>). Because of an expected
> dramatic increase in diabetes in young people over the next forty
> years, the <u>association</u> encourages "strategies for implementing
> childhood obesity prevention programs and primary prevention
> programs for youth at risk of developing type 2 diabetes"
> (<u>"Number"</u>).

■ **10. Two or more works by the same author,** continued

Titles of articles and other short works are placed in quotation marks; titles of books and other long works are italicized.

In the rare case when both the author's name and a short title must be given in parentheses, separate them with a comma.

> Researchers have estimated that "the number of youth with type 2 [diabetes] could quadruple and the number with type 1 could triple" by 2050, "with an increasing proportion of youth with diabetes from minority populations" (American Diabetes, "Number").

■ **11. Two or more works in one citation**   To cite more than one source in the parentheses, list the authors (or titles) in alphabetical order and separate them with semicolons.

> The prevalence of early-onset type 2 diabetes has been well documented (Finn 68; Sharma 2037; Whitaker 118).

■ **12. Repeated citations from the same source**   If you cite a source more than once in a paragraph, you may omit the author's name after the first mention as long as it is clear that you are still referring to the same source. Later citations may include only the page number.

> Family expectations are at the heart of *Everything I Never Told You*, a debut novel in which a daughter shrinks from a mother who forces her to read books on science and medicine "to inspire her, to show her what she could accomplish" (Ng 73). But teenage Lydia commits herself to standing up to her overbearing mother, promising that "she will tell her mother: enough" (274).

■ **13. Encyclopedia or dictionary entry**   When an encyclopedia or dictionary entry does not have an author, mention the word or entry and give the page number on which the entry may be found.

> The word *crocodile* has a complex etymology ("Crocodile" 139).

■ **14. Entire work** Use the author's name in a signal phrase or a parenthetical citation. There is no need to use a page number.

> Pollan explores the issues surrounding food production and consumption from a political angle.

■ **15. Selection in an anthology or a collection** Put the name of the author of the selection (not the editor of the anthology) in the signal phrase or the parentheses.

> In "How to Write Iranian-America, or the Last Essay," Khakpour details degrading experiences with English language instructors "who look to you with the shine of love but the stench of pity" (3).

In the list of works cited, the work is alphabetized under Khakpour, the author of the essay, not under the name of the editor of the anthology. (See item 27 in 57b.)

■ **16. Government document** In a signal phrase, include the name of the agency or governing body as given in the works cited list. In a parenthetical citation, shorten the name.

> In fact, the amount of money the United States spends to treat chronic illnesses is increasing so rapidly that the Centers for Disease Control has labeled chronic disease "the public health challenge of the 21st century" (National Center 1).

If you cite more than one agency or department from the same government in your essay, you may choose to standardize the names by beginning with the name of the government (see item 55 in 57b). In that case, when shortening names of government agencies, give enough of the name to differentiate the authors: (United States, Department of Transportation); (United States, Environmental Protection). See 58b for an essay that uses standardized government authors.

■ **17. Historical document** For a historical document, such as the Constitution of the United States or the Canadian Charter of Rights and Freedoms, provide the document title, neither italicized nor in quotation marks, along with relevant article and section numbers. In parenthetical citations, use abbreviations such as "art." and "sec." See the next page for an example.

■ **17. Historical document,** continued

> While the Constitution provides for the formation of new states
> (art. 4, sec. 3), it does not explicitly allow or prohibit the secession
> of states.

Cite other historical documents as you would any other work, by the first element in the works cited entry (see item 56 in 57b).

■ **18. Legal source** For a legislative act (law) or court case, name the act or case either in a signal phrase or in parentheses. Italicize the names of cases but not the names of acts. (See also items 57 and 58 in 57b.)

> The CARES Act of 2020 provided loans for small businesses.

> *Dred Scott v. Sandford*, which concluded that both free and enslaved
> Black people could not be citizens of the United States, may have
> been the US Supreme Court's worst decision.

■ **19. Visual such as a table, a chart, or another graphic** To cite a visual that has a figure number in the original source, use the abbreviation "fig." and the number in place of a page number in your parenthetical citation: (Manning, fig. 4). If you refer to the figure in your text, spell out the word "figure."

To cite a visual that appears in a print source without a figure number, use the visual's title or a description in your text and cite the author and page number as for any other source.

For a visual not in a print source, identify the visual in your text and then in parentheses use the first element in the works cited entry: the artist's or photographer's name or the title of the work. (See items 49–53 in 57b.)

> Photographs such as *Woman Aircraft Worker* (Bransby) and *Women*
> *Welders* (Parks) demonstrate the US government's attempt to
> document the contributions of women during World War II.

■ **20. Personal communication and social media** Cite a personal letter, a personal interview, an email message, or a social media post by the name listed in the works cited entry, as you would for any other source. Identify the type of source in your text if you think it is necessary for clarity. (See items 11 and 59–62 in 57b.)

■ **21. Web source** Your in-text citation for a source from the web should follow the same guidelines as for other sources. If the source lacks page numbers but has numbered paragraphs, sections, or divisions, use those numbers with the appropriate abbreviation in your parenthetical citation: "par.," "sec.," "ch.," "pt.," and so on. Do not add such numbers if the source itself does not use them; simply give the author or title in your in-text citation.

> Sanjay Gupta, CNN chief medical correspondent, explains that "limited access to fresh, affordable, healthy food" is one of America's most pressing health problems.

■ **22. Indirect source (source quoted in another source)** When a writer's or a speaker's quoted words appear in a source written by someone else, begin the parenthetical citation with the abbreviation "qtd. in." In the following example, Gostin and Gostin are the authors of the source given in the works cited list; their work contains a quotation by Beauchamp.

> Public health researcher Dan Beauchamp has said that "public health practices are communal in nature, and concerned with the well-being of the community as a whole and not just the well-being of any particular person" (qtd. in Gostin and Gostin 217).

Literary works and sacred texts

Literary works and sacred texts are usually available in a variety of editions. Your list of works cited will specify which edition you are using, and your in-text citation will usually consist of a page number from the edition you consulted as for any other work. When possible, give additional information — such as book parts, play divisions, or line numbers — so that readers can locate the cited passage in any edition of the work, as in the examples on the next page.

■ **23. Literary work or play** If a literary work has numbered divisions, include the page number followed by a semicolon and the section, part, or chapter number(s). For a play without line numbers, include the act/and or scene numbers after the page number: (37; sc. 1).

> In utter despair, Dostoyevsky's character Mitya wonders aloud about
> the "terrible tragedies realism inflicts on people" (376; bk. 8,
> ch. 2).

■ **24. Verse play or poem** For verse plays, give act, scene, and line numbers that can be located in any edition of the work. Use arabic numerals and separate the numbers with periods.

> In Shakespeare's *King Lear*, Gloucester learns a profound lesson from
> a tragic experience: "A man may see how this world goes / with no
> eyes" (4.2.148–49).

For a poem, cite the part, stanza, and line numbers, if it has them, separated by periods.

> The Green Knight claims to approach King Arthur's court
> "because the praise of you, prince, is puffed so high, / And
> your manor and your men are considered so magnificent"
> (1.12.258–59).

For poems that are not divided into numbered parts or stanzas, use line numbers. For the first citation, use the word "lines": (lines 5–8). Thereafter use just the numbers: (12–13).

■ **25. Sacred text** The first time you cite the work, give the title of the work as in the works cited entry, followed by the book, chapter, and verse (or their equivalent), separated with periods. Common abbreviations for books of the Bible are acceptable in a parenthetical citation. Omit the work's title from the parentheses in all citations after the first.

> Consider the words of Solomon: "If your enemy is hungry, give him
> bread to eat; and if he is thirsty, give him water to drink" (*Oxford
> Annotated Bible*, Prov. 25.21).

The title of a sacred work is italicized when it refers to a specific edition of the work, as in the preceding example. If you refer to the book in a general sense in your text, neither italicize it nor put it in quotation marks.

The Bible and the Qur'an provide allegories that help readers understand how to lead a moral life.

57b MLA list of works cited

Your list of works cited, which you will place at the end of your paper, guides readers to the sources you have quoted, summarized, and paraphrased. Ask yourself: *What would readers need to know to find this source for themselves?* Usually, you will provide basic information common to most sources, such as author, title, publisher, publication date, and location (page numbers or URL, for example).

Throughout this section of the book, you'll find models organized by type (article, book, website, multimedia source, and so on). But even if you aren't sure exactly what type of source you have (*Is this a blog post or an article?*), you can follow two general principles:

Gather key publication information about the source — the citation elements.

Organize the basic information about the source using what MLA calls "containers."

The author's name and the title of the work are needed for many (though not all) sources and are the first two pieces of information to gather. For the remaining pieces of information, you might find it helpful to think about whether the work is contained within one or more larger works. Some sources are self-contained. Others are nested in larger containers. The chart on the next page illustrates different kinds of sources and their containers.

☐	**SELF-CONTAINED**	a *book* a *film*
☐☐	**ONE CONTAINER**	an *article* in a scholarly journal a *poem* in a collection of poetry a *video* posted to YouTube a *fact sheet* on a government website
☐☐	**TWO CONTAINERS**	an *article* in a journal within a database (JSTOR, etc.) an *episode* from a TV series within a streaming service (Netflix, etc.)

Keep in mind that most sources won't include all of the following pieces of information, so gather only those that are relevant to and available for your source.

Author.		
Title of source.		
Title of container,	*If there is a second container, gather the same information for it (if available).*	→ Title of container 2,
Contributors,		Contributors,
Version (or edition),		Version (or edition),
Number,		Number,
Publisher,		Publisher,
Date,		Date,
Location (page numbers, URL, DOI, etc.).		Location.

WORKS CITED ENTRY, ONE CONTAINER (SELECTION IN AN ANTHOLOGY)

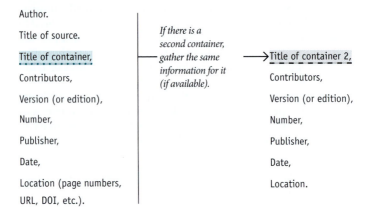

Smith, Zadie. "Speaking in Tongues." *The Glorious American Essay: One Hundred Essays from Colonial Times to the Present,* edited by Phillip Lopate, Pantheon, 2020, pp. 886–900.

WORKS CITED ENTRY, TWO CONTAINERS (ARTICLE IN A JOURNAL IN A DATABASE)

author — title of article

Carey, Craig. "Realism and Recording: Remixing Literary and Media History."

CONTAINER 1

| journal title | volume, issue | date | location (pages) |

American Literary Realism, vol. 53, no. 3, spring 2021, pp. 198–203.

CONTAINER 2

| database title | location (DOI) |

JSTOR, https://doi.org/10.5406/amerlitereal.53.3.0198.

Once you've gathered the relevant and available information about a source, you will organize the elements using the list above as your guideline. Note the punctuation after each element in that list. In this section you will find many examples of how elements and containers are combined to create works cited entries.

General guidelines for listing authors

The formatting of authors' names in items 1–11 applies to all sources — books, articles, websites — in print, on the web, or in other media. For more models of specific source types, see items 12–62.

■ 1. Single author

Bowker, Gordon. *James Joyce: A New Biography*. Farrar, Straus and Giroux,

2012.

■ 2. Two authors   Put the first author's last name first; present the second author's name in the normal order.

Gourevitch, Philip, and Errol Morris. *Standard Operating Procedure*.

Penguin Books, 2008.

■ 3. Three or more authors   Name the first author followed by "et al." (Latin for "and others"). For in-text citations, see item 7 in 57a.

Cunningham, Stewart, et al. *Media Economics*. Palgrave Macmillan, 2015.

GENERAL GUIDELINES FOR THE WORKS CITED LIST

In the list of works cited, include only sources that you have quoted, summarized, or paraphrased in your paper. MLA's guidelines apply to a wide variety of sources. You can adapt the guidelines and models in this section to source types you encounter in your research.

Gathering information and organizing entries

The elements needed for a works cited entry are the following:

- The author (if a work has one)
- The title
- The title of the larger work in which the source is located, if it is contained in a larger work (MLA calls the larger work a "container" — a collection, a journal, a magazine, a website, and so on)
- As much of the following information as is available about the source and the container:

    Editor, translator, director, performer

    Version or edition

    Number

    Publisher

    Date of publication

    Location of the source: page numbers, URL, DOI, and so on

Not all sources will require every element. See specific models in this section for more details.

Authors

- Arrange the list alphabetically by authors' last names or by titles for works with no authors.
- For the first author in a works cited entry, list the last name first, followed by a comma and the first name. Put a second author's name in typical order (first name followed by last name). For three or more authors, use "et al." after the first author's name.
- For organization authors, list the name in the normal order. If the name begins with an article (*A, An,* or *The*), omit it.
- Spell out "editor," "translator," "edited by," and so on.

Titles

- In titles of works, capitalize all words except articles (*a, an, the*), prepositions, coordinating conjunctions, and the *to* in infinitives — unless the word is first or last in the title or subtitle.

GENERAL GUIDELINES FOR THE WORKS CITED LIST, continued

- Use quotation marks for titles of articles and other short works. Place single quotation marks around a quoted term or a title of a short work that appears within an article title; italicize a term or title that is normally italicized.
- Italicize titles of books and other long works, including websites. If a book title contains another title that is normally italicized, neither italicize the internal title nor place it in quotation marks. If the title within the title is normally put in quotation marks, retain the quotation marks and italicize the entire book title.

Publication information

- Use the complete version of publishers' names, except for terms such as *Inc.* and *Co.*; retain terms such as *Books* and *Press*. For university publishers, use *U* and *P* for *University* and *Press*.
- For a book, take the name of the publisher from the title page (or from the copyright page if it is not on the title page). For a website, the publisher might be at the bottom of a page or on the "About" page. If a work has two or more publishers, separate the names with slashes.
- If the title of a website and the publisher are the same or similar, give the title of the site but omit the publisher.

Dates

- For a book, give the most recent year found on the title page or the copyright page.
- For an article from a periodical like a journal or a magazine, use the most specific date given, whether it is a month and year, a full date, or a season (*spring 2021*).
- For a web source, use the posting date, the copyright date, or the most recent update date. Use the complete date as listed in the source. If a web source has no date, give your date of access at the end: Accessed 24 Feb. 2020.
- Abbreviate all months except May, June, and July, and give the date in inverted form: 13 Mar. 2020.

Page numbers

- For most articles and other short works, give page numbers when they are available, preceded by "pp." (or "p." for only one page).
- Do not use the page numbers from a printout of a web source.
- If a short work does not appear on consecutive pages, give the number of the first page followed by a plus sign: 35+.

➔

GENERAL GUIDELINES FOR THE WORKS CITED LIST,
continued

URLs and DOIs

- Give a DOI (digital object identifier) if a source has one. Include the protocol and host (*https://doi.org/*).
- If a source does not have a DOI, include a permalink if possible. Copy the permalink provided by the website.
- If a source does not have a permalink or a DOI, include the full URL for the source. Copy the URL directly from your browser. It is optional to remove the protocol (*http://* or *https://*) when you do not need to provide live links for your readers. Do not insert any line breaks or hyphens into the URL.
- If a URL is longer than three lines on the works cited page, you may shorten it, leaving at least the website host (for example, *cnn.com* or *www.usda.gov*) in the entry.

■ **4. Organization or company as author** Begin with the organization name, omitting any initial articles (*A*, *An*, or *The*). Your in-text citation also should treat the organization as the author (see item 8 in 57a).

Human Rights Watch. *World Report of 2015: Events of 2014.* Seven Stories

Press, 2015.

■ **5. No author listed** Begin the entry with the work's title. Alphabetize by the first word in the title (ignoring, but not omitting, the articles *The*, *A*, or *An*).

"CEO Activism in America Is Risky Business." *The Economist,* 17 Apr.

2021, www.economist.com/business/2021/04/14/ceo-activism

-in-america-is-risky-business.

NOTE: In web sources, often the author's name is available but is not easy to find. It may appear at the end of a web page, in tiny print, or on another page of the site, such as the home page. Also, an organization or a government may be the author (see items 4 and 55).

■ **6. Two or more works by the same author or group of authors** Alphabetize the works by title (ignoring the article *A*, *An*, or *The* at the beginning of a title). Use the author's name or authors' names for the first entry; for subsequent entries, use three hyphens or dashes and a period. The three hyphens must stand for exactly the same name or names, in the same order, that appear in the first entry.

Coates, Ta-Nehisi. *Between the World and Me*. Spiegel and Grau, 2015.

---. *We Were Eight Years in Power: An American Tragedy*. One World, 2018.

Eaton-Robb, Pat, and Susan Haigh. "Pandemic May Lead to Long-Term Changes in

School Calendar." *AP News*, 15 Apr. 2021, apnews.com/article

/pandemics-connecticut-ned-lamont-975d41076ae6b985030c133614685f33.

---. "Rock Star Van Zandt Helping Connecticut Students Re-engage." *AP*

News, 20 Apr. 2021, apnews.com/article/health-music-education

-arts-and-entertainment-entertainment

-5b038c218b30863d76031134db46fa5d.

■ **7. Editor or translator**   Begin with the editor's or translator's name. After the name, add "editor" or "translator." Use "editors" or "translators" for two or more (see also items 2 and 3 for how to handle multiple contributors).

Horner, Avril, and Anne Rowe, editors. *Living on Paper: Letters from Iris*

Murdoch, 1934–1995. Princeton UP, 2016.

■ **8. Author with editor or translator**   Begin with the name of the author. Place the editor's or translator's name after the title.

Ullmann, Regina. *The Country Road: Stories*. Translated by Kurt Beals, New

Directions Publishing, 2015.

■ **9. Graphic narrative or other illustrated work**   If a work has both an author and an illustrator, the order in your citation will depend on which contributor's work you emphasize in your paper. If there are multiple contributors but you are not discussing a specific contributor's work in your essay, you may begin with the title. If the author and illustrator are the same person, cite as you would a book with one author (see items 1 and 23).

Gaiman, Neil. *The Sandman: Overture*. Illustrated by J. H. William III, DC

Comics, 2015.

Martínez, Hugo, illustrator. *Wake: The Hidden History of Women-Led Slave*

Revolts. By Rebecca Hall, Simon and Schuster, 2021.

HOW TO

Answer the basic question "Who is the author?"

PROBLEM: Sometimes when you need to cite a source, it's not clear who the author is. This is especially true for sources on the web and other nonprint sources, which may have been created by one person and uploaded by a different person or an organization. Whom do you cite as the author in such a case? How do you determine who *is* the author?

EXAMPLE: The video "Surfing the Web on the Job" (see below) was uploaded to YouTube by CBSNewsOnline. Is the person or organization that uploads the video the author of the video? Not necessarily.

STRATEGY: After you view or listen to the source a few times, ask yourself whether you can tell who is chiefly responsible for creating the content in the source. It could be an organization. It could be an identifiable individual. This video consists entirely of reporting by Daniel Sieberg, so the author is Sieberg.

Surfing the Web on The Job

 CBSNewsOnline · 42,491 videos

▶ Subscribe   85,736

Uploaded on Nov 12, 2009
As the Internet continues to emerge as a critical facet of everyday life, CBS News' Daniel Sieberg reports that companies are cracking down on employees' personal Web use.

CITATION: To cite the source, you would use the basic MLA guidelines for a video found on the web (item 40).

author:
last name first   title of video   website title

Sieberg, Daniel. "Surfing the Web on the Job." *YouTube*, uploaded by

upload information   upload date   URL

CBSNewsOnline, 12 Nov. 2009, www.youtube.com/watch?v=1wLhNwY-enY.

■ **10. Author using a pseudonym (pen name)** Use the author's name as it appears in the source, followed by the author's real name in brackets, if you know it. Alternatively, if the author's real name is more well-known, you may start with the real name followed by *published as,* italicized, and the pen name in brackets.

North, Claire [Catherine Webb]. *The Pursuit of William Abbey*. Orbit,

2019.

Franklin, Benjamin [*published as* Richard Saunders]. "Poor Richard, 1773."

1773. *Founders Online*, National Archives, founders.archives.gov

/documents/Franklin/01-01-02-0093.

■ **11. Screen name or social media account** Start with the account display name, followed by the screen name or handle (if available) in brackets. If the account name is a first and last name, invert it. If the account name and handle are very similar (for example, ACLU SoCal and @ACLU_SoCal), you may omit the handle.

Gay, Roxane [@rgay]. "The shortness of cultural memory is always

astonishing." *Twitter*, 25 Apr. 2021, twitter.com/rgay/status

/1386507940601995274?.

Partlycloudy. Comment on "Is This the End?" *The New York Times*, 25 Nov.

2012, nyti.ms/3nPkY5j#permid=7726753.

Articles and other short works

■ **12. Basic format for an article or other short work** After the author's name, provide the title of the article, followed by the title of the publication and other publication information.

a. Print

Tilman, David. "Food and Health of a Full Earth." *Daedalus*, vol. 144,

no. 4, fall 2015, pp. 5–7.

■ **12. Basic format for an article or other short work,** continued

b. Web   Include the article's online location (such as the DOI, permalink, or URL).

Florez, Nina. "Chicago Rally Held in Support of Colombian Protesters."
   NBC 5 Chicago, 9 May 2021, www.nbcchicago.com/news/local
   /chicago-rallies-held-in-support-of-colombian-protesters/2505612.

c. Database   Include the database title at the end of your citation.
If the database provides a DOI or a permalink, use that after the
title. Otherwise, provide the URL to the article in the database.

Harris, Ashleigh May, and Nicklas Hållén. "African Street Literature: A
   Method for an Emergent Form beyond World Literature." *Research in
   African Literatures*, vol. 51, no. 2, summer 2020, pp. 1–26. *JSTOR*,
   https://doi.org/10.2979/reseafrilite.51.2.01.

■ **13. Article in a journal**   Provide the volume and issue numbers.

a. Print

Matchie, Thomas. "Law versus Love in *The Round House*." *The Midwest
   Quarterly*, vol. 56, no. 4, summer 2015, pp. 353–64.

b. Online journal

McGuire, Meg. "Women, Healing, and Social Community: Cyberfeminist
   Activities on Reddit." *Kairos*, vol. 25, no. 2, spring 2021, kairos
   .technorhetoric.net/25.2/topoi/mcguire/index.html.

c. Database

Maier, Jessica. "A 'True Likeness': The Renaissance City Portrait."
   Renaissance Quarterly, vol. 65, no. 3, fall 2012, pp. 711–52. *JSTOR*,
   https://doi.org/10.1086/668300.

CITATION AT A GLANCE

Article in an online journal

To cite an article in an online journal in MLA style, include the following elements:

1 Author(s) of article
2 Title and subtitle of article
3 Title of journal
4 Volume and issue numbers
5 Date of publication (including month or season, if any)
6 Page number(s) of article, if given
7 Location of source (DOI, permalink, or URL)

Online journal article

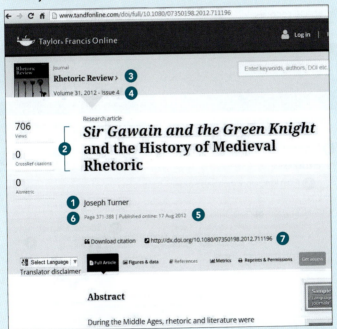

WORKS CITED ENTRY FOR AN ARTICLE IN AN ONLINE JOURNAL

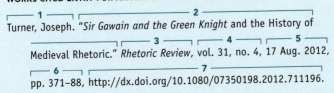

Turner, Joseph. "*Sir Gawain and the Green Knight* and the History of Medieval Rhetoric." *Rhetoric Review*, vol. 31, no. 4, 17 Aug. 2012, pp. 371–88, http://dx.doi.org/10.1080/07350198.2012.711196.

For more on citing online articles in MLA style, see items 12–15.

CITATION AT A GLANCE

Article from a database

To cite an article from a database in MLA style, include the following elements:

1 Author(s) of article
2 Title and subtitle of article
3 Title of journal, magazine, or newspaper
4 Volume and issue numbers (for journal)
5 Date of publication (including month or season, if any)

6 Page number(s) of article, if any
7 Name of database
8 DOI or permalink, if available; otherwise, URL to article

Database record

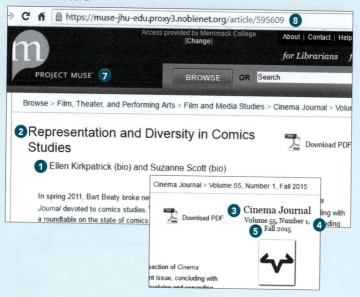

WORKS CITED ENTRY FOR AN ARTICLE FROM A DATABASE

Kirkpatrick, Ellen, and Suzanne Scott. "Representation and Diversity in Comics Studies." *Cinema Journal*, vol. 55, no. 1, fall 2015. *Project Muse*, muse-jhu-edu.proxy3.noblenet.org/article/595609.

For more on citing articles from a database in MLA style, see items 12 and 13.

■ **14. Article in a magazine** Include the <u>full publication date</u> given in the magazine.

Owusu, Nadia. "Head Wraps." *The New York Times Magazine*, <u>7 Mar. 2021</u>,
    p. 20.

Stuart, Tessa. "New Study Suggests Burning Fossil Fuels Contributed to
    1 in 5 Deaths in 2018." *Rolling Stone*, <u>17 Feb. 2021</u>, www
    .rollingstone.com/politics/politics-news/fossil-fuels-air
    -pollution-premature-deaths-statistics-1127586/.

■ **15. Article in a newspaper** Include the <u>full publication date</u> and the <u>section and page number</u>, if available.

Corasaniti, Nick, and Jim Rutenberg. "Record Turnout Hints at Future of
    Vote in U.S." *The New York Times*, <u>6 Dec. 2020</u>, <u>pp. A1+</u>.

Jones, Ayana. "Chamber of Commerce Program to Boost Black-Owned
    Businesses." *The Philadelphia Tribune*, <u>21 Apr. 2021</u>, www.phillytrib.com
    /news/business/chamber-of-commerce-program-to-boost-black-owned
    -businesses/article_6b14ae2f-5db2-5a59-8a67-8bbf974da451.html.

■ **16. Editorial or opinion** List the <u>author as it appears in the source</u>. You may add the word "Editorial" or "Op-ed" to the end of the entry if it is not clear from the author or title of the source.

<u>Kansas City Star Editorial Board</u>. "Kansas Considers Lowering Concealed
    Carry Age to 18. Why It's Wrong for Many Reasons." *The Kansas
    City Star*, 9 Mar. 2021, www.kansascity.com/opinion/editorials
    /article249793143.html.

■ **17. Letter to the editor** Use the <u>label "Letter"</u> as the title if the letter has no title or headline.

Carasso, Roger. <u>Letter</u>. *The New York Times*, 4 Apr. 2021, Sunday Book
    Review sec., p. 5.

■ **18. Comment on an online article** List the author's name as it appears on the comment (see item 11). After the name, include "Comment on" followed by the article's publication information. Include the URL directly to the comment, if possible; otherwise, use the URL for the article.

satch. Comment on "No Compassion," by Roy Edroso. *Alicublog*, 20 Mar.

2021, 9:50 a.m., disq.us/p/2fu0ulk.

■ **19. Review** If the review is untitled, use the label "Review of" and the title and author or director of the work reviewed. Then add information for the publication in which the review appears.

Jopanda, Wayne Silao. Review of *America is Not the Heart*, by Elaine

Castillo. *Alon: Journal for Filipinx American and Diasporic Studies*,

vol. 1, no. 1, Mar. 2021, pp. 106–08. *eScholarship*, escholarship

.org/uc/item/0d44t8wx.

Bramesco, Charles. "*Honeyland* Couches an Apocalyptic Warning in a

Beekeeping Documentary." *The A.V. Club*, G/O Media, 23 July 2019,

film.avclub.com/honeyland-couches-an-apocalyptic-warning-in-a

-beekeepin-1836624795.

■ **20. Interview** Begin with the person interviewed. Include the name of the interviewer after the title (or after the interviewee if the interview is untitled). For an interview that you conducted, use "the author" as the interviewer.

Harjo, Joy. "The First Native American U.S. Poet Laureate on How Poetry

Can Counter Hate." Interview by Olivia B. Waxman. *Time*, 22 Aug.

2019, time.com/5658443/joy-harjo-poet-interview/.

Kendi, Ibram X. Interview by Eric Deggans. *Life Kit*, NPR, 24 Oct. 2020.

Akufo, Rosa. Interview with the author. 10 Nov. 2020.

■ **21. Article in a dictionary or an encyclopedia (including a wiki)** List the author of the entry (if there is one), the title of the entry, and publication information for the reference work. For an online source that is continually updated, such as a wiki entry, use the most recent update date.

Robinson, Lisa Clayton. "Harlem Writers Guild." *Africana: The Encyclopedia of the African and African American Experience*, edited by Kwame Anthony Appiah and Henry Louis Gates Jr., 2nd ed., Oxford UP, 2005, p. 163.

"House Music." *Wikipedia: The Free Encyclopedia,* Wikimedia Foundation, 8 Apr. 2021, en.wikipedia.org/wiki/House_music.

■ **22. Letter in a collection**   List the title as it appears in the collection (or, if untitled, "Letter to" and the recipient), followed by the date of the letter. End with the title and publication information for the collection.

Murdoch, Iris. Letter to Raymond Queneau. 7 Aug. 1946. *Living on Paper: Letters from Iris Murdoch, 1934–1995*, edited by Avril Horner and Anne Rowe, Princeton UP, 2016, pp. 76–78.

Oblinger, Maggie. "Letter from Maggie Oblinger to Charlie Thomas, March 31, 1895." 31 Mar. 1895. *Prairie Settlement: Nebraska Photographs and Family Letters, 1862–1912*, Library of Congress / American Memory, memory.loc.gov/cgi-bin/query/r?ammem /ps:@field(DOCID+l306)#l3060001.

Books and other long works

► Citation at a glance: Book **430**
► Citation at a glance: Selection from an anthology or a collection **432**

■ **23. Basic format for a book**

a. Print book or e-book   If you have used an e-book, indicate "e-book ed." before the publisher's name.

Porter, Max. *Lanny*. Graywolf Press, 2019.

Cabral, Amber. *Allies and Advocates: Creating an Inclusive and Equitable Culture*. E-book ed., Wiley, 2021.

CITATION AT A GLANCE
Book

To cite a print book in MLA style, include the following elements:

1 Author(s)
2 Title and subtitle
3 Publisher
4 Year of publication (latest year)

Title page

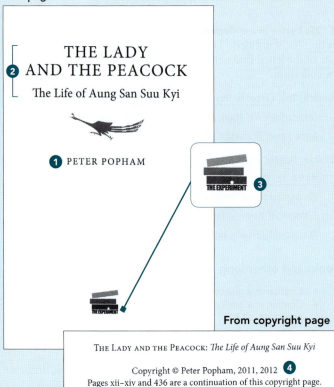

THE LADY AND THE PEACOCK
The Life of Aung San Suu Kyi

2

1 PETER POPHAM

3 THE EXPERIMENT

From copyright page

THE LADY AND THE PEACOCK: *The Life of Aung San Suu Kyi*

Copyright © Peter Popham, 2011, 2012 **4**
Pages xii–xiv and 436 are a continuation of this copyright page.

WORKS CITED ENTRY FOR A PRINT BOOK

        1   2
Popham, Peter. *The Lady and the Peacock: The Life of Aung San Suu Kyi*.
        3   4
    The Experiment, 2012.

For more on citing books in MLA style, see items 23–30.

■ **23. Basic format for a book,** continued

b. Web Give whatever print publication information is available for the work, followed by the title of the website and the URL. If the book's original publication date is not available, include the date of online publication.

Piketty, Thomas. *Capital in the Twenty-First Century*. Translated by Arthur

Goldhammer, Harvard UP, 2014. *Google Books*, books.google.com

/books?isbn=0674369556.

c. Audiobook After the title, include the phrase "Narrated by" followed by the narrator's full name. If the author and narrator are the same, include only the last name. Then include "audiobook ed.," the publisher, and the date of release.

de Hart, Jane Sherron. *Ruth Bader Ginsburg: A Life*. Narrated by Suzanne

Toren, audiobook ed., Random House Audio, 2018.

■ **24. Parts of a book (foreword, introduction, preface, or afterword)**

Coates, Ta-Nehisi. Foreword. *The Origin of Others*, by Toni Morrison,

Harvard UP, 2017, pp. vii–xvii.

Sullivan, John Jeremiah. "The Ill-Defined Plot." Introduction. *The*

Best American Essays 2014, edited by Sullivan, Houghton Mifflin

Harcourt, 2014, pp. xvii–xxvi.

■ **25. Book in a language other than English** Capitalize the title according to the conventions of the book's language. If your readers are not familiar with the language of the book, include a translation of the title in brackets.

Vargas Llosa, Mario. *El sueño del celta* [*The Dream of the Celt*]. Alfaguara

Ediciones, 2010.

■ **26. Entire anthology or collection** An anthology is a collection of works on a common theme, often with different authors for the selections and usually with an editor for the entire volume.

Marcus, Ben, editor. *New American Stories*. Vintage Books, 2015.

CITATION AT A GLANCE

Selection from an anthology or a collection

To cite a selection from an anthology in MLA style, include the following elements:

1 Author(s) of selection
2 Title and subtitle of selection
3 Title and subtitle of anthology
4 Editor(s) of anthology
5 Publisher
6 Year of publication
7 Page number(s) of selection

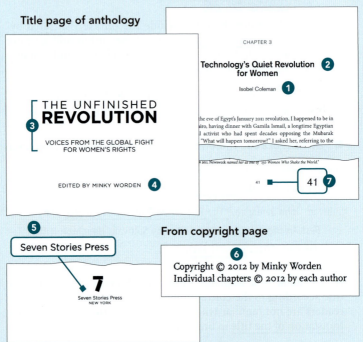

Title page of anthology

First page of selection

CHAPTER 3

Technology's Quiet Revolution for Women 2

Isobel Coleman 1

THE UNFINISHED
REVOLUTION 3

VOICES FROM THE GLOBAL FIGHT
FOR WOMEN'S RIGHTS

EDITED BY MINKY WORDEN 4

...the eve of Egypt's January 2011 revolution, I happened to be in ...iro, having dinner with Gamila Ismail, a longtime Egyptian ...l activist who had spent decades opposing the Mubarak ... "What will happen tomorrow?" I asked her, referring to the

...w 2011, Newsweek named her as one of "150 Women Who Shake the World."

41 ━ 41 7

From copyright page

5
Seven Stories Press

6
Copyright © 2012 by Minky Worden
Individual chapters © 2012 by each author

7
Seven Stories Press
NEW YORK

WORKS CITED ENTRY FOR A SELECTION FROM AN ANTHOLOGY

┌─── 1 ───┐ ┌────────── 2 ──────────┐ ┌─
Coleman, Isobel. "Technology's Quiet Revolution for Women." *The*
─────────── 3 ───────────
Unfinished Revolution: *Voices from the Global Fight for Women's*
┌──── 4 ────┐ ┌───── 5 ─────┐ ┌ 6 ┐ ┌── 7 ──┐
Rights, edited by Minky Worden, Seven Stories Press, 2012, pp. 41–49.

For more on citing selections from anthologies in MLA style, see items 26–28.

■ 27. One selection from an anthology or a collection

Sayrafiezadeh, Saïd. "Paranoia." *New American Stories*, edited by Ben
Marcus, Vintage Books, 2015, pp. 3–29.

■ 28. Two or more selections from an anthology or a collection
Provide an entry for the entire anthology (see item 26) and a shortened entry for each selection. Alphabetize the entries by authors'
or editors' last names. Here, the Eisenberg and Sayrafiezadeh
selections appear in Marcus's anthology, *New American Stories.*

Eisenberg, Deborah. "Some Other, Better Otto." Marcus, pp. 94–136.

Marcus, Ben, editor. *New American Stories.* Vintage Books, 2015.

Sayrafiezadeh, Saïd. "Paranoia." Marcus, pp. 3–29.

■ 29. Edition other than the first   If the book has a translator
or an editor in addition to the author, give the name of the translator or editor before the edition number (see item 8 for a book
with an editor or a translator).

Eagleton, Terry. *Literary Theory: An Introduction.* 3rd ed., U of Minnesota
P, 2008.

■ 30. Multivolume work   Include the total number of volumes
at the end of the entry, using the abbreviation "vols." If the volumes were published over several years, give the inclusive dates
of publication.

Cather, Willa. *Willa Cather: The Complete Fiction and Other Writings.* Edited
by Sharon O'Brien, Library of America, 1987–92. 3 vols.

If you cite only one volume in your paper, include the volume's
title (if the volumes are individually titled) and number and give
the date of publication for that volume.

Cather, Willa. *Willa Cather: Later Novels.* Edited by Sharon O'Brien, Library
of America, 1990. Vol. 2 of *Willa Cather: The Complete Fiction and
Other Writings.*

■ **31. Sacred text** Give the title of the edition (taken from the title page), italicized; the editor's or translator's name (if any); and publication information. Add the name of the version, if there is one, before the publisher.

The Oxford Annotated Bible with the Apocrypha. Edited by Herbert G. May
    and Bruce M. Metzger, Revised Standard Version, Oxford UP, 1965.

Quran: The Final Testament. Translated by Rashad Khalifa, Authorized
    English Version with Arabic Text, Universal Unity, 2000.

■ **32. Dissertation**

Kabugi, Magana J. *The Souls of Black Colleges: Cultural Production,*
    Ideology, and Identity at Historically Black Colleges and Universities.
    2020. Vanderbilt U, PhD dissertation. *Vanderbilt University*
    Institutional Repository, hdl.handle.net/1803/16103.

Web sources

▶ Citation at a glance: Work from a website **436**

■ **33. An entire website** Include the website's sponsor or publisher and the update date. If the website name is the same or similar to the publisher, do not include it; if no date is provided, include the date you accessed the source, as in the example at the top of the next page.

Lift Every Voice. Library of America / Schomburg Center for Research in
    Black Culture, 2020, africanamericanpoetry.org/.

The Newton Project. 2021, www.newtonproject.ox.ac.uk/.

■ **34. Work from a website**

a. Short work (article, individual web page) Place the title in quotation marks. If there is no posting date or update date, include the date you accessed the source.

Enzinna, Wes. "Syria's Unknown Revolution." *Pulitzer Center,* 24 Nov.
    2015, pulitzercenter.org/projects/middle-east-syria-enzinna
    -war-rojava.

"Bali, Karan. "Shashikala." *Upperstall*, upperstall.com/profile/shashikala/.

Accessed 22 Apr. 2021.

b. Long work (book, report) Italicize the title. If a book's original publication date is not available, include the date of online publication.

Euripides. *The Trojan Women*. Translated by Gilbert Murray, Oxford UP,

1915. *Internet Sacred Text Archive*, www.sacred-texts.com/cla

/eurip/trojan.htm.

■ **35. Blog post** Cite a blog post as you would a work from a website (see item 34), with the title of the post in quotation marks. (To cite a comment on a blog, follow the guidelines in item 18.)

Horgan, John. "My Quantum Experiment." *Cross-Check*, 5 June 2020,

blogs.scientificamerican.com/cross-check/my-quantum-experiment/.

Scientific American.

Edroso, Roy. "No Compassion." *Alicublog*, 18 Mar. 2021, alicublog

.blogspot.com/2021/03/no-compassion.html.

■ **36. Social media post** Cite as a work from a website (see item 34). Begin with the author (see item 11 for citing screen names). Use the caption or full text of the post as the title, if it is brief; if the post is long, use the first few words followed by an ellipsis. If the post has no text, or if you focus on a visual element in your paper, provide a description of the post, as in the last example.

Abdurraqib, Hanif [@NifMuhammad]. "Tracy Chapman really one of

the greatest Ohio writers." *Twitter*, 30 Mar. 2021, twitter.com

/NifMuhammad/status/1377086355667320836.

ACLU. "Public officials have . . ." *Facebook*, 10 May 2021, www.facebook

.com/aclu/photos/a.74134381812/10157852911711813.

Rosa, Camila [camixvx]. Illustration of nurses in masks with fists raised.

Instagram, 28 Apr. 2020, www.instagram.com/p/B_h62W9pJaQ/.

CITATION AT A GLANCE

Work from a website

To cite a work from a website in MLA style, include the following elements:

1 Author(s) of work, if any
2 Title and subtitle
3 Title of website
4 Publisher of website (unless it is the same as the title of site)
5 Update date
6 URL of page
7 Date of access (if no update date on site)

Internal page from a website

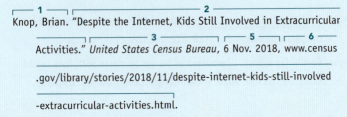

WORKS CITED ENTRY FOR A WORK FROM A WEBSITE

Knop, Brian. "Despite the Internet, Kids Still Involved in Extracurricular

Activities." *United States Census Bureau*, 6 Nov. 2018, www.census

.gov/library/stories/2018/11/despite-internet-kids-still-involved

-extracurricular-activities.html.

For more on citing sources from websites in MLA style, see item 34.

Audio, visual, and multimedia sources

■ **37. Podcast series or episode** Include the <u>distributor or production company</u> and the <u>site or service where you accessed the podcast</u>.

"Childish Gambino: *Because the Internet*." *Dissect*, hosted by Cole Cuchna,

season 7, episode 1, <u>Spotify</u>, Sep. 2020. *<u>Spotify</u> app*.

Dolly Parton's America. Hosted by Jad Abumrad, produced and reported by

Shima Oliaee, <u>WNYC Studios</u>, 2019, <u>www.wnycstudios.org/podcasts</u>

<u>/dolly-partons-america</u>.

■ **38. Stand-alone audio segment**

"The Past Returns to Gdańsk." Written and narrated by Michael Segalov, *BBC*,

26 Apr. 2021, www.bbc.co.uk/sounds/play/m000vh4f.

■ **39. Film** Generally, begin the entry with the title, followed by the <u>director</u>, as in the first example. If your paper emphasizes one or more people involved with the film, you may begin with those names, as in the second example. If you viewed the film on a streaming service, include the <u>app or website name and URL</u>.

Judas and the Black Messiah. <u>Directed by Shaka King</u>, Warner Bros. Pictures,

2021.

<u>Kubrick, Stanley, director</u>. *A Clockwork Orange*. Hawk Films / Warner Bros.

Pictures, 1971. *<u>Netflix</u>, <u>www.netflix.com</u>*.

■ **40. Supplementary material accompanying a film** Begin with the <u>title of the supplementary material</u>, in quotation marks, and the names of any important contributors. End with information about the film, as in item 39, and about the <u>location of the supplementary material</u>.

"<u>Sweeney's London</u>." Produced by Eric Young. *Sweeney Todd: The Demon*

Barber of Fleet Street, directed by Tim Burton, DreamWorks, 2007,

<u>disc 2. DVD</u>.

■ **41. Video from the web** If the video is viewed on a video sharing site such as *YouTube* or *Vimeo*, put the <u>name of the uploader</u> after the name of the website. If the video emphasizes a single speaker or presenter, list that person as the author.

"The Art of Single Stroke Painting in Japan." *YouTube*, <u>uploaded</u>

<u>by National Geographic</u>, 13 July 2018, www.youtube.com

/watch?v=g7H8IhGZnpM.

Kundu, Anindya. "The 'Opportunity Gap' in US Public Education — and How

to Close It." *TED*, May 2019, www.ted.com/talks/anindya_kundu_the

_opportunity_gap_in_us_public_education_and_how_to_close_it.

■ **42. Video game** List the <u>developer or author</u> of the game (if any); the title, italicized; the version, if there is one; and the <u>distributor</u> and date of publication. If the game can be played on the web, add information as for a work from a website (see item 34).

<u>Gearbox Software</u>. *Borderlands 3: Deluxe Edition*. <u>2K Games</u>, 2019.

■ **43. Computer software or app** Cite as a video game (see item 42), giving whatever information is available about the <u>version</u>, distributor, and date.

NYT Cooking. <u>Version 4.36</u>, The New York Times, 2021.

■ **44. TV or radio episode or program** After the episode and/ or series title, provide relevant information about the program, such as contributors; the episode number (if any); the <u>network, distributor, or production company</u>; and the date of broadcast or upload. If you viewed the program <u>on a website or in an app</u>, include that information.

"Umbrellas Down." *This American Life*, hosted by Ira Glass, <u>WBEZ</u>, 10 July

2020.

"Shock and Delight." *Bridgerton*, season 1, episode 2, <u>Shondaland /</u>

<u>Netflix</u>, 2020. <u>*Netflix*</u>, www.netflix.com.

Hillary. Directed by Nanette Burstein, <u>Propagate Content / Hulu</u>, 2020.

<u>*Hulu*</u> app.

HOW TO

Cite a source reposted from another source

PROBLEM: Some sources that you find on the web, particularly on blogs or on video-sharing sites, did not originate with the person who uploaded or published the source online. In such a case, how do you give proper credit to the source?

EXAMPLE: Say you need to cite President John F. Kennedy's inaugural address. You have found a video on YouTube that provides footage of the address (see image). The video was uploaded by PaddyIrishMan2 on October 29, 2006. But clearly, PaddyIrishMan2 is not the author of the video or of the address.

STRATEGY: Start with what you know. The source is a video that you viewed on the web. For this particular video, John F. Kennedy is the speaker and the author of the inaugural address. PaddyIrishMan2 is identified as the person who uploaded the source to YouTube.

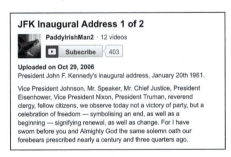

JFK Inaugural Address 1 of 2

PaddyIrishMan2 · 12 videos

▶ Subscribe ◁ 403

Uploaded on Oct 29, 2006
President John F. Kennedy's inaugural address, January 20th 1961.

Vice President Johnson, Mr. Speaker, Mr. Chief Justice, President Eisenhower, Vice President Nixon, President Truman, reverend clergy, fellow citizens, we observe today not a victory of party, but a celebration of freedom — symbolising an end, as well as a beginning — signifying renewal, as well as change. For I have sworn before you and Almighty God the same solemn oath our forebears prescribed nearly a century and three quarters ago.

CITATION: To cite the source, you can follow the basic MLA guidelines for a video found on the web (see item 40).

author/speaker: last
name first   title of video   website title

Kennedy, John F. "JFK Inaugural Address: 1 of 2." *YouTube*,

          upload information   update date   URL

     uploaded by PaddyIrishMan2, 29 Oct. 2006, www.youtube.com

/watch?v=xE0iPY7XGBo.

NOTE: If your work calls for a primary source, you should try to find the original source of the video; a reference librarian can help.

■ **45. Transcript** Cite the source (interview, radio or television program, video, and so on), and add the label "Transcript" at the end of the entry.

Kundu, Anindya. "The 'Opportunity Gap' in US Public Education — and

How to Close It." *TED*, May 2019, https://www.ted.com/talks

/anindya_kundu_the_opportunity_gap_in_us_public_education_and

_how_to_close_it/transcript. Transcript.

■ **46. Live performance** Begin with either the title of the work performed or the author, composer, or main performer if relevant. Include relevant contributors; the theater, ballet, or opera company, if any; the date of the performance; and the location.

Beethoven, Ludwig van. *Piano Concerto No. 3*. Conducted by Andris

Nelsons, performed by Paul Lewis and Boston Symphony Orchestra,

9 Oct. 2015, Symphony Hall, Boston.

Schreck, Heidi. *What the Constitution Means to Me*. Directed by Oliver

Butler, 16 June 2019, Helen Hayes Theater, New York City.

■ **47. Lecture or public address** Begin with the speaker's name, the title of the lecture, the sponsoring organization, the date, and the location. If you viewed the lecture on the web, cite as you would an online video (see item 41). If the lecture or address has no title, use the label "Lecture" or "Address" after the speaker's name.

Gay, Roxane. "Difficult Women, Bad Feminists and Unruly Bodies." Beatty

Lecture Series, 18 Oct. 2018, McGill University.

■ **48. Musical score** Begin with the composer's name; the title of the work, italicized; and the date of composition. For a print source, give the publisher and date. For an online source, give the title of the website, the publisher, the date, and the URL.

Beethoven, Ludwig van. *Symphony no. 5 in C Minor, Opus 67*. 1807. *Center*

for Computer Assisted Research in the Humanities, 2008, scores

.ccarh.org/beethoven/sym/beethoven-sym5-1.pdf.

■ **49. Music recording** Begin with the name of the person you want to emphasize: the composer, conductor, or performer. After the song and/or album title, give the names of relevant performers, the record company, and the date. If you accessed the recording on a website or app, include that information.

Bach, Johann Sebastian. *Bach: Violin Concertos*. Performances by Itzhak

Perlman, Pinchas Zukerman, and English Chamber Orchestra, EMI,

2002.

Bad Bunny. "Vete." *YHLQMDLG*, Rimas, 2020. *Apple Music* app.

■ **50. Artwork, photograph, or other visual art** Begin with the artist and the title of the work, italicized. If you viewed the original work, give the date of composition followed by a comma and the location. If you viewed the work online, give the date of composition followed by a period and the website title, publisher (if any), and URL. If you viewed the work reproduced in a book, cite as a work in an anthology or a collection (item 27), giving the date of composition after the title.

Bradford, Mark. *Let's Walk to the Middle of the Ocean*. 2015, Museum of

Modern Art, New York.

Lange, Dorothea. *Migrant Mother, Nipomo, California*. Mar. 1936. *MOMA*,

www.moma.org/collection/works/50989.

Kertész, André. *Meudon*. 1928. *Street Photography: From Atget to Cartier-*

Bresson, by Clive Scott, Tauris, 2011, p. 61.

■ **51. Visual such as a table, a chart, or another graphic** Cite a visual as you would a short work within a longer work. Add a descriptive label at the end if the type of visual is not clear from the title or if it is important for your work.

"New COVID-19 Cases Worldwide." *Coronavirus Resource Center*, Johns

Hopkins U and Medicine, 3 May 2021, coronavirus.jhu.edu

/data/new-cases. Chart.

"Number of Measles Cases Reported by Year 2010–2019." *Centers for*

Disease Control and Prevention, 22 Feb. 2019, www.cdc.gov/measles

/cases-outbreaks.html. Table.

■ **52. Cartoon or comic strip** Give the cartoonist's name; the title of the cartoon, if it has one, in quotation marks, or the label "Cartoon" or "Comic Strip" without quotation marks in place of a title; and publication information. Cite an online cartoon as a work from a website (item 34).

Shiell, Mike. Cartoon. *The Saturday Evening Post*, Jan.–Feb. 2021, p. 8.

Munroe, Randall. "Heartbleed Explanation." *xkcd*, xkcd.com/1354/.

Accessed 10 Oct. 2020.

■ **53. Advertisement** If the advertisement has no title, begin with the label "Advertisement for" and what is being advertised, followed by the publication information for the source in which the advertisement appears. For some special advertisement formats, you may want to end with a label describing it, such as "Billboard."

Advertisement for Better World Club. *Mother Jones*, Mar.–Apr. 2021, p. 2.

"The Whole Working-from-Home Thing — Apple." *YouTube*, uploaded by

Apple, 13 July 2020, www.youtube.com/watch?v=6_pru8U2RmM.

■ **54. Map** Cite a map as you would a short work within a longer work. If the map is published on its own, cite it as a book or another long work. Use the label "Map" at the end if it is not clear from the title.

"Map of Sudan." *Global Citizen*, Citizens for Global Solutions, 2011,

globalsolutions.org/blog/bashir#.VthzNMfi_FI.

"Vote on Secession, 1861." *Perry-Castañeda Library Map Collection*, U of

Texas at Austin, 1976, www.lib.utexas.edu/maps/atlas_texas/texas

_vote_secession_1861.jpg. Map.

Government and legal documents

■ **55. Government document** Treat the government agency as the author. In most situations, give the name of the publishing agency as presented by the source, as in the first example. If you are using several government sources, you may want to standardize your list of works cited by listing the name of the government, spelled out, followed by the name of any agencies and subagencies, as in the second example.

U.S. Bureau of Labor Statistics. "Consumer Expenditures Report 2019."

> *BLS Reports*, Dec. 2020, www.bls.gov/opub/reports/consumer
>
> -expenditures/2019/home.htm.

United States, Department of Transportation, Federal Highway

> Administration. *Environmental Justice Analysis in Transportation*
>
> *Planning and Programming: State of the Practice*. Feb. 2019, www
>
> .fhwa.dot.gov/environment/environmental_justice/publications
>
> /tpp/fhwahep19022.pdf.

■ **56. Historical document** The titles of most historical documents, such as the US Constitution and the Canadian Charter of Rights and Freedoms, are neither italicized nor put in quotation marks.

Constitution of the United States. 1787. *America's Founding Documents*,

> US National Archives and Records Administration, www.archives.gov
>
> /founding-docs/constitution.

■ **57. Legislative act (law)** Begin with the name of the legislative body and the act's Public Law number. Then give the publication information for the source in which you found the act.

United States, Congress. Public Law 116–136. *United States*

> *Statutes at Large*, vol. 134, 2019, pp. 281–615. *U.S. Government*
>
> *Publishing Office*, www.govinfo.gov/content/pkg/PLAW-116publ136
>
> /uslm/PLAW-116publ136.xml.

■ **58. Court case** List the name of the court. Then provide the title of the case, the date of the decision, and publication information.

United States, Supreme Court. *Utah v. Evans*. 20 June 2002. *Legal*

> *Information Institute*, Cornell Law School, www.law.cornell.edu
>
> /supremecourt/text/536/452.

Personal communication and course materials

■ **59. Personal letter**   Include the <u>letter's format</u>.

Nadir, Abdul. Letter to the author. 6 May 2021. <u>Typescript</u>.

■ **60. E-mail message**

Lewis-Truth, Antoine. E-mail to the Office of Student Financial Assistance.
    30 Aug. 2020.

■ **61. Text message**

Primak, Shoshana. Text message to the author. 6 May 2021.

■ **62. Course materials**   For materials posted to an online learning management system, include as much information as is available about the source (author, title or description, and any publication information); then give the course, instructor, platform, institution name, date of posting, and URL. For materials delivered in a print or PDF course pack, include author and title of the work; the words "Course pack for" with the course number and name; "compiled by" with the instructor's name; the term; and the institution name.

Rose, Mike. "Blue Collar Brilliance." Introduction to College Writing,
    taught by Melanie Li. *Blackboard*, Merrimack College, 9 Sept. 2020,
    blackboard.merrimack.edu/ultra/courses/_25745_1/cl/readings.

57c MLA information notes (optional)

Researchers who use the MLA system of parenthetical documentation may also use information notes for one of two purposes:

1. to provide additional material that is important but might interrupt the flow of the paper
2. to refer to several sources that support a single point or to provide comments on sources

Information notes may be either footnotes or endnotes. Footnotes appear at the foot of the page; endnotes appear on a separate page at the end of the paper, just before the list of works cited. For either style, the notes are numbered consecutively throughout the paper. The text of the paper contains a raised arabic numeral that corresponds to the number of the note.

TEXT

In the past several years, employees have filed a number of lawsuits against employers because of online monitoring practices.[1]

NOTE

[1] For a discussion of federal law applicable to electronic surveillance in the workplace, see Kesan 293.

58 MLA format; sample research paper

The following guidelines are consistent with advice given in the *MLA Handbook*, 9th edition (MLA, 2021), and with typical requirements for student papers. For a sample MLA research paper, see 58b.

58a MLA format

Formatting the paper: The basics

Papers written in MLA style should be formatted as shown on the next page.

Harba 1

Heading includes the student's name, instructor's name, course, and date.

Sophie Harba

Professor Baros-Moon

Engl 1101

9 November 2017

Center the **title**. Add no extra space above or below it, and use no quotation marks or italics.

What's for Dinner? Personal Choices vs. Public Health

Should the government enact laws to regulate healthy eating choices? Many Americans would answer an emphatic "No," arguing that what and how much we eat should be left to individual choice rather than unreasonable laws.

Use Times New Roman or another easy-to-read font.

Others might argue that it would be unreasonable for the government not to enact legislation, given the rise of chronic diseases that result from harmful diets. In this debate, both the definition of reasonable regulations and the role of government to legislate food choices are at stake. In the name of public health and safety, state governments have the responsibility to shape health policies and to regulate healthy eating choices, especially since doing so offers a potentially large social benefit for a relatively small cost.

Use a 1-inch margin on all sides of the page, and **double-space** the text.

Debates surrounding the government's role in regulating food have a long history in the United States. According to Lorine Goodwin, a food historian, nineteenth-century reformers

Formatting the paper: Other concerns

Group projects   If you are writing a group project, create a cover page with all members' names, the professor's name, the course, and the date, all aligned left on separate double-spaced lines. Center the title on a new line a few spaces down. Starting on the first text page, include all members' last names and the page number, aligned top and right, on every page. If all last names will not fit on a single line, include only the page number.

Capitalization, italics, and quotation marks   In titles of works, capitalize all words except articles (*a, an, the*), prepositions (*to, from, between,* and so on), coordinating conjunctions (*and, but, or, nor, for, so, yet*), and the *to* in infinitives — unless the word is first or last in the title or subtitle. Follow these guidelines in your paper even if the title appears in all capital or all lowercase letters in the source.

   Italicize the titles of books, journals, magazines, and other long works, such as websites. Use quotation marks around the titles of articles, short stories, poems, and other short works.

Long quotations   When a quotation is longer than four typed lines of prose or three lines of poetry, set it off from the text by indenting the entire quotation one-half inch from the left margin. Do not use quotation marks when a quotation has been set off from the text by indenting. See page 454 for an example.

Headings   While headings are generally not needed for brief essays, readers may find them helpful for long or complex essays. Place each heading in the same style and size. If you need subheadings (level 2, level 3), be consistent in styling them. Place headings at the left margin without any indent. Capitalize headings as you would titles.

Visuals   MLA classifies visuals as tables and figures (figures include graphs, charts, maps, photographs, and drawings). Place visuals in your essay as near as possible to the relevant text. Label and number each table ("Table 1"), and provide a clear title. Capitalize as you would the title of a work (see above). Place the table number and title on separate lines above the table, flush with the left margin.

   For a table that you have borrowed or adapted, give the source below the table in a note like the following:

Source: Boris Groysberg and Michael Slind, "Leadership Is a
Conversation," *Harvard Business Review*, June 2012, p. 83.

   All other visuals should be labeled "Figure" (abbreviated "Fig."), numbered, and captioned. The label and caption should appear on the same line, aligned left, underneath the visual. Capitalize the caption as you would a sentence; include source information. If your caption includes full source information and you do not cite the source anywhere else in your essay, it is not necessary to include an entry in your list of works cited. Remember to refer to each visual in your text (*see table 1; as shown in figure 2*), indicating how it contributes to the point you are making. See page 450 for an example of a figure in a paper.

Preparing the list of works cited

Begin the list of works cited on a new page at the end of the paper. Center the title "Works Cited" one inch from the top of the page. Double-space throughout. See pages 456 and 457 for a sample list of works cited.

Alphabetizing the list   Alphabetize the list by the last names of the authors (or editors); if a work has no author or editor, alphabetize by the first word of the title other than *A*, *An*, or *The*.

Indenting   Do not indent the first line of each works cited entry, but indent any additional lines one-half inch. This technique, called a hanging indent, highlights the names of the authors, making it easy for readers to scan the alphabetized list. See the works cited list in on page 456.

URLs and DOIs   Do not insert line breaks, spaces, or hyphens into URLs or DOIs in works cited entries. If the entire URL moves to another line, creating a short line, you may leave it that way. See also the instruction on page 419 for treating URLs and DOIs.

58b Sample MLA research paper

On the following pages is a research paper on the topic of the role of government in legislating food choices, written by Sophie Harba, a student in a composition class. Harba's paper is documented with in-text citations and a list of works cited in MLA style. Annotations in the margins of the paper draw your attention to Harba's use of MLA style and her effective writing.

Harba 1

Sophie Harba

Professor Baros-Moon

Engl 1101

9 November 2015

What's for Dinner? Personal Choices vs. Public Health

Should the government enact laws to regulate healthy eating choices? Many Americans would answer an emphatic "No," arguing that what and how much we eat should be left to individual choice rather than unreasonable laws. Others might argue that it would be unreasonable for the government not to enact legislation, given the rise of chronic diseases that result from harmful diets. In this debate, both the definition of reasonable regulations and the role of government to legislate food choices are at stake. In the name of public health and safety, state governments have the responsibility to shape health policies and to regulate healthy eating choices, especially since doing so offers a potentially large social benefit for a relatively small cost.

Debates surrounding the government's role in regulating food have a long history in the United States. According to Lorine Goodwin, a food historian, nineteenth-century reformers who sought to purify the food supply were called "fanatics" and "radicals" by critics who argued that consumers should be free to buy and eat what they want (77). Thanks to regulations, though, such as the 1906 federal Pure Food and Drug Act, food, beverages, and medicine are largely free from toxins. In addition, to prevent contamination and the spread of disease, meat and dairy products are now inspected by government agents to ensure that they meet health requirements. Such regulations can be considered reasonable because they protect us from harm with little, if any, noticeable consumer cost. It is not considered an unreasonable infringement on personal

Title is centered.

Opening question engages readers.

Writer highlights the research conversation.

Thesis answers the question and presents main point.

Signal phrase names the author. Page number is in parentheses.

Harba provides historical background and introduces a key term, *reasonable*.

Marginal annotations indicate MLA-style formatting and effective writing.

Harba 2

choice that contaminated meat or arsenic-laced cough drops are *un*available at our local supermarket. Rather, it is an important government function to stop such harmful items from entering the marketplace.

Even though our food meets current safety standards, there is a need for further regulation. Not all food dangers, for example, arise from obvious toxins like arsenic and *E. coli*. A diet that is low in nutritional value and high in sugars, fats, and refined grains—grains that have been processed to increase shelf life but that contain little fiber, iron, and B vitamins—can be damaging over time (United States, Department of Agriculture 36). A graph from the government's *Dietary Guidelines for Americans, 2010* shows that Americans consume about three times more fats and sugars and twice as many refined grains as is recommended but only half of the recommended foods (see fig. 1).

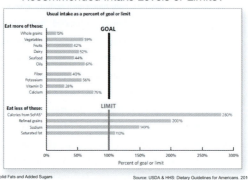

How Do Typical American Diets Compare to Recommended Intake Levels or Limits?

Fig. 1. United States, Department of Agriculture, fig. 5-1.

Annotations (left margin):

Harba establishes common ground with the reader.

Transition helps readers move from one paragraph to the next.

Harba uses a graph to illustrate Americans' poor nutritional choices.

Visual includes a caption with a figure number and source information. A full entry for this source appears in the works cited list.

Harba 3

Michael Pollan, who has written extensively about Americans' unhealthy eating habits, notes that "[t]he Centers for Disease Control estimates that fully three quarters of US health care spending goes to treat chronic diseases, most of which are preventable and linked to diet: heart disease, stroke, type 2 diabetes, and at least a third of all cancers." In fact, the amount of money the United States spends to treat chronic illnesses is increasing so rapidly that the Centers for Disease Control has labeled chronic disease "the public health challenge of the 21st century" (United States, Department of Health 1). In fighting this epidemic, the primary challenge is not the need to find a cure; the challenge is to prevent chronic diseases from striking in the first place.

Legislation, however, is not a popular solution when it comes to most Americans and the food they eat. According to a nationwide poll, seventy-five percent of Americans are opposed to laws that restrict or put limitations on access to unhealthy foods (Neergaard and Agiesta). When New York mayor Michael Bloomberg proposed a regulation in 2012 banning the sale of soft drinks in servings greater than twelve ounces in restaurants and movie theaters, he was ridiculed as "Nanny Bloomberg." In California in 2011, legislators failed to pass a law that would impose a penny-per-ounce tax on soda, which would have funded obesity prevention programs. And in Mississippi, legislators passed "a ban on bans—a law that forbids . . . local restrictions on food or drink" (Conly).

Why is the public largely resistant to laws that would limit unhealthy choices or penalize those choices with so-called fat taxes? Many consumers and civil rights advocates find such laws to be an unreasonable restriction on individual freedom of choice. As health policy experts Mello and others point out, opposition to food and

No page number is available for this web source.

Harba emphasizes the urgency of her argument.

Harba treats both sides fairly.

No page number is provided for a one-page source.

Harba anticipates objections to her idea. She counters opposing views and supports her argument.

Harba 4

beverage regulation is similar to the opposition to early
tobacco legislation: the public views the issue as one of
personal responsibility rather than one requiring government
intervention (2602). In other words, if a person eats
unhealthy food and becomes ill as a result, that is his or her
choice. But those who favor legislation claim that freedom of
choice is a myth because of the strong influence of food and
beverage industry marketing on consumers' dietary habits.
According to one nonprofit health advocacy group, food
and beverage companies spend roughly two billion dollars
per year marketing directly to children. As a result, kids see
nearly four thousand ads per year encouraging them to eat
unhealthy food and drinks ("Facts"). As was the case with
antismoking laws passed in recent decades, taxes and legal
restrictions on junk food sales could help to counter the
strong marketing messages that promote unhealthy products.

The United States has a history of state and local public
health laws that have successfully promoted a particular
behavior by punishing an undesirable behavior. The decline
in tobacco use as a result of antismoking taxes and laws
is perhaps the most obvious example. Another example
is legislation requiring the use of seat belts, which have
significantly reduced fatalities in car crashes. One government
agency reports that seat belt use saved an average of more
than fourteen thousand lives per year in the United States
between 2000 and 2010 (United States, Department of
Transportation 231). Perhaps seat belt laws have public
support because the cost of wearing a seat belt is small,
especially when compared with the benefit of saving fourteen
thousand lives per year.

Laws designed to prevent chronic disease by
promoting healthier food and beverage consumption also

Marginal notes:

Shortened title provided in parentheses for a source with no named author.

Analogy extends Harba's argument.

A government or organization author's name is shortened in parentheses.

Harba 5

have potentially enormous benefits. To give just one example, Marion Nestle, New York University professor of nutrition and public health, notes that "a 1% reduction in intake of saturated fat across the population would prevent more than 30,000 cases of coronary heart disease annually and save more than a billion dollars in health care costs" (7). Few would argue that saving lives and dollars is not an enormous benefit. But three-quarters of Americans say they would object to the costs needed to achieve this benefit— the regulations needed to reduce saturated fat intake.

> Harba introduces a quotation with a signal phrase and shows readers why she chose to use the source.

Why do so many Americans believe there is a degree of personal choice lost when regulations such as taxes, bans, or portion limits on unhealthy foods are proposed? Some critics of anti-junk-food laws believe that even if state and local laws were successful in curbing chronic diseases, they would still be unacceptable. Bioethicist David Resnik emphasizes that such policies, despite their potential to make our society healthier, "open the door to excessive government control over food, which could restrict dietary choices, interfere with cultural, ethnic, and religious traditions, and exacerbate socioeconomic inequalities" (31). Resnik acknowledges that his argument relies on "slippery slope" thinking, but he insists that "social and political pressures" regarding food regulation make his concerns valid (31). Yet the social and political pressures that Resnik cites are really just the desire to improve public health, and limiting access to unhealthy, artificial ingredients seems a small price to pay. As legal scholars L. O. Gostin and K. G. Gostin explain, "[I]nterventions that do not pose a truly significant burden on individual liberty" are justified if they "go a long way towards safeguarding the health and well-being of the populace" (214).

> Harba acknowledges critics and counterarguments.

> Including the source's credentials makes Harba more credible.

Harba 6

To improve public health, advocates such as Bowdoin College philosophy professor Sarah Conly contend that it is the government's duty to prevent people from making harmful choices whenever feasible and whenever public benefits outweigh the costs. In response to critics who claim that laws aimed at stopping us from eating whatever we want are an assault on our freedom of choice, Conly offers a persuasive counterargument:

> [L]aws aren't designed for each one of us individually. Some of us can drive safely at 90 miles per hour, but we're bound by the same laws as the people who can't, because individual speeding laws aren't practical. Giving up a little liberty is something we agree to when we agree to live in a democratic society that is governed by laws.

As Conly suggests, it's important to move from either/or thinking (either we have complete freedom of choice *or* we have government regulations and lose any freedom) to seeing health as a matter of public good, not individual liberty. Proposals such as Mayor Bloomberg's that seek to limit portions of unhealthy beverages aren't about giving up liberty; they are about asking individuals to choose substantial public health benefits at a very small cost.

Despite arguments in favor of regulating unhealthy food as a means to improve public health, public opposition has stood in the way of legislation. Americans freely eat as much unhealthy food as they want, and manufacturers and sellers of these foods have nearly unlimited freedom to promote such products and drive increased consumption, without any requirements to warn the public of potential hazards. Yet mounting scientific evidence points to unhealthy food as a significant contributing factor to

---

Signal phrase names the author.

Long quotation is set off from the text. Quotation marks are omitted.

Quotation is followed by comments that connect the source to Harba's argument.

Conclusion sums up Harba's argument and provides closure.

Harba 7

chronic disease, which is straining our health care system, decreasing Americans' quality of life, and leading to unnecessary premature deaths. Americans must consider whether to allow the costly trend of rising chronic disease to continue in the name of personal choice or whether to support the regulatory changes and public health policies that will reverse that trend.

Works Cited

Conly, Sarah. "Three Cheers for the Nanny State." *The New York Times*, 25 Mar. 2013, p. A23.

"The Facts on Junk Food Marketing and Kids." *Prevention Institute*, www.preventioninstitute.org/focus-areas/were-not-buying-it-get-involved/were-not-buying-it-the-facts-on-junk-food-marketing-and-kids. Accessed 16 Oct. 2015.

Goodwin, Lorine Swainston. *The Pure Food, Drink, and Drug Crusaders, 1879–1914.* McFarland, 2006.

Gostin, L. O., and K. G. Gostin. "A Broader Liberty: J. S. Mill, Paternalism, and the Public's Health." *Public Health*, vol. 123, no. 3, Mar. 2009, pp. 214–21, https://doi.org/10.1016/j.puhe.2008.12.024.

Mello, Michelle M., et al. "Obesity—the New Frontier of Public Health Law." *The New England Journal of Medicine,* vol. 354, no. 24, 15 June 2006, pp. 2601–10, https://doi.org/10.1056/NEJMhpr060227.

Neergaard, Lauran, and Jennifer Agiesta. "Obesity's a Crisis but We Want Our Junk Food, Poll Shows." *The Huffington Post*, 4 Jan. 2013, www.huffingtonpost.com/2013/01/04/obesity-junk-food-government-intervention-poll_n_2410376.html.

Nestle, Marion. *Food Politics: How the Food Industry Influences Nutrition and Health*. U of California P, 2013.

Pollan, Michael. "The Food Movement, Rising." *The New York Review of Books*, 10 June 2010, www.nybooks.com/articles/2010/06/10/food-movement-rising.

Resnik, David. "Trans Fat Bans and Human Freedom." *The American Journal of Bioethics*, vol. 10, no. 3, Mar. 2010, pp. 27–32.

Works cited list begins on a new page. Heading is centered.

Access date used for an undated online source.

List is alphabetized by authors' last names (or by title if no author).

First line of each entry is at the left margin; extra lines are indented ½".

Double-spacing is used throughout.

United States, Department of Agriculture and Department
of Health and Human Services. *Dietary Guidelines
for Americans, 2010,* health.gov/dietaryguidelines
/dga2010/dietaryguidelines2010.pdf.

----, Department of Health and Human Services, Centers for
Disease Control and Prevention, National Center for
Chronic Disease Prevention and Health Promotion.
The Power of Prevention, 2009, www.cdc.gov
/chronicdisease/pdf/2009-Power-of-Prevention.pdf.

----, Department of Transportation, National Highway Traffic
Safety Administration. *Traffic Safety Facts 2010: A
Compilation of Motor Vehicle Crash Data from the
Fatality Analysis Reporting System and the General
Estimates System,* 2010, www.nrd.nhtsa.dot
.gov/Pubs/811659.pdf.

Author names are standardized for multiple government sources.

Writing Papers in
APA Style

Note: An in-text citation is a reference to a source that you place within your paper. A reference list entry is a reference to a source that you include at the end of your paper.

Most instructors in the social sciences and some instructors in other disciplines will ask you to use the American Psychological Association (APA) system for documenting sources. When writing an APA-style paper that draws on sources, you face three main challenges:

1. supporting a thesis statement (59)
2. citing your sources accurately and avoiding plagiarism (60)
3. integrating source material effectively (61)

Examples in sections 59–61 are drawn from one student's research for a review of the literature on technology's role in the shift to student-centered learning. April Bo Wang's paper appears in 63b.

59 Supporting a thesis

▶ Testing your thesis statement **378**

Once you have read a range of sources, considered your subject from different perspectives, and chosen an entry point in the research conversation, you are ready to focus your research paper by forming a thesis statement and supporting that thesis with well-organized evidence. In a paper reviewing the literature on a topic, the thesis analyzes conclusions drawn by a variety of researchers.

59a Form a working thesis statement.

A thesis statement expresses your informed answer to your research question — an answer about which people might disagree. Start by developing a working thesis statement to help you narrow your ideas and clarify your purpose. As your ideas develop, you'll revise your working thesis to make it more specific and focused.

Here, for example, is a research question posed by April Bo Wang, a student in an education class, followed by her working thesis in response.

RESEARCH QUESTION

Can educational technology improve student learning and solve the problem of teacher shortages?

Educational technology can help solve teacher shortages by shifting the focus from teachers to students.

After you have written a rough draft and perhaps done more reading, you may decide to revise your thesis, as Wang did, to give it a sharper focus and to show readers why the thesis matters.

REVISED THESIS STATEMENT

In the face of mounting teacher shortages, public schools should embrace educational technology that promotes student-centered learning in order to help all students become engaged and successful learners.

The thesis usually appears at the end of the introductory paragraph. To read April Bo Wang's thesis in the context of her introduction, see 63b.

See 54a for guidelines for testing your working thesis statement.

59b Organize your ideas.

The American Psychological Association (APA) encourages the use of headings to help readers follow the organization of a paper. For an original research report, the major headings often follow a standard model: "Method," "Results," "Discussion." The introduction does not have a heading; it consists of the material between the title of the paper and the first heading.

For a literature review, headings will vary. Student writer April Bo Wang used three questions to focus her research (see her final paper in 63b); the questions then became headings in her paper:

- In what ways is student-centered learning effective?
- Can educational technology help students drive their own learning?
- How can public schools effectively combine teacher talent and educational technology?

59c Consider how sources will contribute to your research paper.

The source materials you have gathered can play many different roles to support and develop your argument. As you consider using a source, ask yourself what you learned from the source and how it might function to answer your research question.

Providing context or background information

Readers need some background information and context to anchor their understanding of your topic and the debate around it. Describing a research study or offering facts and statistics, as student writer April Bo Wang does, can help readers grasp your topic's significance.

> In the United States, most public school systems are struggling with teacher shortages, which are projected to worsen as the number of applicants to education schools decreases (Donitsa-Schmidt & Zuzovsky, 2014, p. 420). Citing federal data, *The New York Times* reported a 30% drop in "people entering teacher preparation programs" between 2010 and 2014 (Rich, 2015, para. 10).

Explaining terms or concepts

If readers are unfamiliar with a term or concept important to your topic, you will want to define or explain it. Quoting or paraphrasing a source can help you define terms and concepts in accessible language. April Bo Wang uses a source to define a key concept, student-centered learning.

> According to the International Society for Technology in Education (2016), "student-centered learning moves students from passive receivers of information to active participants in their own discovery process" (What Is It? section).

Supporting your claims

As you draft, make sure to back up your assertions with facts, examples, and other evidence from your research (see also 7f). April Bo Wang, for example, uses one source's findings to support her claim that a combination of certified teachers and educational technology can promote student-centered learning.

> Many schools have already effectively paired a reduced faculty with educational technology to support successful student-centered

learning. For example, Watson (2008) offered a case study of the Cincinnati Public Schools Virtual High School, which brought students together in a physical school building to work with an assortment of online learning programs. Although there were only 10 certified teachers in the building, students were able to engage in highly individualized instruction according to their own needs, strengths, and learning styles, using the 10 teachers as support (p. 7).

Lending authority to your argument

Expert opinion can add credibility to your argument (see also 7f). But don't rely on experts to make your points for you. State your ideas in your own words and, when appropriate, cite the judgment of an authority in the field to support your position.

Horn and Staker (2011) concluded that the chief benefit of technological learning was that it could adapt to the individual student in a way that whole-class delivery by a single teacher could not. Their study examined various schools where technology enabled student-centered learning.

Anticipating and countering objections

Do not ignore sources that seem contrary to your position. Instead, use them to state potential objections to your argument before you counter them (see 7g). Readers often have objections in mind already, whether or not they agree with you. April Bo Wang uses a source to acknowledge that some teachers oppose student instruction driven by technology.

Some researchers have expressed doubt that schools are ready for student-centered learning — or any type of instruction — that is driven by technology. In a recent survey conducted by the Nellie Mae Education Foundation, Moeller and Rietzes (2011) reported not only that many teachers lacked confidence in their ability to incorporate technology in the classroom but that 43% of polled high school students said that they lacked confidence in their technological proficiency going into college and careers.

60 Citing sources; avoiding plagiarism

▶ How to be a responsible research writer **386**

In a research paper, you draw on the work of other research-ers and writers, and you must document their contributions by citing your sources. Sources are cited for two reasons:

1. to tell readers where your information comes from — so that they can assess its reliability and, if interested, find and read the original source

2. to give credit to the writers from whom you have borrowed words and ideas

You must include a citation when you quote from a source, when you summarize or paraphrase, and when you borrow visuals, statistics, and facts that are not common knowledge. Borrowing another writer's language, sentence structure, or ideas without proper acknowledgment is plagiarism. The only exception is common knowledge — information that your readers may know or could easily locate in any number of reference sources.

60a Understand how the APA system works.

The American Psychological Association (APA) recommends an author-date system of citations. Here is how the APA citation system works.

1. The source is introduced by a signal phrase that includes the last name of the author followed by the date of publication in parentheses.

2. The material being cited is followed by a locator (such as a page number, paragraph number, or heading) in parentheses.

3. At the end of the paper, an alphabetized list of references gives complete publication information for the source.

IN-TEXT CITATION

Lanier (2018) argued that through the pervasiveness of social media, "what once might have been called advertising must now be understood as continuous behavior modification on a titanic scale" (p. 6).

ENTRY IN THE LIST OF REFERENCES

Lanier, J. (2018). *Ten arguments for deleting your social media accounts right now*. Henry Holt and Company.

NOTE: This basic APA format varies for different types of sources and situations; for example, a locator is not required for a summary or paraphrase. For a detailed discussion and other models, see 62.

60b Understand what plagiarism is.

To be fair and responsible, you must document the work of others by citing your sources. When you acknowledge and document your sources, you avoid *plagiarism*, a form of academic dishonesty. The only exception to this requirement is common knowledge — but if you are unsure whether something is or isn't common knowledge, acknowledge the source. (See also 52c.)

Three different acts are considered plagiarism:

1. failing to cite quotations and borrowed ideas
2. failing to enclose borrowed language in quotation marks
3. failing to put summaries and paraphrases in your own words and sentence structure

Definitions of plagiarism vary; it's a good idea to find out how your school defines and addresses academic dishonesty.

60c Use quotation marks around borrowed language.

To indicate that you are using a source's exact phrases or sentences, you must enclose them in quotation marks unless they have been set off from the text by indenting (see 61b). To omit the quotation marks is to claim — falsely — that the language is your own, as in the following example. Such an omission is plagiarism even if you have cited the source.

ORIGINAL SOURCE

Student-centered learning, or student centeredness, is a model which puts the student in the center of the learning process.

— Z. Çubukçu, "Teachers' Evaluation of Student-Centered Learning Environments" (2012), p. 50

PLAGIARISM

According to Professor Zuhal Çubukçu (2012), student-centered learning . . . is a model which puts the student in the center of the learning process (p. 50).

BORROWED LANGUAGE IN QUOTATION MARKS

According to Professor Zuhal Çubukçu (2012), "student-centered learning . . . is a model which puts the student in the center of the learning process" (p. 50).

NOTE: Quotation marks are not used when quoted sentences are set off from the text by indenting (see 61b).

60d Put summaries and paraphrases in your own words.

A summary condenses information from a source; a paraphrase conveys the information using roughly the same number of words as the original source. When you summarize or paraphrase, it is not enough to name the source. You must present the source's meaning using your own words and sentence structure. (See also 52c and 61a.) Half-copying the author's sentences either by using the author's phrases in your own sentences without quotation marks or by plugging synonyms into the author's sentence structure (sometimes called *patchwriting*) is a form of plagiarism.

The following paraphrases are plagiarism — even though the source is cited — because their language or sentence structure is too close to that of the source.

ORIGINAL SOURCE

Student-centered teaching focuses on the student. Decision-making, organization and content are determined for most by taking individual students' needs and interests into consideration. Student-centered teaching provides opportunities to develop students' skills of transferring knowledge to other situations, triggering retention, and adapting a high motivation for learning.

— Z. Çubukçu, "Teachers' Evaluation of Student-Centered Learning Environments" (2012), p. 52

PLAGIARISM: UNACCEPTABLE BORROWING OF PHRASES

According to Professor Zuhal Çubukçu (2012), student-centered teaching takes into account the needs and interests of each student, making it possible to foster students' skills of transferring knowledge to new situations and triggering retention (p. 52).

PLAGIARISM: UNACCEPTABLE BORROWING OF STRUCTURE

According to Zuhal Çubukçu (2012), this new model of teaching centers on the student. The material and flow of the course are chosen by considering the students' individual requirements. Student-centered teaching gives a chance for students to develop useful, transferable skills, ensuring they'll remember material and stay motivated (p. 52).

To avoid plagiarizing an author's language, resist the temptation to look at the source while you are summarizing or paraphrasing. After you have read the passage you want to paraphrase, set the source aside. Ask yourself, "What is the author's meaning?" In your own words, state your understanding of the author's basic point. Then return to the source and check that you haven't used the author's language or sentence structure or misrepresented the author's ideas. Following these steps will help you avoid plagiarizing the source.

ACCEPTABLE PARAPHRASE

In his research, Çubukçu (2012) has documented the numerous benefits of student-centered teaching in putting the student at the center of teaching and learning. When students are given the option of deciding what they learn and how they learn, they are motivated to apply their learning to new settings and to retain the content of their learning (p. 52).

NOTE: APA does not require a page number or other locator for a paraphrase, but you can choose to include one when doing so might help a reader locate the passage in the source.

For more advice on being a responsible research writer, see the guide in 55d.

61 Integrating sources

Summaries, paraphrases, quotations, and data will help you support your argument, but they cannot speak for you. You need to find a balance between the words of your sources and your own voice, so that readers always know who is speaking in your paper. You can use several strategies to integrate research sources into your paper while maintaining your own voice.

- Use sources as concisely as possible so that your own thinking and voice aren't lost (61a and 61b).

- Use signal phrases to indicate the boundary between your words and the source's words (61c).

- Discuss and analyze your sources to show readers how each source supports your points and how sources relate to one another (61d).

61a Summarize and paraphrase effectively.

In your academic writing, keep the emphasis on your ideas and your language; use your own words to summarize and paraphrase sources and to explain your points. How you choose to use a source — as summary or paraphrase — depends on your purpose.

Summarizing

When you summarize a source, you express another writer's ideas in your own words, condensing the author's key points and using fewer words than the author. Even though a summary is in your own words, the original ideas remain the intellectual property of the author, so you must include a citation. Summarizing allows you to state the source's main idea simply before you respond to or counter it.

See "When to summarize" (p. 388) for more advice.

Paraphrasing

When you paraphrase, you express an author's ideas in your own words and sentence structure, using approximately the same number of words and details as in the source. Even though the words are your own, the original ideas are the author's intellectual property, so you must give a citation. Paraphrasing allows you to capture a source's ideas but perhaps simplify or reorder them.

See "When to paraphrase" (p. 388) for more advice. For a step-by-step guide to paraphrasing effectively, see the box in 56a.

61b Use quotations effectively.

When you quote a source, you borrow some of the author's exact words and enclose them in quotation marks. Quotation marks show your readers that both the idea and the words belong to the author. Use quotations when your source's language is especially vivid or when exact wording is needed for technical accuracy.

See "When to use quotations" (p. 388) for more advice.

Limiting your use of quotations

Keep the emphasis on your own ideas, and, as much as possible, keep your ideas in your own voice. It is not always necessary to quote full sentences from a source. Often you can integrate words and phrases from a source into your own sentence structure quite effectively.

> Citing federal data, *The New York Times* reported a 30-percent drop in "people entering teacher preparation programs" between 2010 and 2014 (Rich, 2015, para. 10).

> Bell (2010) has argued that the chief benefit of student-centered learning is that it connects students with "real-world tasks," thus making learning more engaging as well as more comprehensive (p. 39).

Using the ellipsis

To condense a quoted passage, you can use an ellipsis — a series of three spaced periods — to indicate that you have omitted words. What remains must be grammatically complete.

> Demski (2012) noted that "personalized learning . . . acknowledges
> and accommodates the range of abilities, prior experiences, needs,
> and interests of each student" (p. 33).

The writer has omitted the phrase "a student-centered teaching
and learning model that" from the source.

If you leave out one or more full sentences, use a period
before the ellipsis.

> According to Demski (2012), "In any personalized learning
> model, the student — not the teacher — is the central figure. . . .
> Personalized learning may finally allow individualization and
> differentiation to actually happen in the classroom" (p. 34).

Ordinarily, do not use an ellipsis at the beginning or at the
end of a quotation. Your readers will understand that you have
taken the quoted material from a longer passage. The only exception occurs when you feel it is necessary, for clarity, to indicate
that your quotation begins or ends in the middle of a sentence.

> ★ **Using sources responsibly** Make sure omissions and ellipses do
> not distort the meaning of your source's words.

Using brackets

Brackets allow you to insert your own words into quoted material
to clarify a confusing reference or to keep a sentence grammatical in your context.

> Demski's (2012) research confirms that "implement[ing] a true
> personalized learning model on a national level" is difficult for a
> number of reasons (p. 36).

To indicate an error such as a misspelling in a quotation, insert
"[*sic*]," italicized and in brackets, right after the error.

Setting off long quotations

When you quote forty or more words from a source, set off the
quotation by indenting it one-half inch from the left margin, and
use the normal right margin.

Long quotations should be introduced by an informative sentence, often followed by a colon. Quotation marks are

unnecessary because the indented format tells readers that the passage is taken word for word from the source.

> Svokos (2015) described popular educational games developed by the nonprofit organization GlassLab and used in thousands of U.S. classrooms:
>
> > Some of the company's games are education versions of existing ones — for example, its first release was SimCity EDU — while others are originals. Teachers get real-time updates on students' progress as well as suggestions on what subjects they need to spend more time perfecting. (5. Educational Games section)

NOTE: The parenthetical citation with a locator (page number, paragraph number, or heading) goes outside the final mark of punctuation. When a quotation is run into your text, the opposite is true. See the sample citations on page 470.

For more advice on how to punctuate quotations, see "Quotation marks with other punctuation" in 56b.

61c Use signal phrases to integrate sources.

Whenever you include a paraphrase, summary, or direct quotation of another writer's work in your paper, prepare your readers for it with a signal phrase — or what APA calls a "narrative citation." A signal phrase usually names the author of the source, gives the publication year in parentheses, and often provides some context. It is generally acceptable in APA style to call authors by their last name only, even on a first mention. If your paper refers to two authors with the same last name, use their first initials as well.

When you write a signal phrase, choose a verb that fits with the way you are using the source (see 59c). Are you providing background, explaining a concept, supporting a claim, lending authority, or refuting an argument? See the chart on the next page for a list of verbs commonly used in signal phrases.

See "Using sentence guides to integrate sources" in 56c for templates you can use to introduce sources in your writing.

NOTE: APA requires using verbs in the past tense or present perfect tense ("explained" or "has explained") to introduce source material. Use the present tense only for discussing the applications or effects of your own results ("the data suggest") or knowledge that has been clearly established ("researchers agree").

USING SIGNAL PHRASES IN APA PAPERS

To avoid monotony, try to vary both the language and the placement of your signal phrases.

Model signal phrases

In the words of Mitra (2013), ". . ."

As Bell (2010) has noted, ". . ."

Donista-Schmidt and Zuzovsky (2014) pointed out that ". . ."

". . . ," claimed Çubukçu (2012, Introduction section).

". . . ," explained Demski (2012), ". . ."

Horn and Staker (2011) have offered a compelling argument for this view: ". . ."

In a recent study, Sharon et al. (2019) found that ". . ."

Verbs in signal phrases

admitted	compared	explained	refuted
agreed	confirmed	insisted	rejected
argued	contended	noted	reported
asserted	declared	observed	responded
believed	denied	pointed out	suggested
claimed	emphasized	reasoned	wrote

Marking boundaries

Readers need to move smoothly from your words to the words of a source. Avoid dropping a direct quotation into your text without warning. Provide a clear signal phrase, including at least the author's name and the year of publication. A signal phrase marks the boundary between source material and your own words and can also tell readers why a source is worth quoting. (The signal phrase is highlighted in the second example.)

DROPPED QUOTATION

Many educators have been intrigued by the concept of blended learning but have been unsure how to define it. "Blended learning is a formal education program in which a student learns at least in part through online delivery of content and instruction with some element of student control over time, place, and pace" (Horn & Staker, 2011, p. 4).

QUOTATION WITH SIGNAL PHRASE

Many educators have been intrigued by the concept of blended learning but have been unsure how to define it. As Horn and Staker (2011) have argued, "blended learning is a formal education program in which a student learns at least in part through online delivery of content and instruction with some element of student control over time, place, and pace" (p. 4).

Using signal phrases with summaries and paraphrases

Introduce most summaries and paraphrases with a signal phrase that names the author and the year and places the material in the context of your argument. Readers will then understand that everything between the signal phrase and the parenthetical citation summarizes or paraphrases the cited source.

Without the signal phrase (highlighted) in the following example, readers might think that only the last sentence was being cited, when in fact the whole paragraph is based on the source.

Watson (2008) reported that for American postsecondary students, technology is integral to their academic lives. Nearly three-quarters own their own laptops, and 83% have used a course management system for an online component of a class. Watson pointed out that online and blended learning models are even more widespread outside of the United States (p. 15).

There are times, however, when a summary or a paraphrase does not require a signal phrase naming the author. When the context makes clear where the cited material begins, you may omit the signal phrase and include the author's name and the year in parentheses.

A Stanford study came to the same conclusion; researchers examined four schools that had moved from teacher-driven instruction to student-centered learning (Friedlaender et al., 2014).

Integrating statistics and other data

When you cite a statistic or other data, a signal phrase may be used, but it is often not necessary. In most cases, readers will understand that the citation refers to the data and not the whole paragraph.

> Of polled high school students, 43% said that they lacked confidence in their technological proficiency going into college and careers (Moeller & Rietzes, 2011).

Putting source material in context

Readers should not have to guess why source material appears in your paper; you must put the source in context. If you use another writer's words, you must explain how they relate to your point. It is a good idea to sandwich each quotation between sentences of your own, introducing it with a signal phrase and following it with comments that link the quotation to your paper's argument. (See also 61d.)

> **QUOTATION WITH EFFECTIVE CONTEXT (QUOTATION SANDWICH)**
>
> According to the International Society for Technology in Education (2016), "student-centered learning moves students from passive receivers of information to active participants in their own discovery process" (What Is It? section). The results of student-centered learning have been positive, not only for academic achievement but also for student self-esteem. In this model of instruction, the teacher acts as a facilitator, and the students actively participate in the process of learning and teaching.

61d Synthesize sources.

When you synthesize multiple sources in a research paper, you create a conversation about your research topic. You show readers how the ideas of one source relate to those of another by connecting and analyzing the ideas in the context of your argument. Keep the emphasis on your own writing. The thread of your argument should be easy to identify and to understand, with or without your sources.

SAMPLE SYNTHESIS (APA STYLE)

Student writer April Bo Wang begins with a claim that needs support.

Signal phrase indicates how the source contributes to Wang's paper and shows that the ideas that follow are not her own.

Wang extends the argument and sets up two additional sources.

Wang closes the paragraph by interpreting the source and connecting it to her claim.

Student writer

Source 1

Student writer

Source 2

Source 3

Student writer

It is clear that educational technology will continue to play a role in student and school performance. Horn and Staker (2011) acknowledged that they focused on programs in which integration of educational technology led to improved student performance. In other schools, technological learning is simply distance learning — watching a remote teacher — and not student-centered learning that allows students to partner with teachers to develop enriching learning experiences. That said, many educators seem convinced that educational technology has the potential to help them transition from traditional teacher-driven learning to student-centered learning. All four schools in the Stanford study heavily relied on technology (Friedlaender et al., 2014). And indeed, Demski (2012) argued that technology is not supplemental but instead is "central" to student-centered learning (p. 33). Rather than turning to a teacher as the source of information, students are sent to investigate solutions to problems by searching online, emailing experts, collaborating with one another in a wiki space, or completing online practice. Instead of relying on a teacher for the answer to a question, students are driven to perform— driven to use technology to find those answers themselves.

In this synthesis, Wang uses her own analysis to shape the conversation among her sources. She does not simply string quotations and statistics together or allow her sources to overwhelm her writing. The final sentences, written in her own voice, give her an opportunity to explain to readers how her sources support and extend her argument.

When synthesizing sources, use the following guidelines:

- Be sure your sources address your research question.
- Think about how your sources converse with each other. How do they support, extend, or counter each other?
- Be sure that your synthesis is more than a series of quotations and paraphrases strung together. You can do this by connecting and analyzing sources in your own voice.
- Ask: Is my argument easy to identify and to understand, with or without my sources? The answer should be yes.

62 Documenting sources in APA style

In most social science classes, you will be asked to use the APA system for documenting sources, which is set forth in the *Publication Manual of the American Psychological Association*, 7th ed. (2020).

APA recommends in-text citations that refer readers to a list of references. An in-text citation gives the author of the source (often in a signal phrase), the year of publication, and often a page number in parentheses. At the end of the paper, a list of references provides publication information for each cited source; the list is alphabetized by authors' last names (or by titles for works with no authors). The direct link between the in-text citation and the entry in the reference list is highlighted in the following example.

IN-TEXT CITATION

Bell (2010) reported that students engaged in this kind of learning performed better on both project-based assessments and standardized tests (pp. 39–40).

ENTRY IN THE LIST OF REFERENCES

Bell, S. (2010). Project-based learning for the 21st century: Skills for the future. *The Clearing House, 83*(2), 39–43.

For a reference list that includes this entry, see 63b.

List of APA in-text citation models

List of APA reference list models

GENERAL GUIDELINES FOR LISTING AUTHORS

ARTICLES AND OTHER SHORT WORKS

BOOKS AND OTHER LONG WORKS

→

List of APA reference list models, continued

62a APA in-text citations

APA's in-text citations provide the author's last name and the year of publication, usually before the cited material, and a page number in parentheses directly after the cited material. In the models in this section, certain elements of the citation are underlined.

NOTE: APA style requires the use of the past tense or the present perfect tense in signal phrases introducing cited material: Smith (2020) reported; Smith (2020) has argued.

■ **1. Basic format for a quotation** Ordinarily, introduce the quotation with a <u>signal phrase</u> that includes the author's last name followed by the year of publication in parentheses. Put the <u>page number</u> (preceded by "p.," or "pp." for more than one page) in parentheses after the quotation. For sources from the web without page numbers, see item 3 in this section.

> <u>Çubukçu (2012) argued</u> that for a student-centered approach
> to work, students must maintain "ownership for their goals and
> activities" <u>(p. 64)</u>.

If the author is not named in the signal phrase, place the author's name, the year, and the page number in parentheses after the quotation: (Çubukçu, 2012, p. 64). (See items 6 and 14 for citing sources that lack authors.)

NOTE: Do not include a month in an in-text citation, even if the entry in the reference list includes the month.

■ **2. Basic format for a summary or a paraphrase** As for a quotation (see item 1), include the <u>author's last name and the year</u> either in a signal phrase introducing the material or in parentheses following it. A <u>page number or other locator</u> is not required for a summary or a paraphrase, but include one if it would help readers find the information or if your instructor requires it.

> <u>Watson (2008)</u> offered a case study of the Cincinnati Public Schools
> Virtual High School, in which students were able to engage in highly
> individualized instruction according to their own needs, strengths,
> and learning styles, using 10 teachers as support <u>(p. 7)</u>.
>
> The Cincinnati Public Schools Virtual High School brought students
> together to engage in highly individualized instruction according to

their own needs, strengths, and learning styles, using 10 teachers as support (Watson, 2008, p. 7).

■ **3. Quotation from a source without page numbers**   If your source does not include page numbers, include another locator — information from the source such as a section heading, paragraph number, figure or table number, slide number, or time stamp — to help readers find the cited passage:

> Lopez (2020) has noted that ". . ." (Symptoms section).
>
> Myers (2019) extolled the benefits of humility (para. 5).
>
> Brezinski and Zhang (2017) traced the increase . . . (Figure 3).
>
> The American Immigration Council has recommended that ". . ." (Slide 5).
>
> In a recent TED Talk, Gould (2019) argued that ". . ." (13:27).

If you shorten a long heading, place it in quotation marks: ("How to Apply" section).

■ **4. Work with two authors**   Name both authors in the signal phrase or in parentheses each time you cite the work. In the signal phrase, use "and" between the authors' names; in the parentheses, use "&."

> According to Donitsa-Schmidt and Zuzovsky (2014), "demographic growth in the school population" can lead to teacher shortages (p. 426).

> In the United States, most public school systems are struggling with teacher shortages, which are projected to worsen as the number of applicants to education schools decreases (Donitsa-Schmidt & Zuzovsky, 2014, p. 420).

■ **5. Work with three or more authors**   Use the first author's name followed by "et al." (Latin for "and others") in either a signal phrase or a parenthetical citation.

> In 2013, Harper et al. studied teachers' perceptions of project-based learning (PBL) before and after participating in a PBL pilot program.

> Researchers studied teachers' perceptions of project-based learning (PBL) before and after participating in a PBL pilot program (Harper et al., 2013).

■ **6. Work with an unknown or anonymous author**   If the author is unknown, include the <u>work's title</u> (shortened if more than a few words) in the in-text citation.

> Collaboration increases significantly among students who own or
> have regular access to a laptop (<u>"Tech Seeds,"</u> 2015).

All titles in in-text citations are set in title case: Capitalize the first and last words of a title and subtitle, all significant words, and any words of four letters or more. For books and most stand-alone works (except websites), italicize the title; for most articles and other parts of larger works, set the title in quotation marks.

Only in rare cases when "Anonymous" is specified as the author, use the word "Anonymous" in the author position: (Anonymous, 2020). (Also use the word "Anonymous" at the start of the reference list entry.)

NOTE: Titles are treated differently in reference list entries. See 62b.

■ **7. Organization as author**   If the author is an organization or a government agency, name the <u>organization</u> in the signal phrase or in parentheses the first time you cite the source.

> According to the <u>International Society for Technology in Education</u>
> (2016), "Student-centered learning moves students from passive
> receivers of information to active participants in their own discovery
> process" (What Is It? section).

For an organization with a long name, you may abbreviate the name of the organization in citations after the first.

FIRST CITATION	(Texas Higher Education Coordinating Board [THECB], 2019)
LATER CITATIONS	(THECB, 2019)

For a work by a government agency or large organization with multiple, nested departments, list the most specific agency or department as the author, as in the reference list (see item 33 in 62b).

■ **8. Authors with the same last name**   To avoid confusion, use <u>first initials</u> with the last names in your in-text citations. If authors share the same initials, spell out each author's first name.

> Research by <u>E.</u> Smith (2019) revealed that . . .

> One 2018 study contradicted . . . (<u>R.</u> Smith, p. 234).

■ **9. Two or more works by the same author in the same year** In your reference list, you will use lowercase letters ("a," "b," and so on) with the year to order the entries (see item 8 in 62b). Use those same letters with the year in the in-text citations.

> Research by Durgin (2013b) has yielded new findings about the role of smartphones in the classroom.

■ **10. Two or more works in the same parentheses** Put the works in the same order that they appear in the reference list, separated by semicolons: (Nazer, 2015; Serrao et al., 2014).

■ **11. Multiple citations to the same work in one paragraph** If you give the author's name in the text of your paper (not in parentheses) and you mention that source again in the text of the same paragraph, give only the author's name, not the date, in the later citation. If any subsequent reference in the same paragraph is in parentheses, include both the author and the date in the parentheses.

> Bell (2010) has argued that the chief benefit of student-centered learning is that it can connect students with "real-world tasks," thus making learning more engaging as well as more comprehensive (p. 42). For example, Bell observed a group of middle-school students who wanted to build a social justice monument for their school. Students engaged in this kind of learning performed better on both project-based assessments and standardized tests (Bell, 2010).

■ **12. Part of a source (section, figure)** To cite a specific part of a source, such as a section of a web page or a figure or table, identify the element in parentheses. Don't abbreviate terms such as "Figure," "Chapter," or "Section"; "page" is abbreviated "p." (or "pp." for more than one page). Cite the source as a whole in your reference list.

> The data support the finding that peer relationships are difficult to replicate in a completely online environment (Hanniman, 2010, Figure 8-3).

■ **13. Indirect source (source quoted in another source)** When a published source is quoted in a source written by someone else, cite the original source first; include "as cited in" before the author and date of the source you read. In the following example,

Chow is the author of the source in the reference list; that source contains a quotation by Brailsford.

> Brailsford (1990) commended the writer and educator's "sure
> understanding of the thoughts of young people" (as cited in Chow,
> 2019, para. 9).

■ **14. Web source**   Cite sources from the web as you would cite any other source, giving the author and the year when that information is available.

> Atkinson (2011) found that children who spent at least four hours
> a day engaged in online activities in an academic environment
> were less likely to want to play video games or watch TV after
> school.

Usually a page number is not available; occasionally a web source will lack an author or a date (see 14a–14c).

a. No page numbers   When quoting a web source that lacks stable numbered pages, include a paragraph number or a section heading, or both, to help readers locate the passage being cited.

Some sources have numbered paragraphs; if a source lacks both numbered paragraphs and headings, count the paragraphs manually. When quoting an audio or video source, use a time stamp to indicate the start of the quotation.

> Crush and Jayasingh (2015) pointed out that several other school
> districts in low-income areas had "jump-started their distance
> learning initiatives with available grant funds" (Funding Change
> section, para. 6).

If a heading in a source is long, you may use a shortened version of the heading in quotation marks: (Gregor, 2017, "What Happens When" section).

b. Unknown author   If no author is named in the source, mention the title of the source in a signal phrase or give the first word or two of the title in parentheses (see also item 6). (If an organization serves as the author, see item 7.)

> A student's IEP may, in fact, recommend the use of mobile
> technology ("Considerations," 2012).

c. Unknown date When the source does not give a date, use the abbreviation "n.d." (for "no date").

> Administrators believe 1-to-1 programs boost learner engagement (Magnus, n.d.).

■ **15. An entire website** If you mention an entire website from which you did not pull specific information, give the URL in the text of your paper but do not include it in the reference list.

> The Berkeley Center for Teaching and Learning website (https:// teaching.berkeley.edu/) shares ideas for using mobile technology in the classroom.

■ **16. Personal communication** Interviews that you conduct, memos, letters, email messages, and similar communications that would be difficult for your readers to retrieve should be cited in the text only, not in the reference list. (Use the first initial with the last name either in your text sentence or in parentheses.)

> One of Yim's colleagues, who has studied the effect of social media on children's academic progress, has contended that the benefits of this technology for children under 12 years old are few (F. Johnson, personal communication, October 20, 2020).

■ **17. Course materials** Cite lecture notes from your instructor or your own class notes as personal communication (see item 16). If your instructor's material contains publication information, cite as you would the appropriate source. See also item 56 in 62b.

■ **18. Work available in multiple versions** If you consulted a reprinted, republished, or translated work, include both the date of original publication and the date of the version you used, and separate the dates with a slash: (Padura, 2009/2014).

■ **19. Sacred or classical text** Identify the text (specifying the version or edition you used), the publication date(s), and the relevant part (book, chapter, verse).

> Peace activists have long cited the biblical prophet's vision of a world without war: "And they shall beat their swords into plowshares, and their spears into pruning hooks; nation shall not lift up sword against nation, neither shall they learn war any more" (*Holy Bible Revised Standard Edition*, 1952/2004, Isaiah 2:4).

62b APA list of references

As you gather sources for an assignment, you will likely find them in print, on the web, and in other places. The information you will need for the reference list at the end of your paper will differ slightly for some sources, but the main principles apply to all sources: You should identify an author, a creator, or a producer whenever possible, give a title, and provide the date on which the source was produced. In most cases, you will provide page numbers or other locator or retrieval information.

Section 62b provides specific requirements for and examples of many of the sources you are likely to encounter. When you cite sources, your goals are to show that the sources you've used are reliable and relevant to your work, to provide your readers with enough information so that they can find your sources easily, and to provide that information in a consistent way according to APA conventions.

In the list of references, include only sources that you quote, summarize, or paraphrase in your paper.

General guidelines for listing authors

The formatting of authors' names in items 1–11 applies to all sources in print and on the web — books, articles, websites, and so on. For more models of specific source types, see items 12–59.

■ 1. Single author

Yanagihara, H. (2015). *A little life*. Doubleday.

■ 2. Two to twenty authors
List up to twenty authors by last names followed by initials. Use an ampersand (<u>&</u>) before the name of the last author. (See items 4 and 5 in 62a for citing works with multiple authors in the text of your paper.)

Kim, E. H., Hollon, S. D., <u>&</u> Olatunji, B. O. (2016). Clinical errors in

cognitive-behavior therapy. *Psychotherapy*, *53*(3), 325–330. https://

doi.org/10.1037/pst0000074

GENERAL GUIDELINES FOR THE REFERENCE LIST

In APA style, the alphabetical list of works cited, which appears at the end of the paper, is titled "References." In general, an APA-style reference consists of four parts:

- the **author**'s (or authors') name(s).
- the **date** of publication.
- the **title** of the work.
- the **source** of the work (the retrieval information).

Insert a period following each of these four parts.

Authors and dates

- The author is the person or people most responsible for the work: For a book or article, for example, the author is the person or people who wrote it; for a movie, the person most responsible is the director; for a government report, the author might be the specific agency that produced the work.
- Alphabetize entries in the list of references by authors' last names; if a work has no author, alphabetize it by its title.
- For all authors' names, put the last name first, followed by a comma; use initials for the first and middle names.
- With two or more authors, separate the names with commas. Include names for up to twenty authors, with an ampersand (&) before the last author's name. For twenty-one or more authors, list the first nineteen authors, an ellipsis, and the last author.
- If the author is a company or an organization, give the name in normal order.
- Put the date of publication immediately after the first element of the citation. Enclose the date in parentheses, followed by a period (outside the parentheses).
- Use the date as given in the publication. Generally, give the year for books and journals (2021); the year and month for monthly magazines (2021, April); and the year, month, and day for weekly magazines and for newspapers (2021, April 9). Use the season when a publication gives the season. For web sources, use the date of posting, if it is available. Use "(n.d.)" if no date is given.

Titles

- Italicize the titles and subtitles of books, journals, and other stand-alone works. If a book title contains another book title or an article title, do not italicize the internal title and do not put quotation marks around it.
- Use no italics or quotation marks for the titles of articles. If an article title contains another article title or a term usually placed in

GENERAL GUIDELINES FOR THE REFERENCE LIST, continued

quotation marks, use quotation marks around the internal title or term. If it contains a title or term usually italicized, place the title or term in italics.

- For books and articles, capitalize only the first word of the title and subtitle and all proper nouns.
- For the titles of journals, magazines, and newspapers, capitalize all words of four letters or more (and all nouns, pronouns, verbs, adjectives, and adverbs of any length).

Source information

- In publishers' names, omit business designations such as "Inc." or "Ltd." Otherwise, write the publisher's name exactly how it appears in the source.
- For online sources, list the name of the website in the publisher position: Twitter; YouTube; U.S. Census Bureau.
- If the publisher is the same as the author, do not repeat the name in the publisher position.
- Provide locations only for works associated with a single location (such as a conference presentation).
- Include the volume and issue numbers for any journals, magazines, or other periodicals that have them. Italicize the volume number and put the issue number, not italicized, in parentheses: $26(2)$.
- When an article appears on consecutive pages, provide the range of pages: 87–96. When an article does not appear on consecutive pages, give all page numbers: A1, A17.
- Use "p." and "pp." only before page numbers for selections in edited books. Do not use "p." and "pp." with magazines, journals, and newspapers.

URLs, DOIs, and other retrieval information

- For articles and books from the web, use the DOI (digital object identifier) if the source has one. If a source does not have a DOI, give the URL.
- If a URL or DOI is long and complicated and your readers are not likely to be able to use it to access the source, you may use a permalink (if the website provides one) or create one using a shortening service such as shortdoi.org or bitly.com.
- Use a retrieval date for a web source only if the content is likely to change (such as content on a website's home page or in a social media profile).

■ **3. Twenty-one or more authors** List the first nineteen authors, followed by an <u>ellipsis</u> (. . .) and the last author's name.

Sharon, G., Cruz, N. J., Kang, D.-W., Gandal, M. J., Wang, B., Kim, Y.-M.,
Zink, E. M., Casey, C. P., Taylor, B. C., Lane, C. J., Bramer, L. M.,
Isern, N. G., Hoyt, D. W., Noecker, C., Sweredoski, M. J., Moradian,
A., Borenstein, E., Jansson, J. K., Knight, R., <u>. . .</u> Mazmanian, S. K.
(2019). Human gut microbiota from autism spectrum disorder
promote behavioral symptoms in mice. *Cell, 177*(6), 1600–1618.
https://doi.org/10.1016/j.cell.2019.05.004

■ **4. Organization as author**

American Psychiatric Association. (2013). *Diagnostic and statistical
manual of mental disorders* (5th ed.).

■ **5. Unknown author** Begin the entry with the work's <u>title</u>.
Alphabetize by the first word in the title (not including the articles "The," "A," or "An").

<u>Pushed out</u>. (2019, August 24). *The Economist, 432*(9157), 19–20.

■ **6. Author using a screen name, pen name, or stage name** Use
the author's real name, if known, and give the screen name or
pen name in brackets exactly as it appears in the source. If only
the <u>screen name</u> is known, begin with that name and do not use
brackets. (See also items 58 and 59 on citing screen names in
social media.)

<u>dr.zachary.smith</u>. (2019, October 3). What problem are they trying to
solve? [Comment on the article "Georgia is purging voter rolls
again"]. *Slate*. https://fyre.it/sjSPFyza.4

If the author uses just a single name ("Prince," "Sophocles") or a
two-part name in which the two parts are essential ("Cardi B"),
give the name with no abbreviations or alterations.

■ **7. Two or more works by the same author** Use the author's
name for all entries. List the entries by <u>year</u>, the earliest first.

Abdurraqib, H. (<u>2017</u>). *They can't kill us until they kill us*. Two Dollar
Radio.

Abdurraqib, H. (<u>2021</u>). *A little devil in America: Notes in praise of Black
performance*. Random House.

■ **8. Two or more works by the same author in the same year** List the works by date. In the parentheses, add "a," "b," and so on after the year. (Use these same letters when giving the year in the in-text citations.) If the works have identical dates, list the works alphabetically by title. (See also item 9 in 62a.)

Conover, E. (2019a, June 8). Gold's origins tied to collapsars. *Science News*, 195(10), 10. https://bit.ly/31JTgKD

Conover, E. (2019b, June 22). Space flames may hold secrets to soot-free fire. *Science News*, 195(11), 5. https://bit.ly/2p0Xj89

■ **9. Editor** Begin with the name(s) of the editor(s); place the abbreviation "Ed." (or "Eds." for more than one editor) in parentheses following the name(s).

Yeh, K.-H. (Ed.). (2019). *Asian indigenous psychologies in the global context*. Palgrave Macmillan.

■ **10. Author and editor** Begin with the author and the date. After the title, place the name(s) of the editor(s) and the abbreviation "Ed." (or "Eds.") in parentheses.

Sontag, S. (2018). *Debriefing: Collected stories* (B. Taylor, Ed.). Picador.

■ **11. Translator** Begin with the name of the author. After the title, in parentheses place the name of the translator (in normal order) and the abbreviation "Trans." (for "Translator"). Add the original date of publication at the end of the entry.

Calasso, R. (2019). *The unnamable present* (R. Dixon, Trans.). Farrar, Straus and Giroux. (Original work published 2017)

Articles and other short works

■ **12. Article in a journal** After the author's name, provide the title of the article first, followed by the title of the publication and other publication information. Include the volume and issue numbers and the article's page range. If an article from the web has no DOI, include the URL for the article. If an article from a database has no DOI, do not include a URL. See the models on the next page.

■ **12. Article in a journal (*cont.*)**

a. Print

Ganegoda, D. B., & Bordia, P. (2019). I can be happy for you, but not all
the time: A contingency model of envy and positive empathy in the
workplace. *Journal of Applied Psychology, 104*(6), 776–795.

b. Web

Bruns, A. (2019). The third shift: Multiple job holding and the
incarceration of women's partners. *Social Science Research, 80*(1),
202–215. https://doi.org/dfgj

Vicary, A. M., & Larsen, A. (2018). Potential factors influencing attitudes
toward veterans who commit crimes: An experimental investigation
of PTSD in the legal system. *Current Research in Social Psychology,
26*(2). https://www.uiowa.edu/crisp/sites/uiowa.edu.crisp/files/
crisp_vol_26_2.pdf

c. Database

Maftsir, S. (2019). Emotional change: Romantic love and the university
in postcolonial Egypt. *Journal of Social History, 52*(3), 831–859.
https://doi.org/10.1093/jsh/shx155

■ **13. Article in a magazine**   Include full publication date of the
magazine, plus the volume and issue numbers and page range if
available. If an article from the web has no DOI, use the URL
for the article. If an article from a database has no DOI, do not
include a URL.

a. Print

Andersen, R. (2019, April). The intention machine: A new generation of
brain-machine interface can deduce what a person wants. *Scientific
American, 320*(4), 24–31.

b. Web

Srinivasan, D. (2019, June 4). How digital advertising markets really
work. *The American Prospect.* https://prospect.org/article/
how-digital-advertising-markets-really-work

c. Database

Greengard, S. (2019, August). The algorithm that changed quantum machine learning. *Communications of the ACM, 62*(8), 15–17. https://doi.org/10.1145/3339458

■ **14. Article in a newspaper** Include the full publication date and the page and section, if available.

a. Print

Finucane, M. (2019, September 25). Americans still eating too many low-quality carbs. *The Boston Globe*, B2.

b. Web

Daly, J. (2019, August 2). Duquesne's med school plan part of national trend to train more doctors. *Pittsburgh Post-Gazette*. http://bit.ly/2CbUZOX

■ **15. Comment on an online article** Include the first twenty words of the comment, followed by the title of the source article in brackets.

lollyl2. (2019, September 25). My husband works in IT in a major city down South. He is a permanent employee now, but for years [Comment on the article "The Google workers who voted to unionize in Pittsburgh are part of tech's huge contractor workforce"]. *Slate*. https://fyre.it/ORT8HmeL

■ **16. Supplemental material** If an article on the web contains supplemental material that is not part of the main article, cite the material as you would an article and add the label "Supplemental material" in brackets following the title.

Blasi, D. E., Moran, S., Moisik, S. R., Widmer, P., Dediu, D., & Bickel, B. (2019). Human sound systems are shaped by post-Neolithic changes in bite configuration [Supplemental material]. *Science, 363*(6432). https://doi.org/10.1126/science.aav3218

CITATION AT A GLANCE

Online article in a journal or magazine

To cite an online article in a journal or magazine in APA style, include the following elements:

1 Author(s)
2 Year of publication for journal; complete date for magazine
3 Title and subtitle of article
4 Name of journal or magazine
5 Volume and issue numbers
6 DOI (digital object identifier), if article has one; otherwise, URL for article

Online article

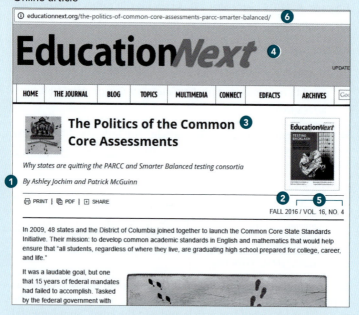

REFERENCE LIST ENTRY FOR AN ONLINE ARTICLE IN A JOURNAL OR MAGAZINE

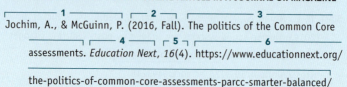

Jochim, A., & McGuinn, P. (2016, Fall). The politics of the Common Core assessments. *Education Next, 16*(4). https://www.educationnext.org/the-politics-of-common-core-assessments-parcc-smarter-balanced/

For more on citing online articles in APA style, see items 12–14.

CITATION AT A GLANCE

Article from a database

To cite an article from a database in APA style, include the following elements:

1 Author(s)

2 Year of publication for journal; complete date for magazine or newspaper

3 Title and subtitle of article

4 Name of periodical

5 Volume and issue numbers

6 Page number(s)

7 DOI (digital object identifier)

Database record

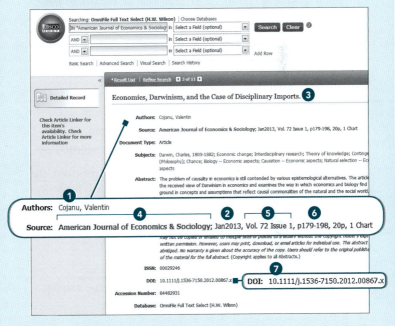

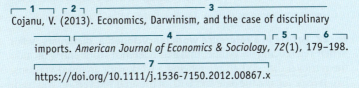

REFERENCE LIST ENTRY FOR AN ARTICLE FROM A DATABASE

┌── 1 ──┐ ┌ 2 ┐ ┌─────────────────── 3 ───────────────────

Cojanu, V. (2013). Economics, Darwinism, and the case of disciplinary

┌──────────────────── 4 ────────────────────┐ ┌ 5 ┐ ┌─ 6 ─┐

imports. *American Journal of Economics & Sociology, 72*(1), 179–198.

┌─────────────────── 7 ───────────────────┐

https://doi.org/10.1111/j.1536-7150.2012.00867.x

For more on citing articles from a database in APA style, see items 12–13.

■ **17. Letter to the editor** Insert the words "Letter to the editor" in brackets after the title of the letter. If the letter has no title, use [Letter to the editor] as the title.

Doran, K. (2019, October 11). When the homeless look like grandma or grandpa

[Letter to the editor]. *The New York Times*. https://nyti.ms/33foDOK

■ **18. Editorial or other unsigned article**

Gavin Newsom wants to stop rent gouging. Will lawmakers finally stand

up for tenants? [Editorial]. (2019, September 4). *Los Angeles Times*.

https://lat.ms/2lBlRm1

■ **19. Newsletter article** Cite as you would an article in a magazine, giving whatever retrieval information is available. If it is not clear that you are citing a newsletter, you may include the label "[Newsletter]" following the title.

Bond, G. (2018, Fall). Celebrities as epidemiologists. *American*

College of Epidemiology Online Member Newsletter. https://www.

acepidemiology.org/assets/ACE_Newsletter_Fall_2018%20FINAL.pdf

■ **20. Review** In brackets, give the type of work reviewed, the title, and the director for a film or the author for a book. If the review has no author or title, use the description in brackets as the title.

Douthat, R. (2019, October 14). A hustle gone wrong [Review of the film

Hustlers, by L. Scafaria, Dir.]. *National Review, 71*(18), 47.

Hall, W. (2019). [Review of the book *How to change your mind:*

The new science of psychedelics, by M. Pollan]. *Addiction, 114*(10),

1892–1893. https://doi.org/10.1111/add.14702

■ **21. Published interview**

Remnick, D. (2019, July 1). Robert Caro reflects on Robert Moses, L.B.J., and

his own career in nonfiction. *The New Yorker*. https://bit.ly/2Lukm3X

■ **22. Article in a reference work (encyclopedia, dictionary, wiki)**
When referencing an online, undated reference work entry, include the retrieval date. When referencing a work with archived versions, like *Wikipedia*, use the date and URL of the archived version you read.

Brue, A. W., & Wilmshurst, L. (2018). Adaptive behavior assessments.

In B. B. Frey (Ed.), *The SAGE encyclopedia of educational research,*

measurement, and evaluation (pp. 40–44). SAGE Publications.
https://doi.org/10.4135/9781506326139.n21

Merriam-Webster. (n.d.). Adscititious. In *Merriam-Webster.com dictionary*.
Retrieved September 5, 2021, from https://www.merriam-webster.
com/dictionary/adscititious

Behaviorism. (2019, October 11). In *Wikipedia*. https://en.wikipedia.
org/w/index.php?title=Behaviorism&oldid=915544724

■ 23. Paper or poster presented at a conference or meeting (unpublished)

Wood, M. (2019, January 3–6). *The effects of an adult development course on
students' perceptions of aging* [Poster session]. Forty-First Annual National
Institute on the Teaching of Psychology, St. Pete Beach, FL, United States.
https://nitop.org/resources/Documents/2019%20Poster%20Session%20II.pdf

Books and other long works

▶ Citation at a glance: Book **496**

■ 24. Basic format for a book

a. Print

Treuer, D. (2019). *The heartbeat of Wounded Knee: Native America from
1890 to the present.* Riverhead Books.

b. Web (or online library) Give the URL for the page where you accessed the book.

Obama, M. (2018). *Becoming*. Crown. https://books.google.com/
books?id=YbtNDwAAQBAJ

c. E-book Include the DOI or, if a DOI is not available, the URL for the page from which you downloaded the book.

Coates, T.-N. (2017). *We were eight years in power: An American tragedy.*
One World. https://www.amazon.com/dp/B01MT7340D/

d. Database If the book has a DOI, include it. If not, do not list a URL or database name.

Kilby, P. (2019). *The green revolution: Narratives of politics, technology
and gender*. Routledge. http://doi.org/dfgt

CITATION AT A GLANCE
Book

To cite a print book in APA style, include the following elements:

1 Author(s)   **3** Title and subtitle
2 Year of publication   **4** Publisher

Title page

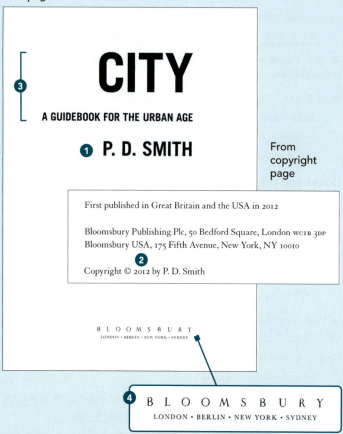

3 CITY

A GUIDEBOOK FOR THE URBAN AGE

1 P. D. SMITH

From copyright page

First published in Great Britain and the USA in 2012

Bloomsbury Publishing Plc, 50 Bedford Square, London WC1B 3DP
Bloomsbury USA, 175 Fifth Avenue, New York, NY 10010

2

Copyright © 2012 by P. D. Smith

BLOOMSBURY
LONDON · BERLIN · NEW YORK · SYDNEY

4 BLOOMSBURY
LONDON · BERLIN · NEW YORK · SYDNEY

REFERENCE LIST ENTRY FOR A PRINT BOOK

┌── **1** ──┐ ┌ **2** ┐ ┌─────────── **3** ───────────┐ ┌─ **4** ─┐
Smith, P. D. (2012). *City: A guidebook for the urban age.* Bloomsbury.

For more on citing books in APA style, see items 24–30.

■ **25. Edition other than the first** Include the edition number (abbreviated) in parentheses after the title.

Dessler, A. E., & Parson, E. A. (2019). *The science and politics of global climate change: A guide to the debate* (3rd ed.). Cambridge University Press.

■ **26. Selection in an anthology or a collection** An anthology is a collection of works on a common theme, often with different authors for the selections and usually with an editor for the entire volume.

a. Entire anthology

Lindert, J., & Marsoobian, A. T. (Eds.). (2018). *Multidisciplinary perspectives on genocide and memory*. Springer.

b. Selection in an anthology

Pettigrew, D. (2018). The suppression of cultural memory and identity in Bosnia and Herzegovina. In J. Lindert & A. T. Marsoobian (Eds.), *Multidisciplinary perspectives on genocide and memory* (pp. 187–198). Springer.

■ **27. Multivolume work** If you have used only one volume of a multivolume work, indicate the volume number after the title of the complete work; if the volume has its own title, add that title after the volume number.

a. All volumes

Zeigler-Hill, V., & Shackelford, T. K. (Eds.). (2018). *The SAGE handbook of personality and individual differences* (Vols. I–III). SAGE Publications.

b. One volume, with title

Zeigler-Hill, V., & Shackelford, T. K. (Eds.). (2018). *The SAGE handbook of personality and individual differences: Vol. II. Origins of personality and individual differences*. SAGE Publications.

■ **28. Dictionary or other reference work**

Leong, F. T. L. (Ed.). (2008). *Encyclopedia of counseling* (Vols. 1–4). SAGE Publications.

■ **29. Republished book**

Fremlin, C. (2017). *The hours before dawn*. Dover Publications. (Original work published 1958)

■ **30. Book in a language other than English** Place the English translation, not italicized, in brackets.

Carminati, G. G., & Méndez, A. (2012). *Étapes de vie, étapes de soins* [Stages of life, stages of care]. Médecine & Hygiène.

■ **31. Dissertation** If you accessed the dissertation from a specialty database, indicate it at the end of the citation.

Bacaksizlar, N. G. (2019). *Understanding social movements through simulations of anger contagion in social media* [Doctoral dissertation, University of North Carolina at Charlotte]. ProQuest Dissertations & Theses.

■ **32. Conference proceedings**

Srujan Raju, K., Govardhan, A., Padmaja Rani, B., Sridevi, R., & Ramakrishna Murty, M. (Eds.). (2018). *Proceedings of the third international conference on computational intelligence and informatics*. Springer.

■ **33. Government document** If no author is listed, begin with the department that produced the document. Any broader organization listed can be included as the publisher of the document, as in the first example below. If a specific report number is provided, include it after the title.

National Park Service. (2019, April 11). *Travel where women made history: Ordinary and extraordinary places of American women.* U.S. Department of the Interior. https://www.nps.gov/subjects/travelwomenshistory/index.htm

Berchick, E. R., Barnett, J. C., & Upton, R. D. (2019, September 10). *Health insurance coverage in the United States: 2018* (Report No. P60-267). U.S. Census Bureau. https://www.census.gov/library/publications/2019/demo/p60-267.html

■ **34. Report from a private organization**

Ford Foundation International Fellowships Program. (2019). *Leveraging higher education to promote social justice: Evidence from the IFP alumni tracking study.* https://p.widencdn.net/kei61u/IFP-Alumni-Tracking-Study-Report-5

■   **35. Legal source**   The title of a court case is italicized in an in-text citation, but it is not italicized in the reference list.

Sweatt v. Painter, 339 U.S. 629 (1950). http://www.law.cornell.edu/
supct/html/historics/USSC_CR_0339_0629_ZS.html

■   **36. Sacred or classical text**   Cite a sacred or classical text as a book, using the title, year, and editor/translator (if any) of the version you are using. If an original date is known, include it at the end of the citation. If the year is approximate, include "ca." (for "circa"); use "B.C.E." for ancient texts.

The Holy Bible 1611 edition: King James version. (2006). Hendrickson
Publishers. (Original work published 1611)

Homer. (2018). *The odyssey* (E. Wilson, Trans.). W. W. Norton & Company.
(Original work published ca. 725–675 B.C.E.)

Websites and parts of websites

▶ Citation at a glance: Page from a website **500**

■   **37. Entire website**   If you retrieved specific information from the home page of a website, include the website name, retrieval date, and URL in your reference list entry. If you only mention the website in the body of your paper, do not include it in your reference list. See items 14 and 15 in 62a for advice about how to cite web sources in the text of your paper.

■   **38. Page from a website**   Use one of the models below only when your source doesn't fit into any other category. These models are for content found on an interior page of a website and not published elsewhere. The website name follows the page title unless the author and website name are the same.

National Institute of Mental Health. (2016, March). *Seasonal affective*
disorder. National Institutes of Health. https://www.nimh.nih.gov/
health/topics/seasonal-affective-disorder/index.shtml

BBC News. (2019, October 31). *California fires: Goats help save*
Ronald Reagan Presidential Library. https://www.bbc.com/news/
world-us-canada-50248549

CITATION AT A GLANCE

Page from a website

To cite a page from a website in APA style, include the following elements:

1 Author(s)

2 Date of publication or most recent update ("n.d." if there is no date)

3 Title of web page

4 Name of website (if not the same as author)

5 URL of web page

Page from a website

REFERENCE LIST ENTRY FOR A PAGE FROM A WEBSITE

―――――― **1** ―――――― ┌ **2** ┐ ┌―――――― **3** ――――――

Minnesota Department of Health. (n.d.). *2010 Minnesota health statistics*

―――――――― ┐ ┌―――――― **5** ――――――

annual summary. http://www.health.state.mn.us/divs/chs/

―――――――――――――

annsum/10annsum/index.html

For more on citing documents from websites in APA style, see items 37–39.

■ **39. Document on a website**   Most documents published on websites fall into other categories, such as an article, a government document, or a report from an organization (items 12–14, 33, and 34).

Tahseen, M., Ahmed, S., & Ahmed, S. (2018). *Bullying of Muslim youth:*

    A review of research and recommendations. The Family and Youth

    Institute. http://www.thefyi.org/wp-content/uploads/2018/10/

    FYI-Bullying-Report.pdf

■ **40. Blog post**   Cite a blog post as you would an article in a periodical. Treat a comment on a blog post as you would a comment on an online article (see item 15).

Fister, B. (2019, February 14). Information literacy's third wave.

    Library Babel Fish. https://www.insidehighered.com/blogs/

    library-babel-fish/information-literacy%E2%80%99s-third-wave

Audio, visual, and multimedia sources

■ **41. Podcast**

a. Series

Abumrad, J., Miller, L., & Nasser, L. (Hosts). (2002–present). *Radiolab*

    [Audio podcast]. WNYC Studios. https://www.wnycstudios.org/

    podcasts/radiolab/podcasts

b. Episode

Longoria, J. (Host & Producer). (2019, April 19). Americanish [Audio

    podcast episode]. In J. Abumrad & R. Krulwich (Hosts), *Radiolab*.

    WNYC Studios. https://www.wnycstudios.org/podcasts/radiolab/

    articles/americanish

■ **42. Video or audio on the web (YouTube, TED Talk)**

The New York Times. (2018, January 9). *Taking a knee and taking*

    down a monument [Video]. YouTube. https://www.youtube.com/

    watch?v=qY34DQCdUvQ

Wray, B. (2019, May). *How climate change affects your mental*

    health [Video]. TED Conferences. https://www.ted.com/talks/

    britt_wray_how_climate_change_affects_your_mental_health

■ **43. Transcript of an audio or video file**

Gopnik, A. (2019, July 10). *A separate kind of intelligence* [Video
transcript]. Edge. https://www.edge.org/conversation/alison_
gopnik-a-separate-kind-of-intelligence

■ **44. Film**   If the film is a special version, such as an extended
cut, include that information in brackets after the title.

Peele, J. (Director). (2017). *Get out* [Film]. Universal Pictures.

Hitchcock, A. (Director). (1959). *The essentials collection: North by
northwest* [Film; special ed. on DVD]. Metro-Goldwyn-Mayer;
Universal Pictures Home Entertainment.

■ **45. TV or radio series or episode**

Waller-Bridge, P., Williams, H., & Williams, J. (Executive Producers).
(2016–2019). *Fleabag* [TV series]. Two Brothers Pictures; BBC.

Waller-Bridge, P. (Writer), & Bradbeer, H. (Director). (2019, March 18).
The provocative request (Season 2, Episode 3) [TV series episode].
In P. Waller-Bridge, H. Williams, & J. Williams (Executive Producers),
Fleabag. Two Brothers Pictures; BBC.

■ **46. Music recording**

Nielsen, C. (2014). *Carl Nielsen: Symphonies 1 & 4* [Album recorded by
New York Philharmonic Orchestra]. Dacapo Records. (Original work
published 1892–1916)

Carlile, B. (2018). The mother [Song]. On *By the way, I forgive you*. Low
Country Sound; Elektra.

■ **47. Lecture, speech, address, or recorded interview**   Cite the
speaker or interviewee as the author.

Warren, E. (2019, September 16). *Senator Elizabeth Warren speech
in Washington Square Park* [Speech video recording]. C-SPAN.
https://www.c-span.org/video/?464314-1/senator-elizabeth-
warren-campaigns-york-city

■ 48. Data set or graphic representation of data (chart, table)

Reid, L. (2019). *Smarter homes: Experiences of living in low carbon homes 2013–2018* [Data set]. UK Data Service. https://doi.org/10.5255/ UKDA-SN-853485

Pew Research Center. (2018, November 15). *U.S. public is closely divided about overall health risk from food additives* [Chart]. https://www.pewresearch.org/science/2018/11/19/ public-perspectives-on-food-risks/

■ 49. Mobile app   Begin with the developer of the app, if known.

Google. (2019). *Google Earth* (Version 9.3.3) [Mobile app]. App Store. https://apps.apple.com/us/app/google-earth/id293622097

■ 50. Video game

ConcernedApe. (2016). *Stardew Valley* [Video game]. Chucklefish.

■ 51. Map

Desjardins, J. (2017, November 17). *Walmart nation: Mapping the largest employers in the U.S.* [Map]. Visual Capitalist. https://www. visualcapitalist.com/walmart-nation-mapping-largest-employers-u-s/

■ 52. Advertisement

America's Biopharmaceutical Companies [Advertisement]. (2018, September). *The Atlantic, 322*(2), 2.

Centers for Disease Control and Prevention. (n.d.). *A tip from a former smoker: Beatrice* [Advertisement]. U.S. Department of Health and Human Services. https://www.cdc.gov/tobacco/campaign/tips/ resources/ads/pdf-print-ads/beatrices-tip-print-ad-7x10.pdf

■ 53. Work of art or photograph   When citing a physical piece of art, include the location of the piece.

O'Keeffe, G. (1931). *Cow's skull: Red, white, and blue* [Painting]. Metropolitan Museum of Art, New York, NY, United States. https://www.metmuseum.org/art/collection/search/488694

Browne, M. (1963). *The burning monk* [Photograph]. Time. http://100photos.time.com/photos/malcolm-browne-burning-monk

■ **54. Brochure or fact sheet**

National Council of State Boards of Nursing. (2018). *A nurse manager's guide to substance use disorder in nursing* [Brochure].

World Health Organization. (2019, July 15). *Immunization coverage* [Fact sheet]. https://www.who.int/news-room/fact-sheets/detail/immunization-coverage

■ **55. Press release**

New York University. (2019, September 5). *NYU Oral Cancer Center awarded $2.5 million NIH grant to study cancer pain* [Press release]. https://www.nyu.edu/about/news-publications/news/2019/september/nyu-oral-cancer-center-awarded--2-5-million-nih-grant-to-study-c.html

■ **56. Lecture notes or other course materials** Cite posted materials as you would a document on a website (see item 39). Cite material from your instructor that is not available to others as personal communication in the text of your paper (see item 16 in 62a).

Chatterjee, S., Constenla, D., Kinghorn, A., & Mayora, C. (2018). *Teaching vaccine economics everywhere: Costing in vaccine planning and programming* [Lecture notes and slides]. Department of Population, Family, and Reproductive Health, Johns Hopkins University. http://ocw.jhsph.edu/index.cfm/go/viewCourse/course/TeachVaccEconCosting/coursePage/lectureNotes/

Personal communication and social media

■ **57. Email** Email messages, letters, and other personal communication are not included in the list of references. See item 16 in 62a for citing these sources in the text of your paper.

■ **58. Social media post (Twitter, Instagram)** If the writer's real name and screen name are given, put the real name first, followed by the screen name in brackets. If only the screen name is known, begin with the screen name without brackets. For the title, include up to the first twenty words (including hashtags or emojis) of the title, caption, or post. After the title, list any attachments (such as a photo or link) and the type of post in separate brackets. List the website or app in the publisher position. Include the URL for the post. Cite posts that are not accessible to all readers as personal communication in the text of your paper.

National Science Foundation [@NSF]. (2019, October 13). *Understanding how forest structure drives carbon sequestration is important for ecologists, climate modelers and forest managers, who are working on* [Thumbnail with link attached] [Tweet]. Twitter. https://twitter.com/NSF/status/1183388649263652864

Smithsonian [@smithsonian]. (2019, October 7). *You're looking at a ureilite meteorite under a microscope. When illuminated with polarized light, they appear in dazzling colors, influenced* [Photograph]. Instagram. https://www.instagram.com/p/B3VI27yHLQG/

■ **59. Social media profile or highlight**   Because profiles are designed to change over time, include the date you viewed the page.

National Science Foundation [@NSF]. (n.d.). *Tweets* [Twitter profile]. Twitter. Retrieved August 15, 2021 from https://twitter.com/NSF

Smithsonian [@smithsonian]. (n.d.). *#Apollo50* [Highlight]. Instagram. Retrieved January 5, 2021, from https://www.instagram.com/stories/highlights/17902787752343364/

63 APA format; sample research paper

The guidelines in this section are consistent with advice given in the *Publication Manual of the American Psychological Association*, 7th ed. (APA, 2020), and with typical requirements for undergraduate papers. For a sample APA research paper, see 63b.

63a APA format

Formatting the paper

The guidelines in this section describe APA's recommendations for formatting the text of a paper written for an undergraduate college course and for preparing the reference list.

Font If your instructor does not require a specific font, use one that is standard and easy to read (such as 12-point Times New Roman).

Title page Put the page number 1 at the right margin one-half inch from the top of the page. A few lines down the page, center the full title of your paper in bold. After a blank line, include your name, and then add the following assignment details on separate lines: the department and the school, the course code and name, your instructor's name, and the due date. See page 510 for a sample title page.

Page numbers and running head Starting with the title page, number all pages in the upper-right corner one-half inch from the top of the page. Professional (submitted for publication) papers also require a running head, a shortened version of the paper's title (no more than 50 characters) on every page. If your assignment requires one, type the running head in the upper-left corner in all capital letters. See page 522 for an example of a running head.

Margins, line spacing, and paragraph indents Use margins of one inch on all sides of the page. Left-align the text.

Double-space throughout the paper. Indent the first line of each paragraph one-half inch.

Capitalization, italics, and quotation marks In headings and in titles of works that appear in the text of the paper, capitalize all words of four letters or more (and all nouns, pronouns, verbs, adjectives, and adverbs of any length). Capitalize the first word following a colon in a title or a heading, and capitalize the first word following a colon in the body of your paper if the word begins a complete sentence.

In the body of your paper, italicize the titles of books, journals, magazines, and other long works, including websites. Use quotation marks around the titles of articles, short stories, and other short works named in the body of your paper.

NOTE: APA has different requirements for titles in the reference list. See page 508.

Long quotations When a quotation is forty or more words, indent it one-half inch from the left margin. Double-space the quotation. Do not use quotation marks around it. (See p. 515 for an example. See also 61b for more information about integrating long quotations.)

Footnotes Insert footnotes using the footnote function in your word processing program. The callout number in the text should immediately follow a word or any mark of punctuation except a dash. The text of the footnote should be single-spaced.

Abstract If your assignment requires an abstract — a 150-to-250-word summary paragraph — include it on a new page after the title page. Center the word "Abstract" (in bold) one inch from the top of the page. Double-space the abstract and do not indent the first or subsequent lines. For an example, see page 522.

Headings Although headings are not always necessary, their use is encouraged in the social sciences. For most undergraduate papers, one level of heading is usually sufficient. (See the paper in 63b.)

First-level headings are centered and boldface. In research papers and laboratory reports, the major headings are "Method," "Results," and "Discussion." In other types of papers, the major headings should be informative and concise, conveying the structure of the paper. In all headings, capitalize the first and last words and all words of four or more letters (and nouns, pronouns, verbs, adjectives, and adverbs of any length).

First-Level Heading Centered

Second-Level Heading Aligned Left

Third-Level Heading Aligned Left

Visuals APA classifies visuals as tables and figures (figures include graphs, charts, drawings, and photographs). Place each visual immediately after the paragraph in which it is called out, or place it on the following page if it does not fit on the same page as the callout.

Number each table or figure (Table 1, Table 2; Figure 1, Figure 2) and provide a clear title. The label and title should appear on separate lines above the visual, flush left and double-spaced. Type the number in bold font; italicize the title.

Table 2

Effect of Nifedipine (Procardia) on Blood Pressure in Women

If you have used data from an outside source or have taken or adapted the visual from a source, give the source information in a note below the table. Begin with the word "Note," italicized and followed by a period. Notes can also include additional information or context for the visual. For an example of a visual with a note, see page 513.

Preparing the list of references

Begin your list of references on a new page at the end of the paper. Center the title "References" in bold one inch from the top of the page. Double-space throughout. For a sample reference list, see page 520.

Indenting entries   Type the first line of each entry at the left margin and indent any additional lines one-half inch.

Alphabetizing the list   Alphabetize the reference list by the last names of the authors (or editors) or by the first word of an organization name (if the author is an organization). When a work has no author or editor, alphabetize by the first word of the title other than "A," "An," or "The."

If your list includes two or more works by the same author, arrange the entries by year, the earliest first. If your list includes two or more works by the same author in the same year, arrange the works alphabetically by title. Add the letters "a," "b," and so on within the parentheses after the year. For journal articles, use only the year and the letter: (2012a). For articles in magazines and newspapers, use the full date and the letter in the reference list: (2012a, July 7); use only the year and the letter in the in-text citation.

Authors' names   Invert all authors' names and use initials instead of first names. Separate the names with commas. For two to twenty authors, use an ampersand (&) before the last author's name. For twenty-one or more authors, give the first nineteen authors, followed by an ellipsis and the last author (see item 3 in 62b).

Titles of books and articles   In the reference list, italicize the titles and subtitles of books. Do not italicize or use quotation marks around the titles of articles and other stand-alone works. For both books and articles, capitalize only the first word of the title and subtitle (and all proper nouns). Capitalize names of journals, magazines, and newspapers as you would capitalize them normally (see 46c).

Abbreviations for page numbers   Abbreviations for "page" and "pages" ("p." and "pp.") are used before page numbers of selections in anthologies and other edited books (see item 26 in 62b). Do not use "p." or "pp." before page numbers of articles in journals and magazines (see items 12 and 13 in 62b).

Breaking a URL or DOI   Do not insert any line breaks into a URL or DOI (digital object identifier). Any line breaks that your word processor makes automatically are acceptable. Do not add a period at the end of a URL or DOI.

63b Sample APA research paper

On the following pages is a research paper on the use of educational technology in the shift to student-centered learning, written by April Bo Wang, a student in an education class. Wang's assignment was to write a literature review paper documented with APA-style citations and references. Following Wang's paper is a sample abstract and running head, used for professional papers. (If you are not sure what your assignment requires, check with your instructor.).

All pages are numbered, starting with the title page.

1

Paper title is boldface, followed by one blank (double-spaced) line. Writer's name, department and school, course, instructor, and date follow on separate double-spaced lines.

Technology and the Shift From Teacher-Delivered to Student-Centered Learning: A Review of the Literature

April Bo Wang

Department of Education, Glen County Community College

EDU 107: Education, Technology, and Media

Dr. Julien Gomez

October 29, 2017

Marginal annotations indicate APA-style formatting and effective writing.

2

Technology and the Shift From Teacher-Delivered to Student-Centered Learning: A Review of the Literature

In the United States, most public school systems are struggling with teacher shortages, which are projected to worsen as the number of applicants to education schools decreases (Donitsa-Schmidt & Zuzovsky, 2014, p. 420). Citing federal data, *The New York Times* reported a 30% drop in "people entering teacher preparation programs" between 2010 and 2014 (Rich, 2015, para. 10). Especially in science and math fields, the teacher shortage is projected to escalate in the next 10 years (Hutchison, 2012). In recent decades, instructors and administrators have viewed the practice of student-centered learning as one promising solution. Unlike traditional teacher-delivered (also called "transmissive") instruction, student-centered learning allows students to help direct their own education by setting their own goals and selecting appropriate resources for achieving those goals. Though student-centered learning might once have been viewed as an experimental solution in understaffed schools, it is gaining credibility as an effective pedagogical practice. What is also gaining momentum is the idea that technology might play a significant role in fostering student-centered learning. This literature review will examine three key questions:

1. In what ways is student-centered learning effective?
2. Can educational technology help students drive their own learning?
3. How can public schools effectively combine teacher talent and educational technology?

In the face of mounting teacher shortages, public schools should embrace educational technology that promotes student-centered learning in order to help all students become engaged and successful learners.

Sources provide background information and context.

In-text citation for a quotation from a source without page numbers includes a paragraph number or another locator.

Wang sets up her organization by posing three questions.

Wang states her thesis.

In What Ways Is Student-Centered Learning Effective?

According to the International Society for Technology in Education (2016), "Student-centered learning moves students from passive receivers of information to active participants in their own discovery process. What students learn, how they learn it, and how their learning is assessed are all driven by each individual student's needs and abilities" (What Is It? section). The results of student-centered learning have been positive, not only for academic achievement but also for student self-esteem. In this model of instruction, the teacher acts as a facilitator, and the students actively participate in the process of learning and teaching. With guidance, students decide on the learning goals most pertinent to themselves, they devise a learning plan that will most likely help them achieve those goals, they direct themselves in carrying out that learning plan, and they assess how much they learned (Çubukçu, 2012, Introduction section). The major differences between student-centered learning and instructor-centered learning are summarized in Table 1.

Bell (2010) has argued that the chief benefit of student-centered learning is that it can connect students with "real-world tasks," thus making learning more engaging as well as more comprehensive (p. 42). For example, Bell observed a group of middle-school students who wanted to build a social justice monument for their school. They researched social justice issues, selected several to focus on, and then designed a three-dimensional playground to represent those issues. In doing so, they achieved learning goals in the areas of social studies, physics, and mathematics and practiced research and teamwork. Students engaged in this kind of learning performed better on both project-based assessments and standardized tests (Bell, 2010).

Wang uses a source to define the key term "student-centered learning."

Locator is included for a paraphrase to help readers find the source in a long article without page numbers.

Page number or other locator is not necessary for a paraphrase from a short article.

4

Table 1

Comparison of Two Approaches to Teaching and Learning

Teaching and learning period	Instructor-centered approach	Student-centered approach
Before class	• Instructor prepares lecture/instruction on new topic. • Students complete homework on previous topic.	• Students read and view new material, practice new concepts, and prepare questions ahead of class. • Instructor views student practice and questions, identifies learning opportunities.
During class	• Instructor delivers new material in a lecture or prepared discussion. • Students — unprepared — listen, watch, take notes, and try to follow along with the new material.	• Students lead discussions of the new material or practice applying the concepts or skills in an active environment. • Instructor answers student questions and provides immediate feedback.
After class	• Instructor grades homework and gives feedback about the previous lesson. • Students work independently to practice or apply the new concepts.	• Students apply concepts/skills to more complex tasks, some of their own choosing, individually and in groups. • Instructor posts additional resources to help students.

Note. Adapted from *The Flipped Class Demystified*, by New York University, n.d. (https://www.nyu.edu/faculty/teaching-and-learning-resources/instructional-technology-support/instructional-design-assessment/flipped-classes/the-flipped-class-demystified.html).

A Stanford study came to a similar conclusion; researchers examined four schools that had moved from teacher-driven instruction to student-centered learning (Friedlaender et al., 2014). The study focused on students from a mix of racial, cultural, and socioeconomic

Wang creates a table to compare and contrast two key concepts for her readers.

In a citation of a work with three or more authors, the first author's name, followed by "et al.," is given in parentheses or in a signal phrase.

backgrounds, with varying levels of English-language proficiency. The researchers predicted that this mix of students, representing differing levels of academic ability, would benefit from a student-centered approach. Through interviews, surveys, and classroom observations, the researchers identified key characteristics of the new student-centered learning environments at the four schools:

- teachers who prioritized building relationships with students

- support structures for teachers to improve and collaborate on instruction

- a shift in classroom activity from lectures and tests to projects and performance-based assessments (pp. 5–7)

After the schools designed their curriculum to be personalized to individual students rather than standardized across a diverse student body and to be inclusive of skills such as persistence as well as traditional academic skills, students outperformed peers on state tests and increased their rates of high school and college graduation (Friedlaender et al., 2014, p. 3).

Authors and year are given earlier in the paragraph, so only page numbers are provided at the end of the paraphrase.

Can Educational Technology Help Students Drive Their Own Learning?

When students engage in self-directed learning, they rely less on teachers to deliver information and require less face-to-face time with teachers. For content delivery, many school districts have begun to use educational technology resources that, in recent years, have become more available, more affordable, and easier to use. For the purposes of this paper, the term "educational technology resources" encompasses the following: distance learning, by which students learn from a remote instructor online; other online education programming such as slide shows and video or

Headings, centered and boldface, help readers follow the organization.

6

audio lectures; interactive online activities, such as quizzing or games; and the use of computers, tablets, smartphones, SMART Boards, or other such devices for coursework.

Much like student-centered learning, the use of educational technology began in many places as a temporary measure to keep classes running despite teacher shortages. A Horn and Staker study (2011) examined the major patterns over time for students who subscribed to distance learning, for example. A decade ago, students who enrolled in distance learning often fell into one of the following categories: They lived in a rural community that had no alternative for learning; they attended a school where there were not enough qualified teachers to teach certain subjects; or they were homeschooled or homebound. But faced with tighter budgets, teacher shortages, increasingly diverse student populations, and rigorous state standards, schools recognized the need and the potential for distance learning across the board.

As the teacher shortage has intensified, educational technology resources have become more tailored to student needs and more affordable. Pens that convert handwritten notes to digital text and organize them, backpacks that charge electronic devices, and apps that create audiovisual flash cards are just a few of the more recent innovations. Some educational technology resources entertain students while supporting student-centered learning. Svokos (2015) described popular educational games developed by the nonprofit organization GlassLab and used in thousands of U.S. classrooms:

> Some of the company's games are education versions
> of existing ones — for example, its first release was
> SimCity EDU — while others are originals. Teachers get
> real-time updates on students' progress as well as

Wang develops her thesis.

In a signal phrase, the word "and" links the names of two authors; the date is given in parentheses.

Quotation of 40 or more words is indented without quotation marks.

suggestions on what subjects they need to spend more time perfecting. (5. Educational Games section) Many of the companies behind these products offer institutional discounts to schools where such devices are used widely by students and teachers.

Locator (section title) is used for a direct quotation from an online source with no page numbers.

Horn and Staker (2011) concluded that the chief benefit of technological learning was that it could adapt to the individual student in a way that whole-class delivery by a single teacher could not. Their study examined various schools where technology enabled student-centered learning. For example, Carpe Diem High School in Yuma, Arizona, hired only six certified subject teachers and then outfitted its classrooms with 280 computers connected to online learning programs. The programs included software that offered "continual feedback, assessment, and incremental victory in a way that a face-to-face teacher with a class of 30 students never could. After each win, students continue to move forward at their own pace" (p. 9). Students alternated between personalized 55-minute courses online and 55-minute courses with one of the six teachers. The academic outcomes were promising. Carpe Diem ranked first in its county for student math and reading scores. Similarly, Rocketship Education, a charter network that serves low-income, predominantly Latino students, created a digital learning lab, reducing the need to hire more teachers. Rocketship's academic scores ranked in the top 15 of all California low-income public schools.

Wang uses her own analysis to shape the conversation among her sources in this synthesis paragraph.

It is clear that educational technology will continue to play a role in student and school performance. Horn and Staker (2011) acknowledged that they focused on programs in which integration of educational technology led to improved student performance. In other schools, technological learning is simply distance learning— watching a remote teacher—and not student-centered

8

learning that allows students to partner with teachers to develop enriching learning experiences. That said, many educators seem convinced that educational technology has the potential to help them transition from traditional teacher-driven learning to student-centered learning. All four schools in the Stanford study heavily relied on technology (Friedlaender et al., 2014). And indeed, Demski (2012) argued that technology is not supplemental but instead is "central" to student-centered learning (p. 33). Rather than turning to a teacher as the source of information, students are sent to investigate solutions to problems by searching online, emailing experts, collaborating with one another in a wiki space, or completing online practice. Instead of relying on a teacher for the answer to a question, students are driven to perform—driven to use technology to find those answers themselves.

How Can Public Schools Effectively Combine Teacher Talent and Educational Technology?

Some researchers have expressed doubt that schools are ready for student-centered learning—or any type of instruction—that is driven by technology. In a recent survey conducted by the Nellie Mae Education Foundation, Moeller and Reitzes (2011) reported not only that many teachers lacked confidence in their ability to incorporate technology in the classroom but that 43% of polled high school students said that they lacked confidence in their technological proficiency going into college and careers. The study concluded that technology alone would not improve learning environments. Yet others argued that students adapt quickly to even unfamiliar technology and use it to further their own learning. For example, Mitra (2013) caught the attention of the education world with his study of how to educate students in the slums of India. He installed

Wang uses a source to introduce a counterargument.

an Internet-accessible computer in a wall in a New Delhi urban slum and left it there with no instructions. Over a few months, many of the children had learned how to use the computer, how to access information over the Internet, how to interpret information, and how to communicate this information to one another. Mitra's experiment was "not about making learning happen. [It was] about letting it happen" (16:31). He concluded that in the absence of teachers, even in developing countries less inundated by technology, a tool that allowed access to an organized database of knowledge (such as a search engine) was sufficient to provide students with a rewarding learning experience.

> Brackets indicate Wang's change in the quoted material.

> For a direct quotation from a video, a time stamp indicates the start of the quotation.

According to the Stanford study, however, the presence of teachers is still crucial (Friedlaender et al., 2014). Their roles will simply change from distributors of knowledge to facilitators and supporters of self-directed student-centered learning. The researchers asserted that teacher education and professional development programs can no longer prepare their teachers in a single instructional mode, such as teacher-delivered learning; they must instead equip teachers with a wide repertoire of skills to support a wide variety of student learning experiences. The Stanford study argued that since teachers would be partnering with students to shape the learning experience, rather than designing and delivering a curriculum on their own, the main job of a teacher would become relationship building. The teacher would establish a relationship with each student so that the teacher could support whatever learning the student pursues.

Many schools have already effectively paired a reduced faculty with educational technology to support successful student-centered learning. For example, Watson (2008)

10

offered a case study of the Cincinnati Public Schools Virtual
High School, which brought students together in a physical
school building to work with an assortment of online learning
programs. Although there were only 10 certified teachers
in the building, students were able to engage in highly
individualized instruction according to their own needs,
strengths, and learning styles, using the 10 teachers as
support (p. 7). Commonwealth Connections Academy (CCA),
a public school in Pennsylvania, also brings students into
a physical school building to engage in digital curriculum.
However, rather than having students identify their own
learning goals and design their own curriculum around those
goals, CCA uses educational technology as an assessment
tool to identify areas of student weakness. It then partners
students with teachers to address those areas (pp. 8–9).

Conclusion

Public education faces the opportunity for a shift
from the model of teacher-delivered instruction that has
characterized American public schools since their foundation
to a student-centered learning model. Not only has student-
centered learning proved effective in improving student
academic and developmental outcomes, but it can also
synchronize with technological learning for widespread
adaptability across schools. Because it relies on student
direction rather than an established curriculum, student-
centered learning supported by educational technology can
adapt to the different needs of individual students and a
variety of learning environments—urban and rural, well
funded and underfunded. Similarly, when student-centered
learning relies on technology rather than a corps of uniformly
trained teachers, it holds promise for schools that would
otherwise suffer from a lack of human or financial resources.

> Tone of the
> conclusion
> is objective
> and presents
> answers to
> Wang's three
> organizational
> questions.

11

References

List of references begins on a new page. Heading is centered and boldface.

Bell, S. (2010). Project-based learning for the 21st century: Skills for the future. *The Clearing House, 83*(2), 39–43.

Çubukçu, Z. (2012). Teachers' evaluation of student-centered learning environments. *Education, 133*(1).

Demski, J. (2012, January). This time it's personal. *THE Journal (Technological Horizons in Education), 39*(1), 32–36.

Donitsa-Schmidt, S., & Zuzovsky, R. (2014). Teacher supply and demand: The school level perspective. *American Journal of Educational Research, 2*(6), 420–429. https://doi.org/10.12691/education-2-6-14

List is alphabetized by authors' last names. All authors' names are inverted.

Friedlaender, D., Burns, D., Lewis-Charp, H., Cook-Harvey, C. M., & Darling-Hammond, L. (2014). *Student-centered schools: Closing the opportunity gap* [Research brief]. Stanford Center for Opportunity Policy in Education. https://edpolicy.stanford.edu/sites/default/files/scope-pub-student-centered-research-brief.pdf

First line of an entry is at the left margin; subsequent lines indent 1/2".

Horn, M. B., & Staker, H. (2011). *The rise of K-12 blended learning*. Innosight Institute. http://www.christenseninstitute.org/wp-content/uploads/2013/04/The-rise-of-K-12-blended-learning.pdf

Hutchison, L. F. (2012). Addressing the STEM teacher shortage in American schools: Ways to recruit and retain effective STEM teachers. *Action in Teacher Education, 34*(5/6), 541–550. https://doi.org/10.1080/01626620.2012.729483

Double-spacing is used throughout.

International Society for Technology in Education. (2016). *Student-centered learning*. http://www.iste.org/connected/standards/essential-conditions/student-centered-learning

12

Mitra, S. (2013, February). *Build a school in the cloud*
        [Video]. TED. https://www.ted.com/talks/sugata_
        mitra_build_a_school_in_the_cloud?language=en

Moeller, B., & Reitzes, T. (2011, July). *Integrating
        technology with student-centered learning*.
        Nellie Mae Education Foundation. http://www.
        nmefoundation.org/research/personalization/
        integrating-technology-with-student-centered-learn

Rich, M. (2015, August 9). Teacher shortages spur a
        nationwide hiring scramble (credentials optional). *The
        New York Times*. https://nyti.ms/1WaaV7a

Svokos, A. (2015, May 7). 5 innovations from the past
        decade that aim to change the American classroom.
        Huffpost. https://www.huffpost.com/entry/
        technology-changes-classrooms_n_7190910

Watson, J. (2008, January). *Blended learning: The
        convergence of online and face-to-face education*. North
        American Council for Online Learning. http://www.
        inacol.org/wp-content/uploads/2015/02/NACOL_PP-
        BlendedLearning-lr.pdf

Additional elements: Abstract and running head

The following elements are required for professional (submitted for publication) papers.

A running head consisting of a shortened title is flush left on all pages.

The abstract appears on a new page after the title page.

The abstract is a fewer than 250-word overview of the paper.

Keywords help readers search for a paper online or in a database.

Abstract

In recent decades, instructors and administrators have viewed student-centered learning as a promising pedagogical practice that offers both the hope of increasing academic performance and a solution for teacher shortages. Differing from the traditional model of instruction in which a teacher delivers content from the front of a classroom, student-centered learning puts the students at the center of teaching and learning. Students set their own learning goals, select appropriate resources, and progress at their own pace. Student-centered learning has produced both positive results and increases in students' self-esteem. Given the recent proliferation of technology in classrooms, school districts are poised for success in making the shift to student-centered learning. The question for district leaders, however, is how to effectively balance existing teacher talent with educational technology.

Keywords: digital learning, student-centered learning, personalized learning, education technology, transmissive, blended

Models of professional writing

Good document design promotes readability and increases the chances that you will achieve your purpose for writing and reach your readers. How you design a document — how you format it for the printed page or for a computer screen, for example — affects your readers' response to it. Most readers have expectations about document design and format, usually depending on the context and the purpose of the piece of writing.

This gallery features pages from business documents. The annotations on the sides of the pages point out design choices as well as important features of the writing.

Standard academic formatting

Use the manuscript format that is recommended for your academic discipline. In most English and some other humanities classes, you will be asked to use MLA (Modern Language Association) format (see section 58). In most social science classes, such as psychology and sociology, and in most business, education, and health-related classes, you'll be asked to use APA (American Psychological Association) format (see section 63).

Standard professional formatting

It helps to look at examples when you are preparing to write a professional document such as a letter, a memo, or a résumé. In general, business and professional writing is direct, clear, and courteous, and documents are designed to be read easily and quickly. When writing less formal documents such as email messages in academic contexts, it is just as important to craft the document for easy readability.

Business report with a visual

Report formatted in typical business style, with citations in APA style.

Doug Ames, manager of operations for OAISYS, noted that some of these issues keep the company from outperforming expectations: "Communication is not timely or uniform, expectations are not clear and consistent, and some employees do not contribute significantly yet nothing is done" (personal communication, February 28, 2021).

Recommendations

It appears that a combination of steps can be used to unlock greater performance for OAISYS. Most important, steps can be taken to strengthen the corporate culture in key areas such as communication, accountability, and appreciation. Employee feedback indicates that these are areas of weakness or motivators that can be improved. This feedback is summarized in Figure 1.

Visual referred to in body of report.

A plan to use communication effectively to set expectations, share results in a timely fashion, and publicly offer appreciation to specific contributors will likely go a long way toward aligning individual motivation with corporate goals. Additionally, holding individuals accountable for results will bring parity to the workplace.

Figure, a bar graph, appears at bottom of page on which it is mentioned. Figure number and caption are placed below figure.

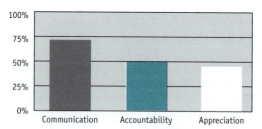

Figure 1. Areas of greatest need for improvements in motivation.

Business letter in full block style

Latinx Voice

March 16, 2021 ———— Date

Jonathan Ríos
Managing Editor
Latinx World Today ——— Inside address
2971 East Oak Avenue
Boston, MA 00000

Dear Mr. Ríos: ———— Salutation

Thank you very much for taking the time yesterday to speak to the University of Bedford's Latinx Club. A number of students have told me that they enjoyed your presentation and found your job search suggestions to be extremely helpful.

As I mentioned to you, the club publishes a monthly newsletter, *Latinx Voice*. Our purpose is to share up-to-date information and expert advice with members of the university's Latinx population. Considering how much students benefited from your talk, I would like to publish excerpts from it in our newsletter.

I have transcribed parts of your presentation and organized them into a question-and-answer format for our readers. Would you mind looking through the enclosed article and letting me know if I may have your permission to print it? I'm hoping to include this article in our next newsletter, so I would need your response by April 4.

Once again, Mr. Ríos, thank you for sharing your experiences with us. I would love to be able to share your thoughts with students who couldn't hear you in person.

Paragraphs single-spaced, not indented; double-spacing between paragraphs.

Body

Sincerely, ———— Close

Jeffrey Richardson (signature)

Jeffrey Richardson
Associate Editor

———— Signature

Enc. ————

Indicates something enclosed with letter.

Résumé

Limit résumé to one page if possible, two pages at most.

Information organized into clear categories— Education, Experience, etc.—and formatted for easy scanning.

Information presented in reverse chronological order.

Present-tense verbs (*work, provide*) used for current activities.

Bulleted lists organize information.

Alexis A. Smith

404 Ponce de Leon NE, #B7
Atlanta, GA 30308

404-231-1234
asmith@smith.localhost

EDUCATION

Bachelor of Arts, English
Georgia State University, Atlanta, GA

expected May 2021

- Emphasis areas: journalism and communication
- Study Abroad, Ecuador (Fall 2019)
- Dean's List (Fall 2018, Fall 2019, Spring 2020)

EXPERIENCE

Copyeditor
The Signal, Atlanta, GA

Sept. 2019-present

- Copyedit articles for spelling, grammar, and style
- Fact-check articles
- Prepare copy for web publication in Dreamweaver

Writing Tutor
Georgia State University Writing Studio, Atlanta, GA

Oct. 2018-present

- Work with undergraduate and graduate students on writing projects in all subject areas
- Provide technical support for multimedia projects

OUTREACH AND ACTIVITIES

- Publicity Director, English Department
  Student Organization   Aug. 2019-present
- Coordinator, Georgia State University
  Relay for Life Student Team   April 2019, 2020

SKILLS

- Writing: competent communicating to different audiences, using a range of written forms (articles, reports, flyers, pamphlets, memos, letters)
- Design: capable of creating visually appealing, audience-appropriate documents; skilled at taking and editing photographs
- Technical: proficient in Microsoft Office; comfortable with Dreamweaver, Photoshop, InDesign
- Language: fluent in spoken and written Spanish

Professional memo

COMMONWEALTH PRESS
MEMORANDUM

February 26, 2021

To: Editorial assistants, Advertising Department

cc: Stephen Chapman

From: Helen Brown

Subject: Training for new database software

The new database software will be installed on your computers next week. I have scheduled a training program to help you become familiar with the software and with our new procedures for data entry and retrieval.

Training program

A member of our IT staff will teach in-house workshops on how to use the new software. If you try the software before the workshop, please be prepared to discuss any problems you encounter.

We will keep the training groups small to encourage hands-on participation and to provide individual attention. The workshops will take place in the training room on the third floor from 10:00 a.m. to 2:00 p.m.

Lunch will be provided in the cafeteria.

Sign-up

Please sign up by March 5 for one of the following dates by adding your name in the department's online calendar:

- Monday, March 8
- Wednesday, March 10
- Friday, March 12

If you will not be in the office on any of those dates, please let me know by March 5.

Annotations (right margin):

Date, name of recipient(s), name of sender on separate lines.

Subject line describes topic concisely.

Introduction states point of memo.

Headings guide readers and promote quick scanning of document.

List calls attention to important information.

Answers to lettered exercises

EXERCISE 6–2, page 87

a. hasty generalization; b. false analogy; c. either/or fallacy;
d. stereotypes; e. non sequitur

EXERCISE 8–1, page 110 *Possible revisions:*

a. The Prussians defeated the Saxons in 1745.
b. Ahmed, the producer, manages the entire operation.
c. The tour guides expertly paddled the sea kayaks.
d. Emphatic and active; no change
e. The senator heard the protesters' shouts as she walked up the Capitol steps.

EXERCISE 8–2, page 111

a. passive; b. active; c. passive; d. active; e. active

EXERCISE 9–1, page 114 *Possible revisions:*

a. Bluetooth technology is used with personal computers, mobile phones, and audio devices.
b. Hannah told her rock-climbing partner that she bought a new harness and that she wanted to climb Otter Cliffs.
c. It is more difficult to sustain an exercise program than to start one.
d. During basic training, I was told not only what to do but also what to think.
e. Jan wanted to drive to the wine country or at least to Sausalito.

EXERCISE 10–1, page 118 *Possible revisions:*

a. A grapefruit or an orange is a good source of vitamin C.
b. The golden eagle's wingspan is nearly as wide as the bald eagle's.
c. Looking out the family room window, Sarah saw that her favorite tree, which she had climbed as a child, was gone.
d. The graphic designers are interested in and knowledgeable about producing posters for the balloon race.
e. The Great Barrier Reef is larger than any other coral reef in the world.

EXERCISE 11–1, page 121 *Possible revisions:*

a. Using surgical gloves is a precaution now taken by dentists to prevent contact with patients' blood and saliva.
b. A career in medicine, which my brother is pursuing, requires at least ten years of challenging work.
c. The pharaohs had bad teeth because tiny particles of sand found their way into Egyptian bread.
d. Recurring bouts of flu caused the team to forfeit a record number of games.
e. This box contains the key to your future.

EXERCISE 12–1, page 124   *Possible revisions:*

a. The manager asked her employees to submit their reports on Friday if they had time.
b. Many students graduate from college with debt totaling more than fifty thousand dollars.
c. It is a myth that humans use only 10 percent of their brains.
d. When Daria looked in the closet, she found the old nightgown she used to wear to sleep.
e. Not all geese fly beyond Narragansett for the winter.

EXERCISE 12–2, page 126   *Possible revisions:*

a. To complete an online purchase with a credit card, you must enter the expiration date and the security code.
b. Though Martha was only sixteen, UCLA accepted her application.
c. As I settled in the cockpit, the pounding of the engine was muffled only slightly by my helmet.
d. After studying polymer chemistry, Letitia found computer games less complex.
e. When I was a young man, my mother enrolled me in ballet and tap dance classes.

EXERCISE 13–3, page 131   *Possible revisions:*

a. An incredibly talented musician, Ray Charles mastered R&B, soul, and gospel styles. He even performed country music well.
b. Environmentalists point out that shrimp farming in Southeast Asia is polluting water and making farmlands useless. They warn that governments must act before it is too late.
c. We observed the samples for five days before we detected any growth. *Or* The samples were observed for five days before any growth was detected.
d. In his famous soliloquy, Hamlet contemplates whether death would be preferable to his difficult life and, if so, whether he is capable of committing suicide.
e. The lawyer told the judge that Miranda Hale was innocent and asked that she be allowed to prove the allegations false. *Or* The lawyer told the judge, "Miranda Hale is innocent. Please allow her to prove the allegations false."

EXERCISE 13–4, page 131   *Possible revisions:*

a. We want to play volleyball this afternoon, but we have to reserve the court through the fitness center before we can use it.
b. The interviewer asked if we had brought our proof of citizenship and our passports.
c. Experienced reconnaissance scouts know how to make fast decisions and use sophisticated equipment to keep their teams from being detected.
d. After the animators finish their scenes, the production designer arranges the clips according to the storyboard and makes synchronization notes for the sound editor and the composer.
e. Madame Defarge is a sinister figure in Dickens's *A Tale of Two Cities*. On a symbolic level, she represents fate; like the Greek Fates, she knits the fabric of individual destiny.

EXERCISE 14–1, page 134   *Possible revisions:*

a. Williams played for the Boston Red Sox from 1939 to 1960, and he managed the Washington Senators and Texas Rangers for several years after retiring as a player.
b. In 1941, Williams finished the season with a batting average of .406; no player has hit over .400 for a season since then.
c. Although he acknowledged that Joe DiMaggio was a better all-around player, Williams felt that he was a better hitter than DiMaggio.
d. Williams was a stubborn man; for example, he always refused to tip his cap to the crowd after a home run because he claimed that fans were fickle.
e. Williams's relationship with the media was unfriendly at best; he sarcastically called baseball writers the "knights of the keyboard" in his memoir.

EXERCISE 14–2, page 136   *Possible revisions:*

a. The X-Men comic books and Japanese woodcuts of kabuki dancers, all part of Marlena's research project on popular culture, covered the tabletop and the chairs.
b. The students organized a petition to change the school motto, which was "A man's greatest strength is his education."
c. Employees can apply for a spot in the leadership program, which teaches management and communication skills.
d. Shore houses were flooded up to the first floor, beaches were washed away, and Brant's Lighthouse was swallowed by the sea.
e. Laura Thackray, an engineer at Volvo Car Corporation, addressed women's safety needs by designing a pregnant crash-test dummy.

EXERCISE 14–3, page 137   *Possible revisions:*

a. These particles, known as "stealth liposomes," can hide in the body for a long time without detection.
b. Irena, a competitive gymnast majoring in biochemistry, intends to apply her athletic experience and her science degree to a career in sports medicine.
c. Because students, textile workers, and labor unions have loudly protested sweatshop abuses, apparel makers have been forced to examine their labor practices.
d. Developed in a European university, IRC (Internet relay chat) was created as a way for a group of graduate students to talk about projects from their dorm rooms.
e. The cafeteria's new menu, which has an international flavor, includes everything from pizza to pad thai.

EXERCISE 14–4, page 139   *Possible revisions:*

a. To help the relief effort, Gina distributed food and medical supplies.
b. Janbir, who spent every Saturday learning tabla drumming, noticed that with each hour of practice his memory for complex patterns was growing stronger.
c. When the rotor hit, it gouged a hole about an eighth of an inch deep in my helmet.

d. My grandfather, who was born eighty years ago in Puerto Rico, raised his daughters the old-fashioned way.
e. By reversing the depressive effect of the drug, the Narcan saved the patient's life.

EXERCISE 15–1, page 142   *Possible revisions:*

a. Across the hall from the fossils exhibit are the exhibits for insects and spiders.
b. After growing up desperately poor, Sayuri becomes a successful geisha.
c. Researchers who have been studying Mount St. Helens for years believe that earthquakes may have caused the 1980 eruption.
d. Ice cream typically contains 10 percent milk fat, but premium ice cream may contain up to 16 percent milk fat and has less air in it.
e. If home values climb, the economy may recover quickly.

EXERCISE 16–1, page 146   *Possible revisions:*

a. Martin Luther King Jr. set a high standard for future leaders.
b. Alice has loved cooking since she could first peek over a kitchen tabletop.
c. Bloom's race for the governorship is futile.
d. A successful graphic designer must have technical knowledge and an eye for color and balance.
e. You will deliver mail to all employees.

EXERCISE 17–1, page 149   *Possible revisions:*

a. When I was young, my family was poor.
b. This conference will help me serve my clients better.
c. I am unemployed because my company laid me off last fall.
d. Government studies show a need for after-school programs.
e. Let's thoroughly analyze sales and share our findings.

EXERCISE 17–3, page 152   *Possible revisions:*

a. Dr. Geralyn Farmer is the chief surgeon at University Hospital. Dr. Paul Green is her assistant.
b. All applicants want to know how much they will earn.
c. Elementary school teachers should understand the concept of nurturing if they intend to be effective.
d. Our company is going to hire a new I.T. employee. This employee will update the server and set up remote desktops.
e. If we do not stop polluting our environment, we will perish.

NOTE: Since it is acceptable to use the pronoun *they* to refer to an indefinite pronoun or a generic noun, sentences b, c, and d could have alternative revisions. For example, this sentence is also acceptable: *Every applicant wants to know how much they will earn.*

EXERCISE 18–2, page 155   *Possible revisions:*

a. Queen Anne was so angry with Sarah Churchill that she refused to see her again.
b. Jean-Pierre is going to try to finish his sociology project this weekend.
c. The parade moved off the street and onto the beach.
d. The experienced hikers plan to make the dangerous trek across the mountains.
e. Correct

EXERCISE 18–3, page 157   *Possible revisions:*

a. John stormed into the room like a hurricane.
b. Some people insist that they'll always be available to help, even when they haven't been before.
c. The Cubs easily beat the Mets, who were in trouble early in the game today at Wrigley Field.
d. We worked out the problems in our relationship.
e. My mother accused me of evading her questions when in fact I was just saying the first thing that came to mind.

EXERCISE 19–1, page 172   *Possible revisions:*

a. Listening to the playlist her sister had created, Blanca was overcome with a mix of emotions: happiness, homesickness, and nostalgia.
b. Cortés and his soldiers were astonished when they looked down from the mountains and saw Tenochtitlán, the magnificent capital of the Aztecs.
c. Although my spoken Spanish is not very good, I can read the language with ease.
d. There are several reasons for not eating meat. One reason is that dangerous chemicals are used throughout the various stages of meat production.
e. To learn how to sculpt beauty from everyday life is my intention in studying art and archaeology.

EXERCISE 20–1, page 178   *Possible revisions:*

a. Martina recently started working at a new company that designs and manufactures educational toys.
b. The building is being renovated, so at times we have no heat, water, or electricity.
c. I don' think I will buy the new model of smartphone. Why spend the money when my current phone works perfectly?
d. Walker's coming-of-age novel is set against a gloomy scientific backdrop; the earth's rotation has begun to slow down.
e. City officials had good reason to fear a major earthquake: Most [*or* most] of the business district was built on landfill.

EXERCISE 20–2, page 179   *Possible revisions:*

a. Wind power for the home is a supplementary source of energy that can be combined with electricity, gas, or solar energy.
b. Correct
c. In the Middle Ages, when the streets of London were dangerous places, it was safer to travel by boat along the Thames.
d. "He's not drunk," I said. "He's in a state of diabetic shock."
e. Are you able to endure extreme angle turns, high speeds, frequent jumps, and occasional crashes? Then supermoto racing may be a sport for you.

EXERCISE 21–1, page 189

a. One of the main reasons for elephant poaching is the profits received from selling the ivory tusks.
b. Correct
c. A number of students in the seminar were aware of the importance of joining the discussion.

d. Batik cloth from Bali, blue and white ceramics from Delft, and a bocce ball from Turin have made Angelie's room the talk of the dorm.
e. Correct

EXERCISE 22–1, page 194 *Possible revisions:*

a. Every presidential candidate must appeal to a wide variety of ethnic and social groups to win the election.
b. Either Tom Hanks or Denzel Washington will win an award for his lifetime achievement in cinema.
c. The aerobics teacher motioned for all the students to move their arms in wide, slow circles.
d. Correct
e. Applicants should be bilingual if they want to qualify for this position.

NOTE: Since it is acceptable to use the pronoun *they* to refer to an indefinite pronoun or a generic noun, sentences a, c, and e could have alternative revisions. For example, this sentence is also acceptable: *The aerobics teacher motioned for everyone to move their arms in wide, slow circles.*

EXERCISE 23–1, page 197 *Possible revisions:*

a. Some professors say that engineering students should have hands-on experience with dismantling and reassembling machines.
b. Because she had decorated her bedroom wall with posters from chamber music festivals, her virtual classmates thought that she was interested in classical music. Actually, she preferred rock.
c. In my high school, students didn't need to get all A's to be considered a success; they just needed to work to their ability.
d. Marianne told Jenny, "I am worried about your mother's illness." [*or* ". . . about my mother's illness."]
e. Though Lewis cried for several minutes after scraping his knee, eventually his crying subsided.

EXERCISE 24–1, page 201

a. Correct [But the writer could change the end of the sentence: . . . *than he was.*]
b. Correct [But the writer could change the end of the sentence: . . . *that she was the coach.*]
c. She appreciated his telling the truth in such a difficult situation.
d. The director has asked you and me to draft a proposal for a new recycling plan.
e. My roommate and I dreamed of renting a station wagon, packing it with food, and driving two hundred miles to Mardi Gras.

EXERCISE 25–1, page 204

a. Correct
b. The environmental policy conference featured scholars whom I had never heard of. [*or* . . . scholars I had never heard of.]
c. Correct
d. Kartik always gives a holiday donation to whoever needs it.
e. So many singers came to the audition that Natalia had trouble deciding whom to select for the choir.

EXERCISE 26–1, page 209

a. Do you expect to perform well on the exam next week?
b. With the budget deadline approaching, our office has hardly had time to handle routine correspondence.
c. Correct
d. The customer complained that he hadn't been treated nicely by the agent on the phone.
e. Of all the smart people in my family, Aunt Ida is the cleverest. [*or* . . . the most clever.]

EXERCISE 27–1, page 213

a. When I get the urge to exercise, I lie down until it passes.
b. Grandmother had driven our new hybrid to the sunrise church service, so we were left with the station wagon.
c. A pile of dirty rags was lying at the bottom of the stairs.
d. How did the game know that the player had gone from the room with the blue ogre to the hall where the gold was heaped?
e. Abraham Lincoln took good care of his legal clients; the contracts he drew for the Illinois Central Railroad could never be broken.

EXERCISE 27–2, page 217

a. The glass sculptures of the Swan Boats were prominent in the brightly lit lobby.
b. Visitors to the glass museum were not supposed to touch the exhibits.
c. The electrician went to the security office to repair the closed-circuit TV.
d. Christos didn't know about Marlo's promotion because he never listens. He is [*or* He's] always talking.
e. Correct

EXERCISE 27–3, page 224   *Possible revisions:*

a. Correct
b. Discovered in 1930, Pluto is an icy dwarf planet that exists at the edge of our solar system.
c. When city planners proposed rezoning the waterfront, did they know that the mayor had promised to curb development in that neighborhood?
d. Tonight's lecture begins at 7:30. If it were earlier, I'd consider attending.
e. Correct

EXERCISE 28–1, page 231

a. In the past, tobacco companies denied any connection between smoking and health problems.
b. The volunteer's compassion has touched many lives.
c. I want to register for a summer tutoring session.
d. By the end of the year, the state will have opened a dozen career and employment centers..
e. The golfers were prepared for all weather conditions.

EXERCISE 28–2, page 233

a. A major league pitcher can throw a baseball more than ninety-five miles per hour.
b. The writing center tutor will help you revise your essay.

c. A reptile must adjust its body temperature to its environment.
d. Correct
e. My uncle, a cartoonist, could sketch a face in less than two minutes.

EXERCISE 28–3, page 236 *Possible revisions:*

a. The electrician might have discovered the broken circuit if she had inspected the wires thoroughly.
b. If Verena wins a scholarship, she will go to graduate school.
c. Whenever a rainbow appears after a storm, everybody comes out to see it.
d. Sarah did not understand the terms of her internship.
e. If I lived in Budapest with my cousin Szusza, she would teach me Hungarian cooking.

EXERCISE 28–4, page 239 *Possible answers:*

a. I enjoy riding my motorcycle.
b. The tutor told Samantha to revise her thesis statement.
c. The team hopes to work hard and win the championship.
d. Ricardo and his brothers miss surfing during the winter.
e. Jon remembered to lock the door. *Or* Jon remembered seeing that movie years ago.

EXERCISE 29–1, page 248

a. Doing volunteer work often brings satisfaction.
b. Although Gemma now lives on the West Coast, she grew up in Cape Cod.
c. Melina likes to drink her coffee with lots of cream.
d. Correct
e. I completed my homework assignment quickly. *Or* I completed the homework assignment quickly.

EXERCISE 30–1, page 251

a. There are some cartons of ice cream in the freezer.
b. I don't use the subway because I am afraid.
c. The prime minister is the most popular leader in my country.
d. We tried to get in touch with the same manager whom we spoke to earlier.
e. Recently there have been a number of earthquakes in Turkey.

EXERCISE 30–2, page 253

a. Listening to everyone's complaints all day was irritating.
b. The all-day online classes were exhausting.
c. Correct
d. After a great deal of research, the scientist made a fascinating discovery.
e. Surviving that tornado was one of the most frightening experiences I've ever had.

EXERCISE 30–3, page 254

a. an intelligent young Vietnamese sculptor
b. a dedicated Catholic priest
c. her old blue wool sweater
d. Elias's delicious Scandinavian bread
e. many beautiful antique jewelry boxes

EXERCISE 31–1, page 256

a. Whenever we eat at the Centerville Café, we sit at a small table in the corner of the patio.
b. Correct
c. On Thursday, Nancy will attend her first home repair class at the community center.
d. Correct
e. We decided to go to the grocery store because there was no fresh food in the refrigerator.

EXERCISE 33–1, page 268

a. Alisa brought the injured bird home and fashioned a splint out of Popsicle sticks for its wing.
b. Considered a classic of early animation, *The Adventures of Prince Achmed* used hand-cut silhouettes against colored backgrounds.
c. If you complete the evaluation form and return it within two weeks, you will receive a free breakfast during your next stay.
d. J. R. R. Tolkien finished writing his draft of *The Lord of the Rings* trilogy in 1949, but the first book in the series wasn't published until 1954.
e. As an intern, I learned most aspects of the broadcasting industry, but I never learned about fundraising.

EXERCISE 33–2, page 269

a. The cold, impersonal atmosphere of the university was unbearable.
b. An ambulance threaded its way through police cars, fire trucks, and irate citizens.
c. Correct
d. After two broken arms, three cracked ribs, and one concussion, Ken quit the varsity football team.
e. Correct

EXERCISE 33–3, page 273

a. Choreographer Alvin Ailey's best-known work, *Revelations*, is more than just a crowd-pleaser.
b. Correct
c. Correct
d. A member of an organization that provides job training for teens was also appointed to the education commission.
e. Brian Eno, who began his career as a rock musician, turned to meditative compositions in the late 1970s.

EXERCISE 33–4, page 276

a. Cricket, which originated in England, is also popular in Australia, South Africa, and India.
b. At the sound of the starting pistol, the horses surged forward toward the first obstacle, a sharp incline three feet high.
c. After seeing an exhibition of Western art, Gerhard Richter escaped from East Berlin and smuggled out many of his notebooks.
d. Corrie's new wet suit has an intricate blue pattern.
e. We replaced the rickety old spiral staircase with a sturdy new ladder.

EXERCISE 33–6, page 277

a. On January 16, 2017, our office moved to 29 Commonwealth Avenue, Mechanicsville, VA 23111.
b. Correct
c. Ms. Carlson, you are a valued customer whose satisfaction is very important to us.
d. Mr. Mundy was born on July 22, 1939, in Arkansas, where his family had lived for four generations.
e. Correct

EXERCISE 34–1, page 281

a. Correct
b. Tricia's first artwork was a bright blue clay dolphin.
c. Some modern musicians (trumpeter Jon Hassell is an example) blend several cultural traditions into a particular sound.
d. Myra liked hot, spicy foods such as chili, kung pao chicken, and buffalo wings.
e. On the display screen was a soothing pattern of light and shadow.

EXERCISE 35–1, page 285

a. Strong black coffee will not sober you up; the truth is that time is the only way to get alcohol out of your system.
b. Margaret was not surprised to see hail and vivid lightning; conditions had been right for violent weather all day.
c. There is often a fine line between right and wrong, good and bad, truth and deception.
d. Correct
e. Severe, unremitting pain is a ravaging force, especially when the patient tries to hide it from others.

EXERCISE 36–1, page 287

a. Correct [Either *It* or *it* is correct.]
b. If we have come to fight, we are far too few; if we have come to die, we are far too many.
c. Each of the gift baskets included a greeting card, a scarf, and homemade cookies.
d. The news article portrays the land use proposal as reckless, although 62 percent of the town's residents support it.
e. Activist and politician Stacey Abrams asks readers of her book *Lead from the Outside* a powerful question: "How do I banish doubts and get out of my own way?" (xxvii).

EXERCISE 37–1, page 290

a. Correct
b. The innovative shoe fastener was inspired by the designer's young son.
c. Each day's menu features a different European country's dish.
d. Lottie worked overtime to increase her family's earnings.
e. Ms. Jacobs is unwilling to listen to students' complaints about computer failures.

EXERCISE 38–1, page 296

a. As for the advertisement "Sailors have more fun," if you consider chipping paint and swabbing decks fun, then you will have plenty of it.
b. Correct
c. After winning the lottery, Juanita said that she would give half the money to charity.
d. After the movie, Vicki said, "The reviewer called this flick 'trash of the first order.' I guess you can't believe everything you read."
e. Correct

EXERCISE 40–1, page 302

a. A client left a [*or* their] cell phone in our conference room after the meeting.
b. The films we made of Kilauea on our trip to Hawaii Volcanoes National Park illustrate a typical spatter cone eruption.
c. Correct
d. Of three engineering fields — chemical, mechanical, and materials — Keegan chose materials engineering for its application to toy manufacturing.
e. Correct

EXERCISE 41–1, page 306

a. Correct
b. All of the students must meet with the professor to discuss their final projects.
c. Correct
d. A gluten-free diet is not always the best strategy for shedding pounds.
e. The work of Dr. Anand Khan [*or* The work of Anand Khan, PhD,] has helped practitioners better understand post-traumatic stress.

EXERCISE 42–1, page 307

a. *MLA style:* The carpenters located three maple timbers, twenty-one sheets of cherry, and ten oblongs of polished ebony for the theater set. *APA style:* The carpenters located three maple timbers, 21 sheets of cherry, and 10 oblongs of polished ebony for the theater set.
b. Correct
c. Correct
d. Eight students in the class signed up for tutoring.
e. The Vietnam Veterans Memorial in Washington, DC, had 58,132 names inscribed on it when it was dedicated in 1982.

EXERCISE 43–1, page 309

a. André De Shields, who starred in Broadway musicals like *The Wiz* and *Hadestown*, won his first Tony Award in 2019.
b. The old man screamed his anger, shouting to all of us, "I will not leave my money to you worthless layabouts!"
c. I learned the Latin term *ad infinitum* from an old nursery rhyme about fleas: "Great fleas have little fleas upon their back to bite 'em, / Little fleas have lesser fleas and so on *ad infinitum.*"
d. Correct
e. Neve Campbell's lifelong interest in ballet inspired her involvement in the film *The Company*, which portrays a season with the Joffrey Ballet.

EXERCISE 45–1, page 315

a. Correct
b. The swiftly moving tugboat pulled alongside the barge and directed it away from the oil spill in the harbor.
c. Correct
d. Your dog is well known in our neighborhood.
e. Roadblocks were set up along all the major highways leading out of the city.

EXERCISE 46–1, page 318

a. Assistant Dean Shirin Ahmadi recommended offering more world language courses.
b. Correct
c. Kalindi has an ambitious semester, studying differential calculus, classical Hebrew, brochure design, and Greek literature.
d. Lydia's aunt and uncle make modular houses as beautiful as modernist works of art.
e. The labs in Ohio began their research in the spring, and we expect clinical trials to start at our Cleveland lab next summer.

EXERCISE 47–1, page 320

a. stage, confrontation, proportions; b. courage, nurses, inspiration, community; c. need, guest, honor, fog; d. defense (noun/adjective), attorney, appeal, jury; e. museum, women (noun/adjective), artists, 1987

EXERCISE 47–2, page 323

a. his; b. that, our (pronoun/adjective); c. he, himself, some, his (pronoun/adjective); d. I, my (pronoun/adjective), you, one; e. no one, her

EXERCISE 47–3, page 325

a. told; b. were, killed; c. brought down; d. Stay, 'll [will] arrive;
e. struggled, was trapped

EXERCISE 47–4, page 326

a. Adjectives: weak, unfocused; b. Adjectives: The (article), Spanish, flexible; adverb: wonderfully; c. Adjectives: The (article), fragrant, the (article), steady; adverb: especially; d. Adjectives: hot, cold; adverbs: rather, slightly, bitterly; e. Adjectives: The (article), its (pronoun/adjective), wicker (noun/adjective); adverb: soundly

EXERCISE 48–1, page 332

a. Complete subjects: The hills and mountains, the snow atop them; simple subjects: hills, mountains, snow; b. Complete subject: points; simple subject: points; c. Complete subject: (You); d. Complete subject: hundreds of fireflies; simple subject: hundreds; e. Complete subject: The evidence against the defendant; simple subject: evidence

EXERCISE 48–2, page 334

a. Subject complement: expensive; b. Direct object: death; c. Direct object: their players' efforts; d. Subject complement: the capital of the Russian Empire; e. Subject complement: bitter

EXERCISE 48–3, page 334

a. Direct objects: adults and children; object complement: weary; b. Indirect object: students; direct object: healthy meal choices; c. Direct object: the work; object complement: finished; d. Indirect objects: the agent, us; direct objects: our tickets, boarding passes; e. Direct object: community service; object complement: her priority

EXERCISE 49–1, page 336

a. In northern Italy (adverb phrase modifying *met*); as their first language (adverb phrase modifying *speak*); b. for beginners (adjective phrase modifying *routine*); with ease (adverb phrase modifying *completed*); c. To my boss's dismay (adverb phrase modifying *was*); for work (adverb phrase modifying *late*); d. of Mayan artifacts (adjective phrase modifying *exhibit*); into pre-Columbian culture (adjective phrase modifying *insight*); e. In 2002, in twelve European countries (adverb phrases modifying *became*)

EXERCISE 49–2, page 339

a. Updating your software (gerund phrase used as subject); b. decreasing the town budget (gerund phrase used as object of the preposition *in*); identifying nonessential services (gerund phrase used as subject complement); c. to help her mother by raking the lawn (infinitive phrase used as direct object); raking the lawn (gerund phrase used as object of the preposition *by*); d. Understanding little (participial phrase modifying *I*); passing my biology final (gerund phrase used as object of the preposition *of*); e. Working with animals (gerund phrase used as subject)

EXERCISE 49–3, page 342

a. so that every vote would count (adverb clause modifying *adjusted*); b. that targets baby boomers (adjective clause modifying *campaign*); c. After the Tambora volcano erupted in the southern Pacific in 1815 (adverb clause modifying *realized*); that it would contribute to the "year without a summer" in Europe and North America (noun clause used as direct object of *realized*); d. that at a certain point there will be no more oil to extract from the earth (noun clause used as direct object of *implies*); e. when you are rushing (adverb clause modifying *are overlooked*)

EXERCISE 50–1, page 345

a. Complex; that are ignited in dry areas (adjective clause); b. Compound; c. Simple; d. Complex; Before we leave for the station (adverb clause); e. Compound-complex; when you want to leave (noun clause)

Index

550 INDEX

Credits

Multilingual Menu

Editing Marks

Boldface numbers refer to sections of the handbook.

abbr	faulty abbreviation **41**	no ,	no comma **34**
add	add needed word **10**	;	semicolon **35**
adj/adv	misuse of adjective or adverb **26**	:	colon **36**
agr	faulty agreement **21, 22**	,	apostrophe **37**
appr	inappropriate language **17**	❝ ❞	quotation marks **38**
art	article (*a, an, the*) **29**	. ?	period, question mark **39a–b**
awk	awkward	!	exclamation point **39c**
cap	capital letter **46**	— ( )	dash, parentheses **40a–b**
case	error in case **24, 25**	[ ] . . .	brackets, ellipsis **40c–d**
cliché	cliché **18d**	/	slash **40e**
coh	coherence **2c**	¶	new paragraph **2d**
coord	faulty coordination **14a**	pass	ineffective passive **8**
cs	comma splice **20**	pn agr	pronoun agreement **22**
dev	inadequate development **2b**	proof	proofreading problem **3g**
dm	dangling modifier **12e**	ref	pronoun reference **23**
-ed	*-ed* ending **27d**	run-on	run-on sentence **20**
emph	emphasis **14**	-s	*-s* ending **21, 27c**
ESL	English as a second language, multilingual **28–32**	sexist	sexist language **17e, 22a**
		shift	distracting shift **13**
exact	inexact language **18**	sl	slang **17d**
frag	sentence fragment **19**	sp	misspelled word **44**
fs	fused sentence **20**	sub	subordination **14a**
gl/us	see glossary of usage **18f**	sv agr	subject-verb agreement **21, 27c**
hyph	hyphen **45**		
idiom	idiom **18c**	t	verb tense **27f**
inc	incomplete construction **10**	trans	transition needed **2c**
irreg	irregular verb **27a**	usage	see glossary of usage **18f**
ital	italics **43**	v	voice **8a**
jarg	jargon **17b**	var	lack of variety in sentence structure **14, 15**
lc	lowercase letter **46**		
mix	mixed construction **11**	vb	verb problem **27, 28**
mm	misplaced modifier **12a–d**	w	wordy **16**
mood	mood **27g**	//	faulty parallelism **9**
num	use of numbers **42**	^	insert
om	omitted word **10, 30b**	#	insert space
p	error in punctuation	⌒	close up space
⌃,	comma **33**		

Detailed Menu